Points of Influence

Points of Influence

A Guide to Using Personality Theory at Work

Morley Segal

Jossey-Bass Publishers • San Francisco

Substantial discounts on bulk quantities of Jossey-Bass books are available to corporations, professional associations, and other organizations. For details and discount information, contact the special sales department at Jossey-Bass Inc., Publishers (415) 433–1740; Fax (800) 605–2665.

For sales outside the United States, please contact your local Simon & Schuster International Office.

 Manufactured in the United States of America on Lyons Falls Pathfinder Tradebook. This paper is acid-free and 100 percent totally chlorine-free.

Library of Congress Cataloging-in-Publication Data

Segal, Morley.
   Points of influence : a guide to using personality theory at work
/ Morley Segal.
      p.   cm. — (The Jossey-Bass business and management series)
   Includes bibliographical references and index.
   ISBN 0–7879–0260–8 (alk. paper)
   1. Personality.   2. Personality and situation.   3. Personality and
occupation.   I. Title.   II. Series: Jossey-Bass business &
management series.
BF698.S4233   1997
158.7—dc20   96–30381

FIRST EDITION
HB Printing 10 9 8 7 6 5 4 3 2 1

The Jossey-Bass
Business & Management Series

*To Maurine Poppers and the students of the
American University/NTL Masters Program in
Organization Development*

Contents

Part One: The Internal Being: Points of Influence Beyond Our Awareness

Part Two: Thought and Feeling: Points of Influence Within Our Awareness

Part Three: The Individual and the Environment: External Points of Influence

Preface

Theories of personality, explicitly or implicitly, have always been important for those who work in organizations. It is impossible to work with people in an organization without some idea of how and why they behave as they do. Although many current books focus on human processes, none that deal with life and work in organizations focus explicitly on theories of personality. Similarly, works on personality theory do not focus on life and work in organizations. *Points of Influence* fills that gap.

I first became aware of the organizational relevance of personality theory when I developed a course on leadership for the American University/NTL* Masters Program in Human Resource Development (now Organization Development). The students in this program were practitioners—practicing midcareer professionals in organizational consulting, training, and management. At first I drew upon theories of leadership, group dynamics, and organizational behavior. These theories provided some help, but each theory also left unanswered questions about the root causes of human behavior. My students asked, and I was unable to answer, why individuals seemed to consistently go through the developmental sequence outlined in the theory of Situational Leadership or why people in groups seemed to so predictably follow the path from dependence to rebellion to intimacy found in many theories of group development. I found myself asking the time-honored question of why people behave as they do and was drawn toward theories of personality as a way to answer that question.

I found that first and foremost these theories answered the "why" question by providing an *understanding* of the forces and causal relationships behind human behavior. In addition, I found

---

*Formerly The National Training Laboratories.

that they provided a stimulus for my own personal *awareness* as well as a number of frameworks for *action*.

This book pays attention to all three contributions; however, as a book of theories, the first consideration is understanding. Awareness comes into play as we focus on the special effectiveness of practitioners when they use themselves—their thoughts, feelings, awareness, and behavior—as instruments of change. In addition, a number of examples and applications are presented for each theory.

The best way to sample the flavor of this book is to examine my assumptions regarding the relative importance of these three essential processes and the interrelationships between them. This book is written with the assumption that understanding a whole theory matters. It is not uncommon in the organizational field to see the work of a theorist such as Sigmund Freud or Carl Jung reduced to a few paragraphs or sometimes even a few lines. Although I have tried to minimize the more abstruse aspects of each thinker, I have presented each theory with all of its major components, including a short section on how the theorist developed that theory. I did this because I believe that in order to *use* a theory in varying situations with confidence, skill, and impact, a practitioner must know more than the rudiments of that theory. Put another way, I have the old-fashioned liberal arts bias that the greater an individual's depth of understanding, the more he or she will be able to use that understanding in widely varying—and even unpredictable—circumstances. I believe that this apparently old-fashioned idea is not really outmoded for those who work in organizations. It is, in fact, very timely, because today's practitioner works in just such a varying and unpredictable environment.

This book is written with the assumption that "the being" or personal awareness—meaning the thoughts, feelings, values, and attitudes of the practitioner—play an important role in every action and intervention. This assertion is commonly accepted in the organizational literature, and "using oneself as an instrument of change" is a familiar statement in many books and articles. The unanswered question is *how* to increase awareness and gain the use of one's full being. What are the dimensions and various forms of such personal awareness, and how does one gain it? Theories of personality are one way to answer these questions, and the theories in this book were selected with an eye toward triggering such awareness.

The book is written with the assumption that applications are important, but also that actions alone, no matter how many, do not make an effective practitioner. I have paid a great deal of attention to applications. Where they have been available in the literature, I have summarized them; where they are not available, I have compiled and synthesized them from my experiences and those of my colleagues. No theory is presented without numerous examples and applications. Still, this is not a cookbook. I use applications to illustrate the theory but not as a formula for management or consulting. My assumption is, again, the liberal arts notion that if practitioners understand the theory and the basic outlines of how it can be applied, they will be able to choose and develop their own suitable applications for each situation.

We in the organizational field have drawn on theories of personality for a long time, but we have not had easy access to the full implications of the theories we were using. I hope that this book makes that task easier.

Acknowledgments

Many people helped me in the long process of writing this book. The book was born and nurtured in my "Leadership" and "Individual and the Organization" classes in the American University/ NTL Masters program. I want to thank the students—from 1980 to the present—whose patience, creativity, and humor have made those classes the brightest moments in my professional life.

I also want to thank Edie Seashore, my partner in founding the American University/NTL Masters Program and the "Why Interventions Work" workshop held in Bethel, Maine, and my colleagues in teaching who have provided the right combination of support and confrontation to help me stay on track: Katherine Farquhar, Jeff Fishel, Barbara Greig, Beth Lister, and Bob Marshak.

Don Zauderer, Lisa Levy, and Al Cooke, the three successive directors of the American University/NTL Masters Program, and Neil Kerwin, dean, and Bernard Ross, department chair, gave me the freedom and encouragement to explore the new ways of teaching that eventually found their way into this book.

Bill Hicks of Jossey-Bass had the faith and vision to give me the green light for a book that didn't fit into any existing category. Cedric Crocker, also at Jossey-Bass, had the combination of patience, support, and appropriate deadlines that helped me get the job done.

This book attempts to walk the fine line between an honest and responsible exposition of theories and a lively and practical guide to applications. This means that I needed the help of both scholars and practitioners. Specialists in individual theories who were kind enough to read and comment on draft chapters are David Cain, John Carter, John Corlett, Pat Commela, Michael Diamond, Albert Ellis, Sandra Folzer, Roberta Gilbert, Joyce Holly, Nel Kandel, Manfred Kets de Vries, Larry Kirkhart, Howard Kirschenbaum, Bob Kramer, Miriam Lewin, Henry Malcolm, Alexandra Merrill, Michael Merrill, Ed Nevis, Ed Olson, Bernard Paris, Carol Pearson, and Mark Young.

Consultants and managers who read drafts and kept reminding me to keep it practical include John Adams, Steve Anderson, Neale Clapp, George Ford, Bob Lapidus, Larry Porter, Ric Reichard, Al Templeton, Paul Tremlett, Ted Tschudy, Judith Vogel, and Marvin Weisbord.

Four graduate assistants provided invaluable help in proofreading, finding sources, and checking citations: Rachel Grossman, Maria Leland, John McCormick, and Laura Stephens.

I of course accept full responsibility for all errors of fact and interpretation.

Cara O'Connor of The Feet First Jazz and Tap Studio, Bethesda, Maryland, introduced me to my Shadow. Without the energy from that mysterious part of my own personality, this book would not have been written.

Finally I want to thank Maurine Poppers, my life partner, who read every chapter and used her natural empathy to support my spirits. She also placed herself in the position of the reader and kept me focused on clarity and directness.

San Francisco, California   Morley Segal
August 1996

About the Author

Morley Segal is co-founder of the American University/NTL Joint Masters Program in Organization Development. He was trained as a historian and political scientist and in the early 1970s began to study and work with intrapersonal and interpersonal behavior in organizations. Since 1975 he has consulted with public and private organizations and developed courses and curriculum that welcome the whole person—thoughts, actions, and feelings—into the college classroom.

Segal received both his B.A. degree (1957) in history and his M.A. degree (1959) in international relations from San Francisco State University. He received his Ph.D. degree (1962) in government from Claremont Graduate School. He has been a high school teacher, lumber mill worker, dishwasher, and staff member in the California Legislature and the United States Congress. He is an amateur tap dancer.

Segal is a member of NTL Institute and since 1975 has conducted T Groups for NTL and as part of American University's program in public administration.

Introduction
Understanding and Affecting Behavior in the Workplace

Organizations have been changing at an accelerating rate. New technologies, global competition, and new relationships with customers and clients have all led to new ways of working together. Groups, teams, and networks have become commonplace, but with all this change one element remains the same. The basic ingredient for all of these new activities and formations is still the individual employee. The individual human is still the basic building block for organizations as well as the final recipient of all of today's change strategies.

Managers and consultants (hereafter called practitioners) who work in these new structures cannot avoid the age-old constants of human nature. They must still struggle with the same human dilemmas that plagued and inspired pioneer management theorist Frederick Winslow Taylor almost one hundred years ago.

In Peter Vaill's words, practitioners must "be in this world with responsibility." By this he refers to "what it means to be a whole person with purposes in a situation with others who have their own purposes" (Vaill, 1989, p. 42). In such a situation, intellectual understanding—even interpersonal skills—are necessary, but not sufficient. Practitioners must be able to make a difference in terms of action, and this includes being aware of and influencing the purpose and behavior of themselves and others. Where can today's practitioners find the wisdom and distilled experience of thinkers who have struggled with the classic questions of how to live and work with their fellow humans? This book offers the wisdom of several important theories of personality as guides to meet that challenge.

Theories of personality as a variety of all the theories that deal with human behavior are particularly well suited to this broad task. This is because personality theories are general theories of behavior, in contrast to a single-domain theory such as a theory of perception. They are *holistic* and *integrative.* Holistic because they deal with the overall functioning of individuals, and integrative because they focus upon how individuals function in their natural environment (Hall and Lindzey, 1978, pp. 1–17). This broad focus parallels the task of the organizational practitioner who must also deal with the total personality of individuals in their total work environment, or, again in Peter Vaill's words, the "wholeness of oneself in relation to the wholeness of others" (Vaill, 1989, p. 43).

An important caveat to this mandate is that although the focus of practitioners is to use theories of personality to influence others, the practitioner is always part of the equation. A prerequisite to understanding others is to first understand oneself. Such self-understanding is an integral part of most of the theories in this volume. Where it is not an integral part of the theory itself, it is part of the discussion of that theory.

One application of such self-understanding that has come to be a fundamental part of organization development is the use of oneself as an instrument of change. This means being aware of and expressing one's own thought and feeling as a way of triggering awareness in others and modeling the behavior one is encouraging in others.

Points of Influence

Theories of personality address the goal of understanding oneself and influencing others by identifying *points of influence* in the human personality. A point of influence is an aspect or part of the human personality that guides or has an effect on the rest of the personality—and ultimately behavior—*and* is open to people or forces outside of the individual.

Why Not Use Just One Good Theory and One Good Point of Influence?

Many fine books on organizational change focus on a single influence point in the personality. Edwin Nevis, in *Organizational Con-*

sulting: A Gestalt Approach, explores Fritz and Laura Perls's view that the whole system meets its needs by reacting to its environment. Fred Luthans and Robert Kreitner, in *Organization Behavior Modification and Beyond,* highlight our tendency to respond to B. F. Skinner's reinforcing environment. These books focus on a single point of influence in the human personality. This volume takes a different approach by focusing on multiple points of influence. It does so because not every influence point can be useful to every practitioner in every situation. Some situations, for example, are more responsive to confrontation, and others are more appropriately dealt with through empathy and support. Some practitioners are more comfortable and adept at using ideas and thought as a means of communication, whereas others work more effectively with feelings.

The theories in this volume have been selected so that each displays a distinctly different point of influence. Each theory provides the practitioner with a different way of influencing human behavior. Two chapters identify two points of influence. Chapter One (Freud) deals with one point of influence identified by Freud and the object relations point of influence identified by Melanie Klein. Chapter Two (Jung) deals with two points of influence identified by Jung: archetypes and psychological type.

The theories are grouped on the basis of the location of that point of influence. Three of the theorists—Freud, Jung, and Horney—focus internally and largely outside of our conscious awareness. Two of the theories—those of Rogers and Ellis and Beck—focus internally, but are still potentially within our conscious awareness. Four theorists—Skinner, Lewin, the Perls, and Bowen—define an external boundary between individuals and part of their environment. These last four theorists vary in how they define the relevant environment.

Part One: Points of Influence Beyond Our Awareness

If some aspects of our inner being were not beyond our conscious awareness, life in organizations—indeed, life itself—would be much simpler. If we were aware of and in control of all aspects of our being, Management by Objectives (MBO) would be the ultimate organizational intervention. Managers or supervisors and workers or teams would meet, set mutual goals, define mileposts, and then periodically monitor the process and eliminate barriers to achieving their goals. MBO, however, has not become such an ultimate intervention, because much that influences us is beyond our conscious awareness and hence our conscious control. Managers and supervisors enter an MBO goal-setting meeting carrying unknown influences on their behavior. These influences remain after the meeting and often confuse and frustrate their efforts to implement their goals.

Thus, much of our inner life remains beyond our awareness and is a powerful influence on our behavior. Fortunately, however, this inner life is not completely beyond detection. It speaks indirectly in the form of indirect clues that give us a chance to understand the hidden influences on our motivation and behavior. Those who can decipher these clues and access these hidden processes possess an important point of influence with which to affect human behavior. The exact nature of these clues, as well as the nature of the hidden influences, remains a source of fundamental disagreement among personality theorists. My book begins by examining four influence points, each of which is the product of a different view of the part of our psyche that remains beyond consciousness.

Chapter One is concerned with the influence point of the *instinctive unconscious* as developed by Sigmund Freud and *object relations* as identified by Melanie Klein. Freud's point of influence is the unconscious conflict between certain defined instincts and civilization, as the latter is incorporated in the other parts of our personality. Freud focused on the urge toward life (popularly viewed as sexuality) to the exclusion of most other possibilities. In his view, the ego is a relatively weak voice of reason caught between the raw instincts of the id (urge toward life) and the superego (morality). Understanding this fundamental internal conflict provides a point of influence with which to strengthen the ego in its continual struggle with instincts and rigid morality.

Melanie Klein identified objects or images in our mind that become very important. We start to develop these objects as infants, and they influence our behavior for the rest of our lives. Fortunately, we can change the way we relate to these objects or images in later life. This section deals with how that is possible.

Chapter Two turns to the influence point of the archetype, which was developed by Carl Jung. Jung points out how over generations, experiences and responses are inscribed into the nervous system, so that when a similar experience occurs, basic parameters exist within which behavior reoccurs. These predispositions are termed *archetypes,* or encoded patterns for experience; they are common to all humans and are stored in what Jung terms *the collective unconscious.* Archetypes become known to us indirectly through symbols, myths, stories, and legends. Understanding these clues to archetypes provides an influence point with which to influence these basic guiding patterns of human behavior.

Jung's second point of influence is *psychological type.* Jung's theory of psychological type identified basic differences between individuals that could be a key to both understanding and influence.

Chapter Three looks at still another point of influence in our unconscious—our *social unconscious*—as identified by Karen Horney. Throughout our early years, we collect a cluster of memories, feelings, images, and inner conflicts that give us the self-image or self-images that influence our behavior. Horney first identified within what I term the social unconscious the image of a "real self" that embodied the healthy growth aspects later developed by Abraham Maslow. She also identified the images of the "ideal self" and its two forms: grandiose and despised. Internal conflict between these images of "self" can be particularly powerful. Understanding these images and how they conflict with one another provides a powerful and effective way to influence workplace behavior.

Part Two: Points of Influence That Are Potentially Within Our Awareness

Thought and feeling are by definition within our awareness, although in practice either can become at least partially hidden. Because they can be almost completely within conscious awareness, some theorists have seized upon these processes as fundamental to the operation of the human psychic system. Their theories emphasize ways to bring these processes within our conscious awareness and then to use them as powerful points of influence.

Chapter Four uses the work of Albert Ellis and Aaron Beck to center on the same point of influence: thinking and the cognitive processes. Both Ellis and Beck point out that often it is not what happens, but how we view what happens, that influences our behavior. Albert Ellis terms these views *beliefs,* and these beliefs can be rational or irrational. Aaron Beck terms them *schema or schemas;* they are verbal or pictorial events based on assumptions from previous experiences. In either case the most highly developed aspect of humans—their thinking process—is available to alter how they react to these views. Understanding the powerful influence of thought upon how we react to the world provides a powerful point of influence with which to influence human behavior.

Chapter Five moves on to focus on feelings as a point of influence, using the work of Carl Rogers as a theoretical foundation. For Rogers, feelings bridge the inner aspects of instincts and reactions that often remain hidden and the outer aspects of our psyche with which we relate to others. In practice, feelings themselves often remain partly hidden from complete awareness. Understanding how to make these feelings available and acceptable provides a powerful point of influence with which to understand inner instincts and reactions and influence behavior.

Part Three: External Points of Influence

The environment (including other people) is a powerful influence on our life and our behavior. The entire environment, however, is too large and complex to be used as a point of influence. How can we narrow down and define the part of the environment that influences our behavior? Chapters Six through Nine present four ways of doing this and four views of the environment as points of influence.

Chapter Six focuses on the total environment and the process of reinforcing behavior as a point of influence. The individual most clearly identified with this point of view is B. F. Skinner. Skinner's theory asserts that the best way to understand the impact of the environment is to focus on behavior and then identify the part of the environment that is active when the behavior reoccurs. Put another way, Skinner's theory maintains that humans have a tendency to repeat behavior that is reinforced and that the environment (including other people) is the chief source of that reinforcement. Understanding how to diagnose behavior to determine what is reinforcing it provides a powerful point of influence that makes this behavior more likely to be repeated.

Chapter Seven focuses on Kurt Lewin's theory of the self-perceived environment as a point of influence. Lewin's theory illustrates how human perception filters the environment: individuals select from within their own self and from the environment to create a life space or private world. This space contains all the influences bearing on the individuals at a given moment. Understanding Lewin's formula, $B = f(P, E)$, which says that behavior (B) is a function (f) of the combined personal (P) and environmental (E) factors that make up an individual's life space at a particular moment in time, provides a powerful point of influence bearing on that individual.

Chapter Eight builds on Kurt Lewin's view of the self-perceived environment but adds the notion of the Gestalt cycle of experience as a point of influence. This theory comes from the combined work of Fritz and Laura Perls and Gestalt-oriented practitioners at the Gestalt Institute of Cleveland. These individuals have described still another way of defining the relationship between the individual and the environment. Their contribution is to view humans as self-regulating systems that are parts of other whole systems. In this view, the human organism, like other parts of nature, has the inherent drive and resources to regulate itself, survive, and meet its own needs through a well-defined cycle of experience. Understanding what the system is doing or could do to satisfy its needs and intervening in a way that removes blockages and allows the cycle to complete itself provides another powerful point of influence.

Chapter Nine ends the book with the family system theory of Murray Bowen. Bowen's theory defines the emotional system as a point of influence. In Bowen's view, humans, in common with other forms of life, continue to hold powerful instinctive forces. These forces not only influence individual behavior but—at an almost invisible level—form networks or communication patterns between individuals in a system. These instinctive forces influence much of our social behavior in and out of the workplace including mating, nurturing, fighting, fleeing, imitation, a predisposition to routine and ritual, and displacement (inappropriate behavior for a given situation when a creature is under stress). Understanding the emotional system and its basis in instinct provides a powerful point of influence.

Conclusion

The final chapter reexamines all eleven points of influence in terms of the three essential tasks or processes faced by all practitioners: understanding human behavior, taking effective action, and increasing their own personal awareness (Friedlander, 1976).

Using Influence Points to Influence Behavior

It is not easy to know how and when to use individual points of influence in an organizational context or to decide which personality theory should apply. It is relatively easy to use different influence points simply to sway individual behavior. The task becomes far more complex when the practitioner decides to intervene at the individual level in order to create an organizational change.

One way to convert individual interventions into organizational change is to identify important processes in which the needs of the individual and the organization meet. An individual intervention involving one of these processes is more likely to have an impact on the organization. We have identified three such processes:

1. The terms and processes by which the individual becomes and remains part of an organization, or *joining*
2. The process by which the individual works and relates to others in the organization under some degree of contention and stress, or *conflict management*
3. The process by which the individual changes and grows within the context of the organization, or *psychological growth*

Two of these processes are familiar and part of the traditional individual-organization relationship. Both joining, which includes hiring, retention, and motivation, and managing conflict have been core processes in organizations for most of recorded history. The process of fostering psychological growth in an organizational environment, however, has only recently come into prominence. Whether they are well-established or new phenomena, these processes identify areas in which interventions with individuals can have a broad organizational impact.

The Process of Joining the Organization

Organizations have been changing the basic parameters through which individuals join. To meet the challenge of the global marketplace, they have restructured, replacing traditional hierarchies with a variety of other arrangements. These changes do not mean that the older boundaries and distinctions no longer exist. They remain, but they are now more flexible and they increasingly exist within the mind of each member of the organization. Companies, for example, are replacing vertical hierarchies with horizontal networks, linking separate functions with cross-functional teams and forming strategic alliances with suppliers, customers, and even competitors. Understanding the overall mission is no longer only the responsibility of top and middle managers but is increasingly an expectation of every employee (Hirschhorn and Gilmore, 1992, p. 104).

With all of these changes, the conditions under which an individual joins and remains in the organization are important in shaping his or her future relationship with the organization. They affect the individual's commitment to the organization, views on the nature of legitimate organizational authority, belief in his or her ability to influence the organization, and response to efforts at organizational change. The changes point in the same direction: the decreasing importance of established, formal boundaries and the increasing importance of boundaries that originate in the mind.

Personality theory helps us to understand the individual process that creates and nurtures these new mental boundaries and the ways we can influence that process. Each of the nine chapters in this volume offers a different point or points of influence in the personality and a different way to influence perceptions of the boundary between the individual and the organization. The increasing importance of these individually perceived boundaries is reflected in the way organizations now deal with authority, tasks, organizational politics, identities, and careers.

The Authority Boundary

At one time, organizational authority could be described as an overall relationship. One individual not only was in charge but was presumed to be so because she or he had the information and ability to make most decisions.

This authority still exists and many managers still lead others, but the leader is not always the same person. An engineer with technical expertise, for example, may lead a project team that includes the engineer's boss. The engineer must be able to inform and disagree with her boss, and the boss must be open to that information and be able to respond in a nonpunishing way (Hirschhorn and Gilmore, 1992, p. 110).

> *Sample intervention:* Practitioners can use personality theory to identify influence points in the authority boundary. They can then use these influence points to help them design experiences that will help individuals to become aware of how their own thoughts, feelings, early experiences, and so on influence and even distort the way they react to authority.

The Task Boundary

Task boundaries once allowed individuals to develop expertise in performing their job with the expectation that others would do the same and that their expertise would be respected (Hirschhorn and Gilmore, 1992, p. 108).

Today, individuals increasingly depend on others whom they can't control, as well as having to invest the time and energy to understand other people's jobs. An accountant in a large firm might have worked in relative isolation from other members of the firm. Now he or she is a member of several teams that provide varied support and assistance to the firm's customers. The accountant's role changes depending upon the task of each team. At times the accountant is the expert in what is being done and at other times he or she must rely on the expertise of others.

> *Sample intervention:* Practitioners can use personality theory to identify influence points in the personality in order to design experiences that will help organizational members become aware of the effect of their feelings, beliefs, values, and attitudes on their ability to shift and adjust their internal task boundary.

Change in Political Boundaries

The existence of political boundaries once meant that one unit's gain was another unit's loss. When these units met over a political boundary, the result was most often a win-lose process. Today, units must still defend their interests, but because the organization's mission is everyone's responsibility, they must do so without sacrificing the interests of the overall organization and in a way that seeks win-win situations.

For example, at one time Manufacturing could be relatively isolated from both Research and Development (R&D) and Marketing and could focus on keeping costs down and production up; it did not have to continually interact with other parts of the organization. Manufacturing units now are increasingly working on smaller batches of customized products, so all three units—Manufacturing, R&D, and Marketing—must meet over a political boundary and decide what is best, both for themselves and for the organization a whole.

Sample intervention: Practitioners can use the influence points in the various personality theories to design experiences that will help members to understand and accept their tendency to bring various pieces of excess emotional baggage into the conflict process.

Change in the Identity Boundary

In the past, to the extent that members of organizations identified with their unit, they identified less with other units or the organization as a whole. Unit loyalty was a win-lose proposition.

Today, with lines of responsibility constantly being redrawn, individuals must develop unit pride without devaluing others and must learn how to reap the benefits of loyalty without undermining outsiders. Unit identity is now a matter of choosing a win-win solution over a win-lose one (Hirschhorn and Gilmore, 1992, p. 107).

Sample intervention: Practitioners can use influence points in the theories of personality to help them to design experiences that assist members in understanding when organizational issues become issues of personal identity and in increasing their objectivity over this process.

Change in the Career Boundary

Historically, many organizations once offered the promise of life-time employment. Others didn't go this far, but the labor market was stable enough so that employees could still rely on using a defined set of skills, contacts, or knowledge. If they lost a job in one company, they could seek a similar job in another organization.

Not only do organizations now rapidly shift their work-force requirements to meet the needs of the market, but entire areas of specialization and management have shrunk or virtually disappeared. Organizations increasingly rely on supplemental employees and outsourced work functions (Barner, 1994, p. 8). Thus, individuals must now take the responsibility for continually managing their own career. To do so they have to learn how to step outside of themselves and objectively evaluate their future in their area of employment. This may require them to abandon what they have invested time and emotional energy in learning to do. They also may have to find the resources to retrain or reeducate themselves several times in their career (Waterman, Waterman, and Collard, 1994).

> *Sample intervention:* Practitioners can use the various influence points in personality theory to design experiences that will help members of organizations increase their awareness of the aspects of their history and personality that influence their ability to manage their own career.

The Process of Conflict Management

Why humans create and maintain personal, group, and organizational struggles is an age-old question. Though it is often deplored, conflict has always been a part of organizational life. What has changed is the way we deal with it. The old organization could afford to buffer itself from conflict, taking on protective insulating strategies so that avoidance, delay, and compromise on side issues had fewer negative consequences. For example, the organization could tolerate Marketing and Manufacturing having a long-standing feud and minimal communication. Such feuds do cost resources, but in the past, the functions were run separately enough for this to have a minimal impact. The cost could be absorbed by raising prices in a less competitive market.

This is no longer the case. Differences still exist, perhaps even more than before, but now they must be managed in other ways. Organizations that include networks of self-managing teams must deal with differences before they become destructive conflicts and manage conflicts before they become deep-seated divisions or feuds. Dealing with differences in this way is a continual process and a considerable challenge. How do we prepare individuals for such a role?

The Individual and Conflict

Two aspects of individual psychology are crucial to the process of dealing with differences: (1) conflicts may *originate* because of different interests and (2) the personal or perceptual element *maintains* the struggle. The conflict-maintaining process is based upon the individual's inner processes and, as in the issue of joining, what helps us to understand the process is the idea of boundaries. These boundaries, however, are more personal. External boundaries separate the individual from the rest of the world and internal boundaries separate different aspects of each individual's personality.

The External Boundary

This is the boundary that separates the individual from the rest of her or his environment. The location and permeability of this boundary help the individual to determine a feeling of personal responsibility for behavior. This boundary is related to conflict in that it is much easier to maintain tension and conflict with something that is considered foreign or outside oneself than with a part of one's own being. As individuals we have to accept responsibility for what is inside our personal boundary, but we can reject or not even recognize what we view as outside.

> *Sample intervention:* Practitioners can use the various influence points in the human personality to design experiences that will help individuals to become aware of ways in which they resolve or maintain conflict by defining what is inside or outside of themselves.

The Internal Boundary

The second set of boundaries that shape human conflict is internal. Boundaries exist between various aspects of the human personality such as thoughts, values, attitudes, feelings, instincts, and physical reactions. They all can be involved in conflict, but humans vary in their ability to call upon the many aspects of their personality. For example, the boundary around feelings is an impenetrable barrier for some, whereas for others it is a relatively open passageway. Feelings that are encased in a rigid boundary still influence the individual, but they are less available for expression and communication. The degree to which individuals are aware of and can call upon different aspects of their personality shapes how they deal with conflict.

> *Sample intervention:* Practitioners can use the various influence points in theories of personality to design experiences that help members to extend the ways that they call upon different aspects of themselves in dealing with conflict. Such awareness opens the door for members to extend their range of interventions.

Psychological Growth and the Organization

The third fundamental process that helps practitioners to focus on the relationship between individuals and their organization is the way individuals grow in an organizational context. Psychological growth includes becoming aware of new aspects of one's being, including thoughts, feelings, reactions, attitudes, and values. It also includes the process of discovering new ways to relate to other people and to perform tasks at a new and higher level. The end result of psychological growth is to be fully *present* in one's role at work—that is, accessible to work (contributing ideas and effort), to others (being open and empathetic), and to oneself (continuing to grow and learn) (Kahn, 1992, p. 322).

An example of an organizational change that required such psychological growth was the switch from the classic automobile assembly line to self-managed teams. The U.S. automobile industry prospered for a long time with the mass-production assembly line. The production line demanded very little of a psychological nature from the individual worker beyond the ability to withstand the monotony. Now, as a part of a self-governing team, the worker must be able to continually evaluate his or her own work and that of others, confront peers, and take up leadership when the situation demands. This example is part of a century-long trend in which organizations are calling upon an increasingly larger part of the individual worker's being. Three examples follow:

1. Peter Block (1987, pp. 154–156) challenges managers to become aware of and possibly change their "political script" or unconscious influence strategy that they use regardless of actual power realities.
2. Peter Senge (1990, p. 143) applies the concept of personal growth to the entire organization by advocating a "learning organization" in which the organization is more effective because it is committed to fostering growth among its employees.
3. Chris Argyris suggests that simply solving problems (single-loop learning) is insufficient. Argyris maintains that employees must develop the psychological strength to question the conditions that generated the problems. These could include personal characteristics or organizational structure and norms, as well as anything that might cause a problem to reoccur. The ability to take that second step is double-loop learning. To foster double-loop learning, the organization, in turn, must be able to create conditions in which questioning basic procedures is supported and encouraged. Argyris's view is an excellent example of psychological growth at its most challenging level. It requires questioning, at a deep and possibly hidden level, one's own habitual, protective, and defensive reactions (Argyris, 1994).

Sample intervention: Every theory of personality in this volume has a way of defining and fostering psychological growth, and every theory has one or more influence points in the personality for doing so. Practitioners can use the theories to help make the process of psychological growth more visible and understandable so that leaders and members of the organization can use their own influence points to encourage the process.

Conclusion

Many strategies exist for leading, managing, and changing organizations, but all of them ultimately depend for their effectiveness upon the reactions of individuals. Given this simple but powerful reality, how can those who have responsibility in organizations better understand and work with the basic material of their job: the individual employee? This Introduction has outlined how the collected wisdom of eleven powerful thinkers can help. The ideas presented here are not new. What is new is the way these ideas have been arranged to make them more available and usable by practitioners. The key concept in doing so has been the notion of *points of influence* in the human personality. Points of influence are the tie between the driving force or forces of the inner psyche and the outer world. Practitioners who can identify the point of influence that best works for them have a far better chance of accomplishing their goals.

Bibliography

Argyris, C. "Good Communication That Blocks Learning." *Harvard Business Review,* July–Aug. 1994, *72*(4), 77–95.

Barner, R. "The New Career Strategist: Career Management for the Year 2000 and Beyond." *The Futurist,* Sept.–Oct. 1994, *28*(5), 8–14.

Block, P. *The Empowered Manager: Positive Political Skills at Work.* San Francisco: Jossey-Bass, 1987.

Devanna, M. A., and Tichy, N. "Creating the Competitive Organization of the 21st Century: The Boundaryless Corporation." *Human Resource Management,* Winter 1990, *29,* 455–471.

Friedlander, F. "OD Reaches Adolescence: An Exploration of Its Underlying Values." *Journal of Applied Behavioral Science,* 1976, *12*(1), 7–43.

Hall, C. S., and Lindzey, G. *Theories of Personality.* (3rd ed.) New York: Wiley, 1978.

Hirschhorn, L., and Gilmore, T. "The New Boundaries of the 'Boundaryless' Company." *Harvard Business Review,* May–June 1992, *70*(3), 104–115.

Kahn, W. A. "To Be Fully There: Psychological Presence at Work." *Human Relations,* Apr. 1992, *45*(4), 321–349.

Luthans, F., and Kreitner, R. *Organization Behavior Modification and Beyond: An Operant and Social Learning Approach.* Glenview, Ill.: Scott, Foresman, 1985.

Senge, P. M. *The Fifth Discipline: The Art and Practice of the Learning Organization.* New York: Doubleday, 1990.

Vaill, P. B. *Managing as a Performing Art: New Ideas for a World of Chaotic Change.* San Francisco: Jossey-Bass, 1989.

Waterman, R. H., Jr., Waterman, J. A., and Collard, B. A. "Toward a Career-Resilient Workforce." *Harvard Business Review,* July–Aug. 1994, *72*(4), 87–95.

Part One

The Internal Being

Points of Influence
Beyond Our Awareness

Chapter One

Sigmund Freud
The Internal Conflict Between Instinct and Civilization

Why Sigmund Freud? An Overview of Organizational Applications

The best-laid organizational plans often fall apart as individuals respond to powerful messages from their unconscious mind. Freud will help you to understand thoughts and behavior under conditions of anxiety. Freud's focus on this less cheerful aspect of the human condition is crucial for anyone hoping to work with organizations in conditions of stress and rapid change.

Freud's Theory as an Organizational Image or Metaphor

Sometimes organizations behave like irrational individuals. Freud's view of the flow of psychic energy will help you to understand why and how individuals in a collective setting simultaneously experience and react to powerful and irrational forces.

Freud's Theory as a Point of Influence for Dealing with Conflict

One root cause of conflict is the human tendency to distort experiences. The Freudian explanation of transference and defense mechanisms will help you to understand and deal with this phenomenon at the individual, group, and organizational level.

Freud's Theory as a Point of Influence for Dealing with Psychological Growth

Unlike plants and animals, humans create many barriers to their own development. Freud identifies these obstacles and suggests strategies to minimize them.

Freud's Theory as a Point of Influence for Dealing with the Dilemmas of Joining

Commitment and allegiance to groups and organizations is both a rational and an emotional process. Freud's focus on the adult reappearance of childhood needs will help you to work with the process through which humans satisfy a need by identifying with a sign or symbol. The concept of projective identification will help you to work with the collective image of the organization in each member's mind.

Freud's Theory as a Basis for Other Organizationally Relevant Theories

Freud was the pioneer explorer of the unconscious mind. He established the foundation for understanding subsequent theories, even those that opposed his view. This chapter describes how Melanie Klein, Wilfred Bion, and other object relations theorists built their theories from the Freudian base. Their theories are particularly relevant for work in organizations because they focus on the reaction to authority.

Limitations of Freud's Theory for Use in Organizations

Freud's view of women reflects his Victorian-era origins and alienates many woman and men today from his entire theory. His focus on the sexual drive brings up aspects of individuals' lives and backgrounds that are awkward to discuss in work settings. Freud's emphasis on the sexual drive as *the* overarching explanation of human behavior ignores other important human qualities such as spirituality. For many, this emphasis seems simplistic. However, Freud's theories continue to provide a unique and valuable view of the less rational aspects of human behavior.

How Freud Developed His Ideas

Sigmund Freud opened up an entire new realm of human functioning, our unconscious mind, and like his theory, his life was one of conflict and struggle. Freud was born to a lower-middle-class Jewish family in Freiberg, Moravia, now in the Czech Socialist Republic. His father suffered financial reverses when Freud was four, and the family moved to Vienna. Freud wished to become a researcher in the basic sciences, but a lack of financial resources forced him to compromise, and he obtained a medical degree instead. As a young Viennese physician in the late 1880s, Freud specialized in diseases of the nervous system. Then, as it is now in many organizations, human behavior was presumed to be essentially logical and rational. People understood their own and others' motives in terms of their stated thoughts and preferences.

Hysterical paralysis, or paralysis induced by psychological rather than physical causes, was then a common problem. The sufferers, who were mostly female, received little sympathy or understanding and were often regarded as lazy or malingering. Seeking a way to help them, Freud first studied with the famous French psychiatrist Jean Charcot. Charcot used hypnotism to provide a few of his patients with temporary relief from some of their paralytic symptoms. Seeking a more permanent cure, Freud then worked with another Viennese physician, Josef Breuer. Breuer had found that talking about memories related to the origins of symptoms often resulted in relief of the symptoms themselves. The notion was that some aspect of these patients' minds of which they were totally unaware could induce physical paralysis. The finding that painful memories that were suppressed in some part of the mind still affected the body in the form of paralysis challenged the medical wisdom and common sense of the times. Freud had identified the unconscious part of the mind, but his discovery raised even more questions. He now sought to find out *why* the manifestations of the unconscious took the particular form that they did. In answering this question, he developed his most important theories, lost Breuer as a colleague, and set the stage for a lifetime of controversy.

The origin of the controversy and the basis for Freud's theory lie in the remarks of his first patients. As Freud spoke to them, he noted that most of their early traumatic experiences relating to paralysis were sexual in origin: the common theme was a sexual advance to a female child from a father or other close male relative. Freud acknowledged the reality of childhood sexual abuse, but as time went by, he came to distrust whether this was the sole source of his patients' problems.

He later concluded that such a large number of previously unknown accounts of child abuse could not all be factual. He then asked himself, if they were not factual, what was their origin? Freud's conclusion remains controversial today. He concluded that these reports of incest were based on fantasy—the child's fantasy or wish to have a sexual relationship with the parent of the opposite sex. From this conclusion, Freud deduced his controversial theory of a basic sexual drive that underlies many other drives and behaviors. This theory included the notion of infant sexuality, which shocked his Victorian colleagues. From this notion of a driving life force inherently at odds with the restraints of civilized society, Freud developed a methodology (psychoanalysis) for exploring these unconscious and inner conflicts. Freud continued his practice and writing until he was driven out of Vienna by the Nazis in 1938. He died London in 1939.

Freud's Point of Influence

Life in organizations, even in the freest and most creative ones, involves harnessing and limiting some of our most powerful inner drives. *Freud's point of influence is the unconscious conflict between these hidden instincts and civilization as it is incorporated in the other parts of our personality.* Understand this fundamental internal conflict, says Freud's theory, and you have a focus for understanding and influencing behavior in its most basic form.

The conflict between primitive drives and today's complex world is embodied in Freud's map of our personality. Writing in the latter part of the nineteenth century, Freud was influenced by Charles Darwin's theory of evolution. If humans had indeed evolved from other, more primitive forms of life, then it would not be surprising to find some physical remnants of these earlier stages. Our appendix and tailbone are examples of our evolutionary heritage. Mental remnants of this earlier era also remain, such as the stress reactions that ready the body to fight or flee, no matter how socially inappropriate that reaction may be. Freud noted that these and other mental remainders of our prehistoric past continue to send out the same messages that were sent out eons ago.

Contemporary theorists and researchers now emphasize relational influences on human behavior, but Freud's basic model of the personality remains important by identifying the conflict between three universal forces: instinct, morality, and reason. This conflict is the basis for understanding the major Freudian applications in this chapter. The three psychic subsystems are the id, which represents raw instinct; the superego, which represents morality; and the ego, which represents reason. These subsystems do not exist as particular organs, but rather as patterns of interactions within the brain and between the brain and the rest of the body. Freud's point of influence in the personality takes place at the point where these three subsystems interact.

Preview: When to Use Sigmund Freud's and Melanie Klein's Points of Influence in the Workplace.

The Id

The id is composed of our basic instincts that are present at birth and is the strongest member of the trio. The id provides us with basic drives such as hunger, response to threat, and sexual desire, but it can do very little to satisfy those needs. The id is neither moral nor rational. Freud said, "The logical laws of thought do not apply in the id, and this is true above all of the law of contradiction. Contrary impulses exist side by side, without canceling each other out or diminishing each other. . . . Impressions, too, which have been sunk into the id by repression, are virtually immortal; after the passage of decades they behave as though they had just occurred" (Freud, [1932] 1964a, pp. 73–74).

The id may be likened to a constant source of energy like the sun or a nuclear reactor. As long as the system is operating, the sun and the reactor send out energy. Control and variation come from other parts of the system. It becomes cooler on earth when clouds block the sun, and the impact of the nuclear reactor is controlled by devices that block its flow of energy. In neither case does the source of energy cease and so it is with the system of instinctive energy called the id. *It never stops and it never changes.* If we wish to limit or change the influence of energy from the id, we must intervene with the ego or superego.

The Superego

The superego is our internalized conscience and the carrier of inner do's and don'ts. The superego draws its energy from the id and is the internalized repository of the instructions from parents and the expectations of others and society. The superego also includes the "ego ideal," which can set forth the emotional map for the unfolding of a life pattern. Like the id, the superego has no built-in limitations. It often displays "a severity for which no model has been provided by the real parents, and . . . calls the ego to account not only for its deeds but equally for its thoughts and unexecuted intentions" (Freud, [1938] 1964b, p. 205).

The Ego

The ego is our *rational* link with the external world and is the internal manager of the rest of the system. Unlike the id, the ego is able

to learn from experience. According to Freud, "Ego learns to re-
nounce immediate satisfaction, to postpone the obtaining of pleasure, to put up with a little unpleasure and to abandon certain
sources of pleasure all together" (Freud, [1917] 1963, p. 357).
Through the process of *identification,* the ego finds a way to help
satisfy some of the demands of the id. Identification also refers to
the developmental process through which individuals incorporate part of the personality of others as they form their own. In
doing so, they can also unconsciously influence decisions about
their career.

Ironically, despite its responsibility as our major mechanism
for coping with reality, the ego is the weakest of the three systems.
It does not have an independent source of energy or an independent base of power. Whatever power or energy the ego has is
drawn from the id. The ego can be overwhelmed by the id and
the superego. The ego serves three tyrannical masters—the external world, the superego, and the id—"and does what it can to
bring their claims and demands into harmony with one another.
These claims are always divergent and often seem incompatible.
No wonder that the ego so often fails in its task" (Freud, [1932]
1964a, p. 77).

Since Freud's point of influence identifies inner psychic workings in which a weak ego is a major source of problems, the principal application of this point of influence is to strengthen the ego.

In Situations of Anxiety

When Freud speaks of anxiety, he is not referring to the everyday
use of the term, as when one is anxious because of being late for
an appointment. Freud's anxiety involves "the combination of un-
pleasurable feelings, impulses of discharge and bodily sensations"
(Freud, [1917] 1963, p. 396) that leads to a feeling of *mortal danger* whereby "the affective state becomes paralysing" (Freud, [1932]
1964a, p. 82) and as a result the operations of the ego (thinking
and problem solving) are shut down or greatly impaired. Examples at the individual and group levels follow.

Individual Level
At the individual level, such anxiety can render a practitioner virtually incapable of effective action.

> While conducting a session, a trainer feels provoked and angered by a comment from a participant but does not feel that he can respond. As the session continues, the trainer finds it hard to remember the design and, as questions are raised by the participants, he finds it difficult to think clearly.

This trainer may have been experiencing any or all of the following three types of anxiety described by Freud ([1932] 1964a, pp. 78–82):

1. Real anxiety, in which the ego perceives an actual threat or danger in the external world
2. Unreasonable anxiety (termed *neurotic* by Freud), in which the ego is aware of the power of instincts—for example, to answer the participant with anger—and fears that this anger will get out of control and result in punishment
3. Moral anxiety, in which a powerful superego punishes an individual for a deed or even the thought of a deed (embarrassing the participant) that is based on an instinct or urge that is contrary to the individual's moral code

Group and Organizational Levels

The same external circumstances could trigger all three types of anxiety in different members of a group:

> A civil engineer is privy to a confidential memo on reorganization that might threaten her job. *Real* anxiety is experienced as she anticipates what it would be like if this reorganization cost her her job. *Neurotic* anxiety is experienced as she thinks of how she could use this information and considers the imagined risks or punishment that might result if she did so. *Moral* anxiety is triggered as she realizes that she could save her job by using this information in a way that would violate her own moral code.

Understanding can bring relief from these symptoms. To the extent that the engineer can become aware of and separate the real threats from her own inner reactions, she will be in a better position to cope with the situation. *The delineation of these three types of anxiety can also help a consultant or manager understand what is going on in the engineer's office.*

The real anxiety in the office pulls energy away from day-to-day work to respond to the crisis. An added air of tension occurs in the office as people who normally work well together become testy or spend a good deal of energy fantasizing about the future. This happens because the id, in response to the threatened reorganization, sends increased energy to the reality-coping ego. For the moment, however, fear of punishment stops the ego from utilizing it and temporarily immobilizes it (neurotic anxiety). Finally, the issue of job security is important enough and the real facts of what this reorganization means are cloudy enough so that individuals are thrown back on their worst fantasies. Individuals are aware, at some level, of tactics such as back-stabbing, going around the boss, or using inside information to save one's position. These methods violate some individuals' code of conduct. For those people the very thought of such behavior triggers energy for their superegos (moral anxiety).

Alleviating Anxiety

In its early days psychoanalysis was called the "talking cure." Individuals experienced some relief of symptoms through simply talking about them. The talking cure is still relevant in situations of anxiety such as those described above. Practitioners can perform a valuable function by utilizing the action research methods of Kurt Lewin (see Chapter Seven) or the empathic listening methods of Carl Rogers (see Chapter Five) to open up the subject for discussion.

When Individuals Experiencing Stress Distort What They See, Hear, or Feel to Relieve Internal Pressure (Defense Mechanisms)

For the civil engineer in the previous example, the thought of being caught with the secret information or anxiety could be so great that her ego would defend itself by rejecting or distorting the message. Instead of acknowledging her anger at the reorganization, the engineer states that the head of the office is angry with her (projection). This is the definition of a defense mechanism. The ego relieves the pressure of anxiety by changing or blocking the disturbing impulse.

Of all the ideas of Freudian theory, the notion of *defense mechanisms* is the most useful in describing day-to-day organizational life. Defense mechanisms are the most common responses when the ego cannot discharge energy from the superego or id. Undischarged energy creates anxiety, and defense mechanisms allow the ego to handle the pressure. They do this by deflecting, distorting, or denying primitive messages from the id or moralistic messages from the superego. Actions resulting from these distortions are termed *defensive behavior.* The following defense mechanisms are a familiar part of organizational life.

Projection

We are most likely to feel defensive when we are in danger of being blamed. The emphasis on responsibility in hierarchical situations makes *projection* a popular defense mechanism in organizations. In such situations, the impulse from the id conflicts with that of the organization or whoever speaks for the organization. Thus it appears difficult for the individual to act on, or even state, that impulse. What happens to the unexpressed impulse? Through a quick sleight of mind, the ego projects it on someone else.

> Marie, a salesperson, is speaking to her sales manager, Frank. Frank is unhappy with Marie's report writing. Frank says, "Marie, I'm sorry, but that last report just doesn't make it. You need to give us a better breakdown of your activities. The part on the Reynolds contract was especially weak. You're just going to have to pay more attention to this part of your job." Marie replies, "I'm sorry, Frank, I will try to do a better job next time." But as she walks away from the encounter, she thinks, "That so-and-so is trying to get rid of me. He wants me to leave the company." Later, Marie remarks to a colleague, "Well, it is really clear now. Frank is trying to get rid of me" (the external defensive behavior). In fact, Marie would like to see Frank out of the company. She cannot say this to Frank because she is not fully aware of this feeling herself (the internal defense mechanism). She cannot even say it to herself.

This is the crucial point regarding projection. To defend itself from an impulse that it cannot act upon, Marie's ego projects that impulse onto Frank.

Repression and Denial

Repression and *denial* are similar in that both involve negating an impulse, fact, feeling, or memory. If an individual is repressing, the impulse is pushed back into the unconscious. In the act of denial the impulse surfaces, but it is not acknowledged for what it is. Consider a case of sexual attraction, a common occurrence in the workplace:

> Brenda Forsythe, an account executive in a large advertising agency, is attracted to Alan Calone, the art director, and the feeling is mutual. Soon after meeting Alan, Brenda begins to be irritated by Alan, and again the feeling is mutual. Differences in their methods or approaches are turned into sarcastic comments about competence. Whenever they are in a meeting together, the air is electric and other people feel the tension. Hollywood has made much of situations like this, from the movies of Katharine Hepburn and Spencer Tracy to the present. If anyone asked either Brenda or Alan about the possibility of sexual attraction, they would vigorously deny it and believe their denial.

Not only is it unacceptable for Brenda and Alan to act on the sexual impulse; it is even unacceptable for them to experience it in a conscious way. As a defense against an impulse that creates anxiety, Brenda's and Alan's egos have pushed the impulse back into the unconscious or turned it into outer conflict.

Reaction Formation
Rather than projecting the unacceptable impulse onto another person or pushing it back into the unconscious, in *reaction formation* the ego turns the impulse into its opposite. When Shakespeare said, "The lady doth protest too much," he might well have had reaction formation in mind. It is that special overemphasis of something that causes the listener to wonder if the speaker really means something beyond what she or he is saying.

> Will Finch is in charge of the affirmative action program in a large Southern public utility. He did not ask for the job and is uneasy about the goals of the program, which have to do with increasing the number of women in management positions. No one would ever guess Will's ambivalence upon first meeting him. He speaks glowingly about the goals of the program, and every woman he advocates is described as "absolutely outstanding" or "unusually well qualified." However, some of the executives Will has helped to promote have not been prepared for their positions, and their mediocre performance has reflected badly on the program. Will treats all of the women with exaggerated courtesy.

Will's basic instincts are not comfortable with equal status, let alone a compensatory program for women. His superego clearly states that he *ought* to support such goals, so the impulse from his id is unacceptable. Will's ego solves the problem by turning the impulse into its opposite. The clue that is present in some form in most situations of reaction formation is the exaggerated nature of the response. In this instance, it is Will's enthusiasm for even marginally qualified women and his exaggerated courtesy to all women.

Fixation and Regression

These two defense mechanisms relate to the Freudian developmental cycle. Each of the four phases in this cycle (oral, anal, phallic, and genital), described in the following section, represents a struggle involving the difficulty of socializing our instincts and developing a way to cope with external reality. The transition from one phase to another is neither clear-cut nor one-way. Individuals can and do become stuck at one phase of the cycle (fixation) or temporarily move back to an early phase (regression). Becoming stuck in one phase or moving back to an earlier one can also function as a defense mechanism. If the message or impulse from the id or superego is not acceptable to the ego, then the ego can, so to speak, leave the scene by moving back to an earlier phase of the developmental cycle.

> Roger Martin heads the payroll section of a large retail store. Roger always prided himself on knowing what was going on, preparing for it, and remaining on top of events, but when the Payroll department adopted a new computer system, Roger's job changed noticeably. Skills he developed are no longer needed, and new skills that are not at all comfortable for him are the order of the day. He no longer feels in control. His initial reaction was to clamp down on everything that he could control. He demanded more data before he would do anything and carefully maneuvered every situation so that he would be covered if anything went wrong.

From someone who was merely cautious and precise, Roger has become an immobilized nitpicker—what Freud described as an anal personality. Under stress Roger has gone back (regressed) to some of the excessive traits of an earlier (anal) developmental level.

When Relationships Appear to Be Distorted (Transference)

To understand the source of these issues, we must briefly focus on Freud's view of individual development. Freud identified four developmental stages:

1. The oral stage usually lasts through the first year. In this stage the mouth is the chief source of pleasure and the infant develops the capacity to accept nurturing, trust, and love. Individuals who have an unsatisfactory experience in this time are more likely to have difficulty in trusting and need more assurances of approval.
2. The anal stage takes place in ages one through three. This is the first encounter with authority, rules, and self-control, and it is embodied in the experience of toilet training. In the Freudian framework, a bad experience in this stage results in an overly strict, retentive, "anal" personality or an overly lenient, loose, undisciplined, self-indulgent personality.
3. The phallic stage runs from ages three through five. After this period the Freudian developmental process becomes latent until early adolescence. During the phallic stage, separate identity and gender identity develop. This is also the stage of Freud's most controversial theories: the Oedipus complex in men and penis envy in women.
4. The fourth and final stage is the genital stage, which lasts from late adolescence until death. Successful completion of this and previous stages gives the individual the ability to form satisfactory love relationships and convert sexual energy into nonsexual energy.

How does a seemingly esoteric and sexually tinged cycle relate to life and work in organizations? It does so in two ways. The first was discussed in the description of the defense mechanisms of fixation and regression. Both defense mechanisms temporarily bring an individual back to earlier parts of the developmental cycle. The second link is the process of *transference*.

As young children go through these stages, adult caregivers have many opportunities to avoid fulfilling their expectations. The two-year-old, for example, has neither the intellectual development to comprehend his or her feelings nor the emotional development to manage them, when a parent has to go to work rather than stay home and play. Freud called the later fallout from these disappointments, misunderstandings, and unfulfilled expectations transference. Transference is a reaction in which we unknowingly perceive and respond to someone in the context of an unresolved feeling from our past. Freud observed the process very early in his career, when patients responded to him as if he were a figure larger than life. Managers and consultants today continue to have similar experiences.

> Sheila Wong, a project coordinator, was puzzled. She wanted to help Helen Burtell with her budget, but Helen seemed so much in awe of her that she doubted that Helen could concentrate enough on putting together a budget. In order to help Helen with her budget, Sheila wanted all of Helen's attention, including her critical faculties, but Helen's attention always shifted back to Sheila herself and how well she did things. What was going on?

The problem for Sheila in going over the budget is the same as Freud's in his Victorian consulting room. The ego, our link with reality, is not doing its job. Helen's reaction to Sheila comes not from Sheila, but from Helen's unconscious. This is transference. When we engage in this process we are treating someone as if they were someone else, or someone is responding to us as if we were someone else. This distortion causes all kinds of organizational mischief, from conflict and misunderstandings to major resistance to needed change.

Transference also has a positive side. Short-term transference reactions have a limited positive impact. Feelings of love toward a leader, or toward some representation such as an ideology or a symbol, help bind individuals to each other or to a structure. A leader's ability to inspire this bonding is called charisma, and its base in Freudian theory is the same unfulfilled relationship that was discussed earlier. Just as there are many varieties of unfulfilled relationships, there are many different types of charismatic leaders, each one tapping into a different need. Zaleznik (1974, pp. 223–227) gives these examples:

John F. Kennedy	Youth and Camelot
Charles de Gaulle	Heroism and grandeur
Mahatma Gandhi	Spirituality and revolution
Adolph Hitler	Untransformed sexuality and aggression

The limitation of a leadership situation based on transference is that the relationship does not engage the full abilities of the leader or the follower. Leaders are on a pedestal. If they collude in maintaining the idealized image, the only characteristics they can display are the ones that maintain the idealization. This rules out the full use of their abilities and the less than perfectly honed aspects of their personality, even though some of these qualities may be essential for solving complex problems. The price for the followers is equally high. Leaders who are described as charismatic often develop loyal but passive staffs. The staffs echo their leader's views but withhold, or even remain unaware of, their own preferences and points of view.

Kets de Vries and Miller draw upon the work of contemporary theorists who have built on Freud's original description of transference (Kets de Vries and Miller, 1984, p. 80). Their synthesis describes several forms of transference common to the workplace (pp. 73–94).

Persecutory Transference

One way individuals in a powerless position manage negative feelings is by *splitting* those feelings. Splitting involves taking someone's bad characteristics and attributing them to someone or something else, thereby turning the world into clearly defined camps of bad and good. We are never more powerless than we are as infants, so the pattern of attributing negative characteristics experienced in one's *past* to a figure in one's *present* has solid roots in most people's lives. An example of someone who demonstrates persecutory transference would be the daughter of a strict, pious mother who placed extremely demanding challenges on the daughter. To the world and in the family, the mother was a saint; the child could not possibly be legitimately angry with her. As an adult in the workplace, the daughter worked for a succession of supervisors whom she described as "overly strict, unrealistic, unfeeling, not human."

Splitting allowed the daughter to manage her anxiety by reporting her good and bad feelings about these supervisors. In this way she could feel anger or even rage without feeling guilty (Kets de Vries and Miller, 1984, p. 88). The daughter, so to speak, carried a "punishing mother" slot that most supervisors quickly fit into.

Mirroring Transference

In mirroring transference, individuals fill the void of an unsatisfactory relationship by viewing themselves as they would *like to have been* in that relationship. An example of someone who showed mirroring transference would be a manager who had professionally involved parents and was raised by housekeepers. The housekeepers provided adequate physical care but little love or attention. As an adult, the manager had an overwhelming desire to be noticed and achieved it by taking credit for his subordinates' ideas. His unfulfilled need for recognition was partially achieved by taking the recognition belonging to others and reflecting it back to himself (Kets de Vries and Miller, 1984, p. 85).

Idealizing Transference

In this instance, individuals try to recapture an idealized past by associating with someone who seems omnipotent and perfect. Good features are exaggerated and bad features are minimized. This behavior was demonstrated by an executive from a broken home with an absent father. The executive always seemed to work for superiors whom he initially described as "absolutely incredible, a world-class leader," but who then became "terrible disappointments, absolute frauds." These two extremes were closely connected in that the executive's overblown expectations of an incredible world-class leader often led to disappointment by an absolute fraud. This was a repetition of the cycle he had experienced with his absent father (Kets de Vries and Miller, 1984, p. 82).

Transference keeps repeating itself, but it does not fill the void. In the previous example, even when the superior was regarded as "absolutely incredible," the emotional vacuum from the early years was not filled. This quality of repetition helps to make transference a pervasive and important part of organizational life.

Another reason why transference becomes a by-product of many work relationships is that consultants, trainers, and managers all occupy positions of authority. With such positions, all of the employees' accumulated and unresolved feelings toward authority can reemerge. Under the prevailing norms in most organizations, little opportunity exists for an individual to explore these feelings.

In Group and Organizational Situations in Which Many Individuals Simultaneously Experience Anxiety, Defense Mechanisms, or Transference (Social Defenses)

Social defenses surface in group and organizational situations in which individuals simultaneously experience anxiety, defense, mechanisms, or transference. Freud focuses upon individuals. However, strategies based upon his theory also apply to groups and organizations, because the processes he pinpoints are so universal and powerful that individuals often experience and act upon them *simultaneously*. Zaleznik (1974) points out that it is quite possible for large sections of an entire nation to experience positive transference for a leader such as Charles de Gaulle or John F. Kennedy. It is also possible for a CEO to evoke feelings in an entire organization that were originally formed in response to a parent. Similarly, entire units or departments can experience or be the object of defense mechanisms. Production, Marketing, and Human Resource Management, for example, can experience anger and frustration as a result of downsizing. They can then deposit (project) those feelings onto Accounting.

Freud laid the groundwork for the application of his theories to groups and organizations in a 1921 publication, *Group Psychology and the Analysis of the Ego* (Freud, [1921] 1955). He noted that at the unconscious level uncertainty exists regarding how much individual identity we can maintain and still be a part of a group. The reaction to this uncertainty is intensified affect and reduced intellectual ability.

This is the sign of a weakened ego, and the ego is our bridge between the outside world and our inner psyche (Freud, [1921] 1955, p. 88). In new groups or groups in which the process of group development has been stymied, the ego cannot connect with the external environment. It is thus not doing its job of linking to the outer world. If this happens to group members simultaneously, we have the appearance of a "group mind," but one in which the mind (ego) is functioning at a low level.

A task force comes together to solve a common problem, one that depends upon its members forging a common identity and a common goal as solvers of the problem. Members, however, continue to see themselves as representatives of their own departments, and this inconsistency is never discussed. Group members complain outside of the group that the group is bad, they have trouble thinking clearly in it, they have headaches, and they can't wait for the meetings to be over.

The group has not developed to the point where it serves as a solid environment for the members' egos to function in. Without the boundary-spanning and cushioning functions of the ego, individuals experience the symptoms of anxiety identified by Freud (disturbed thinking, headaches, and so on).

Michael Diamond and Seth Allcorn (1987) offer further examples of what happens in a group when the ego function is weakened. They describe three dysfunctional ways in which work groups create social defenses against anxiety. Then, as a solution to the problems embodied in these groups, they describe how the practitioner can encourage the development of what they term *the intentional group*. Examples of each group are mine.

The Homogenized Group

In the homogenized group, individuals find it difficult, if not impossible, to experience their individuality. Their ego boundary is temporarily dissolved, and they experience themselves as part of a feeling mass. This is the group or organizational situation in which behavior is most akin to mob psychology. Individuals react and behave in a collective fashion based on fear or anger with little thoughtful consideration of the realistic consequences. This situation occurs when there is no leadership or very ineffective leadership, or when outside events make the leadership impotent. It is also the condition of the early period of most unstructured training groups, when a deliberate effort is made by the trainer or group facilitator to abstain from active leadership.

In this situation the ego, which helps us define ourselves as separate from the rest of the world, temporarily functions at a lower level. We experience anxiety, and it feels less safe to be an individual. We then emotionally fuse or blend with other people, but not necessarily in a productive way. Productive interaction and productive work depend upon an acknowledgment of differences. In the emotional fusion process, we experience a sense of primitive "we" that denies differences and limits rational choice.

> For the past eight years the members of a state natural resource agency had worked under an unpredictable director. The director was intelligent and understood the goals and processes of the agency. This made his unpredictability all the more frightening. Every member of the leadership group had at one time been the target of the director's scorn and wrath. When that happened, the director publicly and privately complained about the offending person in a very personal way to all of the other group members. The group members were very uncomfortable when this happened, but efforts to comment about this practice to the director were unsuccessful. The director's unpredictability created a group environment in which the egos of the group members had nothing with which to connect. The survival strategy for group members was to keep as low a profile as possible, say little at meetings, take no risks, and act as if no problems existed. The group behaved as if it were one homogeneous mass.

The Institutionalized Group

In the homogenized group, individuals respond to a weakened ego boundary by joining with others at a primitive emotional level. The absence of strong ego boundaries heightens the threat of what unchecked energy from the id might mean and makes differences between group members very threatening. In the institutionalized group, on the other hand, the boundary function of the ego is achieved by external rules and procedures; it is the classic bureaucracy. In this group, the ego continues to be weak, but the problem is solved by placing all trust and responsibility in a strong external process. The group can accomplish routine tasks but is not flexible or creative.

> The managers' group of the Harbor Bank was confused. For many years the only purpose of their meetings was to receive an update on rules and procedures. Now, as part of a new program in quality service, they were expected to develop a way to measure customer satisfaction and train their clerks in the new procedures. Top management had brought in a consultant to explain the new program, but after the initial explanation the group responded with blank looks. In private conversations after the meeting, they complained that top management did not know what it was doing and was asking the group to

perform an impossible task. As group members, these individuals had turned over the thinking and problem-solving functions of their egos to the bureaucratic routine of their group. It was not safe in this group for members to express diverse opinions and unleash their creativity.

The Autocratic Group

The autocratic group meets the problem of weak ego boundaries in still another way. Instead of retreating into a generalized "we" feeling (the homogenized group) or into rules or procedures (the institutionalized group), members of the autocratic group turn to an all-powerful leader. In doing so, they substitute a representation of their superegos, the ego ideal, for the functioning of their egos. The leader takes over the function of the ego in helping the members of the group to define reality and control their own feelings of aggression. Because it is virtually impossible for any human being to live up to such glorified expectations on a continuous basis, the members are bound to feel some degree of ambivalence toward their leader, and these feelings of ambivalence impair the full functioning of the group.

However, relative to the other two groups, the autocratic group is a functioning group. The members can perform a variety of tasks and, depending upon the ability of the leader and the members' current feelings toward him or her, they can accomplish a good deal. The limitation of the group is that its growth as an entity that can learn from its own mistakes is governed by its dependence on an idealized leader. In addition, unexpressed feelings of ambivalence tend to come out in indirect ways, eventually sabotaging and limiting the group. The exalted position of the leader also seals her or him off from the very feedback that might uncover these ambivalent feelings.

> Nina Martin was chair of the Brownwood County School Board. She had been a member of the board for fifteen years. Board members and school administrators agreed that she was the most knowledgeable member of the board and that she ran a tight ship. There were no permanent subcommittees; Nina appointed ad hoc subcommittees with limited mandates as she saw fit. Board meetings had a tight agenda, with little time wasted and few arguments between board members. This year, Nina's tight control wasn't working. The school board was faced with drastic budget cuts and a taxpayers' revolt that

Nina couldn't fathom. The collective wisdom of the board might have come up with a new approach, but when Nina asked for new ideas, the board members couldn't respond. They looked to Nina to make the board a safe and comfortable place to work and had never explored their own differences or established the give-and-take necessary to do real problem solving.

The Intentional Group

The intentional group has experienced all of the problems of weak ego boundaries that trouble the previous groups. The difference is that this group, with the assistance of a consultant or leader skilled in group dynamics, has learned to spend some time studying its own dynamics and processes. In doing so, it has acknowledged and dealt with its problems. Members have become aware of transference reactions between themselves and the leader. Individual members have become aware of fantasies that they may have about the group and its performance, and an appropriate time is allowed for the group to examine these fantasies. The distinguishing characteristics of the intentional work group is its heightened awareness and a focus on external reactions to unconscious processes.

How to Help a Group to Become More Intentional

The following example illustrates the learning process that helps a group to become intentional.

> The city council of a midsized New England town had been struggling with a citizens' group for almost a year over the location of a new multiservice center. Each side in the controversy held a low opinion of the character and motivation of the other side. The city council was now meeting in a closed session to define a new position and pick a representative to meet with the citizens' group. They decided to send a relatively low-level recent hire from the planning department. A process consultant, who had been working with the group long enough to build some trust, said, "I wonder if your choice of Mr. Hulbert, who, as you know, is inexperienced in this area, reflects your feelings about the citizens' group. Are you really sending someone who in fact represents your low opinion of this group?" At first there were denials, but then one member of the council said, "Well, I hate to admit it, but that may be how I feel about that group." This was followed by a vigorous discussion of how the various council members felt about the citizens' group, and some members acknowledged that they

didn't think much of the group and that the choice of an inexperienced person represented that judgment. This discussion in turn led to a different proposal, and a more experienced person was chosen to present it.

What happened here? The practitioner confronted the group with an *interpretation* of its behavior. After some hesitation, one member of the group confirmed at least the partial truth of this interpretation, and the ensuing discussion helped the group to become aware of its collective assumptions and fantasies and thereby to become more intentional.

Note that the individuals in this group were able to accept and understand the possibility of unconscious motivation on a collective basis that would have been harder to accept on an individual basis. It took only one member of the council to trigger others to acknowledge their feelings toward the citizens' group. This might not have occurred on an individual basis, and it would be unwise and unethical for someone who is not a therapist to offer such interpretations on an individual basis. Skillful use of the group process, however, helped one council member, and then others, to become aware of and accept the unconscious feelings they harbored about the citizens' group.

Applications at the Individual Level

When dealing with individual situations of transference and defense mechanisms, Freud's point of influence is useful in identifying the underlying dynamics of a problem and pointing the way toward the use of other noninterpretative strategies.

Dealing with Defense Mechanisms. The individual defense mechanism of projection was illustrated by Marie, the sales representative who was unable to acknowledge her anger toward Frank, her sales manager. Instead she *projected* her anger by stating that Frank was angry with her. Without interpreting, a practitioner could employ the following strategies:

1. *Confrontation and use of self.* The practitioner says to Marie, "You know, Marie, I noticed that when you said that Frank was angry with you, my own stomach tightened as it sometimes does when I'm with someone who is angry. I also noticed your own

jaw tightening. How do you feel about Frank?" With some degree of trust, this statement might evoke a realization from Marie that she is angry with Frank. For more information on this approach see Chapter Five (Carl Rogers) and Chapter Eight (Fritz and Laura Perls). A less confrontational version would be to simply ask Marie how she would feel if Frank left the company. This question might not bring forth an awareness the first time it is asked, but if the consultant can continue to raise such questions in a nonthreatening manner, Marie may begin to become aware of her own feelings. The next step would be to help Marie accept these feelings.

2. *Sharing of perceptions.* If Marie could be part of a group that she experienced as supportive, she and Frank might *unfreeze* and share some perceptions of what it is like to work with each other. In a supportive atmosphere, Marie might become more aware and accepting of her own feelings. For more information on this strategy see Chapter Seven (Kurt Lewin).

Dealing with Transference. When you are the object of someone's transference, the person treats you as if you were someone you are not. This most likely means that the other person is reacting to you based on some aspect of yourself that triggers old memories or feelings in him or her. The solution is to more clearly establish your full identity in the relationship.

Stephen Quinn is an internal consultant for a large chemical company. He was called in to do team building for an auditing group in the Western regional office. Neither he nor anyone from the internal organization development group had any contact with this office before. From the first contact with the director of the auditing group, he noticed that he was being treated in an odd way. At first the director seemed to give him a great deal of deference, referring to him as "the good doctor." At the same time, the director and his immediate staff would react to Stephen as if he were an immediate threat, saying in a joking way that they had better get in shape "before the good doctor gives us some of his worst medicine." This reaction was not based on anything that Stephen was aware of. He did not feel like a great expert who could solve all their problems, nor was he aware of any tendency to punish the group. On a very personal level, Stephen was aware of a tightening in his stomach and a vague feeling of uneasiness whenever he was with the director.

Transference is a phenomenon of our unconscious mind, so it is not easy to establish its occurrence with absolute certainty. But for Stephen in this situation, the key signs were there. These same signs would also flag the presence of transference in a variety of other management and conflict situations.

Before Stephen had a chance to demonstrate his competence, he was treated with exaggerated deference. This deference, again without any visible change in his own behavior, changed to thinly veiled fear and anxiety. Because Stephen had learned to trust his own internal reactions, he was concerned; whenever he was with the director he felt an emotional and physical reaction that seemed inappropriate to the situation. This raised the possibility that some sort of transference was taking place. Stephen felt that if the director would deal with his true self rather than this caricature of an all-wise and punishing authority figure, his team-building efforts would have a better chance for success.

What could Stephen do to get out of the dynamic of transference? The following interventions and any others that Stephen might follow successfully would only *temporarily* remove the transference from the other individual. They might, however, permanently end his transference process with Stephen. To permanently alter the transference process within the other individual would involve psychotherapy. The removal of transference with Stephen, however, was a worthwhile goal, for until the transference dynamic was out of the way, its presence would obscure anything else Stephen might do. The best possibility in this situation was to use any intervention or combination of interventions that would allow Stephen to emerge as himself. The following interventions could be used:

1.   *Self-disclosure.* This can be tricky, for Stephen must reveal enough of himself without overwhelming the client with facts (this is not the place for a long life story) or emotion. It is also not the place for a confrontation that will leave the client feeling that she or he has been outdone. It is the time to be human and to honestly reveal some facet of his own reactions, feelings, or vulnerabilities that will conflict with the stereotype or slot in which the client has placed him. This self-disclosure must be genuine, yet not overwhelming. If Stephen is unfamiliar with making such disclo-

sures, it will probably be difficult or awkward to do so in this situation. In response to the question, "What do you think we should do?" Stephen could say, "I've found that often my first opinion is way off, and I've gotten into big trouble when I act on it. That is why I need to speak to more of you before I can even speculate as to what we might do."

2. *Creating a New Situation.* This would involve a restructuring of the group so that it is easier for the client to learn more about Stephen. One tactic would be to have the client unit break into small groups and brainstorm questions they would like Stephen to answer about himself. At the same time Stephen poses similar questions to the group. Stephen and the client then take turns asking and responding to questions.

3. *Confrontation.* A confrontation is not a put-down, but it does help clients to see the discrepancies in their own behavior. Stephen might say, "When you call me 'the good doctor,' I get the impression that I'm here to fix you, cure you, or give you some harsh medicine. I see myself as someone working jointly with you to find solutions for some important problems. How do you see me?" Or, in a group session, Stephen might say, "It sounds as if you think I'm here to set all of you straight, is that right?"

Given the nature of this situation, these interventions are the most promising, but given a different situation or combination of personalities, the consultant could also attempt to use the following strategies:

1. *Increasing personal awareness.* The consultant may use active listening (see Chapter Five) to paraphrase a remark by saying, for example, "It sounds as if you think I'm here to keep the group in line."

2. *Expanding awareness for the situation.* The consultant might say, for example, "I wonder if we could take a moment and brainstorm all the resources this group has for dealing with this problem."

3. *Providing support.* This could be done simply through the active listening discussed as part of increasing personal awareness; it could also be done by creating a supportive situation, saying, "You know, it looks as though the directors in the other divisions

might be having a similar problem. I know you people don't usually meet, but I wonder if you could spend some time exploring how other people are working with this issue."

Beyond Freud: Melanie Klein and Wilfred Bion and the Influence Point of Object Relations

Melanie Reizes was born in Vienna in 1882. As a young woman she participated in an arranged marriage with Arthur Klein. In 1910, she and her husband settled in Budapest, where she entered analysis with Sandor Ferenczi, one of Freud's most creative followers. Ferenczi and later the more orthodox Freudian Karl Abraham encouraged Klein to become an analyst and then to apply Freud's ideas to young children. Klein's contribution was to build on Freud's notion of childhood struggle by carrying it back to infancy (Klein, 1959). To do this, she developed a method of analyzing the play of very young children. In this play, she saw not only the peace and innocence commonly associated with the very young but also deep feelings of rage and anger. She found "[l]imbs shall trample, hit and kick; . . . mouth shall devour, swallow and 'kill' (annihilate); eyes kill by a look" (Riviere, quoted in Gross-Kurth, 1986, p. 223). From this experience and this perspective Klein developed her theory of *object relations*.

The Object Relations Point of Influence

The *object relations point of influence* is the ambivalent feeling toward power and authority that is developed as an infant and that later influences adult behavior. The objects in Klein's theory are the images in our mind that we develop as a result of our early experiences. These images or objects form the core of our personality and govern how we experience and react to the world. Klein's special contribution was to focus on the first years, when we were both completely powerless and unable to intellectually understand our experiences. She then pointed out how the ambivalence, rage, and anger that one would expect from someone in this position influences that person's adult behavior.

Klein focused upon the mother as the first and primary object of strong and conflicting emotions. To the infant, the mother provides love, warmth, and nourishment, but it is also true that this mother will at times withhold these benefits. Klein noted that the infant, without being able to grasp it intellectually, feels unconsciously that this and other discomforts are inflicted *intentionally* by hostile forces. The infant at this time is developing a personality by taking in or introjecting the experience of the mother. This introjection is both good and bad, pleasant and unpleasant. Individuals can introject the mother's love and understanding, and these qualities are the basis for their future capacity to have empathy for others. Infants can also take in the mother's anger, annoyance, and impatience. The mother is thus *both* a bad and a good introjected object. The infant, however, has difficulty managing these radically conflicting emotions. The infant's solution is internal and external. It first deals with the problem internally by creating a fantasy about a good mother who provides and a bad mother who punishes by withholding. This is the internal part of object relations in Klein's theory, and it is basic to the development of the personality. We develop our ego and superego by taking in (introjecting) our early experiences.

Klein called the good and bad division of this experience *splitting*. Splitting is a familiar part of the world of childhood, as evidenced by fairy tales that routinely divide the world into the good and bad. Splitting continues to occur in the adult world. Organizational life is filled with situations in which individuals have conflicting feelings; this makes object relations especially relevant to organizations. Usually, some factual basis exists for the splitting, some real event that sets up individuals as projection objects. Larry Hirschhorn (1992, pp. 176–177) describes an example of splitting:

> Two executives, Mr. Cook and Mr. Dry, worked in a bank. Dry was hired from a previous position in which he acted the role of the hard enforcer. Cook, his superior, was concerned that Dry was stirring up the employees too much in his new position. However, despite urging from the consultant, Cook did not pass this information on to Dry.

Consciously or unconsciously, Dry was encouraging a process of splitting. The employees could look upon Dry as the "mean" supervisor and Cook as the benevolent supervisor. Cook was thus an ideal candidate for the projection of good feelings, and Dry was already the recipient of projected bad feelings. The second external part of this process occurred when individuals projected their own good and bad fantasies upon Cook and Dry.

Klein dealt with another interesting phenomenon: our feelings about our feelings. Strong feelings affect us in two ways. The first is our reaction to the feeling itself. The second is the reaction of guilt or depression that the initial feeling triggers in the superego. Klein differed from Freud in maintaining that the superego begins to develop in infancy. The infant or small child faces the task of reconciling its initial reactions of anger and rage toward its main object of love, its mother. The *quality* of later object relationships depends upon both the initial relationship with the mother and what the individual has done subsequently to accept and integrate these internal responses.

Klein defines as a depressed state the reaction that takes place when splitting occurs in adult life and we realize that it has occurred. We are unhappy at having unfairly attributed all that is bad to others. The depressed state, however, offers an opportunity for growth. If we can live with our depressed feelings long enough to hold or contain them, we can reintegrate our split image and reestablish a relationship on new grounds. Klein called this *making reparations*. If it can be done with genuine feelings, relationships can be repaired without groveling or feeling demeaned.

Larry Hirschhorn, an organizational consultant with expertise in object relations theory, describes a situation in which he had an initial interview with a client at a time when he had been feeling depressed and vulnerable. In the interview he had discounted the client's problems and not given them his best attention. When he realized that he had done this, and that he was attributing negative feelings to the client that did not exist, he called the client, acknowledged that he might have been "off" that day, said he was interested in the project, and offered to submit a fresh proposal (the reparations). To do this he had to acknowledge his depressed state without sinking into disabling guilt and to define appropriate compensation (a renewed statement of interest in the project) (Hirschhorn, 1988, pp. 206–209).

Most organizations are based upon some degree of power disparity. Hirschhorn's example illustrates that differences in power, such as those between a consultant and a client, can trigger feelings and behavior that are rooted in old relationships as well as such secondary reactions as guilt. His example illustrates how object relations theory can be used both to trigger self-awareness and to respond positively to the situation by making reparations.

Basic Assumptions as Group Objects

Wilfred Bion, a student of Klein, developed his theory by working with therapy groups that studied their own group process in a British veterans' hospital. Bion (1961) focused on what happens when individuals in a group simultaneously experience the internal processes that Klein identified. He called these processes "basic assumptions," because the group is acting as if it were in fact two groups: one carrying out a conscious task together and another for the purpose of carrying out the psychological processes described in the following paragraphs. On a long-term basis, the internal experience of Bion's basic assumptions are not much of a defense, but they do offer temporary comfort.

The basic assumption of *dependency* offers a group the notion that it will be taken care of by an all-wise and caring leader. This basic assumption is often in place at the very start of a group. The basic assumption of *fight or flight* offers the group the notion that the group has come together to either fight or flee from someone or something. With this assumption, the group has a task. The task might not be based in reality, but even a false task temporarily relieves anxiety. The basic assumption of *pairing* offers the notion that the group has come together to watch two or more individuals perform a task. Again, the notion does not lead to real work because the group was most likely brought together to use the abilities of all of its members and not to function simply as an audience for a few.

Where to Use the Object Relations Point of Influence

Organizations are fertile grounds for evoking the reactions of our earliest object relations. As infants, even with loving parents, we experienced an imbalance of power and a limited ability to express our thoughts and needs. Such imbalances of power and limited communication are also intrinsic to life in organizations. Organizations limit individual options in order to expand collective options. In doing so they re-create the emotions of our earliest object relations. We work in organizations at a task and for a goal we might not have chosen, for a reward that might seem inadequate, and for and with individuals who might not understand or appreciate us. Reactions to these experiences touch on our earliest experiences with power and authority. They are individual reactions, but they take a collective form. The dynamics identified by Klein pervade any organization that would include individuals with the early childhood experiences that Klein describes. They are apt to be most vividly present in (1) organizational groups, task forces, teams, and meetings and (2) the task and culture of an organization.

Organizational Groups

The experience of the Menninger Clinic as an organization illustrates the degree to which object relations and basic assumptions can become embedded in organizational groups and meetings. After a leadership change in the late 1960s, the clinic began sending members of the organization to group process conferences at the A. K. Rice Institute of the Washington School of Psychiatry. The group experience in these conferences is designed to bring Bion's basic assumptions into sharp relief. It does so by focusing on the way in which participants treat group consultants (authority figures) and each other with feelings and attitudes that were shaped by their early experiences with object relations.

A typical example of such behavior would be when a participant defers to the wisdom of a consultant regarding a group incident in which the participant, or the participants collectively, knew as much as if not more than the consultant. The intervention would be for the consultant to say something like the following: "Questions are now being asked of the consultant as if she were the source of all wisdom, even though the information is in the minds of the group members themselves." This phenomenon would illustrate Bion's basic assumption of dependency.

Roy Menninger, president of the Menninger Foundation, offered concrete examples of the impact of group training that is based on Bion's theory. After sending individuals to these training groups for a number of years, he reported the following changes in the organization's meetings (Menninger, 1975, 1985):

- A growing awareness of excessive dependence upon the formal group leader
- A growing awareness of how group members silently colluded in promoting the very conditions they complained about
- Several dramatic examples of the ability to forge a consensus in projects that had previously been stalemated
- A growing ability to deal with conflict rather than smothering it

The Culture of an Organization

The impact of *simultaneous* Kleinan projection, introjection, and splitting is made clear in Isabel Menzies's study of how nurses cope with the powerful and conflicting emotions inherent in caring for the sick (Menzies, 1960). Menzies describes the function of seemingly irrational hospital rules and procedures that prompt nurses to do such things as wake patients up to give them a sleeping pill. She explained this behavior by pointing out that nurses operate under a great deal of stress. Not only must they be in contact with people who are ill and injured, often seriously, but their work involves carrying out tasks that by ordinary standards are distasteful, even frightening. Intimate contact with patients can arouse strong positive and negative feelings: pity, anxiety, love, guilt, hatred, and resentment. Patients and relatives also have complicated feelings toward the hospital and the nurses who represent it: gratitude, affection, respect, envy, and resentment, to name a few. How do the egos of nurses and others involved with patient care handle this daily onslaught of powerful feelings?

Besides the individual mechanisms of defense, the nursing profession and hospitals have developed several institutionalized barriers against feelings. These are social defenses, and they take such forms as having the nurses provide limited care for a large number of patients, thus reducing individual contact. Patients are depersonalized, so that they may be referred to as "the liver in bed seven." Care for a patient is decided by the patient's fit into a category of diseases rather than by personal or idiosyncratic needs. Standardization also builds personal barriers: there is one way to make a bed, one time and one way to wash a patient. Attachment is discouraged. Nurses must be able to move from department to department at a moment's notice, and elaborate systems of checking and counterchecking minimize individual responsibility for decision making (Menzies, 1960).

In Menzies's account, the nurses *introjected* the impersonal authority of the hospital into themselves as a justification for treating patients in an impersonal manner rather than according to individual needs. This is similar to the way a clerk at the Department of Motor Vehicles, bored and frustrated in a routine job, can introject the authority of the office as a way of behaving contrary to his or her own standards.

Menzies also describes the task of nursing as involving a degree of responsibility that is often difficult to bear. If nurses were not responsible enough, patients would suffer or even die. On the other hand, if they assumed the full mantle of responsibility, with all its implications, they might become overly strict. Menzies found that the nurses she observed as a group attributed (*projected*) irresponsible impulses to their juniors and a painfully severe attitude to their seniors. These roles were then accepted by juniors and seniors. The nurses unconsciously projected a feeling or impulse that was unacceptable to themselves onto other groups, and the groups accepted it.

Menzies's nurses were caught between their feelings of compassion and disgust. They were unable to sustain both feelings with balance and continuity. The unconscious solution was to *split* their feelings of authority and responsibility from their personal experience and project them into the ritual of drug administration (Hirschhorn, 1988, p. 2). They were thus able to perform an act that is quite uncomfortable or disturbing for the patient without feeling personally responsible. The stress of life-and-death situations in hospitals accentuates the importance of structures and norms to alleviate anxiety, but hospitals are not unique.

Using the Object Relations Point of Influence at the Group and Organizational Level

How could a consultant use concepts from Klein's theory and Bion's theory to deal with the nurses described by Menzies? Individuals in a group that have been brought together for the purpose of training or consultation usually reproduce workplace behaviors or problems. The training group then becomes a microcosm or miniature version of the workplace, except that in the training situation individuals have an increased opportunity to become aware of their behavior and its implications.

Suppose that these nurses were in a training group and in the course of the workshop one of the nurses was absent. If the nurses behaved in the training group as they did in the hospital, they would deny, muffle, or suppress any anger or sadness they felt over this absence. The group consultant could then raise the possibility that the nurses were dealing with this absence the same way they dealt with their reactions to death and illness in the workplace. Bringing the unconscious to light is a cumbersome and indirect process. Such interpretations are rarely accepted the first time, but, as illustrated by Menninger (1985), the process can be effective.

In another example, Michael Diamond consulted at an organizational level to a state development agency concerning social defenses. In doing so he combined Kurt Lewin's action research (see Chapter Seven) with the interpretative concepts of Bion, Klein, and other object relations theorists. Diamond used conventional interviewing and feedback methodology to present interpretations that highlighted the agency's pattern of conflict avoidance. The interviews revealed that a serious split between the business development and community development units was neither acknowledged nor being dealt with, nor were differences between the leader of community development and the agency head. Bion's fight-or-flight notion guided the consultants as they facilitated a series of group meetings. When organization members inadvertently behaved in a way that confirmed this diagnosis (as when one top manager slipped and said, "The duty of top managers is to avoid"), the consultants pointed this out. The issues came to a head at a role clarification session, and at the end of the consultation the group was beginning to deal with the issues that had been avoided (Diamond, 1993, pp. 163–191).

The person or self of practitioners themselves is also a valuable tool in working with collective images of the organization. Edward Shapiro was invited to serve as an Institute leader for an educational conference of a professional association. Despite the friendly acceptance of his lectures, he found the experience disturbing. As Institute leader, he remained cut off and isolated from integrating experiences with the rest of the Institute that would have enhanced the learning from his lectures. He felt, to use the title of his account of this experience, "Lost in Familiar Places." He was an acknowledged expert delivering lectures to what appeared to be a friendly audience, yet he felt lost. This feeling sensitized him to be aware of other clues regarding what was going on in the association.

Shapiro discovered that a declining business environment for the Institute members had subtly shifted them from the task of seeking the truth to networking for survival. This shift was below the consciousness of the members but was represented in a wide range of behaviors, ranging from expressions of contempt for the Institute's founding fathers to an intent focus on themes of absent or crippled leadership in the program presentations. Shapiro's contradictory role was that of an ambivalent object standing for the members' uncertain feelings about their relationship to the organization. At the end of the Institute, he was invited to share his organizational perceptions; in doing so he precipitated an intense discussion that brought some of these ambivalent feelings to light (Shapiro and Carr, 1991, pp. 88–94). In this example, the conceptual insights of Klein and Bion were combined with the use of self. Use of self is more fully discussed by Carl Rogers in Chapter Five and Fritz and Laura Perls in Chapter Eight.

The Freudian and Object Relations Points of Influence and Joining

Freud and the object relations theorists have identified the process that distorts and discourages individual motivation to join groups and organizations. This process consists of transference and defense mechanisms.

Healthways, a large medical products distributor, had determined that it was going to change its relationship with its suppliers. Rather than dealing with its suppliers at arms' length or in an adversarial way, it was attempting to enter into an alliance with several of its major providers. This meant that many of its own employees would have to make a commitment of time, energy, and trust to periodic meetings with these providers.

The first task was to focus on the process of identification. Individuals would have to join and identify with a new group composed jointly of Healthways members and suppliers. In a Freudian context, a major obstacle to such identification would be the various internal mechanisms of defense and transference that members of the new "alliance groups," as they were now termed, had habitually used to defend themselves from such unacceptable feelings as

anger and fear. Another issue was the degree to which alliance members reacted to other individuals in terms of old associations (transference). The antidote for these feelings and processes was open acknowledgment and
discussion. One way in which situations were structured to encourage such discussion was by building in time and opportunity for Healthways members,
perhaps with a facilitator, to discuss their feelings before and after alliance
group meetings, and then, at a later point, structuring several groups composed of both Healthways members and suppliers to discuss what working in
this alliance was like for each of them.

The actual meetings of each alliance group were also fertile ground for
Bion's basic assumptions and Diamond and Allcorn's social defenses. The antidote was again awareness, along with acceptance and understanding of these
forces. To achieve this result, leadership and/or consultation had to follow Diamond and Allcorn's instructions for building an intentional group.

The Freudian and Object Relations
Points of Influence and Conflict

The main value of these theories in dealing with conflict is that they
help protagonists to stay as close to the actual issues as possible.
They do this by helping the group to identify and at least temporarily neutralize the transference and defenses that color the conflict with the members' intrapsychic (or internal psychological)
history. Several avenues exist for doing this. To the extent that individual defenses are experienced on a group basis and the group
is willing to focus upon this possibility, it can learn to process its own
behavior. This is most likely to occur with the help of a facilitator
trained to work with group-level interpretations. Examples of ways
to work with such transference and defenses on an individual basis
were discussed earlier in this chapter and include Hirschhorn, *The
Workplace Within* (1988); Colman and Bexton (Eds.), *Group Relations
Reader* (1975); and Colman and Geller (Eds.), *Group Relations Reader
2* (1985).

The Freudian and Object Relations Points
of Influence and Psychological Growth

Freud's theory of psychological growth focuses on what happens up
to the age of five and views the rest of life in terms of the repetition

of these incidents. The Freudian and object relations point of influence thus deal mostly with the *obstacles* to growth.

As illustrated in the Introduction, most changes that an organization makes will require some degree of psychological growth from its members. In the process of organizational change, individuals will be asked to consider different information, operate in a different paradigm, relate to people differently, and alter some of their personal boundaries in ways that they have not done before. Transference and defense mechanisms are natural human reactions to such a situation. They are also obstacles to the personal growth needed to respond to such change and must be dealt with. For example, if an organization asked managers who were used to supervising and giving orders to offer a different sort of leadership to self-directed teams, these managers would have to engage in some degree of psychological growth. As a result of their new role they could experience transference and defensive behavior from the individuals they supervise. Without some degree of psychological growth these managers could not function effectively in their new psychological environment. The chapter sections on transference and defense mechanisms offer a number of suggestions for dealing with such problems.

In addition, the object relations point of influence goes beyond Freud's focus on minimizing obstacles to growth and offers a positive step using the notion of *reparations*. Reparations requires the individual to acknowledge his or her depressed position and avoid sinking into a paralyzing state of guilt long enough to define an appropriate way to mend a relationship. In an organization, this might occur, for example, if a police department that was receiving diversity training managed to avoid both a defensive position that denied aspects of the department's possibly racist previous behavior or a position in which members of the department wallowed in and were paralyzed by guilt about such behaviors. The object relations point of influence requires a special brand of realism toward oneself, but the product of this realism can be psychological growth.

Conclusion

The ideas of Freud, Klein, and Bion all emphasize the importance of *repetition*. Individuals singly and collectively tend to repeat life experiences that were previously incomplete or imperfectly completed. Such early experiences are relevant to life in organizations because organizations routinely duplicate the conditions of power disparity that we all experienced as infants and children. We never had less power than when we were very young, and organizations by their nature invariably give more power to some than others. The theories of Freud, Klein, and Bion give us the best handle on understanding our reactions when current experiences trigger such old feelings and reactions.

The chapter then offers two ways to deal with these unconscious impulses. The first way includes the direct noninterpretative responses suggested in the sections on transference and defense mechanisms. The second way is the more interpretative group methods suggested in the section on object relations.

Annotated Bibliography
Original Sources: Readable Freud

All of the following works of Freud are also available in inexpensive paperback editions.

Freud, S. "Group Psychology and the Analysis of the Ego." In J. Strachey (ed.), *The Standard Edition of the Complete Psychological Works of Sigmund Freud.* Vol. 18. London: Hogarth Press and Institute of Psycho-Analysis, 1955. (Originally published 1921.)
This is Freud's only work dealing with groups. It is short and readable and will give you an understanding of how he believes individual dynamics are played out collectively.

Freud, S. "General Theory of the Neuroses." In J. Strachey (ed.), *The Standard Edition of the Complete Psychological Works of Sigmund Freud.* Vol. 16. London: Hogarth Press and Institute of Psycho-Analysis, 1963. (Originally published 1917.)
These are lectures that Freud delivered and are aimed at the general literate public. Like most of Freud's writings, they are clear and gracefully written. They focus on the earlier version of Freud's theory, before he had developed his ideas about the psychic structure, but they do provide an excellent description of his view of the role and importance of dreams and the unconscious.

Freud, S. "New Introductory Lectures on Psychoanalysis." In J. Strachey
    (ed.), *The Standard Edition of the Complete Psychological Works of Sig-
    mund Freud.* Vol. 22. London: Hogarth Press and Institute of Psycho-
    Analysis, 1964. (Originally published 1932.)
Because of Freud's declining health, these lectures were never actually
delivered, but they are written in a clear and graceful style. They do not
supersede the earlier lectures but continue to the full development of
Freud's theory.

Secondary Sources: Books About Freud and His Theories

Gay, P. *Freud: A Life for Our Time.* New York: W. W. Norton, 1988.
Many biographies of Freud exist—some pro, some anti. This work by a
distinguished historian is objective and well written.

Hall, C. S. *A Primer of Freudian Psychology.* New York: New American Li-
    brary, 1954.
This is an excellent summary of Freud's basic ideas.

Mitchell, J. *Psychoanalysis and Feminism.* New York: Pantheon Books, 1974.
It's impossible to consider Freud's ideas today without also considering
his views on women. This work examines Freud's ideas from a feminist
perspective but also with a close examination of the text and a consideration of Freud's times.

Organizational Applications

Colman, A. D., and Bexton, W. H. (eds.). *Group Relations Reader.* Sausalito,
    Calif.: GREX, 1975.
Colman, A. D., and Geller, M. H. (eds.). *Group Relations Reader 2.* Spring-
    field, Va.: A. K. Rice Institute, 1985.
These two readers focus on the theory and applications of Klein's object
relations theory as they are presented in Tavistock group relations conferences.

Hirschhorn, L. *The Workplace Within: Psychodynamics of Organizational Life.*
    Cambridge, Mass.: MIT Press, 1988.
This book provides useful theory and the experiences of a consultant operating in the object relations tradition.

Kets de Vries, M.F.R., and Miller, D. *The Neurotic Organization: Diagnosing
    and Changing Counterproductive Styles of Management.* San Francisco:
    Jossey-Bass, 1984.
This book covers a wide range of managerial and organizational processes
from a broad framework that builds on Freud's theories and includes the

work of many current psychodynamic theorists. It also includes many useful examples and short case studies.

Levinson, H. *Emotional Health in the World of Work.* New York: Harper-Collins, 1964.
This is the closest one gets to the roles and functions of the manager from a purely Freudian perspective.

Menzies, I.E.P. "A Case-Study in the Functioning of Social Systems as a Defense Against Anxiety." *Human Relations,* 1960, *13,* 95–121.
This is a classic case study that has been widely reprinted and quoted from. It contains detailed and specific examples of how Freudian and object relations dynamics can be institutionalized in organizational norms and procedures.

Bibliography

Allcorn, S. *Workplace Superstars in Resistant Organizations.* Westport, Conn.: Quorum Books, 1991.

Bion, W. R. *Experiences in Groups and Other Papers.* New York: Basic Books, 1961.

Diamond, M. A. *The Unconscious Life of Organizations: Interpreting Organizational Identity.* Westport, Conn.: Quorum Books, 1993.

Diamond, M. A., and Allcorn, S. "The Psychodynamics of Regression in Work Groups." *Human Relations,* Aug. 1987, *40,* 525–543.

Fine, G. A. "The Assault on Freud." *Contemporary Sociology,* 1984, *13,* 686–688.

Freud, S. *The Standard Edition of the Complete Psychological Works of Sigmund Freud,* Vol. 18: *Beyond the Pleasure Principle* (J. Strachey, ed.). London: Hogarth Press and Institute of Psycho-Analysis, 1955. (Originally published 1921.)

Freud, S. *Group Psychology and the Analysis of the Ego* (J. Strachey, ed.). New York: Liveright, 1959.

Freud, S. *The Standard Edition of the Complete Psychological Works of Sigmund Freud,* Vol. 16, Part III: *Introductory Lectures on Psycho-Analysis* (J. Strachey, ed.). London: Hogarth Press and Institute of Psycho-Analysis, 1963. (Originally published 1917.)

Freud, S. *The Standard Edition of the Complete Psychological Works of Sigmund Freud,* Vol. 23: *Moses and Monotheism: An Outline of Psychoanalysis and Other Works* (J. Strachey, ed.). London: Hogarth Press and Institute of Psycho-Analysis, 1964b. (Originally published 1938.)

Freud, S. *New Introductory Lectures on Psychoanalysis* (J. Strachey, ed.). New York: W. W. Norton, 1964.

Gross-Kurth, P. *Melanie Klein: Her World and Her Work.* Cambridge, Mass.: Harvard University Press, 1986.

Hirschhorn, L. *The Workplace Within: Psychodynamics of Organizational Life.* Cambridge, Mass.: MIT Press, 1988.

Hirschhorn, L., and Gilmore, T. "The New Boundaries of the 'Boundaryless' Company." *Harvard Business Review,* June 1992, *70*(3), 104–115.

Janis, I. L. *Groupthink: Psychological Studies of Policy Decisions and Fiascoes.* Boston: Houghton Mifflin, 1982.

Kets de Vries, M.F.R., and Miller, D. *The Neurotic Organization: Diagnosing and Changing Counterproductive Styles of Management.* San Francisco: Jossey-Bass, 1984.

Kets de Vries, M.F.R., and Miller, D. *Unstable at the Top: Inside the Troubled Organization.* New York: New American Library, 1988.

Klein, M. "Our Adult World and Its Roots in Infancy." *Human Relations,* 1959, *12,* 291–301.

Levinson, H. *Emotional Health in the World of Work.* New York: HarperCollins, 1964.

McGrath, W. J. *Freud's Discovery of Psychoanalysis: The Politics of Hysteria.* Ithaca, N.Y.: Cornell University Press, 1986.

Malcolm, J. *In the Freud Archives.* New York: Knopf, 1984.

Masson, J. M. *The Assault on Truth: Freud's Suppression of the Seduction Theory.* New York: Farrar, Straus & Giroux, 1984.

Menninger, R. W. "The Impact of Group Relations Conferences on Organizational Growth." In A. D. Colman and W. H. Bexton (eds.), *Group Relations Reader* (pp. 265–280). Sausalito, Calif.: GREX, 1975.

Menninger, R. W. "A Retrospective View of a Hospital-Wide Group Relations Training Program: Costs, Consequences and Conclusions." In A. D. Colman and M. H. Geller (eds.), *Group Relations Reader 2* (pp. 285–298). Springfield, Va.: A. K. Rice Institute: 1985.

Menzies, I.E.P. "A Case-Study in the Functioning of Social Systems as a Defense Against Anxiety." *Human Relations,* 1960, *13,* 95–121.

Rice, A. K. "Selections from: 'Learning for Leadership.'" In A. D. Colman and W. H. Bexton (eds.), *Group Relations Reader* (pp. 71–158). Sausalito, Calif.: GREX, 1975.

Rycroft, C. Review of *The Assault on Truth,* by J. M. Masson. In *New York Review of Books,* Apr. 12, 1984, *31,* 3–4.

Shapiro, E. R., and Carr, A. W. *Lost in Familiar Places: Creating New Connections Between the Individual and Society.* New Haven, Conn.: Yale University Press, 1991.

Zaleznik, A. "Charismatic and Consensus Leaders: A Psychological Comparison." *Bulletin of the Menninger Clinic,* May 1974, *38*(3), 222–238.

Chapter Two

Carl Jung

The Collective Unconscious, Archetypes, and Psychological Types

Why Carl Jung? An Overview of Organizational Applications

Individuals have significant untapped sources of creativity and energy, and today's organizations need those resources. Jung's concept of archetypes and his description of the exchange of energy between the conscious and the unconscious give practitioners access to a source of behavior at both the individual and the organizational levels. His concept of psychological type is a similar avenue to understanding differences in work style.

Jung's Theories as Influence Points for Dealing with Conflict

Individuals and organizations have a hidden side of their personality that is a frequent source of trouble and embarrassment. Jung's identification of the shadow archetype can help in working with this source of conflict and creativity. His view of the masculine image in the female and the feminine image in the male helps both genders deal with differences that lead to conflict.

Jung's Theories as Influence Points for Dealing with Psychological Growth

Psychological growth is now a necessity in many organizations. Jung's theory provides ways to support this development. His theory of lifelong growth focuses on changes that occur during the adult working years. His linking of Eastern thought with Western psychology provides a bridge to the peak performance associated with higher levels of consciousness.

Jung's Theories as Influence Points for Dealing with the Dilemmas of Joining

Jung's theory of archetypes in the unconscious and conscious psychological functions offers the practitioner a wide array of points of influence to the part of the personality that influences an individual's motivation to join a group or organization.

Jung's Theories as Organizational Images or Metaphors

Jung's archetypes are inner patterns that are known by the images, myths, and metaphors they evoke. His framework of archetypes and his combinations of psychological types are rich sources of such organizational images and metaphors. Archetypes can also be a means of expanding capabilities. In addition, Jung's model of the flow of energy from the unconscious to consciousness can be a revealing model for change within organizations.

Jung's Theories as a Basis for Other Organizationally Relevant Theories

Jung's theory of psychological types has spawned a number of written instruments, theories, and application programs for dealing with individual behavior and organizational change. His identification of archetypes has opened the way for a second generation of archetypal theorists. Individuals such as Carol Pearson, discussed later in this chapter, have developed theories of symbols, stories, and myths that can serve as vehicles for understanding organizational culture and organizational diagnosis and change.

Limitations of Jung's Theories for Use in Organizations

Jung's theory is complex and hard to read. He did not focus his writings for use by the layperson, and it is usually necessary to use secondary works to fully understand his theories. Jung's link to

Eastern thought and mysticism, although attractive to some, is liable to alienate managers and consultants who are oriented toward immediate, visible results.

How Jung Developed His Theories

Like B. F. Skinner, Jung spent a lifetime developing his own approach to understanding human behavior and, like Skinner's approach, Jung's reflects his life. However, unlike Skinner's autobiography, Jung's *Memories, Dreams, Reflections* (Jung, 1963) examines his life from the inside out. In this work Jung describes in detail his significant dreams, including some that he had had as a young child. Jung had two selves. Self One was based in consciousness, and his autobiography contains the usual chronology of dates, names, and places. Self Two was based in the unconscious, and his autobiography includes symbols, dreams, reflections, and fantasy. Jung's life and work was about bringing these two selves together.

Carl Jung was born in the small Swiss village of Kesswil in 1875. His maternal grandfather was a distinguished theologian, his paternal grandfather a well-known physician, and his father a village pastor. From his early childhood, religion was a significant presence in his life, not in the sense of strict devotion or piety, but rather in coming to terms with a greater spiritual power. In his autobiography, Jung's Self One was large, muscular, active, and gregarious. But the focus of the autobiography is on Self Two, who was quiet and extremely introspective. Jung questioned man's place in the universe and was disappointed in his father's shallow grasp of theology. One memorable traumatic event gives us a picture of Jung as a child. He wrote an essay so profound that the teacher made the judgment that no child could have written it, and he publicly humiliated young Carl with this accusation. Jung remembered this incident all of his life.

Like Freud, Jung wanted to become an archeologist, but also like Freud, finances forced him to enter the more practical profession of medicine. Jung decided that he could satisfy both urges by becoming a psychiatrist, and he became an assistant to Eugene Blueler, a leading psychiatrist of the time. As a young physician,

Jung became well known. He adapted the Galton word association test to take advantage of the minuscule pause that occurred when a subject responded to a word with some emotional content. This was an early empirical demonstration of the unconscious, and the original publication of the work in 1906 drew Jung to Sigmund Freud (Donn, 1988, p. 66). At their first meeting, the two pioneers were so entranced with each other's ideas and personalities that they conversed for thirteen hours (Brome, 1968, p. 26). Jung corresponded and collaborated with Freud for seven years and joined him in a famous lecture visit to Clark University in the United States. Freud considered Jung his heir apparent. Jung, however, could not accept Freud's sexual hypotheses as *the* explanation of human motivation. He believed that other forces, including the spiritual and "supernatural," were equally, if not more, important.

A fundamental difference also existed in the way the two theorists viewed the unconscious. For Freud the unconscious was a swamp that had to be drained. Jung found that, despite continuous efforts, the swamp was never fully drained. No matter how many dreams or how many slips of the tongue he analyzed, more always remained. This suggested to Jung that the contents of the swamp might be more than remnants of forgotten or repressed experiences. He also found that much of the material from the unconscious did not even relate to the individual's personal experience. From this, Jung hypothesized the *collective unconscious* as a second level of the unconscious. This level is the repository of our common experience as human beings. Far from being a swamp of suppressed memories, it is a treasure trove of potential wisdom, and it influences our attitudes, feelings, and behavior.

Jung's autobiography illustrates the importance he placed upon this level. He stated, "[A]ll the 'outer' aspects of my life should be accidental. Only what is interior has proved to have substance and a determining value" (Jung, 1963, p. ix). In this comment Jung moved from Freud's view of the unconscious as a distorted *reflection* of the external world to a view of the unconscious as an internal *pattern* or causal basis for behavior. These doctrinal differences, combined with personal and stylistic clashes, led to a permanent split between the two thinkers in 1914. Jung was deeply affected by this break, and he suffered what we today would call a nervous breakdown. He called this episode his "journey into his unconscious," kept careful records of his experiences, and spent the rest of his life exploring its significance. He also explored the significance of his personal and stylistic differences with Freud in his 1923 publication *Psychological Types* (Jung, [1923] 1971). This work later was used as a basis for the Myers-Briggs Type Indicator (MBTI). (Further information on the Myers-Briggs appears in the latter part of this chapter.)

Jung believed that the symbols and dreams that emerged in his journey into the unconscious were images of the enduring life forms that he later called *archetypes*. To find out if these same symbols and images had emerged with other people at other times, Jung studied medieval alchemy, comparative religion, and mythology and made two extensive anthropological expeditions—one to study the Pueblo Indians of New Mexico in 1924–25 and the other to visit what is now Kenya in 1925–26. Jung renamed his approach "analytical psychology" to differentiate it from Freud's psychoanalysis and continued to write and see patients well into old age. His complete works total eighteen volumes.

When psychoanalysis was fashionable, Jung was primarily known as an analyst who had broken with Freud. His focus on the supernatural and inner causation kept his theories from achieving wide acceptance in an era when first psychoanalysis and later strict behaviorism were the most accepted theories. With the development and widespread acceptance of the MBTI and the more general acceptance of Eastern philosophies, Jung has finally come into his own. The irony is that Jung's writings do not display the remotest interest in organizations or even much interest in groups. However, his work on the collective unconscious and psychological types has made his ideas relevant to organizations of the 1990s.

Jung's First Point of Influence

Jung theorized that over the generations, experiences and responses are inscribed into the nervous system so that when a similar experience occurs, behavior reoccurs within basic parameters. We have, in effect, a number of innate propensities to reenact universal patterns of our emotional experience. These predispositions are archetypes or encoded patterns for experience. The patterns are part of each individual's psychological heritage. This point of influence works from the inside out. Outer behavior is a reflection of inner patterns. The inner core of the personality is the collective unconscious or the aspect of our personality that contains archetypes. For Jung, psychological energy flows in both directions between the unconscious and consciousness.

As influential as Jung believed archetypes to be, he did not state that they determine behavior or events in detail. Archetypes are broad patterns, and the exact behavior that emerges from these patterns depends upon the surrounding culture and the specifics of the situation. Because Jung believed that archetypes existed for every recurring situation in life, he didn't believe that anyone could enumerate them. The key to psychological growth for Jung was increasing an individual's awareness and access to these unconscious patterns.

When to Use Jung's Influence Point of Archetypes
When Practitioners Need to Diagnose and Intervene in Organization-Wide Problems

A prime focus for Jung was the two-way flow of psychic energy between the conscious and the unconscious. This flow of energy has an impact on organizations in three ways:

**Preview: When to Use Jung's
Point of Influence in the Workplace.**

1. When energy is repressed and then emerges in troublesome or embarrassing forms
2. When energy flows uncontained from the unconscious to the conscious
3. When practitioners are able to help the organization contain unconscious energy so that it can be used in a helpful form

The Suppressed Flow of Energy

Organizations can suppress or deny energy, maintaining it in an archetype Jung called "The Shadow." In this instance the energy inevitably emerges in troublesome and unpredictable forms. This process is described in detail later in this chapter.

The Unconstrained Flow of Psychic Energy

Jung explained Nazi destructiveness as an example of uncondoned energy from the unconscious. He likened the energy fueling Nazi devastation to that of Wotan, the fierce Germanic god of thunder and martial fury. A less extreme, but similar, process can be found in organizations when a goal (even one as presumably worthy as "excellence") taps into powerful but unrecognized inner forces. Murray Stein gives an example (Stein, 1992, p. 3):

> Ruth, an attractive woman in her late thirties, was single and well placed at the executive level of a large corporation. The corporation was an old, established company that badly needed to change its outmoded ways. It was committed to a program of excellence, and this meant a transformation of the whole corporate culture that required reeducation of all of the organization's managers; Ruth was in the center of this exciting process. The worthy goal of excellence soon had Ruth "by her throat." She was working through weekends and into the earliest hours of the morning. She had no private life, felt no sexual desire, and suffered from sleeplessness and anxiety, and the demonic consultant who was heading the project felt free to call her anytime—day or night—with more suggestions.

Stein does not expand on his example, but these demands upon one person could not exist in a vacuum. It is safe to assume that the unrestrained energy that was so damaging to Ruth influenced other people and quite possibly the norms in the organization.

To use a Jungian metaphor, the remedy in such a situation is to "get the genie back in the bottle" so that the energy can be used productively. The first step is to *acknowledge the energy as part of oneself,* either individually, collectively as part of the organizational culture, or both. This acknowledgment gets the genie back in the bottle. In metaphoric terms, the powerful destructive force is part of ourselves. The next step is to *honor this force from the unconscious* and recognize it as a powerful and potentially useful owned part of the individual or collective self. From this point individuals and organizations can proceed to the process of *containment*, described below.

The Contained Flow of Energy

Energy from the unconscious can also be used productively. Examined, accepted, and understood, it can be a positive source of creativity. But to be used, the energy must be "held" or enclosed, and the organization is one vehicle for this process. Practitioners with a Jungian orientation help the organization to examine the stories, the myths, the roles—all the outer manifestations of archetypes that make up its culture and that are unknowingly acted out in the everyday life of the organization. This can happen if the organization can bring some of its unconscious energy to consciousness. People must be able to step out of defined roles and identify ignored but potentially useful aspects of themselves or of the organization's history or culture (Stein, 1992, p. 12).

McWhinney and Batista (1988) explain old myths and legends in light of current events. This process helps today's managers to draw on the founding energy of the organization. Such analysis can provide fresh insights for strategic planning. McWhinney and Batista illustrate how to contain and use the unconscious energy of an organization by describing a consultation with the Walt Disney Company. They called this process *remythologizing*, maintaining that "interpreting the myths and tales in light of current issues reconnect[ed]" those in the organization "with founding energy, [thereby] giving them guidance in strategic directions" (McWhinney and Batista, 1988, p. 53).

> The original Disney creations drew upon Walt Disney's own memories of his childhood, particularly the period up to adolescence. In this period a young boy could focus on the wonders of science, magic, and adventure in which good and evil are clearly delineated—with good usually winning. He also included adult elements of threat and evil, such as the dancing skeleton in

Disney's early Mickey Mouse films. But by the 1970s, Disney's movies and theme parks had lost their early elements of adult sophistication. Walt Disney's successors had made sure that nothing in the park invoked a sense of evil or worldly ways. As a result, nothing was left in the 1970s park "to appeal to the competitive or achievement-oriented impulses of adolescents and young adults" (McWhinney and Batista, 1988, p. 53). The energy from the original myth had been repressed. Without that force and drive, the park had limited opportunities to change and grow.

McWhinney and Batista's goal was to help the organization rediscover the true origin of its own myths, and in doing so they helped it to again contain the energy from its organizational unconscious. To do this, they involved leaders in a deeper analysis of the tales and the origin of the myth of the founders and used Jungian analysis of symbols as the evidence of unseen personal and communal processes. The process also involved looking at deviant behaviors in order to examine behaviors that were not accounted for in the myth. To accomplish this, McWhinney and Batista facilitated discussions that re-created the universe that existed when the original myths were born. In this way organization members could feel the atmosphere, values, and hidden messages of the time. This process evoked some of the same creative energies in today's context that the myth had created in the thirties and forties.

The result was that the Disney executives could reexamine the theme park from the adolescent perspective and then identify what was missing. What they found missing was paradox and absurdity, the kind found in *Mad Comics*. Following this realization, the executives held on to the Disney themes of basic family values, but they formed a subsidiary company, Touchstone Pictures, which applied the basic Disney approach to family values to successful pictures that had an adult appeal, such as *Splash* and *Three Men and a Baby*.

How to Increase Motivation and Commitment

For Jung, as for Karen Horney and Carl Rogers, individuals have an inherent drive to grow and develop. They experience this force as a lifelong quest for meaning. The *Self* is the archetype that drives this search in the form of a process of *differentiation* and *integration*. Individuals become aware of separate and distinct parts (archetypes) of their psyche. They then integrate the function of these archetypes into the whole. We experience this process as we become aware of another feeling, impulse, or value and then relate this newly discovered part of ourselves to the rest of our personality. If an organization wants commitment from its members, it must tap into this process.

When Organizations Wish to Increase Motivation and Commitment

The application of archetypes to solve an organizational problem was illustrated recently by AT&T in an organization-wide effort to improve "quality" (Zuckerman and Hatala, 1992):

> Like many American corporations in the 1980s, AT&T was attempting to improve the quality of its product and services. Their model was the Japanese application of the work of W. Edwards Deming. Deming advocated using statistical methods so that workers themselves "did it right the first time" without depending on quality inspectors. Initial results, however, were disappointing. AT&T, like many American corporations, found that methods that were widely successful in Japan were much less successful in the United States. The explanation that the culture was different in the United States was accurate but only a partial answer. AT&T management needed to know the specific steps that could be taken so that American workers would make quality a prime consideration.

The answer came from an application of archetypal psychology. AT&T engaged G. Clotaire Rapaille, who had applied archetypal psychology to the problems of a number of European corporations, in order to find out what quality meant to American workers. The initial Jungian premise of his investigation was that a cultural quality archetype, an internal pattern peculiar to Americans, operated when an American attempted to produce a quality product. The next question was, What form did the quality pattern take in the American culture? Rapaille involved a number of participants in a series of experiences using free association and other methods of depth psychology to identify and explore their earliest associations with quality.

The findings were that the American archetype of quality emerged from a childhood experience quite different from that of the Japanese. The American experience involved an overwhelming challenge, initial setbacks, perhaps failure, embarrassment, and/or humiliation. From this initial position, Americans, with the right support and coaching, summon the energy to produce great works. This victory is then celebrated. It is a case of *failure breeding success*. The American recoveries from the attack on Pearl Harbor and the early Russian triumphs in space are good examples of this pattern. This energy, however, dissipates with success. It is hard for Americans to find the energy to keep working on an already successful product without some new threat or crisis.

In contrast, the Japanese archetype of quality is played out in a highly disciplined society that regards initial failure or setbacks as a disgrace, something that is avoided at all costs. For the Japanese, *failure does not breed success*. The Japanese are more easily motivated to follow Deming's advice and "do it right the first time." Their highly disciplined society also encourages them not to be bored with success but to seek constant refinements and improvements even though a product seems to be successful at the time.

These findings concluded that AT&T should develop an American formula for quality that accepted early setbacks as inevitable but then legitimated them and limited their impact by designating them as pilots—or, to use Tom Peters's phrase, "fast failures" (1987, p. 259). Jung's concept of archetypes thus supplied the researchers with an avenue to the unconscious that would lead to discovering a distinctly American highway to success.

When Organizations Want Men and Women to Work Together More Productively

Until recently, most men and women accepted, and worked within, relatively narrow roles. The male world was the "harder" world of being aggressive, rational, autonomous, task-oriented, and tough-minded (Sargent, 1981, p. 2). The female world was "soft." It involved expressing and accepting emotions and nurturing, supporting, and building relationships. Following is an organizational example of the results of these stereotypes.

Everett Page was director of marketing for a large New England manufacturer of lighting fixtures. He was forceful and direct in his manner and had a reputation as a strong competitor. Although he was affable and outgoing, few in the office or at home understood Everett's reactions. No one knew how he felt about their relationship. People who wanted to know how he felt spoke to one of two people whom Everett jokingly called his "two wives"—one at home and one at the office. At home, his wife, Gwen, acted as a buffer and explainer between Everett and his two children. At the office, his administrative assistant, Shirley Clark, performed the same role with other members of the office and sales staff. It was hard for Everett to discuss how he felt, but one of the women was usually available to perform that function.

Both of Everett's "wives" had unfinished agendas in their own work life. Gwen had worked in advertising; she had followed Everett's moves but had never stayed in one location long enough to test her potential. Similarly, Shirley had many ideas for marketing lighting fixtures and a keen sense of how to deal with the various personalities of the sales staff. However, she also had never had the opportunity or taken the necessary risks to put forth her ideas and actions as her own. Both women, in different ways, allowed Everett to express this aspect of their personalities.

These stereotypes are beginning to change, but enough of them still survive to limit men and women. Men such as Everett have difficulty expressing emotions, building support, or nurturing. Women such as Gwen and Shirley do not feel free to channel their energies into logic, analysis, and an emphasis on task completion.

A further difficulty is that the repressed tendencies of both genders do not disappear, but surface awkwardly, indirectly, and less productively. Men who are unaware of their need to express and accept emotion do so in indirect ways—for example, by manipulating women to do it for them. Women who are not aware of, or accepting of, their own need for assertion and control also express these needs in indirect and unproductive ways. This was the case for Everett, Shirley, and Gwen.

Occasionally, Everett expressed his emotions. It was not something that he planned for or even anticipated, but occasionally a feeling would just pop to the surface and he would blurt it out. This made him feel uncomfortable, and he usually found a way to weaken this expression. Sometimes he made a joke;

at other times he pledged the recipient to secrecy. This behavior was confusing to his listeners. This aspect of Everett was not used to open expression, and when he declared himself he did not know how to follow up.

A different situation occurred with Shirley. She had a real ability to deal with figures. Her quick perception of math and her sensitivity with people made her an excellent negotiator. She found that when she was discussing the cost of an item, she could do the math in her head so quickly that the person she was dealing with, usually a man, had to concede the point that she was making. In these instances, Shirley laughed nervously, made a self-deprecating remark, and apologized for what she had said. Shirley was as uncomfortable with the logical and assertive parts of her personality as Everett was with his feelings.

Jung's archetypal theory offers a way to free Everett, Shirley, and Gwen from their stereotypical behavior. The notion of the Anima archetype (the feminine within man) and the Animus archetype (the masculine within woman) offers individuals an opportunity to become aware of and accept some of their opposite-gender characteristics.

For Jung, these images are more than passive reflections; they are an internal microcosm of the opposite gender. Within Everett, the Anima archetype is a psychological woman; "an inherited collective image of woman exists in an unconscious, with the help of which he apprehends the nature of woman" (Jung, [1943] 1966, p. 190). It is also a representation of the feminine genes in males (Jung, [1939] 1959, p. 284). Similarly, within Gwen and Shirley in the Animus archetype is a psychological male, and this archetype influences the way women relate to men.

In this example, the Anima and Animus of all three individuals, rather than being integrated with the rest of the personality, were either repressed or projected onto another person. If they were accepted and integrated, they would give Everett, Gwen, and Shirley the combination of task and relationship skills that organizations need from their members. When individuals develop both archetypes, each gender can increase its effectiveness. Jung's theory offers the framework for doing this.

In his earlier writings, Jung defined the *content* of Anima and Animus in a way that reflected the gender stereotypes of his own time. He saw men as *doers* and women as *nurturers*. Anima and Animus were the product of untold generations who had been nurtured by women and protected by men. Contemporary feminists utilize Jung by emphasizing his later work, in which he viewed Anima and Animus as the archetypes, not of genders, but of *opposites*, or as the instinctive tendency to discriminate between "self" and "not self" (Young-Eisendrath and Wiedemann, 1987, p. 40). Jung called it the image in which "[I place] what is felt as not belonging to me and therefore outside of me" (Jung, [1939] 1959, p. 27). The *content* of the "not I" is determined by individual experience within existing cultural and social norms. This view allows an individual to continue to utilize Jung's valuable idea that each person carries an image of the opposite gender that must be integrated into the rest of the personality *without* accepting his earlier beliefs regarding the content of that image.

How to Encourage the Acceptance and Integration of Anima and Animus

Alice Sargent's description of the androgynous manager illustrates Jung's view of the successful integration of Anima or Animus. Androgynous managers are able to draw upon the characteristics of their own gender as well as those of the opposite gender (Sargent, 1981). Since the publication of Sargent's work, practitioners working in organizations have defined a number of practical steps that help men and women to break out of their stereotypes, call upon a broader range of affiliation skills, and work together more effectively. Many such strategies are described in *The Promise of Diversity*, edited by Elsie Cross, Judith Katz, Frederick Miller, and Edith Seashore (1994). One example of such strategies is that of Elizabeth Hostetler, who describes how the feminine characteristics of both female and male leaders have been largely silenced in organizations (Hostetler, 1994, p. 191). She suggests a number of strategies so that leaders—both men and women—can develop and honor the feminine. The following are illustrative (pp. 193–194):

> Be still.
> Be aware of the trap of constant action and cultivate the ability
>   to hold still long enough to receive creativity.

Focus on the whole.

Everything is connected: put this into practice by focusing on
yourself as a whole and move from there.

Become a learner.

When everything is in flux, mastery or control is an illusion.

Nurture the attitude that there is no right or wrong and that
play and experimentation are appropriate responses to life.

Jung's theory thus makes a contribution to contemporary work
on gender in organizations by illustrating how characteristics that
we generally associate with the other gender also exist in ourselves
and can be used productively.

When Individuals or Organizations Have Persistent Patterns of Dysfunction, Conflicts, and Embarrassment

Individuals and organizations both have their reoccurring trouble
spots—types of people or situations that bring out their least effective behavior and performance. For Jung, *persistent* patterns of
such behavior are not a coincidence. They are evidence of the
Shadow archetype. The Shadow is the envelope or container for
the less-developed aspects of our personality. It contains those
vaguely familiar parts of our personalities that were declared unwelcome during our upbringing. Charles Seashore and Henry
Malcolm (1979, p. 8) liken the initial experience of the Shadow to
an inner core of rot and state, "[W]herever I go my core of rot
seems to have gotten there first and spoils everything. For most, it
simply oozes into daily life when least expected, makes itself known
in terrifying dreams, and oddly enough, is the part of us that is the
most transparent to others, despite our best attempts to lock it away
in the vault of the unconscious."

The Shadow archetype also contains positive parts of our biological heritage that might be completely unfamiliar because in
our society these impulses have had no opportunity to surface. In
Jung's view, an example of the latter would be our need for a spiritual connection.

Robert Bly describes the process by which individuals fill the
framework that is the container for the Shadow archetype (Bly,
1988, p. 17):

When we were one or two years old we had what we might visualize as a 360-degree personality. Energy radiated out from all parts of our body and all parts of our psyche. A child running is a living globe of energy. We had a ball of energy, all right; but one day we noticed that our parents didn't like certain parts of that ball. They said things like: "Can't you be still?" Or "It isn't nice to try and kill your brother." Behind us we have an invisible bag, and the part of us our parents don't like, we, to keep our parents' love, put in the bag. By the time we go to school our bag is quite large.

Bly continues to describe the contributions that teachers, adolescent peers, and others make to the ever-growing bag until "out of a round globe of energy the twenty-year-old ends up with a slice. We'll imagine a man who has a thin slice left—the rest is in the bag—and we'll imagine that he meets a woman; let's say they are both twenty-four. She has a thin, elegant slice left. They join each other in a ceremony, and this union of two slices is called marriage" (Bly, 1988, p. 18).

Because the contents of Bly's bag seem to appear at the worst and most unexpected times, the act of bringing this archetype to consciousness is a source of strength. The strength comes both from desensitizing the embarrassment from the disclosure of a "hidden" aspect of one's personality and from drawing upon the positive and creative powers embodied in the Shadow.

The Shadow Archetype at the Individual Level

At the individual level the Shadow archetype consists of unintegrated personal attributes that seem alien, negative, and threatening to an individual. Relegating these attributes to the background does not eliminate them; they then sneak into the foreground to embarrass us. If they are unattractive enough, we may deny their presence within our own personality but project them onto another person. In this instance the Shadow functions as an undiscovered source of conflict. The same process can occur at a collective level, causing groups and organizations to behave as if they have a hidden Shadow as part of their character.

As a child, Felice Gilton was warm, enthusiastic, and naturally empathic with the people around her. The message from her parents, her friends in the neighborhood where she grew up, and her teachers was "Don't show your enthusiasm; don't let anyone take advantage of you." She believed this message, and as she grew up, more and more of her warm and enthusiastic side was placed in the sack that Bly describes. Still, Felice wanted to help people, and she became a social worker and eventually a social work supervisor. She occasionally had twinges of feeling about the plight of people she was helping but dismissed them quickly, often so quickly that she was not aware of them.

Shortly after Felice become a supervisor, Jack Heston was assigned as one of her case workers. Jack had much of the same natural warmth and enthusiasm that Felice had relegated to the Shadow part of her personality, but he displayed it openly. The relationship between Felice and Jack got off to a bad start and didn't improve with time. Felice prided herself on having a cool and professional manner at work, but she quickly lost her objectivity where Jack was concerned. She became very uncomfortable whenever he displayed enthusiasm or feelings regarding the agency's clients or their fellow workers. Felice called this expression unprofessional and quickly changed the subject or left the room. In a few instances she cut Jack off. Despite better-than-average performance for a beginner, Jack received only an average performance rating.

Felice projected the warm and empathic part of her personality onto Jack, and because these attributes were unacceptable to her, she attacked or avoided them when she saw them in him.

The Shadow Archetype at the Group and Organizational Level

Groups and organizations have a collective personality that includes a Shadow side, but it can remain hidden to group members. One way that groups and organizations avoid dealing with this unwelcome element is by scapegoating. In scapegoating, a person or group is viewed as representing an unwelcome aspect of the collective personality. This person or group is identified as bad or threatening, and the remainder of the group or organization coalesces around eliminating or punishing the scapegoat.

Arthur Colman describes the way he consults to the scapegoating process. Organizations call and ask him to justify getting rid of or changing an offending individual or group. As Colman describes it, after some investigation he helps the organization to "redefine the scapegoating system as part of the organization's troubled process rather than its cause" (Colman, 1992, pp. 99–103).

Colman consulted with the management group of a California agency concerned with conservation. The apparent problem was how to deal with a dissident citizens' group. The organization described itself as a "good American family." Colman suspected that the family metaphor masked differences and dissent within the organization that it was unconsciously trying to keep hidden. At one point he asked, "If everything is so good, then who are the public that seem to disagree with your policies?" This and more challenging interpretations were met with vigorous denial until two individuals spoke out against the majority view, stating that they did not accept the "happy family" description but stayed in the organization because they hoped to *change* the very policies that others stated they were so pleased with.

In Colman's view, the crucial step for this organization would be for the management group to explore how the views of the citizens' group they feared symbolized and mirrored their own. Colman believed that the scapegoated citizens' group carried the organization's potential for change, and its differing views needed to be accepted and integrated into the organization.

William Bridges takes a similar tack, illustrating how an organization can deposit its Shadow in one of its major functions. Such organizations end up treating an important function as a disowned part, and this results in important lapses in business strategy (Bridges, 1992, pp. 84–85):

> Kodak, the pioneer in the consumer photographic field, cultivated its existing market but had difficulty developing new technologies. Polaroid, in contrast, became successful by developing the radical new technology of instant photography, but Polaroid then developed an instant movie camera for which it did insufficient market research, creating a major loss.

Both organizations had a Shadow side. Kodak's was its R&D function, which found it hard to take risks and innovate. Polaroid's was its market research, which could not look outward and determine what consumers really wanted rather than looking inward and depending on the company's technical ingenuity. In both cases, this deficiency caught up with the corporation.

Reclaiming the Shadow and Finding New Sources of Energy and Creativity

Because our hidden capacities are unfamiliar, they may be regarded as threatening. This less-developed side of our personality, however, is not inherently evil but is immature and socially *unacceptable*. It is also a source of strength. To illustrate, within the Shadow of Felice Gilton, the social work supervisor in the previous example, was the capacity to be enthusiastic about her agency's programs and to be empathic with her clients. The first time she allowed herself to express these qualities she might appear awkward, and she certainly would feel awkward. Her enthusiasm and empathy, however, are the hidden gold in her personality, just as the ability to be innovative is the hidden gold in Kodak's corporate personality.

Jung dealt with the issue of finding gold or value in what has been disowned and unvalued in a very unlikely place: the disowned and unvalued medieval study of alchemy.

The Relevance of Alchemy

The medieval study of alchemy attempted to turn what appeared to be worthless substances into gold. Jung studied alchemy in order to discover principles of transformation and apply them to the human condition. He found that the alchemist first identified a *prima materia,* a highly ambiguous substance made up of disgusting ingredients. A contemporary analogy might be the fecal matter of organizational life that seems to be part of so many managers' lives. A specific example could be envy reactions and rivalries. One envies someone who has some sort of perceived advantage or access to the self—perhaps in the form of a creative spirit or a privileged access to power. On a systems basis, organizations can also envy other organizations. They can project the organizational self onto some other organization that presumably has some special ability or access to markets.

To deal with this phenomenon the alchemists created the *vas bene clausam* ("the well-sealed vessel"), which could contain the presumably distasteful material so that one could find the gold within. The well-sealed vessel of the organizational practitioner is whatever it takes to create enough trust between individuals so that they can honestly explore their own issues and recognize the hidden gold. What, then, would be the gold in envy? Envy focuses on who we are not. Awareness that we are focusing on who we are not can open the way for us to contain and consider the existence of these presumably undesirable qualities within us. This is the first step toward accepting and integrating a presumably negative quality (with its hidden nugget of gold) into ourselves.

Envy frequently contains the element of ambition. Recognizing and accepting ambition can lead us toward recognizing, accepting, and ultimately harnessing it. In the Jungian metaphor, putting envy back in the bottle so that it can be accepted and understood as part of us is the necessary step in discovering, accepting, and utilizing our ambition (Stein, 1992, p. 7).

An Individual Example of Reclaiming the Shadow and Finding New Sources of Creativity and Energy

Charles Bates suggests the following exercise to help individuals uncover the gold in their shadow. The exercise has two essential ingredients: a stated want and a resistance to that want. Bates asks you to attempt the following (1991, p. 142):

> Think of one intractable problem in your life. Make a list of behaviors around that problem that are acceptable to you. Make another list of behaviors around that problem that are unacceptable to you (things you would not do). From this second list, make a third list called What I Would Do Temporarily As An Experiment. Next, choose one item from this last list around which you will conduct your experiment. This identifies your want. Reflect on the resistance to your want such as embarrassment, fear, a feeling of lack of authenticity, social pressure, etc. Purposefully find a way to bring your want into your everyday experience and notice the resistance and anxiety arising in you as a result. Finally, take note of any benefit that this new behavior might offer you. Assess the benefit, and if you feel more empowered ethically, a deeper sense of connection to yourself, and more power, choose to make the behavior part of your life.

The fourth list is the key to the positive potential of one's Shadow. The payoff comes from reflecting on the resistance to thinking of the items on this list as an experiment. This includes reactions such as embarrassment, fear, lack of authenticity, or social pressure. Individuals are instructed to purposefully find a way to bring that behavior into their everyday experience and then *to notice the resistance and anxiety that arise as they do it*. They are also asked to consider any benefit that the new behavior might offer, noting particularly if they feel more empowered ethically, if they feel a deeper sense of connection to themselves, and if they feel as if they have more power to make that new behavior a part of their life (Bates, 1991, p. 56).

A Group-Level Example of Reclaiming the Shadow and Finding New Sources of Creativity and Energy

This intervention (Gemmill and Costello, 1990, p. 277) is a variation of the classic organization development intergroup intervention used to surface hidden or denied feelings. Group members are asked to brainstorm adjectives that describe:

1. How the group members view their own group
2. How they view another group or groups
3. How they believe the other groups view them

Downplaying the importance of artistic skill, the facilitator asks group members to produce drawings that symbolize their answer to these three questions. Such drawings, like any activity that does not use a polished skill, are more likely to touch the unconscious, which is the home of the Shadow. After finishing the drawings, the group members present them to the other groups and answer clarifying questions. At this point, the facilitator presents the hypothesis that groups often project their own Shadow or aspects of themselves that they would rather not deal with to other groups.

After presenting this hypothesis, the facilitator directs the participants' attention to their own drawings and asks them to examine them to identify the group's Shadow. The facilitator then suggests to the group that when they draw a picture of the other groups or what they believe the other groups are saying about them, they may well have been drawing a picture that symbolizes their feelings about their own group. Given a sufficient level of trust, the next step is for the groups to consider this hypothesis. Figure 2.1 illustrates how this method works.

The first drawing (a) describes how members of one group saw the other group. The drawing is built around a closed circle, and the group described the other group as boring, safe, and polite. At that point they did not want to admit the possibility that any of these traits could also describe their group. The drawing they made of

Figure 2.1. Using Group Drawings to Analyze the Group Shadow (the Dancing Flames Group).

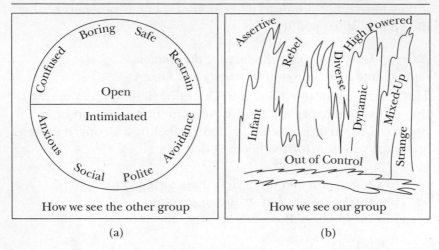

(a)   How we see the other group

(b)   How we see our group

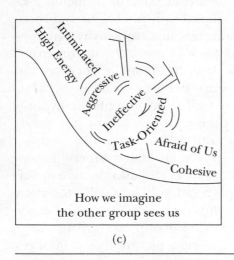

(c)   How we imagine the other group sees us

Source: Gemmill and Costello, 1990. Used by permission of Plenum Publishing.

their own group (b) contained dancing flames, and they described themselves as dynamic, assertive, and rebellious. In later discussion, some members revealed that they were indeed bored within the group but that it was difficult to discuss this issue.

These comments tied into a third drawing (c), in which members of the "dancing flames" group described how they thought the other group viewed them. The drawing pictured a snowball careening down a hill and overtaking skiers in its path. Later discussion revealed that the members of the group were really describing themselves, for although they saw themselves as dynamic and strong, they also feared the aggressiveness of other members and worried that this aggressiveness could get out of control. The drawings revealed that aggressiveness was the Shadow side of the group's excitement and willingness to take risks and that group members had some fear of this quality. By imagining how others might see them, the group members were able to identify their own Shadow or hidden view of themselves (Gemmill and Costello, 1990, p. 279).

When Organizations Need a Vehicle to Tap into Hidden Sources of Energy and Creativity

Joseph Campbell identified myths as a prime indicator of archetypes. In his study, Campbell noted a striking similarity between the myths and stories of many cultures. The common element that he identified throughout history and prehistory he termed the "hero's journey": "A hero ventures forth from the world of common day into a region of supernatural wonder: fabulous forces are there encountered and a decisive victory is won: the hero comes back from this mysterious adventure with the power to bestow boons on his fellow man" (Campbell, 1968, p. 30). Some writers believe that this similarity is the result of diffusion, stating that the stories or myths originated in one place and then spread to others. Others account for the similarity by stating that each group went through a similar experience, such as the need to explain the mysteries of the physical world. Because all groups have similar experiences, they develop similar tales and myths.

Campbell bases his explanation on Jung's theory, which characteristically views external experience as embodied in internal patterns or archetypes (Campbell, 1968, pp. 17–19). The Jungian view of the basic hero myth is that for millions of years animals and, later, humans have had to move from their protected place as an offspring to a position of self-reliance and independence. This is an important physiological and psychological task. We must differentiate ourselves from an old secure position and function independently in the world. Jung notes that we are programmed with a set of potential responses to accomplish this task of differentiation and integration. Generations of external experiences have become an internal set of archetypes. These archetypes are expressed in various symbolic ways as each individual goes through the life experience.

In organizations, myths can be used to identify the underlying (archetypal) reality and help members to experience past, present, and potential. The term *experience* is important because myths have a way of communicating an emotional or spiritual quality beyond rational understanding. They have this impact because they do not have the burden of being verifiable truths. This freedom leaves an open space where individuals can place their own meaning. It is the quality of form with nonspecific substance that allows myths to symbolize archetypes. According to Harrison Owen, "Myth is neither true nor false, but rather *behind* truth—as that body of material through which a culture's values, purpose, and direction come to expression. Myth is not just 'any old story,' it is *the* story which gives shape and focus to Spirit and makes everything make sense" (Owen, 1987, p. 12).

Owen describes his use of myth as a point of influence for change in the U.S. Internal Revenue Service (IRS):

Owen was working with the Appellate Division of the IRS. This division is an intermediate step in taxpayer disputes between the tax examiner and a court of law. Until the early 1980s, individuals in the division were called "appellate conferees" and functioned as an insulated and elite group within the IRS. The emphasis was on fair, impartial judgments, often in favor of the taxpayer. This stance led to appellate conferees being jokingly referred to as "Santa Claus" by some tax examiners, whose findings they had reversed.

By the early 1980s, the increasing complexity of the tax law, the increasing rates of taxation, and the growing tendency to routinely challenge examiners' findings led to an enormous backlog of cases with the appellate conferees. It was determined that the division could no longer operate as an insulated and elite unit. Individuals who had handled the less complex cases were administratively moved and joined with the previously elite group of appellate conferees. In addition, the Appellate Division was placed under the office of the counsel of the IRS. Previously the appellate conferees considered themselves the "teachers" of the IRS lawyers. Now they were placed in a less-independent position in the office of the IRS counsel, thus removing their structural insulation. In addition, the previously independent appellate conferees were placed more directly under a new group of managers who wished to build a statistical record of rapid case closure.

Although most of the older conferees and the newer managers attempted to adjust to the conflict in values and work styles, the solutions were far from perfect. Available resources of human energy and spirit were not being utilized effectively. Owen conducted interviews among both internal groups and related outside groups. He tried to identify the myths that moved both groups. His job was easier with the older appellate conferees, who had a long history as a semiautonomous group carrying the torch of fairness, impartiality, and integrity. In the new situation negative stories illustrated that the current appeals officers felt hampered because they still had the same responsibilities, but they no longer had their previous authority to arrange a settlement without its being reviewed by a manager. The older appeals officers looked at the record of rapid case closure and saw, not something positive, but a surrender of quality to quantity and statistics.

The myth of the new managers was not as poetic as that of the appellate conferees, but their spirit behind their goal of rapid case closures was just as strong as the appellate conferees was behind their goal.

Owen's mode of operation was to interview both groups, asking simple open-ended questions such as "What is this place and what should it be?" In these interviews he listened for the stories that displayed the underlying truth of each group and the Service as a whole. He also played back the story as he was hearing it. The hero of one group's story was often the villain in the other group's.

As Owen listened to stories throughout the IRS, he came to realize that the newly formed Appeals Division fulfilled a function that was not being acknowledged. The United States is the only country in the industrialized world that depends upon the voluntary compliance of the taxpayer. If even 10 to 15 percent of taxpayers were to refuse to cooperate, the system as we know it would break down. The appeals system made a strong contribution to this voluntary compliance because it was the only part of the revenue-collecting process that was not adversarial. It was the only part of the service that had been devoting energy to having the taxpayer feel that he or she was receiving fair treatment. In this context, Owen identified a statistical measure that had validity for both groups: the Taxpayer Confidence Index. This index was based upon a survey of taxpayers after the appeals process that would ask them if they believed that they had received fair treatment. The index would yield a specific number that would be relevant to the newer, statistically minded managers. It also emphasized the unique role played by the Appellate Division in dealing with taxpayer satisfaction.

Owen had identified a myth that could unify both groups. For him this myth exemplified the hidden spirit of the IRS, the underlying force or dynamic that made the system operate. This spirit was not available on the immediate surface, or perhaps it was so obvious that it did not seem to be available. Owen's intervention was to persuade both groups to use the Taxpayer Confidence Index as a measure of organizational effectiveness. The success of his intervention is illustrated in this excerpt from a letter to Owen from IRS director Howard Martin: "You helped us to identify the actual role of Appeals in the Internal Revenue Service. We learned from this that we could establish our identity by telling our story as we believe it should be. . . . All of this story-telling has defined our role now and in the future, and a much healthier organization has resulted. With your assistance, we were able to take the initiative and design our future rather than reacting to others" (Owen, 1987, p. 208).

Carol Pearson's Theory of Archetypes as a Framework for Change

Carol Pearson (1991) is one of a number of writers who have taken the second step of developing a framework of developmental archetypes. Her theory is also built around the hero's journey. It is outlined here because of the relative ease with which it can be applied to individuals, groups, and organizations. Each archetype in her theory also has a Shadow side that draws on the power of the archetype in an excessive, immature, or unproductive way.

Pearson views the metaphorical journey as consisting of three steps, with four archetypes activated in each step. These steps correspond to Campbell's description of the archetypal hero's journey. The first four archetypes help us to prepare for the journey, and the second four help on the journey itself as we encounter our souls and become "real." The final four mediate the return, helping us to express our true self and transform our life (Pearson, 1991, p. 29). I have grouped these twelve tasks into three, which I have renamed *developmental tasks,* that could be applied to individuals and organizations: *defining, developing,* and *discovery.*

Defining marks one's place in the world. At the individual level, it means doing the basic things one must do to establish oneself as a person: establishing boundaries, parameters for trust, and the balance between directed effort and nurturing. At the organizational level it involves the basic tasks of management, finding the right people, training them, setting up systems for reward and motivation, and balancing task and maintenance. Metaphorically, it is the preparation for the journey of individual or organizational life; it involves the Innocent, the Orphan, the Warrior, and the Caregiver archetypes.

The *Innocent* and the *Orphan* balance one another to produce the persona or face we present to the outside world. If we are to be accepted or loved, we must have trust and make some of our inner self available to others. The *Innocent* archetype is the impulse that helps us share who we are. Within organizations, this archetype encourages trust in the organization, optimism, acquiescence to authority, and acceptance of limits and rules, and it enables the organization to present itself to the world. It is termed *Innocent* because it promotes looking at the world as if nothing could cause harm. The Shadow side of this archetype is typically undeveloped and undiscriminating. Under the influence of the Shadow of the Innocent archetype, we are more likely to deny or repress signs of external danger. We are likely to be excessively dependent and to be unrealistic about change, either fearing it too much or becoming inappropriately fearless.

In contrast to Innocents, *Orphans* have to be realistic. Our Orphan archetype tells us that if we want to reach external goals, we cannot share all of our feelings and impulses all of the time. This is the archetype within individuals and organizations that analyzes the situation to see what must be sacrificed or goes underground to present a particular image. Within organizations, the Orphan recognizes the downside of issues, anticipates problems, and names fears, constraints, and limits. Both archetypes are important in shaping the initial image of an organization and defining what it is, what it is not, what can be stated, and what remains hidden. An initial task of management is to implement and maintain these parameters. When the Shadow side of the Orphan is in control, impulses to protect are less discriminating. Individuals and organizations are more likely to blame others for their own actions, expect special treatment because of past wrongs, or attack those who are trying to help them.

The Innocent and the Orphan together establish boundaries with the outside world. The *Warrior* and the *Caregiver* balance the energy within these boundaries between focused task performance and nurturing. Warriors mobilize the raw energy of the instincts. They are disciplined, focused, and assertive. This archetype helps individuals and organizations to plan, be strategic, and direct the energy needed to get the job done.

The Shadow of the Warrior is the excess that leads to acting in a cutthroat way and being overly competitive when cooperation would be more effective. Balancing the Warrior is the Caregiver archetype, which provides support for itself and others. The Caregiver archetype helps individuals to do their job with a clear sense of duty, responsibility, and morality. It also helps them to work hard and long hours, be kind to people when they are in supervisory roles, and be loyal to their own supervisors. As an organizational archetype it helps to balance a focus on the task with an emphasis on nurturing and support. The Shadow of the Caregiver is the suffering martyr. Under its influence we are likely to avoid confrontation, be too passive, give in on issues, appease, be more likely to have job burnout, and use guilt as a manipulative device.

Encouraging the Defining Archetypes Within Organizations

Defining and running the organization corresponds to the general concepts and skills taught in business schools. These are the basics, and it is very easy to ignore these areas and become enamored of the more exciting and esoteric aspects of change, such as finding higher purposes or magical transformations. Doing this would mean neglecting to maintain the integrity (image and boundaries) of the organization, care for and appreciate the people who do the work, balance task and process, and marshal the resources to get the job done. Several useful resources for developing and maintaining this aspect of organizational culture include the following. (These resources usually encompass more than one of the three categories of archetypes.)

Block, P. *The Empowered Manager: Positive Political Skills at Work.* San Francisco: Jossey-Bass, 1987.

Cohen, A. *The Portable MBA in Management.* New York: Wiley, 1993.

Collins, J. C., and Porras, J. I. *Built to Last: Successful Habits of Visionary Companies.* New York: Harper Business, 1994.

Cross, E., Katz, J., Miller, F., and Seashore, E. *The Promise of Diversity: Over Forty Voices Discuss Strategies for Eliminating Discrimination in Organizations.* Homewood, Ill.: Irwin, 1994.

Gardner, J. *On Leadership.* New York: Free Press, 1990.

Kotter, J. *The Leadership Factor.* New York: Free Press, 1988.

Kouzes, J., and Posner, B. *Credibility: How Leaders Gain and Lose It, Why People Demand It.* San Francisco: Jossey-Bass, 1993.

Sayles, L. R. *Leadership: Managing in Real Organizations.* New York: McGraw-Hill, 1989.

Thomas, R. R., Jr. *Beyond Race and Gender: Unleashing the Power of Your Total Work Force by Managing Diversity.* New York: American Management Association, 1991.

Developing means identifying and generating inner capacities. Metaphorically, the individual or organization goes on a journey and returns with a prize, which is a newly differentiated part of himself, herself, or itself. That part must then be integrated. Individually, this involves discovering and marshaling the full range of one's talents and abilities, including the ability to affiliate and be close with others and to envision what one can become. Organizationally, it involves core organization development activities such as strategic planning, culture change, career development, and balancing family and work. It also involves other change strategies such as Total Quality Management and reengineering. Development involves the Seeker, Destroyer, Lover, and Creator archetypes.

The *Seeker* and *Destroyer* archetypes represent the inner capacity to discover the new and make room for discoveries by eliminating the old. The historical record of human achievement supports the idea of an innate urge to move beyond the status quo. Individuals and organizations under the influence of the Seeker are more likely to be searching for new products and new ways of doing things. They are also likely to display independence and integrity in the face of external pressure. In its Shadow form, the Seeker archetype can lead to dilettante behavior in which an individual or organization moves repeatedly from one new project or approach to another without remaining long enough to complete any.

The Destroyer archetype is the voice within us that acknowledges our own mortality, the presence of evil in the world, and the fact that change usually involves giving something up. In the workplace it is the ability to give up the old program or way of doing things and adapt to the new. The Shadow form of the Destroyer consists of the multitude of actions that humans take, individually and collectively, to demolish themselves and others. These actions range from individual substance and emotional abuse to such large-scale destructive acts as riots and war.

The *Lover* and *Creator* archetypes provide the pattern for passion and vision within individuals and organizations. As a species, humans can generate and express passionate commitment in every area of endeavor. In the workplace, the Lover archetype enables individuals to become passionate about work, empathic and understanding of problems, and caring, warm, and appreciative of diversity. The Shadow of the Lover archetype carries in it commitment to excess, encouraging addiction to love or causes and an inability to discriminate. The Creator provides patterns for the total existence of the individual or organization. Highlighting Jung's focus on internal causation, the Creator is the archetype that gives each person the vision of her or his potential.

We all can have fragmentary contact with the Creator at any stage of our development. Useful, mature, and positive contact with the Creator comes when we have internally discovered our unique strengths and message and externally tempered and honed those strengths to meet the world. In the metaphor of the hero's journey, this is expressed as first preparing for the journey with the Innocent, Orphan, Warrior, and Caregiver and then taking the risks necessary to become aware of inner messages with the Seeker, Lover, and Destroyer.

Contact with the Creator suggests that one is close to finding one's treasure; it is an inner intuitive or imaginative guide to a fulfilling and productive life. The next step of the journey is to integrate the Creator into one's life. Under the influence of the Shadow of the Creator, we are apt to be involved with obsessively creating and being involved with so many possibilities that none can be finished.

Encouraging the Developing Archetypes Within Organizations

This is the realm of Organization Development. To develop is to make the most of resources that are already there, and that is the focus of these archetypes. Organizations often look outside for these nurturing qualities, but it is possible to cultivate nurturing processes within the organization. These would include encouraging and supporting the full range and depth of the abilities of *all* organization members and having a vision of what the organization can become if its resources are developed to their full potential. Developing includes having attitudes that are usually considered supportive, such as a high tolerance for diversity, encouragement of individual initiative, affiliation, intimacy, and personal and professional development. To balance the supportive approach, development must also include such critical or discriminating skills as the ability to say no, to confront in a productive manner, to maintain a critical eye on activities and programs, and to eliminate those that are not working in order to make room for the new. Useful resources for development include the following.

Bradford, D. L., and Cohen, A. R. *Managing for Excellence: The Guide to Developing High Performance in Contemporary Organizations.* New York: Wiley, 1984.

Burke, W. W. *Organization Development: A Process of Learning and Changing.* Reading, Mass.: Addison-Wesley, 1994.

Covey, S. R. *Principle-Centered Leadership.* New York: Simon & Schuster, 1990.

De Pree, M. *Leadership Is an Art.* East Lansing: Michigan State University Press, 1987.

French, W. L., and Bell, C. *Organization Development: Behavioral Science Interventions for Organization Improvement.* Englewood Cliffs, N.J.: Prentice-Hall, 1995.

Porras, J. I. *Stream Analysis: A Powerful Way to Diagnose and Manage Organizational Change.* Reading, Mass.: Addison-Wesley, 1987.

Schein, E. H. *Organizational Culture and Leadership.* (2nd ed.) San Francisco: Jossey-Bass, 1992.

Weisbord, M. R. *Productive Workplaces: Organizing and Managing for Dignity, Meaning, and Community.* San Francisco: Jossey-Bass, 1987.

Discovery goes beyond developing what is apparent to unearth processes, talents, and assets that one did not even know existed. Discovery at the individual level includes reaching into the unconscious for creative solutions, wisdom, and whimsy. At the organizational level, it involves processes associated with organizational transformation such as paradigm shifts, open space technology, spirituality, alignment with global and universal forces, creation of learning organizations, fun, and the full range of right-brain activities. This process involves the Ruler, the Magician, the Sage, and the Fool archetypes.

The *Ruler* and the *Magician* archetypes direct the individual and the organization in diverse but complementary ways. The Ruler manages; the Magician guides and leads. The Ruler promotes harmony among the rich diversity of other archetypes within the psyche, linking the spiritual and cosmic forces triggered by the Creator with the day-to-day world. The Ruler in organizations is the capacity to recognize a vision and then turn it into reality. The Shadow side of the Ruler archetype is threatened by the occasional flashes from the unconscious and suppresses them.

The hero's journey as described by Pearson is an expansion of consciousness. Before the journey, the individual has access only to the aspects of the psyche that are controlled by the ego. The journey widens awareness to the realm of the unconscious and the power to tap into new sources of power and creativity. The Magician is the archetype that guides the process from conscious awareness to the realm of the unconscious. This archetype enables individuals or organizations to use such methods as meditation, ritual, fantasy, or renaming an experience to change their conscious state or that of others.

When an individual or organization has access to the Magician, it can creatively come up with new approaches, develop win-win approaches to problem solving, create multiple options, and cope with transitions. The Shadow side of the Magician uses the transformational process in reverse to make better options into lesser options. When they are influenced by this side of the archetype, individuals or organizations use the power of negative thinking to alter perceptions in a negative way. An extreme example is transforming a society's view of a whole group and then scapegoating that group, as Hitler did with the Jews.

The *Sage* and the *Fool* offer contrasting ways to integrate and *move beyond* experience: the Sage through wisdom, the Fool through awareness and unbridled instincts. Not every person or organization feels the need to integrate at this level.

The Sage searches for a broader truth that includes, but goes beyond, intellectual knowledge and that includes, but is not distorted by, the perception of the observer. This truth is what doctors can discern beyond their own subjectivity, the lab tests, and patients' comments. The search for such truth is usually associated with methods of inner exploration such as meditation, which enable individuals to learn by standing beyond thoughts, feelings, and desires. The Sage can help each individual discover personal truth—truth that moves beyond realism, produces commitment, and is valid for that person. If an individual is under the influence of the Shadow side of the Sage archetype, he or she might use the process in a cold, heartless, dogmatic, or hurtful way.

Within organizations, the Sage archetype helps individuals to develop a vision and a global perspective. Organizations themselves call upon the Sage when they must identify a purpose and mode of being beyond the needs of any time or place. Major religious organizations that have appealed to widely diverse groups and cultures and have endured for centuries could not have done so without calling upon the wisdom of the Sage. The original Bell Telephone system may have called upon the wisdom of the Sage when it envisioned the goal of "universal service."

The archetype of the Fool triggers our unbridled instincts—our desire to react to the moment and express ourselves without inhibitions. This archetype is evident in children until they are socialized. Then it is repressed, but, like all repressed archetypes, it continues to function and present itself in ways that can lead to trouble or at least embarrassment. Pearson states that the *Wise Fool*, the individual who is in contact with this spontaneous trigger for enjoying life in the moment and has enriched those impulses with love, can pluck the strings of curiosity or absurdity to reveal such things as the lack of responsibility in a faceless bureaucracy or the real kindness behind a gruff exterior. Organizations with access to the Fool archetype can lighten things up in times of stress, imagine clever ways to get around obstacles, free their members from convention and tradition, and excel at brainstorming and creativity. The Shadow of the Fool archetype consists of lusts and urges without wisdom, compassion, or higher purposes and results in a glutton, sloth, or lecher.

Encouraging the Discovering Archetypes Within Organizations

This is the realm of organizational transformation; it consists of a paradigm shift in the way an organization defines itself, its tasks, and its place in the world. Organizational transformation involves the ability to thrive in chaos, to turn win-lose situations into win-win ones, and then to capitalize on this wizardry and incorporate deep and sweeping changes into the ongoing procedures of the organization. Such transformation is guided by the ability to step back and take a global, philosophical, and spiritual view of all that pertains to the organization and is also guided by the ability to "lighten up," remove the restraints of convention, and use curiosity and absurdity to finish a task or find the truth behind a stalemate. Some useful resources for such a transformation include the following.

Beckhard, R., and Pritchard, W. *Changing the Essence: The Art of Creating and Leading Fundamental Change in Organizations.* San Francisco: Jossey-Bass, 1992.

Fletcher, B. *Organization Transformation Theorists and Practitioners: Profiles and Themes.* New York: Praeger, 1990.

Janov, J. *The Inventive Organization: Hope and Daring at Work.* San Francisco: Jossey-Bass, 1994.

Jick, T. *Managing Change: Cases and Concepts.* Homewood, Ill.: Irwin, 1993.

Kanter, R., Stein, B., and Jick, T. *The Challenge of Organizational Change: How Companies Experience It and Leaders Guide It.* New York: Free Press, 1992.

Kochan, T. A., and Useem, M. *Transforming Organizations.* New York: Oxford University Press, 1992.

Merry, U. *Coping with Uncertainty: Insights from the New Sciences of Chaos, Self-Organization, and Complexity.* New York: Praeger, 1995.

Nadler, D., Shaw, R. B., and Walton, A. E. *Discontinuous Change: Leading Organizational Transformation.* San Francisco: Jossey-Bass, 1995.

Quinn, R. E., and Cameron, K. S. (eds.). *Paradox and Transformation: Toward a Theory of Change in Organization and Management.* Cambridge, Mass.: Ballinger, 1988.

Senge, P. *The Fifth Discipline: The Art and Practice of the Learning Organization.* New York: Doubleday, 1990.

When Organizations Want to Help Individuals with Different Personal Styles to Work Together

Jung's break with Freud was a difficult and painful experience. One way he dealt with his reactions was to try to understand them intellectually and emotionally as deeply as possible. He asked himself how two individuals who seemed to have such an affinity for each other could then see and experience things in a way that led toward such a painful separation (Donn, 1988, p. 182). His answer, our second point of influence, was *psychological types.* This point of influence is a typology of individual differences and consists of *functions* and *attitudes.* These differences are arranged on a continuum, with one end closer to consciousness and the other closer to the unconscious.

Functions are the psychological processes of gathering information and making decisions. Attitudes govern the direction in which psychological energy flows within the functions. Such energy can be directed inward (introversion) or outward (extroversion). The functions and attitudes that are closer to conscious awareness are more developed and available. Those at the other end of the continuum are less developed, closer to the unconscious, and hence less available. Jung termed these functions "inferior." The inferiority refers to their development, not to their power or influence. The less-developed functions have similar Shadow characteristics. They often turn out to have a stronger but more troublesome influence than the "superior" functions.

The Attitudes of Introversion and Extroversion

Jung's first distinction consisted of his observations about *introverts* and *extroverts,* for which he coined these terms. He noted, "Everyone knows those reserved, inscrutable, rather shy people who form the strongest possible contrast to the open, sociable, jovial, or at least friendly and approachable characters who are on good terms with everybody, or quarrel with everybody, but always relate to them in some way and in turn are affected by them" (Jung, [1923] 1971, p. 330).

Jung is talking about the *direction* of psychological energy. Extroverts do not necessarily like people more than introverts, but they are more attuned to and energized by the world around them. Introverts are more attuned to and energized by their own inner world. Jung points out that all individuals have the potential for *both* extroversion and introversion, and what is not developed in the conscious realm remains in the unconscious. The fact that an attitude operates within consciousness, however, does not mean that the individual is aware of it. Neither introverts nor extroverts are necessarily aware of the direction of their psychic energy.

Jung's formula for balancing the consciousness and the unconscious says that extroverts are likely to have an undeveloped path directed inward toward their own psyche, "and this is just [the individual's] weak point, for the tendency of his type is so outer-directed that even the most obvious of all subjective facts, the condition of his own body, receives scant attention" (Jung, [1923] 1971, p. 335).

For Jung, introverts just as extroverts must understand and deal with external reality, but for introverts the route to the external world runs through their unconscious. Our unconscious in many circumstances is not the most effective tool for coping with everyday reality. "The individual's freedom of mind is fettered by the ignominy of his financial dependence, his freedom of action trembles in the face of public opinion, his moral superiority collapses in a morass of inferior relationships" (Jung, [1923] 1971, p. 378).

The Psychological Functions

Jung also addressed the *content* of the flow of energy. This content is what the attitudes of introversion direct inward or outward. To describe this content, Jung focused on two psychological functions, gathering information and making decisions. He then identified two basic approaches to each function.

Two Ways to Gather Information

Sensing takes the world as it is, in its specific terms, at least as it appears to the senses. *Intuition* takes the world in a holistic way, focusing on possibilities and what can be.

Jung noted that individuals vary in the way they rely on their senses. For some, whom Jung termed Sensing types, the senses are both the beginning and the end of the information-gathering activity. The Sensing type has a direct pipeline between data from the senses and the process of decision making. In Jung's framework, however, nothing occurs without an opposite reaction. If Sensing is highly developed, then the opposite function, Intuition, is likely to be repressed (Jung, [1923] 1971, p. 363).

Intuition involves images, perceptions, or relations between things that could not be transmitted any other way. If Sensing tells us what an object is in a way that can be verified by the senses of other people, then Intuition tells us what the object once was or could be in a way that cannot be approximated by the senses. Individuals who favor the intuitive functions still use their senses, but Sensing is the inferior function and is closer to the unconscious. Jung explains, "He does have sensations, of course, but he is not guided by them as such; he uses them merely as starting-points for his perceptions. . . . Facts are acknowledged only if they open new possibilities of advancing beyond them and delivering the individual from their power" (Jung, [1923] 1971, pp. 367–368).

Two Ways to Make Decisions

The next step after gathering information is to use it in some way, which usually involves making a decision. Jung then identified two ways of making decisions: *Thinking* and *Feeling*. Again, these two ways are not absolute, and all individuals have both.

Thinking is impersonal. It is a way of making decisions using criterion outside one's own value system. If one is oriented toward thinking as defined by Jung one looks at logical consistency and asks if the matter in question is true. It is the "psychological function which, following its own laws, brings the content of ideas in conceptual connection with one another" (Jung, [1923] 1971, p. 481).

Feeling, in contrast, focuses on what is of value. A feeling decision imparts a worthiness to what is being considered: it is good or bad, liked or disliked. If one is exercising one's feeling function, then one's sense of right or wrong comes into play. Thinking sets up a criterion for conceptual relations; feeling establishes a criterion for acceptance or rejection.

Jung's Eight Psychological Types

Jung combined functions and attitudes to create a typology of eight personality types. The function listed is the *dominant* one. The opposite function is *inferior.* (Sensing and Intuition are opposites as are Thinking and Feeling.) *Inferior* refers to the level of development, not influence. The inferior function is closer to the unconscious and the Shadow and therefore is potentially influential. At the same time it is less developed and accessible, and because of its proximity to the Shadow it is possibly more troublesome.

If the Dominant Function Is	*The Inferior Function Is*
Extroverted Sensing	Introverted Intuition
Introverted Sensing	Extroverted Intuition
Extroverted Intuition	Introverted Sensing
Introverted Intuition	Extroverted Sensing
Extroverted Thinking	Introverted Feeling
Introverted Thinking	Extroverted Feeling
Extroverted Feeling	Introverted Thinking
Introverted Feeling	Extroverted Thinking

How to Use Jung's Theory of Type

The applications of Jung's second point of influence are as unlimited as the variety of people and situations that occur in the workplace. Jung, however, did not identify a way for the nonclinician to determine or use psychological type. He considered it to be strictly an analytic scheme, and he expressed no willingness to develop a method that would allow his theory to be used by the general public. Nevertheless, others have, and we now examine two instruments that are currently used to apply Jung's theory of type in the workplace. We first examine the widely used Myers-Briggs Type Indicator and then the more recently developed Singer-Loomis.

The Myers-Briggs Type Indicator and Conscious Functions

It is ironic that Jung is best known among organizational practitioners through the MBTI, which focuses almost exclusively on the *conscious* aspect of individual differences.* Jung's principal interest was the exploration of the *unconscious,* but the MBTI deals with unconscious or inferior (Shadow) functions more by implication.

The MBTI was developed by Katherine Briggs and her daughter Isabel Briggs Myers. Jung's theory had three dimensions: Introversion-Extroversion, Sensing-Intuition, and Thinking-Feeling. In the MBTI, Briggs and Myers added a fourth dimension, Judging-Perceiving, which measured an individual's preferred way to gather information (Sensing-Intuiting) or make decisions (Thinking-Feeling).

Scattered throughout Jung's writings are his views of lifelong psychological development. Isabel Briggs Myers's seminal work on the MBTI, *Gifts Differing* (Myers and Myers, 1980) distilled some of these ideas and made them part of the accepted context for applying Jung's theory of type:

- All individuals have some development of *both* sides of each pair of functions and attitudes.
- Each type has advantages and pitfalls. No one type is inherently better than another.
- Accepting and understanding one's type helps an individual to be more effective.
- Understanding the full range of types helps an individual to communicate and work effectively with others.

These principles are the foundation of myriad applications of the MBTI in an organizational setting. As described by Kroeger and Thuesen (1992, p. 11), applications include:

- Matching individual potential with job requirements by understanding individual strengths and weaknesses
- Breaking work-flow bottlenecks by allowing each person to work according to his or her own style and by allowing everyone to know what everyone else is doing

---

*The Myers-Briggs Type Indicator is available in many forms and with a wide range of supporting material from Consulting Psychologists Press, 3803 East Bayshore Road, Palo Alto, CA 94303; (800) 624–1765.

- Setting more realistic and more widely accepted organizational goals by including a broader range of different perspectives, needs, and ideas
- Reducing stress levels by understanding that what can excite and energize one person can stress and drain another
- Meeting deadlines better by realizing that different types deal with time in different ways

The specifics of making these applications have been dealt with in great detail by a number of writers. Following are some of the best sources.

Bridges, W. *The Character of Organizations.* Palo Alto, Calif.: Consulting Psychologists Press, 1992.

Hirsch, S. *Introduction to Type in Organizations: Individual Interpretive Guide.* Palo Alto, Calif.: Consulting Psychologists Press, 1990.

Keirsey, D., and Bates, M. *Please Understand Me: Character and Temperament Types.* (4th ed.) Del Mar, Calif.: Prometheus Nemesis, 1984.

Kroeger, O., and Thuesen, J. M. *Type Talk at Work.* New York: Delacorte Press, 1992.

Using the Myers-Briggs Type Indicator at the Organizational Level

The MBTI's dimensions can also be used to identify the strengths and limitations of an organization, as shown in Exhibit 2.1.

The profiles of United Parcel Service and Federal Express illustrate some of these differences. Both organizations are in the same industry, but the organizations structure themselves and approach their businesses quite differently. United Parcel Service (Introverted, Sensing, Thinking, and Judging) is proud that it runs "the tightest ship in the shipping business." It is an inward-looking organization that provides a standard service and gains its competitive edge through exhaustive standardization and time-and-motion studies. Every aspect of UPS, from the top executive offices to minute instructions to truck drivers, is spartan and standardized. In contrast, outward-looking Federal Express (Extroverted, Intuitive, Thinking, and Judging) entered the world by offering an imaginative, unheard-of product (nationwide overnight delivery)

Exhibit 2.1. Myers-Briggs Type Indicator Dimensions Used in Organizations.

Extraverted Organizations	Introverted Organizations
Have open boundaries	Have closed boundaries
Experiment with several possible lines of action	Explore options in detail, then try one line of action
Trust oral communication	Trust written communication
Turn outside for guidance	Insist that guidance must come from within
Invite outsiders to celebrations	Keep celebrations "in the family"
Have as a motto, "The answer is out there—we just have to find it"	Have as a motto, "The answer is within—we just have to figure it out"

Sensing Organizations	Intuitive Organizations
Are at their best with detail	Are at their best with the big picture
Can handle masses of data	Can spot emerging trends
Prefer solid routines	Are a little careless about routines
See intuitive organizations as lost in the clouds	See Sensing organizations as stuck in the mud
See the future as an extension of the present	Believe that the future can be created
Emphasize targets and plans	Emphasize purposes and vision
Tend to organize functionally	Often use cross-functional teams
Have as a motto, "Change the structure"	Have as a motto, "Change the belief systems"

Thinking Organizations	Feeling Organizations
Make decisions based on principles	Make decisions based on values
Think in terms of rules and exceptions	Think in terms of particular human situations
Value what-is-logical	Value what-we-care-about
Emphasize the objective	Emphasize the people
Believe that criticism leads to efficiency	Believe that support leads to effectiveness
Have as a motto, "Do the right (or intelligent) thing"	Have as a motto, "Work well together"

Judging Organizations	Perceiving Organizations
Drive toward decisions	Keep options open and seek more information
May be weak in information gathering	May be weak in decision making
Set clear, specific standards	Set general standards
Define lots of things in detail	Leave many things vague and undefined
Are often moralistic	Are loose and fairly tolerant
Have as a motto, "Fish or cut bait"	Have as a motto, "Don't miss an opportunity"

Source: Modified and reproduced by special permission of the Publisher, Consulting Psychologists Press, Inc., Palo Alto, CA 94303, from THE CHARACTER OF ORGANIZATIONS by William Bridges. Copyright 1992 by Consulting Psychologists Press, Inc. All rights reserved. Further reproduction is prohibited without the Publisher's written consent.

that customers ultimately bought but at the time didn't even know was possible (Bridges, 1992, p. 4).

The Organizational Character Index (Bridges, 1992, pp. 114–119) allows a group of individuals to assess their organization along the four MBTI dimensions. With this understanding, organizations are in a better position to change than individuals because they have more resources and options. For example, if an individual with an extremely low Sensing score finds that he or she needs to pay more attention to details, others may not be easily available to help. An organization in a similar situation has a better chance of finding some individuals with high Sensing functions within the organization. Bridges's instrument as yet has not been statistically validated, but it is a start in applying Jung's individual concepts at the organizational level.

When Individuals or Organizations Need to Link What They Know and Can Verify (the Conscious) with Other Sources of Information (the Unconscious)

The Singer-Loomis was developed by June Singer and Mary Loomis, both Jungian analysts. It is a newer instrument than the MBTI. It has the usual manuals and interpretive materials, but at this time has only a small number of HRD/OD applications.*

The Singer-Loomis uses the same Jungian theory base as the MBTI, but it is constructed in a way that allows the user to draw more fully on Jung's theory of the unconscious. In this way the Singer-Loomis highlights the inferior function and, ultimately, the Jungian process of transcendence.

How the Transcendent Function Links the Conscious and Unconscious

Consciousness and the unconscious are both important, but they function as two separate universes within the same individual. Both contain valuable material. Consciousness contains all that we know we know. The unconscious contains our personal unconscious, all that we have repressed or forgotten plus all of our archetypal patterns. The unconscious presents a world that is both different and

---

*The Singer-Loomis is available from Moving Boundaries, Inc., 1375 SW Blaine Court, Gresham, OR 97080; (503) 661–4126.

compensatory, emphasizing feelings, situations, and ways of understanding and responding that are ignored in the conscious world.

Both universes demand the whole stage and will, if allowed, completely drown out the other. Under usual conditions, consciousness shuts out the creative interpretation of symbols, which is the language of the unconscious. When the unconscious has the stage, as when we are dreaming, it shuts out logic, the careful screening of data, and the linear thought patterns that are the language of consciousness. In organizations, consciousness and the unconscious can play off each other in a variety of ways.

> A department seemed to follow the directives from the central office but in doing so it left out important details and thereby subverted the intent of the directives. The conscious was following the directives, but the unconscious was finding a way to avoid them.

> An engineering subunit asked for more clarification of an assignment, when in fact it was seeking recognition for work that it had already accomplished. The unconscious was asking for recognition; the conscious was expressing this desire in an indirect and ineffective way.

The challenge for organizational practitioners is to find ways to draw on the wisdom of both. The transcendent function maintains contact with *both levels* simultaneously or serially, letting neither shut out the other. This occurs as long as individuals are able to tolerate the tension that comes from an apparent contradiction.

Using the Inferior Function to Transcend
Consciousness and the Unconscious

As a clinician, Jung linked consciousness and the unconscious through what he called the *transcendent function*. He did this by interpreting dreams, a process he called *active imagination*. In active imagination a patient creates a story by actively adding elements to fantasies. The process of active imagination is not a likely tool for organizational practitioners as it requires in-depth training in Jungian psychology and would not be appropriate in many organizational situations.

There is, however, another way to transcend consciousness and the unconscious: by gaining access to the *inferior function*. Unlike the MBTI, which focuses on the dominant function, the Singer-Loomis also highlights the less-used or inferior function. The dominant function resides in consciousness; the inferior in the unconscious. The inferior function is not identical to the Shadow but rather serves as a link to the Shadow and the unconscious (von Franz, 1979, p. 7). Since it resides almost entirely in the unconscious, it is not readily accessible and is similar to a small child who has little contact with the outside world. For this reason, it can be hard to work with and can tyrannize the individual in whom it resides, as well as those who work with that person. Also like a small child, the inferior function displays a great deal of creativity and energy. The inferior function is where organizations find a sense of renewal within their members. To illustrate this dilemma, consider Resina Gliddens.

> Resina was a software engineer with a small firm in Arizona. Her ability to conceptualize new systems was extraordinary, and her ability to detect the bugs in new software systems and work them out was equally impressive. When she was working alone on a programming problem, Resina could be quite creative. She had a dominant function of introverted thinking and an inferior function of extroverted feeling. Her colleagues had learned that even though Resina acted as if their relationship was of no importance, casual remarks they made could be a source of pain to her. It was simply not easy for her to extrovert her feelings, and when she did, the feelings seemed to burst forth in a torrent.

How can an organization continue to profit from Resina's powerful introverted thinking but, since she must continue to work with other people, help her to deal with her less-developed extroverted feeling? Edwin Olson illustrates how to use the Singer-Loomis to transcend consciousness and the unconscious. To do this, he first pairs individuals with similar unconscious functions to discuss their scores. This is done so that they will gain confidence and relax as they discuss their strengths. He then pairs individuals on the basis of opposite dominant and inferior functions. In this instance Resina would be paired with someone who has a dominant function of extroverted feeling, Resina's least-developed side. This individual would have an inferior function of introverted thinking, Resina's strongest side. Olson reports that this system will frequently pair individuals who already are experiencing conflict.

The goal in this activity is to maintain the tension or contact of opposites long enough for each individual to confront an opposite reality in the form of colleagues who represent the less conscious aspects of his or her personality. To the extent that inferior functions represent the Shadow, these individuals are now meeting with the embodiment of part of their Shadow. Olson reports that as a result of such pairings, individuals are better able to understand those with whom they had been in conflict (Olson, 1992, p. 166).

Other differences in the construction of Singer-Loomis lead toward three additional implications for work in organizations.

1.   *The Singer-Loomis is not bipolar.* This means that it does not assume that the two judging functions (thinking and feeling) or the two perceiving functions (sensation and intuition) are necessarily in opposition to each other. The Singer-Loomis does not assume the pairs of functions operate like a see-saw: when one goes up, the other goes down. Instead it draws on the interpretation of Jung's theory that at certain points the functions can simultaneously develop without changes in one occurring at the expense of the other (Loomis, 1982, p. 61).

> Glenda Sawyer had always considered herself a strong extroverted and feeling person, and her Singer-Loomis test results placed extroverted feeling as her most used function. She returned to graduate school for a Ph.D. degree at the age of forty-three, and after she graduated, she took the Singer-Loomis again. She then found that while extroverted feeling remained her most-used function, introverted thinking had moved from number seven to number three.

2.   *The Singer-Loomis is situational.* Instead of asking an individual in the abstract how he or she responds, which would be context-free measurement, the Singer-Loomis assesses how much the individual uses each of the eight functions in a specific situation. The final score on the instrument is a result of how the individual indicates his or her responses to a variety of situations (Loomis, 1982, p. 62).

> Bill Naguchi considers himself a different person at home than at the office, and he most probably would object to inventories not related to specific contexts. While some depth psychologists might disagree with Bill's dual view of

himself, his conviction would affect the usefulness of an instrument. Bill would be less likely to object to the Singer-Loomis because it asks him to indicate how he behaves in specific situations. For Bill (and others like him), it would be easier to relate the results of the Singer-Loomis to himself and understand many of the implications on his own.

3. *The Singer-Loomis rank orders all eight Jungian functions.* This rank ordering provides a more precise identification and understanding of those functions that reside closer to the unconscious.

Harlow Graham was one of the top creative account executives at a leading Chicago ad agency. He regularly came up with winning campaigns, but anyone who questioned or helped to correct any of his ideas was labeled "anal" or a "nitpicker." It helped Harlow to learn that extraverted sensing was number eight, the least used in his list of functions. This scoring gave him an opportunity to consider whether he was projecting his inferior function on those who were trying to help him.

Conclusion

Jung's primary point of influence for practitioners is his view of archetypes. This is a broad and powerful concept that can be used to understand and influence behavior at all levels. But the very qualities that make archetypes pervasive and influential also make them harder to demonstrate in organizations. Archetypes reside in the unconscious, and exploring the unconscious is not accepted behavior in organizations. However, indirect links to the unconscious can be found; this chapter has explored myths, stories, drawings, visioning, and rituals as ways to tap into the power of archetypes. Jung's second point of influence, psychological type, resides in both the unconscious and consciousness. These aspects of Jung's thought have reached the organizational world and the general public through the widespread use of the MBTI and other instruments.

Both archetypes and psychological type are powerful points of influence in dealing with our three key psychological processes: joining, conflict, and psychological growth.

Joining

Archetypes are links to inner motivation. Practitioners can use archetypal psychology to find out why individuals commit themselves to a collectivity larger than themselves. Archetypes are particularly helpful if the motivation is other than tangible self-interest. By using examples from AT&T, Disney, and the IRS, this chapter demonstrated how symbols, myths, rituals, and stories can link inner motivation with the process of commitment to a group or organization.

At the conscious level, Jung's theory of psychological type describes how individuals differ in a systematic fashion and how these differences can influence commitment to an organization.

Conflict

Jung's unique contribution to understanding and working with conflict is his view of the Shadow archetype. In Jung's view, we all have an underdeveloped side to our personality. If this part is not acknowledged and accepted, we project it onto others, and what was unwelcome in our own personality we find even more objectionable in others. The example of Felice, the social worker, illustrates that the first step in dealing with this type of conflict is to recognize these qualities in ourselves. We also have illustrated how this process takes place and have shown a way to deal with it at the group and organizational levels.

Conflict also originates because individuals have different ways of gathering information, making decisions, and working with each other. Jung's theory of psychological type and its application in the Singer-Loomis and MBTI illustrate a variety of ways to respond to such conflict.

Psychological Growth

Jung's theory is a theory of psychological growth. Archetypes are inner patterns for growth and change. The archetypes in the chapter that pinpoint particular aspects of growth and change are the Self (self-identity and motivation), the Anima/Animus (gender identity), and the Shadow (undeveloped characteristics). Both individuals and organizations face predictable challenges in their process of development. Carol Pearson's framework of archetypes describes the major developmental tasks faced by individuals and organizations as well as some of the pitfalls along the way as exemplified by the Shadow of each archetype.

Annotated Bibliography
Original Sources: Readable Jung

Jung, C. G. *Memories, Dreams, Reflections.* New York: Pantheon Books, 1963.
This is Jung's autobiography presented from his own theoretical perspective, which, as the title indicates, emphasizes his inner life rather than the customary external events.

Jung, C. G. *Man and His Symbols.* New York: Doubleday, 1964.
The opening essay by Jung, "Approaching the Unconscious," is the single best readable account he wrote of his theories. The book is lavishly illustrated and contains essays by other leading Jungian analysts.

Secondary Sources: Books About Jung and His Theories

Bennet, E. A. *What Jung Really Said.* New York: Schocken Books, 1983.
Hill, C. S., and Nordby, V. *A Primer of Jungian Psychology.* New York: Taplinger, 1973.
Both of the above books present Jung's ideas in a clear, concise form.

Organizational Applications

Bridges, W. *The Character of Organizations: Using Jungian Type in Organization Development.* Palo Alto, Calif.: Consulting Psychologists Press, 1992.
This book uses the Myers-Briggs framework at the organizational level to describe how and why organizations operate as they do.

Kroeger, O., and Thuesen, J. M. *Type Talk at Work.* New York: Delacorte Press, 1992.
This book uses the Myers-Briggs framework to describe and present action steps to help individuals of differing types to work together more productively.

Pearson, C. S. *Awakening the Heroes Within: Twelve Archetypes to Help Us Find Ourselves and Transform Our World.* New York: HarperCollins, 1991.
This book defines twelve archetypes taken from the classic "hero's journey." They describe a pattern of individual and organization development from the basics of defining an identity to finding a higher purpose.

Stein, M., and Hollwitz, J. (eds.). *Psyche at Work: Workplace Applications of Jungian Analytical Psychology*. Wilmette, Ill.: Chiron Publications, 1992.

These essays describe the work of current organizational practitioners who utilize Jung's theories. The lead essay by Stein outlines how Jung's view of the flow of energy between the conscious and the unconscious can be applied to organizations.

Bibliography

Bates, C. *Pigs Eat Wolves: Going into Partnership with Your Dark Side*. St. Paul, Minn.: Yes International Publishers, 1991.

Bly, R. *A Little Book on the Human Shadow*. New York: HarperCollins, 1988.

Bolen, J. S. *Goddesses in Everywoman: A New Psychology of Women*. New York: HarperCollins, 1984.

Bolen, J. S. *Gods in Everyman: A New Psychology of Men's Lives and Loves*. New York: HarperCollins, 1989.

Bowles, M. L. "The Organization Shadow." *Organization Studies*, 1991, *12*(3), 387–404.

Bridges, W. *The Character of Organizations: Using Jungian Type in Organization Development*. Palo Alto, Calif.: Consulting Psychologists Press, 1992.

Brome, V. *Freud and His Early Circle*. New York: William Morrow, 1968.

Campbell, J. *The Hero with a Thousand Faces*. Princeton, N.J.: Princeton University Press, 1968.

Campbell, J. (ed.). *The Portable Jung*. New York: Viking, 1971.

Colman, A. "Depth Consultation." In M. Stein and J. Hollwitz (eds.), *Psyche at Work: Workplace Applications of Jungian Analytical Psychology* (pp. 92–117). Wilmette, Ill.: Chiron Press, 1992.

Cross, E., Katz, J., Miller, F., and Seashore, E. *The Promise of Diversity*. Homewood, Ill.: Irwin Professional, 1994.

Donn, L. *Freud and Jung: Years of Friendship and Loss*. New York: Charles Scribner's Sons, 1988.

Gemmill, G., and Costello, M. "Group Mirroring as a Means for Exploring the Group Shadow: A Perspective for Organizational Consulting." *Consultation*, Winter 1990, *9*(4), 277–291.

Hostetler, E. "Leadership: The Silencing of the Feminine." In E. Cross and others, *The Promise of Diversity: Over Forty Voices Discuss Strategies for Eliminating Discrimination in Organizations* (pp. 188–197). Homewood, Ill.: Irwin, 1994.

Jung, C. G. *The Collected Works of C. G. Jung* (R.F.C. Hull, trans.), Vol. 9: *The Archetypes and the Collective Unconscious*. New York: Pantheon Books, 1959. (Originally published 1939.)

Jung, C. G. *Memories, Dreams, Reflections*. New York: Pantheon Books, 1963.

Jung, C. G. *The Collected Works of C. G. Jung* (R.F.C. Hull, trans.), Vol. 7: *Two Essays on Analytical Psychology.* New York: Pantheon Books, 1966. (Originally published 1943.)

Jung, C. G. *The Collected Works of C. G. Jung* (R.F.C. Hull, trans.), Vol. 6: *Psychological Types.* New York: Pantheon Books, 1971. (Originally published 1923.)

Kroeger, O., and Thuesen, J. M. *Type Talk at Work.* New York: Delacorte Press, 1992.

Loomis, M. "A New Perspective for Jung's Typology." *Journal of Analytical Psychology,* 1982, *27,* 59–69.

McWhinney, W., and Batista, J. "How Remythologizing Can Revitalize Organizations." *Organization Dynamics,* Autumn 1988, *17*(3), 46–58.

Myers, I. B., and Myers, P. B. *Gifts Differing.* Palo Alto, Calif.: Consulting Psychologists Press, 1980.

Olson, E. E. "The Transcendent Function in Organizational Change." *Journal of Applied Behavioral Science,* 1990, *26*(1), 69–81.

Olson, E. E. "Opening to the Change Process: The Transcendent Function at Work." In M. Stein and J. Hollwitz (eds.), *Psyche at Work: Workplace Applications of Jungian Analytical Psychology* (pp. 156–173). Wilmette, Ill.: Chiron Press, 1992.

Owen, H. *SPIRIT: Transformation and Development in Organizations.* Potomac, Md.: Abbott Publishing, 1987.

Pearson, C. S. *Awakening the Heroes Within: Twelve Archetypes to Help Us Find Ourselves and Transform Our World.* New York: HarperCollins, 1991.

Pearson, C. S., and Seivert, S. V. *Heroes at Work: A Workbook.* College Park, Md.: A Meristem Project, 1988.

Peters, T. *Thriving on Chaos.* New York: Knopf, 1987.

Sargent, A. G. *The Androgynous Manager.* New York, AMACOM, 1981.

Seashore, C., and Malcolm, H. "Learning to Love Your Core of Rot." *Social Change,* 1979, *9*(2), 8–10.

Stein, M. "Organizational Life as Spiritual Practice." In M. Stein and J. Hollwitz (eds.), *Psyche at Work: Workplace Applications of Jungian Analytical Psychology* (pp. 1–18). Wilmette, Ill.: Chiron Press, 1992.

Stevens, A. *On Jung.* New York: Routledge Kegan Paul, 1990.

von Franz, M. "The Inferior Function." In M. von Franz and J. Hillman (eds.), *Jung's Typology* (pp. 1–72). Irving, Tex.: Spring Publications, 1979.

Wehr, D. S. *Jung and Feminism.* Boston: Beacon Press, 1987.

Young-Eisendrath, P., and Wiedemann, F. L. *Female Authority: Empowering Women Through Psychotherapy.* New York: Guilford Press, 1987.

Zuckerman, M. R., and Hatala, L. J. *Incredibly American: Releasing the Heart of Quality.* Milwaukee, Wis.: ASQC Quality Press, 1992.

Chapter Three

Karen Horney

The Social Unconscious and the Conflict of Self-Images

Why Karen Horney? An Overview of Organizational Applications

Karen Horney identified four aspects of our personality that have a crucial impact upon behavior in organizations. The real self is the basis for positive growth and change, and the ideal self is the basis for much individual and organizational dysfunction. Three movements—toward, against, and away from people—are the basis for much of management style. Horney's description of the development of gender identity also helps men and women to understand many of their differences in attitudes and behavior.

Horney's Theory as a Point of Influence for Dealing with Conflict

Horney's notion of the ideal self and moving toward, against, and away from people as a reflection of developmental struggles is a useful way to understand and work with conflicts. Her description of the internal struggle between the grandiose and despised images of the ideal self is also a helpful way to understand external struggle.

Horney's Theory as a Point of Influence for Dealing with Psychological Growth

Horney's theory focuses on how we replace the real self, which promotes psychological growth, with an ideal self that limits such

111

growth. This understanding can help to promote an organizational environment and activities that support psychological growth.

Horney's Theory as a Point of Influence for Dealing with the Dilemmas of Joining

Horney's concept of the real and ideal selves and the two sides of the ideal self (grandiose and despised) offers an original and insightful basis for understanding why individuals are drawn to identifying with an organization.

Horney's Theory as an Organizational Image or Metaphor

Horney's concepts of the ideal self and moving toward, against, and away from people reflect the negative and limiting messages that individuals receive in their childhood. These internalized messages, embodied in organizational norms and culture, are useful as images or metaphors to describe organizational phenomena.

Horney's Theory as a Basis for Other Organizationally Relevant Theories

Although it is not often acknowledged, Horney's ideas of gender socialization are at the base of much current thinking on androgenous management. Her concept of moving toward, against, and away from people is also similar to the frameworks of many management-style instruments and can be used to help individuals explore the origins of their own management style. Horney's reputation as a dissenter from Freudian orthodoxy also attracted to her three individuals as patients or mentes who later became significant theorists and creators in their own right. These three are Frederick (Fritz) Perls (see Chapter Eight), Albert Ellis (see Chapter Four), and pioneer humanistic psychologist Abraham Maslow.

Limitations of Horney's Theory for Use in Organizations

Horney's theory focuses upon early experiences in socialization, particularly those that have been embedded in the unconscious. Although the theory does not touch upon such strongly private areas as Freud's sexual focus, discussion of these early experiences can still seem intrusive to some. Horney also describes behavior as "neurotic." Practitioners using her theory would have to convert her terms into more current and less clinical language.

How Horney Developed Her Ideas

Karen Horney was born in Hamburg, Germany, in 1885. Her innovative ideas are a reflection of a conflicted and pioneering life. Her father was a ship's captain, sailing the then-dangerous route through the Strait of Magellan to distant ports of South America. When he was at home, he was a stern, pious, and demanding taskmaster. Her mother, seventeen years his junior, was a lively free-thinker who eventually left her husband. This was an unthinkable act for a German woman of her time. Frequently criticized by her father and feeling unattractive, Horney decided at an early age to excel academically. In later life she wrote, "If I couldn't be beautiful I decided I would be smart." This was in spite the fact that she was a strikingly beautiful young girl (Rubins, 1978, p. 14). She then became one of the first women in Germany to earn a medical degree and also one of the first female practicing psychoanalysts. Trained as an orthodox Freudian by one of Freud's most loyal followers, Karl Abraham, Horney soon became a dissenting voice in the psychoanalytic establishment. This rebellious reputation brought her a struggling young doctor, Frederick (Friz) Perls, as an early patient.

In one of her first published papers, Horney broke with the Freudian view that a woman's destiny was dictated by the absence of male genitals. In this paper, Horney questioned the Freudian view that "one-half the human race is discontented with the sex assigned to it" (Horney, [1922] 1967, p. 38). She then proceeded to question Freud's empirical support for his theory of penis envy. Her early feminist views of psychic development earned her the label of a rebel and the disapproval of Freud himself. The final break occurred later, over the influence of social factors in human development.

Emigrating to the United States in 1932, Horney was struck by the difference between her patients in Germany and those in the

United States. For Horney, these differences could not be explained by the Freudian emphasis on instincts. Living in New York, Horney was in the midst of an innovative group of thinkers and writers who focused on the role of culture in the development of the personality. This group included Erich Fromm and Harry Stack Sullivan. Her reputation as an original thinker brought her Albert Ellis as a patient. Ellis later developed his own theory of personality and therapy (see Chapter Four).

In this period Horney and others identified the positive force for growth and development that Horney termed the *real self*. Horney's version is important for organizational work for two reasons. She identified the conditions that could nurture and thwart this force and the neurotic solution (the *ideal self*) that individuals devised in response. At this time she also mentored a young Brooklyn College psychologist who later developed his own theory of human needs, Abraham Maslow. Maslow built on and extended Horney's distinction between satisfaction and safety needs (Hoffman, 1988, p. 66) and then applied this positive conception of human nature to management and organizations.

In 1941 Horney broke formally with the orthodox Freudians, starting her own institute with a small band of followers. Theoretical dissension caused further breaks within this institute, but Horney continued to write and practice her own approach to psychoanalysis until her death in 1952. In the last two decades of her life, she published five books focusing on the importance of culture, early childhood experiences, and the development of the human personality. Her work enjoyed considerable popularity with the public but was either ignored or strongly criticized by the psychoanalytic establishment.

Horney's Point of Influence

Horney's point of influence is the *social unconscious*. This is a depository for the cluster of memories, feelings, images, and inner conflicts that give us the self-image or images that influence our later behavior. Where Freud looked at the conflict between our instincts and society, the instinctive part of our unconscious, Horney looked at the inner conflicts that grew out of our early experiences. The starting point for these experiences is what Horney defined as the real self.

**Preview: When to Use Horney's
Point of Influence in the Workplace.**

When organizations need to identify and support high performance
(the real self) (pp. 121–122, 129–130)

When organizations need to foster more varied and productive
management styles (pp. 122–126, 130–134)

When organizations need to identify and limit the impact of individual
dysfunction (the idealized self) (pp. 126–127, 134, 135)

When issues of gender identity influence work relationships
(pp. 119–121, 127–129, 135–137)

The Real Self

Like Carl Rogers and Abraham Maslow, Horney declared that, if
given the chance, an individual will grow, substantially undiverted,
toward self-realization, or the individual's real self; this individual
develops the "unique alive forces of his real self: the clarity and
depth of his own feelings, thoughts, wishes, interests; the ability to
tap his own resources, the strength of his will power, the special capacities or gifts he may have; the faculty to express himself, and to
relate himself to others with his spontaneous feelings." The real
self is *"that central inner force, common to all human beings and yet
unique to each, which is the deep source of growth"* (Horney, 1950, p. 17,
emphasis in original).

What determines whether the real self develops is what Horney
called "conditions of safety." Here she preceded Maslow's "hierarchy" and made the distinction between conditions of safety (psychological safety) and conditions of satisfaction (such as food and
shelter). Conditions of safety include an atmosphere of warmth that
provides freedom to have one's own feelings and thoughts, guidance, encouragement, and a healthy friction with the wishes and
wills of others. For Horney, this atmosphere was both supportive
and confrontative. To become a healthy and mature individual the
child grows "with others in love and friction." In this way the child
grows "in accordance with his real self" (Horney, 1950, p. 18).

Conditions of safety also mean the absence of direct or indirect
domination, indifference, erratic behavior, lack of respect for the
child's individual needs, disparaging attitudes, too much admiration

or the absence of it, having to take sides in parental disagreements, too much or too little responsibility, isolation from other children, discrimination, and unkept promises.

The real self can only grow in conditions of safety, so when they are missing we respond as best we can. Unfortunately this response is limited. As children we lack the cognitive skills and emotional capacity to deal with our situation, so we adopt one of three defensive *stances:* moving against, moving toward, or moving away from people. These stances are more general than the ad hoc defenses such as projection described by Freud. They are life-style defenses, comprehensive positions toward the rest of the world that shape attitudes, feelings, and behavior. By using them, we pay a high price, abandoning "ourselves in order to protect ourselves" (Paris, 1994, p. 190).

Moving Against People

The "moving against" stance is taken to identify with mastery and deny everything else. For the child it "chiefly entails his determination, conscious or unconscious, to overcome every obstacle—in or outside himself—and the belief that he should be able, and in fact is able, to do so. He should be able to master the adversities of fate, the difficulties of a situation, the intricacies of intellectual problems, the resistances of other people, conflicts in himself. The reverse side of the necessity for mastery is his dread of anything connoting helplessness; this is the most poignant dread he has" (Horney, 1950, p. 192).

When moving against people, the child accepts and takes for granted hostility and determines consciously or unconsciously to fight it or control it. The child implicitly distrusts the feelings and intentions of others and rebels in whatever ways are open. The goal is to be the stronger one, partly for protection and partly for revenge: "He becomes too proud to ask for anything, and cannot receive anything graciously. To be on the receiving end is so humiliating to him that it chokes off any feelings of gratitude. Having smothered positive feelings, he can rely upon only his intellect for the mastery of life" (Horney, 1950, p. 204).

Moving Toward People

In moving toward people, all behavior and motivation that suggest winning and success are forbidden. If we understand the position of the child, an unconscious decision to assume this stance makes sense. When the child is moving toward people, she or he accepts helplessness and, in spite of estrangement, uncertainty, and fears, the child tries to win the affection of others and to lean on them. Only in this way can the child feel safe with them. If the family contains dissenting parties, the child will attach to the most powerful person or group. This attachment brings a feeling of belonging and support that makes the child feel less weak and less isolated. Horney explained this stance by describing a patient's drawing "a baby surrounded by strange and threatening animals. There she stood, tiny and helpless, in the middle of the picture, around her a huge bee ready to sting her, a dog that could bite her, a cat that could jump at her, a bull that could gore her. . . . [T]he more aggressive ones, being the more frightening, are the ones whose 'affection' is the most necessary" (Horney, 1945, pp. 50–51).

For Horney, the important point was that the individual felt helpless, surrounded by forces that were too powerful to fight and too all-encompassing to flee. The only solution was to win their affection. This frightened perception of the world leads to an interpersonal style emphasizing acceptance and affection. In its extreme form it involves a compulsive and overwhelming need to be liked, wanted, desired, or loved. Self-effacing qualities are used without consulting one's thoughts or feelings or the particular merits of a situation. They are used compulsively, and aggressive tendencies are repressed.

Moving Away from People

When moving away from people, the child wants neither to belong or to fight but to keep apart. The child feels little in common with other people and feels that they do not understand him or her anyhow. A private world is built with nature, toys, books, and dreams. Emotions are served, but not experienced. As in the other two examples, the child lacks passion, goals, and awareness and has given up the possibility of having unmet dreams and needs by having no dreams and minimizing needs. In moving away from people, the child shuts the door to the intimacy of moving toward them or the zest and assertiveness of moving against them. The other difficulty is that this is not a conscious choice. The child chooses to move away from people as a strategy of psychological survival. The adult who continues to be locked into this stance is not aware of the price that is being paid for this invisible wall of isolation.

All three stances can be effective at times, but if an individual is *locked into* any one of them, his or her range of behavior is limited. The individual also pays an inner price for such rigidity. Strict adherence to one of the three stances means a loss or denial of part of the real self. For example, someone who is locked into moving toward others is denying or repressing all inclinations toward winning or competition, or gaining perspective by emotionally or intellectually becoming detached from a problem.

How does an individual make peace with such a compromise? Horney describes a solution, but it is again a solution with a price. It is the idealized image of the self.

The Idealized Image of the Self

To fill the void of the denied parts of the self, the individual replaces the real self with an *idealized image*. If this image is accepted into the personality, it becomes what Horney refers to as the *idealized self*. This is an unrealistic and grandiose image of the self that the individual believes he or she *should* be.

The idealized image of the self fills in the void left by denied aspects of the real self and justifies the need to adopt the limiting stance of one of the three movements. For example, the idealized image of someone with a "moving toward" stance is that of a saint, a completely giving person who lives only to help others, and whose motives are always above reproach. Horney refers to the fruitless attempt to actualize such a grandiose image as the "search for glory." The idealized self functions as if it were a separate individual with its own life, claims upon the world, proscriptions to itself, pride and identity, and even its own internal conflicts.

The idealized self is grandiose and godlike. It has unlimited powers and exalted faculties. According to Horney, the individual "becomes a hero, a genius, a supreme lover, a saint, a god" (Horney, 1950, p. 22). Unfortunately, actualizing the ideal self who accomplishes everything is an impossibility. This leads to the formulation of the *despised self*, who because of impossible goals accomplishes little and is therefore an object of disdain. The individual who lives with the vision of becoming a grandiose hero thus lives with the likelihood of becoming a grandiose failure. Idealization leads to self-hate. The grandiose image of the completely giving person, with the hint of one self-centered act, becomes the despised image of the totally selfish person.

The idealized self seldom lays claim to an individual's entire personality, but at the same time few completely escape the influence of such an idealized image of themselves. The individual continues to experience an obscured connection with the real self, through muffled thoughts, feelings, and images.

Gender Identity

Horney's work on gender was completed in Germany before she developed her theory of personality, but it is consistent with the rest of her theory. The link is the images that influence behavior. She explained that our images of gender are socially determined at an early age and then reside at least partially outside of conscious awareness.

In Freud's theory, anatomy was destiny, and the conventions of society that relegated women to domesticity were never questioned. For Freud, the absence of a penis and women's presumed disappointment about this explained their limitations in the economic and political order. Marcia Westkott says, "The yearning to compensate for the lack of a penis, according to Freud, explains female heterosexual desire, rivalry among women, and the gratification of motherhood. It also explains female homosexuality, masochism, and jealous imitation of male behavior. In sum, the Freudian concept of penis envy explains all one needs to understand of female behavior, from passivity and self-denial to active striving and desire" (Westkott, 1986, p. 53).

Horney, in contrast, acknowledged that gender is biologically based but emphasized that society gives gender its meaning. Her ideas, pioneering in her time, shed a great deal of light on today's work-related gender issues. Horney first confronted these ideas by using psychoanalytic thinking to elevate the role of motherhood. Her more enduring contribution was her later application of sociological thought to explain women's lower social and economic status. In "The Flight from Womanhood" ([1926] 1967a), she stated that, based on her clinical experience, men envied women's ability to produce new life (womb envy) at least as much as women envied men because of their sexual organ. She asked with genuine astonishment, "What about motherhood?" inviting her readers to consider the indescribable happiness and excitement when one thinks of bringing a new person into the world. "And the joy when it finally makes its appearance and one holds it for the first time in one's arms?" (p. 60). She questioned whether the great strength of men to achieve in virtually every field of work is not in fact a compensation for playing such a small role in the creation of life (Horney, [1926] 1967a, p. 62). Women's role is placed in mystery by men, and this is one way of keeping women out.

Horney's second contribution was to step away from the psychoanalytic dependence upon instincts and look at gender differences from a social point of view. Anticipating our current concern with masculine and feminine styles of thought and behavior, she drew on the ideas of philosopher Georg Simmel to demonstrate how the masculine basis of our civilization distorts our perception. She pointed out how masculine values define our conception of reality itself. For Simmel, the state, laws, morality, religion, and the sciences are the creation of men. Horney then quotes Simmel, who states: "The requirements of art, patriotism, morality in general and social ideas in particular, correctness in practical judgment and objectivity in theoretical knowledge, the energy and the profundity of life. . . . Supposing that we describe these things, viewed as absolute ideas, by the single word 'objective,' we then find that in the history of our race the equation objective = masculine is a valid one" (Horney, [1926] 1967a, pp. 55–56).

Freudian psychoanalysis reinforces male bias by describing the presumed nature of women from the viewpoint of men. In Freud's view, little boys view little girls as inferior because they lack a penis. From this perception, they develop an idea of feminine psychology in which girls accept the male bias and view themselves as inferior because they lack the male organ. Horney countered this view by pointing out that it is not anatomy that is destiny but what society decides anatomy means. In this instance, the male organ has meant *privilege,* and this is what women envy. It is impossible to tell, according to Simmel, "whether this masculine character of the fundamentals of our civilization has its origins in the essential nature of the sexes or only in a certain preponderance of force in men. In any case this is the reason why, in the most varying fields, inadequate achievements are contemptuously called 'feminine,' while distinguished achievements on the part of women are called 'masculine' as expression of praise" (Horney, [1926] 1967a, p. 56). She then stated that women have accommodated themselves to the needs and desires of men and then accepted this compromise as if it were their own true nature (Horney, [1926] l967a, pp. 56–57).

Identifying and Supporting High Performance (The Real Self)

Super performance in an organization begins with people who can think and feel (Allcorn, 1991, p. 3). This ability to fully engage our thoughts and emotions in action is the organizational embodiment of Horney's real self. Super performance requires the emotional capacity to engage reality fully, know our true thoughts and feelings, communicate valid information effectively, respond constructively and creatively to conflict, and recognize and seize learning opportunities in the face of threat and anxiety (Holmer, 1994, p. 51). A tall order and one that it's hard to imagine filling without an engaged real self.

Organizations cannot undo a childhood without psychological safety. That is a job for individual psychotherapy. Organizations can, however, create a culture that brings out the potential of its members by encouraging the expression of true thoughts and feelings. One clear expression of such a culture is the learning organization described by Peter Senge (1990). Senge notes that learning is a natural act. No one has to teach an infant to learn. The infant and the very young child learn naturally and constantly, a description consistent with Horney's view of the real self. Two of Senge's five conditions for organizational learning are similar to Horney's environmental conditions that encourage the real self. The first is *personal mastery,* which means that organizations encourage individuals to pursue a lifelong quest toward reaching their higher aspirations, or doing what matters. Senge notes that even though the energy that goes into such a drive can be quite valuable to an organization, few organizations take steps to foster personal mastery. The second condition is *dialogue,* or the conditions that allow individuals to suspend assumptions and truly enter into learning together. Senge contrasts dialogue with discussion, which is more likely to involve going back and forth with ideas until one idea dominates or wins (Senge, 1990, pp. 7–11). Although childhood cannot be relived, organizations can take steps to encourage Senge's view of learning expression and the real self.

Fostering More Varied and Productive Management Styles

Horney acknowledges that moving toward, against, and away from can be useful strategies when they are used appropriately. Used inflexibly, however, all three limit performance. This is illustrated as we examine three responses to a team-building effort at AVTRON, a small software company specializing in programs for the airline industry.

AVTRON had gone through an extensive program of attempting to build a company culture and developing an "AVTRON Vision for the 1990s." These efforts achieved some positive results, but the key members of top management were still not working together to achieve the vision that they had labored so hard to develop. Brenda Stratton, an organization development consultant, was called in with the general charge of "building a team." She decided to gather some initial data by asking each member of the team to write her a letter describing the present operation of the team in terms of its strengths and weaknesses. She also asked team members to separately summarize what they saw as their own strengths and limitations and the particular contribution that they could make to the team if it was functioning well. The following letters from the team members illustrate some workplace consequences of rigid adherence to the stances of moving toward, against, and away from people.

The Moving Toward Position

Dear Brenda,

I really appreciate your setting it up so that we could contact you individually, although I prefer personal contact to a letter. When we are working with people it always seems better to communicate face to face. We have some very strong personalities in this company, but I have found that with a little patience and understanding one can get along. As you might know, we recently had a problem regarding our new system for inventory control. I really hate to get involved in these power games. They don't accomplish anything, and someone always gets hurt. In this case we had a slightly different point of view about a product, and this turned into a full-scale war.

I tried to get Bob Lyman, our head of Product Development, together with Walt Jackson, the vice president for Finance, but it didn't work. I thought that if we could meet in a nice, comfortable setting away from the office, then we could get to know each other as people. If we could do that, then we could all see our differences in perspective. Unfortunately, this isn't how it worked out. We had a nice lunch in a private room at my club, but Bob spent most of the time stating and restating his case, and Walt just checked out. I mean he was there physically but he wasn't there mentally. The only thing he said was that he couldn't say much about this without the figures, and, of course, he didn't have them with him. Anyway, the evening was a flop, and I'm not sure what to do with these people.

The one thing that is sure is that we don't trust each other anymore. There was a time when I could be very sure what each person needed to feel OK. Knowing this, I was able to give them what they needed, and they would come around and do what was right. That is not true anymore. People still have their needs, but I can't be sure what they are, so there is no way to help. The hardest part is that I'm getting so that I don't trust my own judgment about people anymore, and that's something I always thought that I could rely on. What I do is just be pleasant to everyone, but I don't really let anyone know too much. I know that this isn't good, but under these circumstances there is not much else that anyone can do.

I want to cooperate, but I must admit that I'm not very optimistic about your efforts to turn us into a team. The basic faith in people isn't there, and without that you can't do anything.

Mary St. Claire, Head of Marketing

Mary has a strong preference for moving toward people. If there is a difference over policy or principle, or even self-interest, she perceives it as a personal difference; she tries to deal with differences by converting them to a personal issue and then using her well-developed personal skills and social grace to bring about agreement. When it is not possible to deal with issues in this way, she feels helpless.

The Moving Against Position

Dear Ms. Stratton:

You have asked me to describe the condition of our team. I must be honest with you. I don't think that it is anything an outsider like yourself can help. Several years ago, in another company, I was involved in something called team building, and it turned out to be a waste of time. We sat around and talked about our feelings, and when it was all over, nothing changed. Despite this experience I'm an open-minded person, so I will supply the information that you are requesting. The situation here is not unique. Business is civilized battle. Everyone has his or her own interests, and most people will do whatever they can to get what they want. This is not cynicism. It is realism, and I am sometimes surprised when otherwise intelligent people don't seem to understand this basic fact.

AVTRON is not unique in this respect, although I think that the people that we are involved with are perhaps not as open and straightforward in this respect as they could be. Mary, like all marketing people, wants a product that she can move so she can rack up the sales figures and make herself look good. She has a really minimal interest in the product and its quality, and the thing that bothers me is that she doesn't admit this. She arranged a dinner for us to get together that was worse than a waste of time. I say worse because when I tried to get her and Walt to come out of the woodwork and say what they were after, they both played games. Mary asked me about my family (which is none of her business) and Walt, as usual, didn't say a damn thing (excuse my French). The result was that I laid out my plans and strategies and they didn't do the same, so now I wonder if I am one down.

Overall, its a hard group for me to work with. I hate to say it, but it isn't really an honest group. None of them say what is really on their mind, and for that reason I can't trust them.

Good luck. You are going to need it.

Bob Lyman, Head of Product Development

For Bob Lyman, it is truly a world of all against all. He makes an immediate interpretation that those working with him are interested solely in advancing their own interests. He is ready to accept that definition of reality and move into a fighting stance himself. His own feelings are forbidden ground to others and to himself as well. He resists all efforts to bring the affective part of himself into the situation.

The Moving Away Position

Dear Ms. Stratton:

I apologize for the delay in answering your letter, but it was time for our quarterly report, and, of course, that required my attention—and in this instance a good deal of it. You have asked for my thoughts regarding how we work together as a team. It's hard for me to answer that because I don't really know what you mean by a team. We each have distinct jobs to do, and, of course, at times we need to supply each other with information. I'm always willing to do that. I must say, however, that I don't always get the same courtesy in return. Neither Mary nor Bob gives me the information that I need when I need it. What their motivation might be I can't possibly imagine. I have found that it's a waste to time to ponder the imponderable, and the motivation of other people fits into that category.

This became very clear when Mary invited us all for dinner. It was a strange evening. Mary, as usual, was asking a lot of irrelevant questions. I say irrelevant in that my outside life has nothing to do with what I do at work. Bob was, as usual, peddling his own point of view, which was fine, but it doesn't have anything to do with my job. My job is to keep this company in as strong a fiscal position as possible, and the best way for me to do that is to have sound, accurate, and timely information. I don't need to know a great deal about their personal lives, nor do they need to know a great deal about mine. I do need to know something about how they are doing their job, and I would get that if they just supplied the information for my quarterly reports on time. I have worked to make those forms concise and objective so nobody's time is wasted, and I don't know why the others can't be as cooperative.

I have answered your questions about what you refer to as a work team. It's an idea that might be relevant to some organizations, but it's not relevant to ours. There are some ways that each of us could do our job more effectively, but that's always possible.

I hope that this information is helpful.

Walt Jackson, Head of Finance

Walt Jackson wants to neither fight nor belong. His prime goal is to move away, remain uninvolved, and use his obvious expertise and interest in the data of the company to keep himself in that position. For Walt, any contact that would involve his feelings is irrelevant, and he does not recognize its relevance for anyone else.

Each of these responses involves behaviors that support one stance toward the world. Unfortunately, each is also a distorted and rigid version of that approach. Power is an inevitable part of life, especially life at work. The "moving against" position, however, makes power an end in itself and encourages people to behave as if life is a constant battle. Love is also an important aspect of human existence, but the "moving toward" position assumes that the only alternative people have is to ingratiate themselves with others. The "moving away" position similarly makes the position of detached objectivity an all-purpose strategy. Horney's point of influence gives us a framework with which to understand where these stances are being used unproductively.

Identifying and Limiting the Impact of Individual Dysfunction (the Idealized Self)

The idealized self at work is not a pretty picture. If it is incorporated into the personality, the image develops artificial strategies to cope with others and override genuine feelings, wishes, and thoughts. An individual thus motivated invests with pride attitudes and activities that actualize the ideal self. For example, a manager whose ideal self is defined in terms of perfect performance invests with pride the ability to find minor errors.

The ideal self's reaction to frustration is intense and not appropriate to the circumstances. Pleasure over an achievement is experienced fleetingly, if at all, and vindicating triumph is more important than actual accomplishment. Drive and motivation are compulsive, and facts, thoughts, feelings, and reality itself are distorted to fit the need. The example of Bill Voss, president of AVTRON, shows the incorporation of the ideal self into an individual.

> Bill's family background illustrates the conditions that foster the image of an ideal self. Bill and his two brothers were taught to compete for their father's attention in every part of their life, especially in school athletics and their social life. Behind this drive for perfection was the message that Bill and his brothers must always exceed expectations. Bill's father did not believe in giving compliments or specific criticism. If Bill performed well his father said little, simply noting that Bill was doing what he was supposed to be doing. If he was dissatisfied with a school paper or something the boys had made, he handed it back and walked away with no comment. He believed that this behavior would teach them to be critical of themselves and find imperfections without his comments. It worked, and Bill and his brothers developed strong and powerful

idealized selves. In Horney's terms, their solution was an idealized image of the self that was a perfect and flawless competitor in every aspect of life. This image in turn led to an image of the despised self that could never succeed and never do enough.

As an adult, Bill became founder and president of AVTRON. AVTRON was the first company to develop several important systems for aircraft parts, flight scheduling, and personnel administration. The company has attracted many talented people who have promised to keep its technology at the leading edge. With these qualities, AVTRON should be demonstrating steady growth, but it is not. It cannot hold onto its top people.

Bill demands perfection but is unable to enjoy success when it occurs. When it doesn't he takes his disappointment out on his subordinates. He demands that the company always be first with any new innovation, and when it is not, he experiences this as a personal failing and describes those around him as "losers." He views other software producers as enemies to be vanquished rather than as competitors. Instead of basing his desires on an objective and attainable standard and giving his engineers specific feedback about their work, Bill preaches about "high standards" but ignores the specific feedback that would help others to define and achieve it. His ideal self has thus limited his awareness of how the company is actually running. As a result, the engineers are murmuring to each other about how impossible it is to work at AVTRON. Those who can have left.

In this profile, "[t]he actual, empirical self becomes the offensive stranger to whom the idealized self happens to be tied, and the latter [ideal self] turns against this stranger with hate and contempt" (Horney, 1950, p. 112). The ideal self punishes the real self through relentless and impossible demands.

Working with Issues of Gender Identity

Problems of gender identity in organizations have an effect on the individual but originate at the group and organizational levels. This process is illustrated in the following scenario.

Wanda Ballinger was a mechanical engineer and the first woman to be employed as an engineer by Purvis-Atkins, a large international consulting group. Wanda was hired with the backing of Elwood Purvis, the managing partner, and the message was clearly stated that she was to be treated fairly: no special privileges, but certainly no discrimination. In her day-to-day duties, which usually meant working on defined projects, Wanda was satisfied. The problem was that by the time she found out how projects were to be divided, it was too late for her input. There seemed to be a general understanding about who would be doing what. This understanding developed informally at the monthly poker game, held the third Wednesday of every month. Wanda was not excluded from this game. In fact, with a deliberate gesture, she had been invited to the game her first week on the job. She turned down the invitation because of a previous engagement, but then she received no more invitations. Six months later, Wanda left the firm.

Wanda's experience illustrates some of the dynamics underlying gender issues in the workplace. The male management of Purvis-Atkins wanted to keep Wanda, but they were not able to understand her experience. For her part, Wanda was not able to discuss her experience, why she was reluctant to say anything that might make anyone uncomfortable, and, finally, why it was so hard for her to explain what was bothering her.

Westkott (1986), in *The Feminist Legacy of Karen Horney,* links Horney's gender theory with her notions of the real and ideal self and offers insights that could have helped both Wanda and the Purvis-Atkins management to understand the situation. For Westkott, the "moving toward" position is the basic solution that most women use when their family environment stifles their real self. The pattern is for the individual to gain reassurance and protection against basic anxiety through the affection of others. To attain this protection, women adopt attitudes of helplessness, docility, and self-effacement. Their techniques include belittling or denying themselves and living according to others' expectations by being unassertive, passive, and self-effacing. In this view, the feminine dependent type (moving toward) is masculine civilization's stepchild. Wanda's self-effacing attitude was a product of a male-dominated culture. The cost of meeting these male expectations was Wanda's alienation from her real self.

Westkott (1986) notes that society imposes this role on women through the processes of *devaluation* and *sexualization*. Devaluation comes from the patriarchal pattern of preference for males and an ideology of male superiority. Elements of this message include the imperative that women nurture men and that this nurturing and attention is something males are entitled to. Mothers cannot or will not protect little girls from having this role imposed upon them. The pattern is rationalized with an ideology of the "higher nature" of women—an inherent female altruism and sense of responsibility for others.

Sexualization, to Westkott, is another form of devaluation. It comes not only from actual sexual abuse but from defining little girls as essentially sexual beings and training them in seductive and sexually aggressive ways. For Westkott, it is also an expression of male power: the power to treat any relationship with sexual overtones. To illustrate the flavor of such sexualization, Westkott quotes from J. Strouse's biography of Alice James, sister of psychologist William James: "He addressed courtly letters to her as 'you lovely babe.'. . . He referred constantly to her physical attributes and drew verbal portraits of her sensual, untutored, indulged feminine nature. He wrote to her, 'a thousand thanks to the cherry lipped apricot nosed double chinned little Bal for her strongly dashed off letter, which inflamed the hearts of her lonely brothers with an intense longing to kiss and slap her cheeks'" (Strouse, quoted in Westkott, 1986, p. 102). Perhaps such language is merely an example of Victorian sentimentality. To Westkott, however, it is an example of how generations of women, with society's blessing, have been taught to develop an identity based on their ability to please and care for men.

Wanda Ballinger, the engineer who found it easier to leave a job she liked than to express feelings that might make her male coworkers uncomfortable, followed this pattern of pleasing others. Wanda was ready for an engineering career in the 1990s. Her ideal self had an aversion to disagreement and a strong appetite for approval. It could not tolerate the corporate culture at Purvis-Atkins.

How to Use Horney's Point of Influence
Encouraging the Growth of the Real Self

Horney's concept of the real self outlines the process of individual psychological growth. What can organizations do to encourage such individual development without involving clinical methodology? Two possibilities are (1) to develop a culture that supports the real self ("the learning organization") and (2) to apply twelve-step programs to encourage individual personal growth.

Twelve-step programs such as Alcoholics Anonymous have developed effective programs that help individuals tap into the potential of their real self and have achieved therapeutic results without psychotherapy. Lee Holmer suggests that such change is possible within organizations provided that the programs are voluntary (1994, p. 67). Most management change programs are top-down: individuals are directed or persuaded to participate by the hierarchy. This process will not work if the goal is support and encouragement of the real self. Ongoing social support must also exist. Participants must be encouraged to build support networks across organizational levels and divisions.

Within this context, the following four principles, all strikingly similar to Horney's definition of the kind of early environment that encourages the development of the real self, form the core of most twelve-step programs (Holmer, 1994, pp. 68–69):

1. A reprieve from cynicism, with a positive safe environment for the expression and pursuit of nonmaterialistic, spiritual, and altruistic values such as personal integrity and organizational ethics
2. A reprieve from perfectionism, with a positive and safe culture for accepting and recognizing one's limitations and their undesirable consequences
3. Norms of self-honesty and self-disclosure
4. Norms of self-mastery, including taking responsibility for oneself rather than analyzing or blaming other people

These norms and processes might seem hard to carry out in today's competitive organizational environment, but they do indicate how individual development can be achieved in such an environment.

Working with Movement Toward, Against, and Away from People

These three movements, as Horney describes them, are inadequate solutions to inadequate parenting. At the same time, Horney acknowledges that, if they are not applied rigidly and compulsively, they are "complementary capacities necessary for good human relations" (Horney, 1950, p. 19), present in all of us without being the least indicative of neurosis (Horney, 1937, p. 102). Horney says little more about the *functional* aspect of these three movements, but here we find an interesting coincidence. Her three movements match the categories in a number of contemporary management-style instruments. These inventories typify the unique way in which individuals make decisions, communicate, and generally conduct themselves in managerial roles. With the exception of the Jung-based MBTI, many current management style frameworks contain:

1. A people-oriented category similar to the "moving toward" position
2. An action-oriented category similar to the "moving against" position
3. An analysis-oriented category similar to the "moving away" position

Table 3.1 illustrates this relationship for two widely used management-style frameworks, LIFO™, which stands for "Life Orientations" (Atkins, 1982) and Social Styles (Merrill and Reid, 1981). Neither LIFO™ nor Social Styles is described by its creators as based on Horney's theory. Stuart Atkins, the creator of LIFO™, cites the writings of Sigmund Freud, Erik Erikson, and Erich Fromm on character formation as important sources of his framework. David Merrill and Roger Reid describe the origin of Social Styles as ignoring *all* preconceived frameworks and being based solely on factor analysis of observed behavior (Atkins, 1981, pp. 266–288; Merrill and Reid, 1981, pp. 210–231).

My view is that the childhood experiences Horney characterized as the foundation for neurotic behavior are also the basis for different styles of productive functioning. Frameworks such as LIFO™ or Social Styles draw upon the same experiences as Horney's three movements. They do so, however, in positive, growth-oriented language that is more appropriate for the workplace. Noting this similarity can be mutually beneficial in two ways.

First, Horney's description can alert practitioners to the sensitive events that may have led individuals to adopt a particular management style. This is important because even though the authors

Table 3.1. Relationship Between Management-Style Frameworks and Horney's Theory.

Framework	Moving Toward People (Relationship-Oriented)	Moving Against People (Action-Oriented)	Moving away from People (Analysis-Oriented)
LIFO™	1. Adapting Dealing 2. Supporting Giving	Controlling Taking	Conserving Holding
Social Styles	1. Amiable 2. Expressive	Driver	Analytic

Note: Both frameworks define two types of people-oriented styles.

of LIFO™ and other frameworks have phrased their instruments in positive, nonclinical language, some individuals still react in a defensive way to the personal application of these categories. Horney's theory offers a possible explanation. A preference for solving problems with people (moving toward), through action (moving against), or through analysis (moving away) could have its roots in painful childhood experiences. Practitioners who are aware of this possibility can then adjust their behavior.

Second, those who are interested in applying Horney's three movements to functional behavior can use the positive, nonthreatening application methodology of instruments such as LIFO™ to:

1. Conceptualize differences in style in a neutral, nonjudgmental fashion and thereby legitimate differences
2. Regard no one style as correct and illustrate how individuals may utilize a number of styles to achieve their goals
3. Help individuals to become aware that each style or approach has strengths and weaknesses
4. Use a knowledge of different styles to help individuals increase the use of their less-used styles and thereby increase their behavioral repertoire
5. Become aware of the styles of others so that individuals can relate to them in a positive way

Mary St. Claire of AVTRON seemed to have a strong preference for solving problems with people by moving toward them. Her Social Style might be described as "amiable." Her LIFO™ preference might be described as "adapting dealing." Using the LIFO™ methodology, a consultant in a consultation or workshop setting could first help Mary to *confirm* her strengths by becoming more aware of her ability to tune into other people's needs and desires and relate to them on a personal basis. Mary would then be urged to consider *capitalizing* on this strength by finding new situations in which it could be used to good advantage.

Now, well aware of her strength in approaching problems from the personal basis, Mary could look at the other sides of her style. She could consider what happens when she uses the personal approach inappropriately or in excess. She could decide how she might moderate her tendency to move toward people. Aware that other ways exist to deal with problems, she would also be encouraged to look at the resources around her and find out how to get help from people with different orientations. She might learn how to extend her own approach and could, for example, experiment with stating her case more objectively and having someone with a detached, "moving away" style, like Walt Jackson, hear her. In doing so she would be learning how to bridge and communicate more effectively with others who have different styles (Atkins, 1981, pp. 119–136).

Working with Problems of the Ideal Self

Horney's theory identifies the image of the ideal self as a focal point of individual and organizational dysfunction. Her solution was psychoanalysis. This approach remains the way clinicians work with this limiting image. A more limited, nonclinical solution is to help individuals refocus on the muffled image of their real self. Following are some organizationally appropriate methods that are described elsewhere in this volume for helping individuals such as Bill Voss of AVTRON to minimize the impact of their ideal self.

Feedback

Kurt Lewin (see Chapter Seven) describes the unfreezing, change, and refreezing process that helps individuals to relax, drop their defenses, and thereby accept feedback. Lewin's theory would help the practitioner to set up a team-building activity that would make it more likely for Bill Voss to hear and understand the responses of his engineers.

Active Listening

Carl Rogers (Chapter Five) describes "conditions of worth" that are very close to Horney's idealized self. The atmosphere of congruence, unconditional positive regard, and empathic listening involved in active listening could be used to help Bill Voss reconnect with the thoughts and feelings of his real self.

Rational Confrontation

Another way of describing the ideal self is as an image produced by irrational or distorted beliefs. Albert Ellis and Aaron Beck (Chapter Four) offer methods for disputing with such belief systems.

Use of Self in a Feeling Confrontation

The real-time responses of the practitioner to Voss's demand for perfection and his punishing stance when he inevitably doesn't get it is another way to help him to gain awareness of the impact of his ideal self. Three other approaches to the use of self are described in the chapters on Carl Rogers, Fritz and Laura Perls, and, in a more detached way, Murray Bowen.

Consulting to the Ideal Self as an Organizational Image

Organizations can and do operate in the image of the ideal self. Bill Voss's ideal self has influenced the norms and culture of AVTRON in a variety of ways, including:

- Poor communication between individuals and units
- An appraisal system that demands perfection and punishes anything short of it
- An office atmosphere that alternates between grandiosity and despair (the two sides of the ideal self)
- A practice and culture of internal competition in which a great deal of creative energy is spent competing for advantage within the company rather than against outside competitors
- An atmosphere in which considerable energy is spent on inter-personal or interunit feuds and getting even

Embodiment of the image of the ideal self into the culture and operation of an organization can result from the influence of leaders such as Bill Voss, from traumatic external circumstances such as loss of a market, or from a combination of both. In any case, the image of an organizational ideal self provides practitioners with a guideline for understanding how the organization is operating and for developing frameworks for intervention. In this instance, data feedback could be used to help organization members examine their appraisal system, noting where it evokes their best efforts and where it evokes defensiveness and efforts to cover their tracks.

Working with Problems of Gender Identity

Horney's identification of unconsciously based ideas of gender-appropriate behaviors is still valid. The initial step in modifying the impact of these unconscious images is to develop self-awareness. This is one aim of diversity training—to help individuals and groups become aware of the unconscious base of their behavior as it relates to gender, race, age, or any other aspect of human diversity. The following exercise is based on gender, but the principles in the exercise are relevant for many aspects of human diversity.

In this exercise, male and female workshop participants meet in a separate space with a trainer of the same gender and brainstorm about the messages they recall as helping them define what it means to be a man or a woman. These messages can originate with parents, peers, school, or the culture as expressed in television, movies, and so on. When the two groups come back together, the results are written down on newsprint; this is followed by a facilitated discussion between groups. The important role of the facilitator is to keep the discussion focused on learning. This does not mean that the discussion cannot become heated. It can, but the goal of the heat is to generate light in the form of awareness of one's own position and understanding of the other person's. An example of such a discussion follows:

> *Male Participant:* I see on your list of what it means to be a female in our organization "to be invisible in meetings." What does that mean?
>
> *Female Participant:* It means that when I make a suggestion in a meeting, a lot of times it's ignored, but when a male makes the same suggestion later people pick up on it.
>
> *Male Participant:* Does that really happen? I've never noticed it.
>
> *Female Participant:* It happened here in this workshop when Marge suggested that we look at our experience on the basis of how long we have been with the company. We didn't pick up on it until Bill suggested it.

This exercise can also reveal the differing degrees of psychological energy behind male and female identity. The facilitator and the groups themselves can observe which group seems to have more instantaneous focus and energy. Horney's theory can be used to understand why the members of one group may appear to have more immediate energy and enthusiasm and to be more enthusiastic just about being grouped together, whereas the members of the other group have difficulty focusing upon themselves as a group. Horney noted that the less privileged group is always more focused on its position. She quoted Simmel, who stated that it is "one of the privileges of the master that he has not constantly to think that he is master, while the position of the slave is such that he can never forget it" (Horney, [1926] 1967a, p. 69).

Goodwill and good intentions are not sufficient to change the unconscious patterns that govern how men and women deal with each other. Horney's theory is useful both to the women who want to pursue organizational careers and the men and women in organizations who want to create the opportunities for them to do so. Horney's concepts of the real and ideal self and the special pattern of pleasing and dependency that has evolved between men and women are useful tools in understanding and changing these old patterns.

Conclusion

Few individuals who are attempting to influence human behavior in organizations would dispute the influence of the unconscious part of our mind. Defining that impact clearly and influencing it in the direction they choose is another matter. It is not easy to do, especially if the unconscious is governed by remote events in an individual's infancy or early childhood. The question is how to work with this powerful force in the context of day-to-day behavior in organizations. Horney's point of influence provides such a tool. Her concepts provide a way to work with unconscious influences on behavior without reference to early developmental events. Horney's pioneering identification of the real self identified the positive force within individuals behind their psychological growth and development. Her identification of the forces of moving toward, against, and away from people identified the origins of effective and dysfunctional management styles. Her identification of the ideal self also helps practitioners to identify and work with the roots of much dysfunctional organizational behavior. And her pioneering work on the social origin of gender identity is still relevant in helping men and women work together.

Although it is written for the psychotherapist, Horney's theory explains the unconscious roots of human behavior in a way that can be useful for today's practitioner in the organization.

Annotated Bibliography
Original Sources: Readable Horney

Horney, K. *The Neurotic Personality of Our Time.* New York: W. W. Norton, 1937.
This, like all of Horney's books, was written for the general public. This was the first book she wrote and it contains the basic elements of her theory with a special emphasis on the importance of early socialization.

Horney, K. *Neurosis and Human Growth: The Struggle Toward Self-Realization.* New York: W. W. Norton, 1950.
This work contains the most complete exposition of Horney's theory, including the later development of the ideas of the idealized self and the various stances toward the world.

Kelman, H. (ed.). *Feminine Psychology.* New York: W. W. Norton, 1967.
This book includes all of Horney's essays, in which she offered one of the first systematic refutations of Freud's view of women, as well as a useful introductory essay by Harold Kelman. These essays contain many of the root ideas of feminism and are still useful reading today. Particularly interesting are "The Flight from Womanhood," "The Dread of Woman," and "The Overvaluation of Love."

Secondary Sources: Books About Horney and Her Theories

Paris, B. J. *Karen Horney: A Psychoanalyst's Search for Self-Understanding.* New Haven, Conn.: Yale University Press, 1994.
This is a careful and scholarly biography that pays particular attention to the way Horney's theories reflect some of her own personal struggles.

Quinn, S. *A Mind of Her Own: The Life of Karen Horney.* New York: Summit Books, 1987.
A warm, admiring biography of Horney, this book emphasizes her role as the first woman in a number of settings.

Westkott, M. *The Feminist Legacy of Karen Horney.* New Haven, Conn.: Yale University Press, 1986.
After Horney came to the United States, she stopped writing about women and feminism and concentrated on her overall theory. Westkott makes the case that her overall theory also addresses the plight of women and that the "moving toward" stance is applicable to most women of Horney's time, and perhaps today.

Bibliography

Allcorn, S. *Workplace Superstars in Resistant Organizations.* New York: Quorum Books, 1991.

Atkins, S. *The Name of Your Game: Four Game Plans for Success at Home and Work.* Beverly Hills, Calif.: Stewart Publishers, 1981.

Hoffman, E. *The Right to Be Human: A Biography of Abraham Maslow.* Los Angeles: Jeremy P. Tarcher, 1988.

Holmer, L. "Developing Emotional Capacity and Organizational Health." In R. H. Kilmann, I. Kilmann, and Associates, *Managing Ego Energy: The Transformation of Personal Meaning into Organizational Success* (pp. 49–72). San Francisco: Jossey-Bass, 1994.

Horney, K. *The Neurotic Personality of Our Time.* New York: W. W. Norton, 1937.

Horney, K. *New Ways in Psychoanalysis.* New York: W. W. Norton, 1939.

Horney, K. *Our Inner Conflicts: A Constructive Theory of Neurosis.* New York: W. W. Norton, 1945.

Horney, K. *Neurosis and Human Growth: The Struggle Toward Self-Realization.* New York: W. W. Norton, 1950.

Horney, K. "Flucht aus der Weiblichkeit" [The Flight from Womanhood]." In H. Kelman (ed.), *Feminine Psychology* (pp. 54–70). New York: W. W. Norton, 1967a. (Originally published 1926.)

Horney, K. "Das Misstrauen zwischen den Geschlechtern" [The Distrust Between the Sexes]. In H. Kelman (ed.), *Feminine Psychology* (pp. 107–118). New York: W. W. Norton, 1967b. (Originally published 1931.)

Maccoby, M. *The Gamesman.* New York: Simon & Schuster, 1976.

Merrill, D. W., and Reid, R. H. *Personal Styles and Effective Performance: Make Your Style Work for You.* Radnor, Penn.: Chilton, 1981.

Paris, B. J. *Karen Horney: A Psychoanalyst's Search for Self-Understanding.* New Haven, Conn.: Yale University Press, 1994.

Rubins, J. L. *Karen Horney: Gentle Rebel of Psychoanalysis.* New York: Dial Press, 1978.

Senge, P. M. *The Fifth Discipline: The Art and Practice of the Learning Organization.* New York: Doubleday, 1990.

Strouse, J. *Alice James: A Biography.* Boston: Houghton Mifflin, 1980.

Westkott, M. *The Feminist Legacy of Karen Horney.* New Haven, Conn.: Yale University Press, 1986.

Part Two

Thought and Feeling

Points of Influence
Within Our Awareness

Chapter Four

Albert Ellis and Aaron Beck
The Power of Thought and Belief

Why Albert Ellis and Aaron Beck?
An Overview of Organizational Applications

One powerful way to influence both behavior and feelings is through our thoughts. The two theorists in this chapter have demonstrated how to influence feelings and behavior by influencing thinking. Albert Ellis and Aaron Beck developed their theories independently, but both focus upon the interaction between cognition, feelings, and behavior. Both also view cognition (thoughts, attitudes, beliefs, and so on) as the most accessible point of influence for feelings and behavior. In addition, both draw upon the familiar methods of reason, empirical investigation, and reframing to change cognition. Their emphasis upon using conscious thought to understand less conscious areas helps to make their methods more acceptable in organizations.

Ellis's and Beck's Theories as an
Organizational Image or Metaphor

Image often governs behavior. Ellis's and Beck's focus on cognition is a powerful point of influence for reformulating image. The chapter also draws significantly from Robert Marshak and Judith Katz's writings and their Covert Processes Model™. This model first uses a prism to identify thought as a cognitive point of influence and then identifies organizationally appropriate ways to use that point of influence (Marshak and Katz, 1991).

Ellis's and Beck's Theories as a Point of Influence for Dealing with Conflict

Conflict can be dealt with as a mental construct. By changing the mental image one has of a presumed opponent or the goal or process of conflict, a practitioner can influence both the nature and the outcome of conflictual situations. On an individual basis, Ellis and Beck illustrate ways to reframe beliefs to avoid viewing others in absolute terms. The cognitive approach also helps to build a greater awareness of the thoughts that shape an individual's views of issues, organizations, and conflict.

Ellis's and Beck's Theories as a Point of Influence for Dealing with Psychological Growth

The ability to grow psychologically is strongly influenced by an individual's internal picture or self-image. Like all images, a self-image is a product of our thinking, and the theorists in this chapter offer specific ways to influence the way we construct our self-image. These include becoming aware of and changing how we regard ourselves, the degree to which we view ourselves as controlled by our individual past history or external events, and the degree to which the actions of others affect our self-image.

Ellis's and Beck's Theories as a Point of Influence for Dealing with the Dilemmas of Joining

Joining a group or organization is a concrete action. The degree of commitment that one brings to this action is a mental and emotional process. The theorists in this chapter offer the practitioner a way to understand and influence the thoughts behind the commitment. Both theorists focus upon the internal network of beliefs, values, attitudes, and cognitive filters that influence the degree to which individuals become committed.

Ellis's and Beck's Theories as a Basis for Other Organizationally Relevant Theories

As psychotherapists, Ellis and Beck focus upon the ways in which individually oriented constructs, such as "I am a good person" or

"I have to perform at a certain level to be worthwhile," influence feelings and ultimately behavior. Behavior in organizations, however, is also influenced by other, less personal, constructs involving the way in which tasks should be done, how people should work together, or what the organization's goals should be. These less personal constructs include beliefs, assumptions and values, formal theories, paradigms, and the organizational and societal culture and values. The chapter describes how organization consultants Robert Marshak and Judith Katz use these more general constructs as part of their framework for individual and organizational change.

Limitations of Ellis's and Beck's Theories for Use in Organizations

The assumption underlying the theories in this chapter is that thought governs affect. Still, not every individual or organization is equally amenable to thinking as a point of influence for change. Some organizations, and some organizational situations, are more suited to dealing with affect first. Organizations that have a strong rational or thinking basis may seek a consultant who will help them to become more comfortable with their affective side. In addition, some consultants are most effective using their own affect and relating to the affect of others. In these instances cognition as a point of influence is not the most appropriate approach. Still, even the most affect-oriented practitioner can benefit by broadening her or his approach with the influence point described by Albert Ellis and Aaron Beck.

Ellis and Beck: Two Approaches to Thinking as a Point of Influence

Albert Ellis and Aaron Beck both use thinking as an influence point for change. They differ in how they define and work with unproductive or dysfunctional thoughts. Ellis's rational emotive behavior therapy (REBT), formerly called rational emotive therapy (RET) (Ellis, 1993a), takes a philosophical approach, defining certain types of thoughts as irrational and vigorously disputing them. Aaron Beck's cognitive therapy is more empirical, with therapist and client jointly exploring the basis and impact of the individual's thoughts (Weinrach, 1988, p. 162).

Albert Ellis pioneered in the modern identification of the thinking process as a point of influence for emotion and behavior. He is particularly clear in his explanation of the influence of what he terms *irrational thinking*. Ellis's strong commitment to his point of view and his unflagging energy have helped to establish and maintain REBT as a significant therapeutic modality. Although REBT practitioners use a wide variety of methods and Ellis limits vigorous disputation when working with some populations, he still maintains that the theory is most effective when the practitioner can vigorously debate and dispute what is termed *irrational thinking*. It is fair to say that REBT "not only tries to rip up clients' anti-empirical unrealistic statements but also reveals the underlying 'musturbatory' premises'" (Ellis, 1980, pp. 329–330).

Such vigorous disputation can be very powerful but is not always possible in nonclinical settings. In psychotherapy, individuals customarily make the commitment to stay with treatment at least through one session or long enough to learn whether the experience, which might be seen initially as threatening, could be useful. Such initial commitment is not always possible when working in organizations. To illustrate how cognition as a point of influence can be used in a wider range of organizational situations, we also examine the cognitive approach of Aaron Beck.

Operating independently of Ellis, but from a similar theory base, Beck brought to cognitive theory a university research base and a less confrontational style. Beck has done less with active disputation but has emphasized cognitive reframing and empirical investigation. The combination of both approaches provides a more complete understanding of how to use the influence point of thinking to change behavior in organizations.

How Albert Ellis Reintroduced the Influence Point of Thinking

Albert Ellis's life and development follow the contours of his theory. By most standards, his early life was not a happy one. However, Ellis maintains that these early circumstances had minimal impact upon his later life because he was able to influence his beliefs about this experience. The following selection from an autobio-graphical article illustrates Ellis's personal style as well as how he has applied his theory to his own life (Ellis, 1972b, pp. 104–107):

In many ways my early life was replete with poor circumstances. For one thing, I was always a semi-orphan. My father, a travelling sales-man and a promoter at that time, was frequently away from home for weeks or months on end. When he was living with us, he was so busy with his daytime business activities and his nighttime pinochle games or running around with attractive women, (or whatever the hell else he did) that my younger brother and sister and I literally spent about five minutes a day with him. . . .

As for my nice Jewish mother, a hell of a lot of help she was! Born at least twenty years before her time, thrown out of school in the sixth grade for compulsive talking, and quite unequipped to deal adequately with either marriage or child rearing, she was much more immersed in her own pleasures and her ego-aggrandizing activities than she was in understanding and taking care of children. . . .

As if all this parental neglect were not enough, I had a few other problems as a child. . . . I went back and forth to Presbyterian Hospital [for nephritis] about eight times, once for a period of ten months. As a result of this hospitalization and my convalescence from it, I was forbidden to take active part in any of the usual child-hood games for months on end. Sportswise, I developed into some-thing of a sissy. . . .

Despite all this, I somehow refused to be miserable. I took my father's absence and my mother's neglect in stride—and even felt good about being allowed so much autonomy and independence. I ignored my physical disabilities and determined to take care of my health in a rigorous manner so that I would no longer have the fre-quent headaches and other pains I then had. I decided not to hate my mother for her ineptness and used it, instead, to turn her round my little finger. . . .

Anyway, my difficult childhood helped me do one important thing: become a stubborn and pronounced problem solver. If life, I said to myself, is going to be so dammed rough and hassle-filled, what the devil can I do to live successfully and happily nevertheless?

The attitudes expressed in these excerpts have set the tone for Ellis's life and career. He has become an active therapist, writer, and problem solver. After graduating from City University of New York with a business degree in 1934, he worked in various office jobs by day and wrote fiction in his free time. He also became involved in the radical politics that flourished in New York City at that time. His interest in radical social change, combined with his personal problem of shyness, led him to read and later write in the area of sex, love, and marriage. This interest in turn led him to pursue a doctorate in clinical psychology at Columbia University, which he received in 1947. While developing an active practice in marriage, family, and sex counseling, he worked with a member of the Karen Horney group and became a practicing psychoanalyst.

However, neither psychoanalysis nor any of the other current therapeutic modalities seemed to suit Ellis's directive personality and style. Ellis recalled that he conquered his problems of shyness with women, not through psychoanalytic insight, but by going to the Bronx Botanical Gardens and compelling himself to speak to as many young women as possible. Most of these conversations were not successful. Ellis convinced himself that he was not a failure, only a person who had happened to fail in striking up sex-love with women (Ellis, 1972b, p. 114). This personal incident illustrates what was to become the essence of REBT: emotion follows from thinking.

During the early 1950s, Ellis gradually abandoned psychoanalysis and focused on the power of individual beliefs to influence feelings and behavior. He published a variety of articles and monographs in the 1950s and the first full exposition of his theory, *Reason and Emotion in Psychotherapy*, in 1962. Since then, Ellis has founded the Institute for Rational Emotive Therapy and published over fifty books, including *Executive Leadership: A Rational Approach* (1972a). His books apply REBT to many areas of human endeavor. He continues to write and conduct numerous public demonstrations.

How Aaron Beck Developed His Approach to Thinking as a Point of Influence

Beck's version of cognitive therapy and his life reflect a pattern of overcoming obstacles through thoughtful, pragmatic, and persistent effort. Like Albert Ellis and other theorists in this volume,

Beck was a practicing psychoanalyst who developed his theory to compensate for what he believed to be inadequacies in that medium. These inadequacies included the inability of psychoanalytic principles to bear up under academic investigation and the whole range of important "automatic thoughts" that didn't show up in free association (Weishaar, 1993, p. 20).

Aaron Beck was born in Providence, Rhode Island, in 1921. His father owned a printing business, and his mother was very active in community affairs. Thought and ideas were important in the Beck family, and the family atmosphere reflected a lively interest in politics, literature, and poetry. Beck's older sister, Beatrice, had died two years before his birth in the influenza epidemic of 1919. As a result, his mother suffered from lifelong symptoms of depression. Beck's initial research, which established his cognitive approach as a new therapeutic model, focused on the problem of depression.

Like Albert Ellis, Beck had a lengthy and unpleasant hospital stay as a young child. A broken arm that led to blood poisoning resulted in his being held back in school and to his view that he was thought of as "genetically and unalterably inferior" (Weishaar, 1993, p. 10). With tutoring help from his two brothers and persistent effort, Beck managed to catch up and end up an academic year ahead of his peers.

As a result of this early illness and other experiences, Beck carried into adulthood anxieties and phobias involving blood and injury, fear of heights, suffocation, and public speaking. As a medical student, his phobia about blood and injury was a particular challenge: "I learned systematic desensitization not through working in a laboratory, but through experience. In anticipation of Surgery [rotation], I started to expose myself in gradual ways so by the time I got into the operating room I was still able to proceed although I was very uncomfortable" (Weishaar, 1993, p. 13). His suffocation anxiety took the form of a tunnel phobia. One day, approaching the Holland Tunnel in New York, he realized that he was interpreting the tightness in his chest as a sign that he was suffocating. As quoted in Weishaar (1993, p. 13), he said, "'After I worked that through *cognitively* [italics mine], . . . I never had it again. I could go through tunnels and I'd still get the tightness, . . . but I would be amused by it because I see it as a kind of residue.'" Here Beck changed his feeling reaction by altering his view of it.

Beck graduated from Brown University in 1942, attended Yale University Medical School in an accelerated wartime program, and graduated in 1946. He entered psychiatry indirectly and reluctantly. Because of a shortage of psychiatrists, all medical residents were required to complete a six-month residency in psychiatry. Beck was intrigued with the ease with which psychoanalysis had "an answer for everything" (Weishaar, 1980, p. 15), but his pragmatic nature continued to seek proof that these answers were valid. He suspended his disbelief long enough to become board-certified in psychiatry and complete analytic training at the Philadelphia Analytic Institute.

In 1959 Beck became an assistant professor of psychiatry at the University of Pennsylvania Medical School and received his first major research grant. At this point he believed that the insights of psychoanalytic theory were important, but he also was aware that they were not accepted by scientifically oriented psychologists. His goal was to substantiate psychoanalytic principles, but instead he founded a version of cognitive therapy.

Psychoanalytic theory explained depression as hostility turned inward. In Beck's research, he compared the dreams of depressed and nondepressed patients. At first the dreams of his subjects confirmed Freudian theory. Depressed individuals apparently did have a need to suffer and did see themselves as losers. The theory broke down when Beck devised various success experiences and the depressed individuals reacted even more favorably than the control group. What seemed to count were their thoughts regarding their success rather than deep unconscious motivation. Dreams, instead of reflecting hidden motivation in the unconscious, seemed to reflect waking thoughts.

Beck hypothesized that an undiscovered type of thinking, rather than some hidden instinctive force, was at the root of human behavior. His suspicions were confirmed when he questioned an analytic patient who was angrily criticizing him. He asked the patient what he was feeling, and the patient first revealed a feeling of guilt and then a running internal dialogue about what he was saying to Beck, such as "He won't like me" and "I'm wrong to criticize him." These running thoughts, which Beck later termed *automatic thoughts,* acted as a buffer between the patient's outward emotion and inner guilty feeling. Thought was thus identified as a crucial internal point of influence.

From these and other experiences Beck deduced his cognitive theory of depression; he tested the theory with a succession of research grants. In 1961, he published his first article on the cognitive theory of depression. Albert Ellis read the article and contacted Beck, and the two theorists developed a cooperative professional relationship, though each continued to independently develop his own approach.

Since 1961, Beck has continued to carefully develop his theory, applying it to new areas of psychological dysfunction. In 1979, with A. John Rush, Brian F. Shaw, and Gary Emery, he published *Cognitive Therapy of Depression.* In 1985, with Gary Emery and Rath Greenberg, he published *Anxiety Disorders and Phobias: A Cognitive Perspective.* In 1988, he applied cognitive theory to problems in marriage in a book directed toward the general public, *Love Is Never Enough: How Couples Can Overcome Misunderstandings, Resolve Conflicts, and Solve Relationship Problems Through Cognitive Therapy,* and in 1990, with Arthur M. Freeman and Associates, he developed a cognitive theory of personality in *Cognitive Therapy of Personality Disorders.*

Thinking as a Point of Influence

Albert Ellis quotes the Roman philosopher Epictetus, who stated that people "are not disturbed by things, but by the *views* which they take of them" (Ellis, 1962, p. 54, italics mine). The point of influence in this chapter refers to those views. Aaron Beck similarly describes such views as *schemas,* or the verbal or pictorial events based on attitudes or assumptions from previous experiences. In Beck's framework, if a person interprets all experience in terms of adequacy or competence, that person's "thinking may be dominated by the schema, 'Unless I do everything perfectly, I'm a failure'" (Beck, Rush, Shaw, and Emery, 1979, p. 3).

We can examine how thinking affects feelings and behavior by focusing on Jerry Lyons, a salesperson in a large, upscale department store.

Preview: When to Use Ellis's and Beck's
Point of Influence in the Workplace.

Jerry's store keeps track of each salesperson's performance, and Jerry was in the top 25 percent until the store implemented a customer-centered quality improvement program. One part of this program was to increase the salesperson's knowledge of a wider variety of merchandise so that individuals could serve in a number of departments. In addition, a major effort was being made to increase each salesperson's capacity to satisfy customers' complaints and requests on the spot. Most of the rules that would prevent a salesperson from offering an on-the-spot exchange or refund or from quickly finding and delivering an item had been eliminated. Salespeople now were also systematically rotated, not only to other sales areas but also to supporting services such as alterations.

Some employees took to the new program with enthusiasm, but not Jerry. Jerry was uneasy with the rotation to different departments and the new responsibility of immediately settling complaints, but he didn't state his concerns. He was not comfortable learning about other lines of merchandise, nor did he like the idea of cutting through red tape or breaking what he saw as rules that should be followed. He had developed some expertise in men's suits, and he wanted to stick with what he knew. In addition, he was afraid that customers would abuse this new policy. In fact, this whole change was very upsetting to Jerry; he felt that his previous work had been ignored and he was very uneasy about how he would perform in the new assignments. He hoped that the negative aspects of the program would be obvious to everyone.

When he was queried about his feelings toward his new assignment, Jerry said that he would try and then dropped a subtle hint that he was not happy with the new way of doing things. His hints went unnoticed, and his unexpressed misgivings turned to anger and began to limit his performance. At the end of his first year, Jerry's sales were decreasing, and he was increasingly calling in sick with various unspecified headaches and stomach disorders. His performance was now merely adequate and fading. He was thinking of resigning.

How Albert Ellis Would Explain Jerry's Situation

Albert Ellis's ABC explanation concisely describes the impact of attitudes and beliefs on situations such as this one. In this framework, "A" signifies an action (Jerry's job was changed) and "C" signifies a consequence (Jerry is unhappy, his sales are falling, and he is thinking of resigning). In between "A" and "C" is "B," which signifies the belief Jerry held that strongly influenced his response to the original action. The intervening, or middle, position, "B," is the crucial variable for both Ellis and Beck. Emotions or feelings are closely linked with what Ellis describes as the other four fundamental life operations: sensing, emoting, moving, and thinking. This influence does not flow in only one direction; it is mutual. Emotions and behavior are both influenced by and influence thinking.

Activating events, belief systems, and resulting feelings and behavior all influence each other (Ellis, 1990, pp. 13–14). The system of interaction is complex, but Ellis focuses on thinking and belief systems as the most effective and efficient point of influence with which to affect the system (Ellis, 1990, p. 5). For him, thinking is the point of influence because he believes it to be the *most amenable to influence*. Ellis hypothesizes that "One may control one's emotion by changing the internalized sentences or self-talk with which one largely created these emotions in the first place" (1962, p. 52).

The essence of Ellis's view of human nature is that through a process of flawed thinking, which is inherent in the human condition

(Ellis, 1987), individuals absorb unquestioned values, goals, and guidelines from their parents and their culture. They hold onto these beliefs long after they have lost their usefulness; in addition, they add on to them and turn what were guidelines into absolutes (Ellis, 1990, p. 6). The result of this process is that the individuals view *unsatisfactory* situations as *terrible and unbearable*. They then react as if these situations are in fact terrible and unbearable. However, humans also have the ability to understand what they are doing and change their irrational thoughts to rational ones (Dryden, 1990, p. 6).

The previous scenario illustrates irrational thinking. Jerry based his reactions on what Ellis terms the three basic types of disturbed thinking (Ellis and Abrahams, 1978, pp. 77–78). These beliefs are:

1. I *must* do well and win others' approval, and isn't it *awful* when I don't!
2. You *must* treat me beautifully and love me when I want you to, and isn't it *terrible* when you don't!
3. The conditions of my life and the world around me *must* give me what I want immediately, without too much effort on my part, and isn't it *horrible* when they don't!

Jerry's unhappiness in this situation is understandable. Ellis does not advocate ignoring problems, taking a Pollyannaish attitude toward life's disappointments, or feeling unemotional about them. Jerry, however, did not stop at being disappointed. In Ellis's framework, although Jerry lacked skills in expressing or asserting his desires to others, within his own mind he *demanded* that he do the work that he enjoyed doing. He then *evaluated* himself on the basis of whether he was able to get others to change and give him what he wanted. When he could not do this he considered resigning. In Ellis's terms, Jerry's internal dialogue or "self-talk" might have gone like this:

How *awful* that I can't continue selling in the way that I was hired to do and that I enjoy. I don't know how long I *can stand* this. What a rotten state of affairs it is that I let people know that I'm not happy breaking my neck to satisfy these unreasonable requests, and they don't pay any attention to me. They

ought to stop asking me to do these things. What an insensitive bunch of people I'm working for. There ought to be some way in which they will be punished, and what kind of person am I to be treated this way? I don't seem to be
able to do anything about this treatment. Maybe I really am a wimp and a
completely unworthy person. Maybe I am just getting what I deserve.

Before Jerry could be empowered to answer the customers' requests, he had to be empowered to satisfy his own. However, his
own belief system stopped him from presenting his needs in a way
that could be answered. For Jerry, the result was, in Ellis's terms,
"awful and catastrophic." Because it was catastrophic, he had little
choice but to go into a depression, develop physical symptoms, and
eventually leave his job.

Jerry's self-talk contained Ellis's three major components of irrational beliefs (Wessler and Wessler, 1980, p. 40):

1. *Awfulizing:* "This is *unbearable,* and I *can't stand* doing this one
   day longer."
2. *Demandingness:* "They *have to* give me back my old assignment."
3. *Evaluation of self:* "Maybe I really *am* a wimp and a *completely unworthy person.*"

How Aaron Beck Would Explain Jerry's Situation

Aaron Beck's framework is less philosophical and more empirical.
Beck views the human personality as a product of thinking. Some
of this thinking is analogous to the rigid, primitive cognitive pro-
cessing that Freud described as *primary process.* Other thinking,
termed *secondary process* by Freud, is more flexible, with much
greater discrimination. Under stress, however, primary process
schemas can override more flexible secondary process thinking
(Beck and Weishaar, 1989, p. 21). The more we remain unaware of
our schemas, particularly the primary schemas, the more they can
control our behavior. Beck advocates using secondary process thinking to become more aware of and less controlled by the schemas
embodied in primary process thinking. For example, it would be
very helpful for a person who tends to hang back when entering a
group that includes unfamiliar people to be aware of a schema that

states, "I am vulnerable because I am inept in new situations" (Beck, Freeman, and Associates, 1990, p. 29). In Jerry's case, Beck might define the schema as "others should understand my needs."

Extending the Influence Point of Thought to Groups and Organizations

In order to apply thought as a point of influence within groups and organizations, we must extend Ellis's and Beck's frameworks in two ways: first, we must find a way to focus upon the more general and less personal level of beliefs and assumptions prevalent in everyday organizational discourse, and second, we must find methods of inquiry and intervention that touch on organizational beliefs. With such methods we will be able to help individuals increase their awareness of the personal and organizational assumptions, biases, and distortions that influence their thinking.

Organization consultants Robert Marshak and Judith Katz's consulting approach and their Covert Processes Model™ offer a way to accomplish both goals. Marshak and Katz do this by extending their examination to include *levels of thought* that occur more frequently in organizations and *types of interventions,* based upon image and symbols, that are more acceptable within the culture of many organizations.

Their approach draws on the work of Ellis, Beck, and the other theorists covered in this book but uses nontechnical language. The overall framework of the Covert Processes Model™ is based on the metaphor of what's "on, over, and under the table" within any organizational situation. This metaphor communicates the sometimes murky concepts of consciousness ("what's on the table"), the unconscious ("what's under the table"), and higher consciousness ("what's over the table") in a clear and concise fashion.

On-the-table issues and topics are those that the individual, group, or organization defines as acceptable, reasonable, and legitimate. They are open to public view and discussion. Below-the-table issues consist of two subcategories. The first category consists of issues that are within awareness but are deemed too risky to openly discuss. An example would be when someone refers to "some issues we may have had in our task force" but chooses not to discuss them. The second category consists of thoughts that at the moment are beyond awareness. Such thoughts have a variety of names in the framework of other theorists, such as "projections" in the work of Freud and "the Shadow" in the work of Jung.

Above-the-table issues are made up of two similar categories: first, those that are "too good to be true"—hopes and aspirations that individuals are aware of but are reluctant to discuss—and second, processes that are untapped or "unacceptable to imagine" and that are aspects of creativity and talent—the outer limits of one's ability that are as yet undiscovered (Marshak and Katz, 1991, pp. 1–5).

As psychotherapists, Ellis and Beck both focus on self-evaluative constructs and basic beliefs, assumptions, and values. These are the first two of five types of thought defined by the Covert Processes Model™. These two types of thinking influence life in organizations, but the other three levels of thought in the model often bear more directly on what is taking place. Much interaction in organizations, both oral and written, is task-oriented, focusing on decisions, plans, policies, and ideas. Individuals make decisions and relate to each other on the basis of assumptions, values, formal theories, paradigms, and the norms and values prevalent in the culture of the organization. This is a relatively neglected area in most psychological approaches. However, thoughts at this less personal level can be just as "irrational," in Ellis's terms, or just as "automatic," in Beck's terms. These thoughts can have as many hidden and distorting biases as those at the more personal level. Organizationally, they deserve as much attention as childhood lessons or even more. Marshak and Katz, in the Covert Processes Model™, add this focus by including an individual, group, and organizational "prism" through which experiences are mediated. Following are the five levels of thought contained within the prism of the Covert Processes Model™ (Marshak and Katz, 1994):

1. *Childhood lessons learned:* These include early childhood memories and messages from parents and other authority figures about what is right and wrong, how one should behave, and what it means to be "a good little boy or girl."

2. *Beliefs, assumptions, and values:* These include an array of concepts that order, judge, link, or otherwise explain events. They include rules of thumb, biases and prejudices, habitual thought patterns, proverbs, sayings, and learned or assimilated ways of thinking about things. Childhood lessons could be included in this group, but so would ideas of more recent origin. They all have the impact of organizing and limiting experience and response.

3. *Formal theories and systems of thought:* These thoughts include what one learns from formal education as well as professional training and/or exposure to religious, philosophical, or professional ideas and concepts. This level of thought shapes how one looks at the world and how things are believed to be associated with each other.

4. *Paradigms:* Paradigms usually exist outside of our conscious awareness, and because of this, they are very powerful. They are the framework that governs *what* we see. Formal theories and systems of thought usually develop and exist within a paradigm, and it is hard to "see" anything that does not exist in our paradigm. Changes in paradigms are rare, but they are so powerful that they are usually considered revolutionary or transformational.

5. *Organizational and societal culture:* This is a special category of ideas drawn from all of the previous levels that is built into the most basic aspects of life in organizations. It is "how things are done" in the organization, and includes the meaning of life and work and concepts such as time, space, and causality. Until these ideas are brought to awareness, they may just seem to be the "natural" way the world operates.

As we examine Ellis's and Beck's individual theories, we will be drawing examples and extensions of their theories from Marshak and Katz's Covert Processes Model™ to illustrate how the principles in Ellis's and Beck's influence point of thought can be used in organizations.

Using Cognition as a Point of Influence to Change Individual Behavior

In the previous example, Jerry's department store took the first step in removing *external* obstacles to Jerry's empowerment through widening his competencies by changing rules and procedures; however, in Jerry's case a second set of significant obstacles existed. These were his internal values, attitudes, and beliefs. They, in turn, influenced his feelings and behavior. Because of these internal values, attitudes, and beliefs, the removal of external obstacles was insufficient. Ellis and Beck each offer a point of influence for limiting the impact of such beliefs.

How Albert Ellis's Theory Influences Individual Behavior

Ellis's favored, but not sole, approach is to actively *dispute* what he terms *irrational beliefs*. These beliefs take the form of an internal dialogue that Ellis calls *self-talk*. Self-talk has a growing and cumulative effect. In Ellis's view, rather than passively waiting to be called upon, we engage attitudes and beliefs in a lively internal conversation and, for all practical purposes, the phrases that we keep saying to ourselves *are* or *become* our thoughts and emotions.

The more Jerry told himself that his new job assignment was terrible and that he was an unworthy person because he could not change it, the more he tended to believe it. Jerry's problem also illustrated how self-talk leads to false and widening generalizations. First, he illogically deduced that because he was not being treated as he wished to be, he deserved to be treated poorly, thus reinforcing his original illogical premise. He then broadened its applicability to a general evaluation of himself.

In Ellis's view, the strong emotion that is triggered in such self-talk can only be countered by an equally vigorous dispute. Without the emotion that is aroused in a spirited exchange, individuals gain an intellectual understanding but lack the emotional force needed to change their underlying beliefs and attitudes. To illustrate, Jerry believed that "people should know what he wanted without his telling them," and he also believed that "human unhappiness is externally caused and that people have little or no ability to control their sorrows and disturbances." These beliefs, like others, could be disputed by two methods, *discriminating* and *defining*.

Discriminating consists of identifying the difference between what is difficult, inconvenient, or unfamiliar and what is impossible and terrible, then making the distinction between logical conclusions drawn from one's experience and various kinds of non sequiturs, inconsistencies, and contradictions. Defining starts off with some definition of terms and ends up with even finer and more discriminating terms. It avoids and undercuts gross generalizations (Ellis and Grieger, 1977, p. 21).

For example, if Jerry were taught to discriminate between feeling disappointed because he was not doing the job he wanted to do or feeling so "awful" that he had trouble functioning, the outcome could be different. In effect, he would be defining the difference between "undesirable" and "terrible." The internal dialogue or self-talk in such a case might look like this:

> "Assuming that it really is exceptionally frustrating and bad that I am not working with customers as I used to, how can I substantiate that something is *unbearable?* The answer is that I can't. For although it may not be pleasant for me to come in every day and do work that I don't enjoy, it is not unbearable. In fact, I am bearing it and I probably could bear it a lot longer. 'Awful' means totally bad or worse than it *should* be. But it *should* be that bad because that's how bad it actually is.
>
> "Saying that *no one* cares about me implies that, no matter what I say or do, no one will respond, and I can't substantiate that idea. I haven't yet told anyone how I feel about catering to customers in the way that they want me to. I don't know if they will listen to me because I haven't yet put it to the test. I have given them hints, but that is not evidence that they don't care at all, for if this were true, they would not have asked me at all or waited for me to answer.
>
> "Saying that I *can't stand* doing this job is a logical impossibility, because I obviously have been doing it up to the present moment, and I could probably stand a lot more, although I can also choose not to stay in this situation. What is different is that now I can choose. I can also choose to say more about this job. Not too long ago, I thought that I couldn't stand it at all, and this didn't give me much choice. What I've learned is that what I *think* about how much I can stand probably has a lot to do with what I can stand."

This scenario contains Ellis's three major derivatives of psychological health (Ellis, 1990, p. 18):

1. *Rating or evaluating badness,* which enables Jerry to place his new job requirements on a more precise 0–100 continuum of desir-

ability and thereby to avoid labeling them as completely awful or unbearable.

2. *Tolerance,* which would help Jerry to accept the reality that something he does not like has occurred but then help him to focus his energy elsewhere and pursue other alternatives.

3. *Acceptance,* which means accepting the conditions as they are at this time but not resigning to circumstances, because they can always be changed. It also means acceptance of self, acceptance of one's human fallibility in a complex world, and avoidance of self-damning.

In addition, Jerry might be pushed to describe the worst possible reaction that could occur if he asked for a different assignment. Someone following Ellis's theory might also give him "homework" where, in a low-risk but embarrassing situation, he repeatedly asks for what he wants. An example of this technique would be to give someone who is extremely shy and avoids talking to strangers the homework assignment of asking three strangers a day for the time or directions.

Using Guided Imagery to Trigger an Internal Myth-Disputing Process

Practitioners of REBT have also developed a methodology termed *rational emotive imagery,* with which individuals can dispute their inappropriate ideas. The methodology has primarily been applied to individuals, but the following example portrays how it can also be applied to groups within organizations. To illustrate, if this method were applied to the irrational belief that every person should be 100 percent competent at all times, the consultant would proceed as follows:

> "I would like you to shut your eyes and imagine that, for some reason or another, you have made a mistake in your work. It is a medium-sized mistake, not trivial, but not so momentous that the firm is going to go out of business. It's a clear error, and people know that you made it. Now I would like you to picture this situation in your mind. Put in as many details as you can. Where

are you sitting? Who else is involved? How are you feeling? (Pause) Now that you have it, imagine that you really feel bad about this mistake. Push the feeling as far as you can. Imagine that you really feel *terrible* about this mistake, and make that feeling as strong and as powerful as possible. Allow yourself to see this as an awful situation, one you really can't stand. (Pause) What is your reaction? Become aware of the feeling. Allow yourself to feel that emotion. Let it sink in. Now what have you been feeling? (Listens to answer) Anxiety, panic, embarrassment, fright, fear, . . . ? OK, keep that image in your head. Remember, you have made a mistake; it's clearly your mistake, and at least some other people know it. Now imagine that instead of feeling panic, fear, embarrassment, or whatever, you are only disappointed and feeling sorrowful."

The consultant then waits a few moments to let the feelings sink in. If people say that they are having trouble making this shift, the consultant asks them to persist until they are able to change the feeling. Most of those in the group are now able to make this shift. The consultant then asks them how they did it. The replies sound like the rational disputing of beliefs that was illustrated earlier. For example:

"So I made a mistake. It's not the first one I've made, and it's probably not the last, although I don't think that I will make this one again. I'm still here doing my job, and the company is still here doing its job. It's too bad that I made this mistake, but that's the way life is. I would much rather that I had done things differently, but it's not the end of the world. I'm not going to pretend that I like it, but I can survive and even learn something from it."

What has happened in this situation is that instead of another person disputing the beliefs, the individuals themselves are now disputing them. After this exercise, the consultant facilitates a discussion in which several people discuss how they have changed and how they feel about office situations in which they had been taking excessive precautions against making minor errors. This is not an overnight cure, but it appears that the belief that it is catastrophic to make a mistake is being changed. Using rational emotive imagery in this way helps the group to realize that, in their own way, they already know how to dispute irrational beliefs (Ellis, 1993c).

How Aaron Beck's Theory Influences Individual Behavior

Beck encourages individuals not to directly dispute thoughts but to investigate the evidence themselves. The following three general questions drawn from his work on anxiety illustrate how his theory can be applied to work in organizations:

1. What's the evidence?
2. What's another way of looking at it?
3. So what if it happens?

What's the Evidence?

Beck assumes the role of a collaborative investigator of underlying thought patterns. Like Ellis, he focuses on faulty logic but with an emphasis on low-key empirical inquiry rather than vigorous dispute. This inquiry takes the form of Socratic questions and hypotheses to be tested empirically. The Socratic questioning is not an attempt to trap an individual in contradictions or to blatantly expose beliefs as fallacious. It is intended to help a person arrive at his or her own answers by carefully crafting a series of questions (Weishaar, 1993, p. 81) that urge clients to:

1. Become aware of their own thoughts
2. Examine them for cognitive distortions
3. Substitute more balanced thoughts
4. Make plans to develop new thought patterns

The awareness process helps individuals to become aware of automatic thoughts, thoughts that seem to have a life of their own, which appear spontaneously and provide an unrequested running commentary on what is going on. Beck often provides a homework assignment and a form on which individuals keep track of these automatic thoughts. By understanding their existence, an individual can bring them more into consciousness and thereby lessen their automatic impact. This is a straightforward approach that clients or workers can be trained to use themselves (Weishaar, 1993, p. 79).

Checking the Evidence at the Individual Level

The concept of automatic thoughts is Beck's way of demystifying the unconscious. He views the conscious and unconscious part of our mind as belonging to a continuum. Becoming aware of automatic thoughts allows an individual to access what is occurring in the less conscious end of the continuum. The following list illustrates how Jerry's case might appear using this aspect of Beck's approach. Individuals are asked to identify a triggering event, termed "Data"; their emotions; and their interpretation. Finally, they are asked to comment on how this situation might appear to an objective outsider.

Data	Emotions	Interpretation (Automatic Thoughts)	Observer's Interpretation
"I said that I would try this new method of working with customers but that I wasn't crazy about it."	Shock; fear; "Look what they are doing to me. I can't do it!"	"They don't care what I think around here, and they are asking me to do the impossible."	There is little to indicate that no one cares what this person thinks because he has only indicated mild disapproval. He also has not tried to do what he defines as impossible.

Other cognitive distortions, as described by Beck and Weishaar (1989, pp. 23–24), include:

- *Arbitrary inference*—drawing a particular conclusion in the absence of substantiating evidence or even in the face of contradictory evidence. An example of this is the working mother who concluded after a busy workday, "I'm a terrible mother."
- *Selective abstraction*—conceptualizing a situation on the basis of a detail taken out of context and ignoring other relevant information. For example, an honoree at a banquet, who was not asked to speak before her admirers, concluded, "They don't really think I'm that great because they didn't ask for a speech."

- *Overgeneralization*—formulating a general rule based on one or a few isolated incidents and applying it broadly to other situations. An example of this is the man who concluded after a brief affair, "I'll never get close to anyone because I can't."
- *Magnification and minimization*—viewing something as far more or far less significant than it actually is. Upon putting a minor dent in her car, a young woman concluded that she was a terrible driver who had had a major collision.
- *Personalization*—attributing external events to oneself in the absence of any causal connection. After being treated brusquely by a supervisor, a man concluded, "I must have written a bad quarterly report."
- *Dichotomous thinking*—categorizing experiences in one of two extremes, for example, as a complete success or a total failure. A doctoral candidate said, "I must be the best student in this department, or I've failed."

Checking the Evidence at the Group Level

Beck's methods for checking the evidence can also be applied at the group level. What he describes as automatic thoughts can take the form of dysfunctional myths or beliefs held collectively by members of a group. In the following example, an approach similar to Beck's Socratic questioning is used to reveal the hidden ideas behind two dysfunctional organizational myths.

Even though the members of the organization in this example possess the information to disprove or at least cast serious doubt on the myth's validity, they have not used this information. These myths are identified as dysfunction because, although they may have been true at one time, they have been inflated by anxiety and passed from one organizational generation to the next. Acceptance of such dysfunctional myths has permitted the individuals to remain passive, dependent, and ultimately irresponsible in coping with the organization's problems (Bradford and Harvey, 1972, p. 247).

To illustrate, Bradford and Harvey (1972, pp. 244–245) offer an example in which members of the organization claim they can't try anything new. The interviewer then asks for evidence that new initiatives are stifled.

Organization Member: I'm sure everybody thinks the same thing. I've never talked to anybody about it because it's so obvious that everybody thinks the same way.

Interviewer: What makes it obvious?

Organization Member: Well, you don't see many new things tried here.

Interviewer: Have you tried something different, or have you seen someone else try something new?

Organization Member: Well, yes. [So-and-so] installed a whole new process of working in her department.

Interviewer: Did it work and was it allowed?

Organization Member: Yes, it did. But I'm sure that was an exception.

A similar dialogue takes place around the myth that the boss will punish you if you don't have a ready answer to every question. The consultant again asks for examples.

Organization Member: Oh, yes. I heard of a person in Department X who really got clobbered by the "old man" for not knowing the answer to something.

Interviewer: Did that happen recently?

Organization Member: Oh, no. That happened sometime ago. The "old man" retired in 1958.

Interviewer: Has your superior ever asked you for information that you didn't immediately have?

Organization Member: Oh, yes.

Interviewer: What happened?

Organization Member: He just asked me to get the information when I had time.

Interviewer: Did he reprimand you? Did anything happen to hurt you later?

Organization Member: No, nothing. But it's very clear around here that you'd better be prepared on any issue concerning your work. It's worth the extra clerical help to be ready.

After making this information available to the group member, the consultant can ask group members to explore whether these "Do's" are accurate or whether the norms are, in fact, myths. The consultant can also ask participants if they have ever violated any of these norms and, if they have, what happened to them. If they have not violated them, can they remember anyone else who has? If the participants cannot identify individuals who have suffered because these norms were broken, they are faced with realizing that they are responding to an organizational myth. The myth, not reality, prevents individuals from trying something new.

If these norms appear to reflect the organization's realities, the next step is to help members to consider whether it is in the firm's interest to continue the conditions that fostered these norms. The consultant can then help the group to define the norms of behavior that the members would like the organization to have and the steps that are necessary to get them. If the consultant discovers that the beliefs behind the norms are not only dysfunctional but a myth that possibly was reflective of reality at one time but is no longer true, the task will be to help the group to get rid of the myth.

What's Another Way of Looking at It?

Here Beck's goal is to change the impact of automatic thoughts by regarding them in a new way. Individuals are asked to keep track of these spontaneous thoughts and then to brainstorm alternative explanations. Beck reports that over time, most individuals find that their later interpretations square more with reality. Individuals are also asked to focus on how much they hold themselves responsible for a negative outcome and then to list other forces that could contribute to such a negative outcome. After looking at the issue from this broader point of view, they are asked to again assess their own personal responsibility for a negative outcome. As before, the broader viewpoint is usually found to be the more accurate and realistic one. The mood of this process is exploratory. The goal is to calmly and systematically develop new explanations and then test them against experience. It is a methodical process that would be consistent with the culture and norms of many organizations.

If Jerry, the clothing salesperson, were to brainstorm alternative explanations of why his mild dissatisfaction about his new assignment was ignored, the list might include the following:

The management only "hears" more forceful comments.

They didn't understand me.

They lack the power to respond to my requests.

The store has to change its service to respond to a new competitive environment.

Sometimes you have to repeat something for people to hear it.

Appreciative Inquiry: Looking at It Another Way by Reframing the Questions

The traditional therapy model involves individual questions or dialogue, with the therapist working with one individual. Organizational intervention is more likely to involve group or organizational data collection and feedback. The questions asked in such data shape the nature of the answers; these questions can also be reframed to serve as a point of influence for encouraging a particular style of thought.

Appreciative inquiry is a data collection approach that encourages the awareness of what *is* working by reframing the process of gathering organizational information so that the questions asked focus on creative, positive, and life-enhancing properties within the organization. The aim is to "*consciously choose* the appreciative schema, the context that guides human knowledge, the breakthroughs that make creative action possible (Srivastva and Barrett, 1990, p. 386). Following are some examples of interview questions that illustrate the process of appreciative inquiry (Rainey, 1990, p. 5):

- Think about your time in your organization. Can you recall an experience when you felt most alive, most excited, or most fulfilled about your involvement in the organization?
- What made this such an exciting experience? Who were the most significant others involved?
- When did you feel most committed to your company and its mission?

- Can you recall a time when there was great cooperation between different groups or individuals in the company? How did this come about?

The focus on peak experiences does not produce only positive data. The experience of those working with this approach is that it helps individuals to identify the aspects of the organization that are really important to them. By identifying an experience with a strong positive value, they are then more open to working with *all* of their experiences—including the obstacles to re-creating the positive experience.

In addition, appreciative inquiry brings into consciousness what Marshak and Katz described in a previous section as "above the table," "too good to be true"—hopes and aspirations that individuals are aware of but reluctant to discuss—or "unacceptable to imagine" processes that are at the outer limits of one's ability and as yet undiscovered.

So What If It Happens (Reframing Your Vision of the Future)

Thoughts of the future can also trigger fear of dire consequences. At times, such fear prompts useful coping behavior. At other times, however, fear is disabling because it far exceeds the likely reality. Beck's approach helps individuals to more accurately assess the likelihood of the disastrous results that they fear. He does this by asking the following four questions:

1. What is the probability of the feared event?
2. What is the degree of its awfulness?
3. What is the individual's ability to prevent the feared event from happening?
4. What is the individual's ability to accept and deal with the worst outcomes?

Beck utilizes a variety of approaches to discover and then alter the beliefs behind a disabling fear. Some involve straightforward reasoning, such as developing a coping plan or reversing roles, which means that the therapist states the reason why the feared event is *going* to happen, and the individual receiving help states the *countering* arguments (Beck and Emery, 1985, p. 209).

Beck also uses mental images as a point of influence to alter thoughts and ultimately feelings and behavior. Mental images are pictures of thoughts, and just as it is easier to change the image of a written text in a computer's memory before it is printed, it is also easier to change the image of a thought before it becomes the basis for feelings or action. Beck provides a variety of methods to change such images. All start with asking the individual to imagine the anxious situation and then to utilize a variety of means of altering the image. These methods include:

- *Turn-off techniques*—using a previously agreed-upon signal such as hand clapping to trigger a positive image that counters or turns off a negative image.
- *Repetition*—asking an individual to repeat an image a number of times. The impact of such repetition is twofold: first, successive repetition reduces the negative charge; second, the contents become more realistic.
- *Time projection*—asking an individual to imagine what the supposed issue would look like at some future time. This process also adds realism.
- *Symbolic images*—asking, for example, an individual with writer's block to simply start writing without any reference to content or quality. The goal is to fill up a certain number of pages, while at the same time imagining a pump that needs to be primed with water. The individual is asked to link the initial writing with the water that primes the pump in order to start it.
- *Substituting imagery*—substituting specific imagery for a fearful or anxious situation, for example, imagining a successful meeting with a problem peer or subordinate, a generally peaceful scene such as a quiet walk in the woods, or whatever would fulfill that purpose for the individual.
- *Exaggeration*—pushing a feared scene to its logical absurdity. An example would be having a person who fears working with a new machine imagine the machine taking on a life of its own (like the broom in *The Sorcerer's Apprentice*), with unwanted products filling the room, the halls, and the building and flowing into the street. The idea is to push the image to its logical absurdity and thereby to help the individual assess the reality of her or his worst fantasies (Beck and Emery, 1985, pp. 210–287).

Using Symbols and Imagery to Reframe at the Group and Organizational Levels

In their work with organizational covert processes, Marshak and Katz extended Ellis's and Beck's theories to include a wider range of symbols and images. Following are four types of symbol systems described in the Covert Processes Model™ (Marshak and Katz, 1992). In using these methods, it is important to remember that individuals do not like to feel "caught" saying something that they did not intend to say. In an organizational context, which has strong norms against confrontation and intrusiveness, the practitioner can easily be tuned out if he or she violates these norms. To minimize defensiveness, the practitioner should emphasize the positive by pointing out that communication is complex and that symbols and metaphors just illustrate how we often know more than we think we know.

Metaphor

Metaphor includes the many forms of word imagery, figures of speech, similes, puns, parables, or any combination of words that paint a verbal picture. For example, do people describe their group as a family? a team? solo performers? a feudal system? Is the culture described as sink-or-swim? May the best person win? Or are we all in this together?

> A consultant working with a group charged with designing and implementing a new way of doing business kept hearing phrases like "If it ain't broke, don't fix it." This gave the consultant the clue that the group was implicitly operating on the basis that the organization was a machine that simply needed minor repairs. This insight enabled the consultant to reframe the task in terms of more fundamental changes in the organization (Marshak and Katz, 1992, pp. 3–4).

In order to have the organization members in the preceding example become more aware of their assumptions about the change process, a consultant might use the metaphor of repairing a house and ask them to complete the following sentence: "If this organization were a house, what that house would need is _____."

Because individuals have widely varied assumptions about the change process, the answers might include:

- Repainting the interior and exterior and fixing the plumbing (fixing and maintaining)
- Adding a bedroom and extending the kitchen (building and developing)
- Moving from a duplex to a single-family dwelling by taking down a wall (moving and relocating)
- Tearing down the whole structure and rebuilding it (liberating and re-creating) (Marshak, 1993, p. 53)

A practitioner using metaphors in this way could help individuals to identify their beliefs, theories, and perhaps other paradigms about change and could provide a common frame of reference for reaching consensus about what is needed.

Gareth Morgan also provides a comprehensive framework for using metaphor by drawing upon our image of the organization. Morgan describes how this image shapes what we believe to be possible within any organization we are consulting to. For example, if we view an organization as a machine, we would focus on structure and the careful arrangement of tasks. A consultant with this image would work to have tasks ordered on the basis of efficient effort, uniformity, and predictability. In contrast, if we view an organization as an organism, we would not focus on the arrangement of tasks but rather on how the organization responds to changes in the environment. Machines and organisms are not mutually exclusive. As complex social phenomena, organizations can simultaneously operate as if they were machines *and* organisms and a good deal more. How a practitioner works with an organization depends upon the image in his or her mind. The image governs the range of actions. Practitioners can improve their communication with clients and extend their diagnostic and intervention possibilities by increasing their own and their clients' awareness of the image they have of the organization.

A consultant was working with an advertising agency founded by two older principal partners and two younger junior partners. When it was founded, the agency was innovative and dynamic. Decisions were made by all four partners. After some time, the senior partners started making decisions without the junior partners and then decided to regularize the operation of the organization. The organization become less creative and more bureaucratic. After a brief period, the two junior partners left and formed their own agency, taking both clients and a good deal of the organization's vitality and energy. The agency now was less effective (Morgan, 1986, pp. 322–325).

The actions of a consultant working with this organization, either before or after the junior partners left, would depend upon her or his image of the organization. Table 4.1 shows some of the possibilities. Each of the images provides a different diagnosis and a different set of actions. Awareness of the function of image helps practitioners to select the appropriate course of action and also helps members of the organization to become aware of the full range of their possible actions.

Music

Music contains many elements that are present but not usually listened to in human interactions. These include voice, tone, pitch, tempo, volume, speed, rhythm, harmony, and melody as well as themes in song and music (Marshak and Katz, 1992, p. 3). Are all voices in tune? Are they heard? in harmony? dissonant? Is there counterpoint? Is the sound shrill? soothing? sharp? flat? As you listen to the group's discussions, do you hear a funeral march? a joyful tune? a melancholy refrain? a wedding song?

A consultant working with a bogged-down planning session noted that one participant was humming a tune. After some thought she was able to identify that it was the theme song of the movie *Gone with the Wind.* The participant then remembered that the film had an introductory narrative that ended with "And an entire way of life was gone with the wind." This revelation helped the group to become aware of their fears and feelings regarding the drastic change that could result from the proposed change. This in turn led to a more productive session (Marshak and Katz, 1992, p. 4).

Movement

Movement includes all forms of kinesthetic expression, including gesture, facial cues, posture, position, spatial relations, dance, and

Table 4.1. How Image Defines the Problem and the Solution.

If the Consultant's Image of the Agency Is:	Problems Are Likely to Be Seen as:	The Focus Would Then Be on:
A machine	Increasing bureaucratization	Fixing inefficient operations
An organism	The agency's relationship to its environment (market)	Strategic planning; redesigning the organization to better compete
A culture	A shared philosophy and values that prevailed "when the agency was operating successfully with four partners"	Analyzing the culture and regaining lost norms, spirit, and values
A political system	The exercise of power and influence among the four partners	The competing aims, aspirations, and life-styles of the four principals and the appropriate power and decision-making processes that would enable them to work together
A psychic prison	The unconscious processes of the four principals	Making the covert overt so that the four partners could continue working together

body language. How are people sitting or standing? Are key people sitting in opposition to one another? Are they lined up in support? How close or far apart are they? Are they looking down? looking up? Are individuals or groups sitting together? apart? scattered? If you are describing the movement or dance of a group, are all members of the group in step? moving at a snail's pace? frolicking? jumping? dragging their feet? Are they moving in circles? Taking three steps forward and one back?

During team building for an interdisciplinary medical team, the doctors maintained that they did not remain separate but worked with everyone as "equal professionals." However, during a small group discussion, they formed a group in the corner with their backs to the other team members. When the consultant asked the whole group to note how they had positioned themselves, one of the doctors acknowledged their position; this triggered an intense discussion of roles and behavior in the teams.

Media

Media includes artistic techniques and expression, including pictures, painting, drawing, sculpture, photography, collage, three-dimensional forms, and slides, as well as all other forms of representational media. Do an organization's logo, brochures, reports, and graphics suggest that it is lined up? boxed in? a network? disconnected or with blurred lines? open-ended? two-dimensional? stuck in the past? unclear about the present?

In a group charged with implementing a vision, a group of middle managers drew some individuals with no eyes. When they were questioned about this, their hesitant response was that the people with no eyes represented top management, who were not aware of what was really going on in the organization. This led to a more thoughtful discussion and a decision to seek a face-to-face meeting with top management (Marshak and Katz, 1992, pp. 1–5).

Three Cognitive Approaches to Dealing with Conflict

This chapter has presented three approaches to the application of thought or mental images to influencing human behavior:

- Albert Ellis, who vigorously disputes what he terms *irrational thought*
- Aaron Beck, who emphasizes empirically testing and reframing thoughts or images behind behavior
- Robert Marshak and Judith Katz, who focus on symbols, imagery, and metaphor at the group and organizational level

The following summarizes how each of these theorists approaches working with conflict.

Albert Ellis's Approach to Conflict

Ellis's approach to conflict is philosophical, but it has a strong practical base. He points out that beneath much, but not all, of human conflict are irrational beliefs, rigid thinking, and viewing others in moral or judgmental terms. The unique quality of his approach is the distinction between human *desire* and *demand,* "between people feeling distinctly displeased and frustrated about their serious differences with others and their feeling angry, resentful, and enraged about these same differences" (Ellis, 1992, p. 86).

The major thrust of Ellis's work in conflict resolution, as well as in other areas, is aimed at undermining the irrational belief that individuals *must* have their own way or the outcome will be *awful.* Instead he stresses that individuals need to recognize that "human differences make for originality, invention, creativity, and other aspects of vital living" (Ellis, 1992, p. 91). By "understanding oneself and others," "choosing an and/also instead of an either/or outlook," "recognizing the importance of preventing conflicts," "accepting differences and disagreements," "agreeing to disagree," and "acquiring a philosophy of collaboration and caring," an individual can avoid conflict and achieve peaceful relationships (Ellis, 1992).

According to Ellis (1992, p. 96), irrational beliefs, questionable attributions, and misleading inferences can be countered by:

- Making rational coping statements that prevent individuals from believing that they *cannot survive* with an *undesirable* situation
- Reframing unfortunate situations that one "awfulizes" about
- Monitoring linguistic and semantic errors that create self-defeating cognition
- Using cognitive distraction methods of interruption and assaultiveness

Aaron Beck's Cognitive Approach to Conflict

Mental processes are an important point of influence for both creating and dealing with conflict. On an individual level, Beck's approach can be used to raise the same empirical questions that he raises for dealing with anxiety.

The first question involves *asking for the evidence*. To someone basing an action on an *assumption* about what another person is thinking, Beck might point the individual in the direction of empirical investigation by asking "How do you know that they are trying to get rid of your program?" "Have you checked this out with them?"

Beck might then suggest *another way of looking at it*. For two feuding departments, he might try to get each department to shift its image of the other by asking both to brainstorm other explanations of their relationship. He might also ask them "What is your definition of a cooperative relationship?" "What are your expectations of the other department?" "What is the payoff for you in being able to prove that you are right?" "What goal are you going to achieve by proving yourself 100 percent right?"

Finally Beck might pursue the question of *so what if it happens*. The strategy in this instance is again to test reality by asking about the probability of a feared event, just how bad it would be, what measures could be taken to prevent it, and how individuals could deal with the worst consequences if they occurred. Individuals and groups can also use a variety of techniques to alter their image of a possible conflict, such as exaggeration or carrying a feared scene to its logical absurdity.

Robert Marshak and Judith Katz's Approach to Conflict

One way to use Marshak and Katz's approach is to deal with literal statements symbolically, and symbolic statements literally (Marshak and Katz, 1992; Marshak, 1993). The use of symbols and imagery in this way is especially applicable to working with groups and organizations. The translation of imagery from one level to the other is likely to trigger powerful discussions among group and organization members.

> Two units of an R&D division in a large chemical company conduct different but sometimes overlapping research. This overlap more often produces competition and conflict than the type of cooperation and synergy that the company leadership intended. Following is part of a conversation moving from literal to symbolic between the consultant and members of one unit.

> *Consultant:* What is your experience working with Department B?
> *R&D Scientist:* Well, they have some able people over there, but they really do
> a number on you. You start working with them, and before
> you know it, they are running the whole show and turning it
> into their own act.
> *Consultant:* (Sample questions, picking up on the symbolic metaphor of a
> show or entertainment) Sounds like your relationship with B
> is some sort of show or entertainment. What kind of a show is
> it? Is it a series of individual acts or a single number? Who are
> the featured players, and who are the audience, the hero, and
> the villain? How do you know you are pleasing the audience?

Questions such as these would help those involved to better understand how
their own assumptions, values, and other ideas contribute to their understanding of and reactions to the conflict. Moving from the symbolic to literal, the
following conversation might occur:

> *Consultant:* You have given me some of the information about how you work
> with Department B; it sounds like some sort of contest. If it were
> a sporting event, what would it be?
> *Scientist:* Well, I don't know; yes, I do know—we're like a college golf
> team. We are all on the same side, but each of us just goes out
> and plays our own game, and we have a lot of internal competi-
> tion. We don't really attack each other, but we don't do anything
> to help each other, either.

The use of metaphor in this instance enables the consultant to go beneath the
surface comment to the speaker's meaning or intent.

The Influence Point of Thinking and Psychological Growth

Ellis and Beck bring private experience into the realm of scientific
inquiry. Both approaches shift attention from the mystery of the
unconscious and the complexity of the environment to the way in
which individuals construct their own experiences. Beck does this
by joining with the client in becoming a researcher into observable
reality. For example:

A practitioner worked with a manager who used dichotomous thinking to convince herself that unless she received consistent praise from all of her peers and subordinates she was a failure.

Consultant: Well, as long as we're talking about evaluation, how do you feel about the other managers at your level? Who do you think does the best job?

Manager: Well, none of them are really incompetent, but I'd say probably Manager V. I would rate him very high.

Consultant: What kind of praise and credit does he get?

Manager: Well, none.

Consultant: Have you ever told him what you told me? Does he seem to get this kind of praise from other people? If he doesn't, what do you think the explanation is?

Ellis approaches psychological growth by defining and disputing the irrational thoughts by which individuals avoid unconditional self-acceptance. He makes what he believes to be an important distinction between *self-esteem* and *self-acceptance*. In his view, the concept of self-esteem means that we rate or evaluate our whole self, being, or personhood. This rating is made on the basis of performance, and a good performance today can become a poor performance tomorrow. In contrast, unconditional self-acceptance means that we always accept goodness whether or not we perform well or are accepted by others. We accept ourselves just because we are human and alive, without regard to performance or acceptance by others.

In Ellis's framework, the major obstacles to unconditional self-acceptance are dysfunctional or irrational beliefs. REBT provides methods for disputing these beliefs. Following are three important irrational beliefs, placed in an organizational context. Such beliefs typically erode self-acceptance in the workplace. Following the beliefs are the arguments that Ellis's theory might use to dispute them.

1.   *An individual should be thoroughly competent and adequate and achieve in all possible respects in order to consider himself or herself worthwhile enough to receive a merit raise.* In Ellis's framework it is not irrational to try to be the best that you can be; the irrationality comes

from demanding that you must be supercompetent and perfect in every way. He calls such beliefs "musturbatory." Built into such demands are constant comparisons with others. This approach is also self-defeating, because it makes the individual other-directed rather than self-directed. In work settings, such beliefs would remove the focus from interest or value in the work one is doing to comparisons with others.

Ellis urges individuals to avoid general evaluations of themselves as a person. For him, there is no rational validity to the statements "I am a bad person" and "I am a good person."

2.　*Human happiness is externally caused, and people have little or no ability to control their sorrows and disturbances, so it's totally up to management to create an environment that motivates people.* Countering this belief is not sufficient for employee empowerment, nor is simply removing obstacles to being more effective on the job. *Together,* however, changing underlying beliefs *and* removing external obstacles can be effective in increasing employee empowerment.

Ellis's role in this process is to point out that happiness and unhappiness are usually a product of our own psyche rather than of external events. In modern society, we are rarely assaulted physically. The damage that other people do is most likely to be psychological. Because the external threat is limited, to the extent that we go beyond feeling regretful about unfortunate happenings, we are inventing irrational beliefs. Disputing such beliefs opens the way for psychological growth because it takes control away from others, the environment, or the system and gives it largely to the individual.

3.　*It is easier to avoid than to face certain life difficulties and responsibilities, so sweep them under the rug.* Organizational norms often support avoiding difficult issues, so Ellis's individual analysis is also relevant organizationally. Ellis focuses on what he calls short-term and long-term hedonism. Short-term hedonism is giving in to the immediate impulses. Long-term hedonism involves disputing the irrational belief that what is temporarily uncomfortable to do is also impossible to do. For example, Ellis would advocate disputing the belief that it might be harder to put in the extra effort to settle a disagreement than to put it off or avoid it. Putting it off would provide short-term hedonism or pleasure. Settling it would provide long-term hedonism or pleasure. Ellis's theory provides the tools to dispute the short-term hedonism of avoidance. Disputing the irrational belief that supports such avoidance can also be growth-producing.

> At a staff meeting, the manager of Purchasing asked the group to do a force-field exercise focusing on the goal, "We will reach an agreement with Data Processing as soon as possible." This activity would encourage the unit to focus on priorities, values, and goals. Such a focus is an essential part of the psychological growth of the unit.

The Influence Point of Thinking and the Process of Joining

Neither Ellis nor Beck specifically comment on the individual's relationship with a group or organization, but they both focus on the way that individual beliefs can sabotage relationships. Ellis, for example, points out that his own beliefs stopped him from initiating a relationship with a woman. More generally, Ellis focuses upon the three "musturbatory" beliefs: *I* must perform well, *you* must treat me kindly, and *conditions* must be favorable and fortunate. All three turn the individual's experience with the organization into absolute demands that are unlikely to be fulfilled. Ellis's methods help the individual to become aware of these demands and then dispute them.

Beck's contribution is to help the individual and the organization to empirically test their experience and their expectations of each other. This means helping both sides to test the degree to which their perceptions of each other were borne out by reality. Beck also asks how the contract between the individual and the organization can be viewed in another way, and he urges individuals to become more precise and definite about the consequences if the relationship is not meeting each party's expectations.

Marshak and Katz, in their Covert Processes Model™, provide useful ideas for identifying more general levels of thought that can influence the individual's relationship to the organization and for utilizing imagery and symbols that are helpful in finding the important thoughts behind the feelings.

Conclusion

Psychological theory was initially used to help individuals in organizations become aware of and accept feelings. T groups, based on Kurt Lewin's theory, and team building, using Carl Rogers's theories of communication and encounter, both did this. The mode for many years was to help organization members "get in touch with their feelings." Little attention was paid to the thinking process as an aspect of interpersonal relationships in organizations. The theorists in this chapter illustrate the importance of thinking as an influence point that affects the whole realm of human functioning.

Albert Ellis focuses mainly on vigorous dispute as a means of helping individuals to identify and get rid of irrational thoughts and beliefs. Aaron Beck emphasizes empirically testing such thoughts and beliefs. Both approaches can be used in an organizational context. In addition, Robert Marshak and Judith Katz demonstrate how more general and abstract levels of thought can be used to influence feelings and behavior at the individual, group, and organizational levels.

Annotated Bibliography
Original Sources: Readable Ellis and Beck

Beck, A. *Depression: Causes and Treatment.* Philadelphia: University of Pennsylvania Press, 1972. (Originally published, 1967, as *Depression, Clinical, Experimental, and Theoretical Aspects.*)

Beck, A. T., Rush, A. J., Shaw, B. F., and Emery, G. *Cognitive Therapy of Depression.* New York: Guilford Press, 1979.

Beck's first focus was on the problem of depression, and these two works represent the development of his ideas. Beck believed that the method of treatment varied with the problem.

Beck, A. T. *Love Is Never Enough.* New York: HarperCollins, 1988.

Written for the general public, Beck's book applies his cognitive theory to the problems of relationships.

Beck, A. and Emery, G., with Greenberg, R. L. *Anxiety Disorders and Phobias: A Cognitive Perspective.* New York: Basic Books, 1985.

Beck, A. T., Freeman, A. M., and Associates. *Cognitive Therapy of Personality Disorders.* New York: Guilford Press, 1990.

These works illustrate the way Beck would vary his method with problems other than depression.

Dryden, W. (ed.). *The Essential Albert Ellis: Seminal Writings on Psychotherapy.* New York: Springer, 1990.
Ellis has written over fifty books, and his theory has evolved over the years. This is the most recent compilation of his basic writings.

Ellis, A. *Reason and Emotion in Psychotherapy.* New York: Lyle Stuart, 1962. This is Ellis's original formulation of his theory. He has modified it since, but this readable book explains the theory more completely and in a more interesting fashion than the later versions.

Secondary Sources: Books About Ellis and Beck and Their Theories
Weishaar, M. E. *Aaron T. Beck.* Newbury Park, Calif.: Sage, 1993.
Yankura, J., and Dryden, W. *Albert Ellis.* London: Sage, 1994.
This series from Sage is built around personal and intellectual biographies that present theorists' lives and the development of their contributions to theory, applications, and critical evaluation. Both of the above biographies are short and readable and include a comprehensive bibliography about the theorist and his work.

Organizational Applications
Ellis, A. *Executive Leadership: A Rational Approach.* Secaucus, N.J.: Citadel Press, 1972.
Ellis applies his ideas to the individual manager. The book focuses on how the executive can develop the following qualities: decisiveness, concentration, relationship skills, self-acceptance, and the ability to overcome hostility.

Marshak, R. J. "Managing the Metaphors of Change." *Organizational Dynamics,* Summer 1993, *22*(1), 44–56.
This provides a useful example of how thought can influence our approach to an important organizational process. It includes numerous examples as well as suggestions.

Morgan, G. *Images of Organization.* Newbury Park, Calif.: Sage, 1986.
This is a thorough examination of the numerous ways in which our mental picture or image of an organization dictates our later diagnosis, interventions, and overall behavior.

Bibliography
Arnold, M. B. *Emotion and Personality.* 2 vols. New York: Columbia University Press, 1960.

Beck, A. T. *Love Is Never Enough: How Couples Can Overcome Misunderstandings, Resolve Conflicts, and Solve Relationship Problems Through Cognitive Therapy*. New York: HarperCollins, 1988.

Beck, A. T., and Emery, G., with Greenberg, R. L. *Anxiety Disorders and Phobias: A Cognitive Perspective*. New York: Basic Books, 1985.

Beck, A. T., Freeman, A. M. and Associates. *Cognitive Therapy of Personality Disorders*. New York: Guilford Press, 1990.

Beck, A. T., Rush, A. J., Shaw, B. F., and Emery, G. *Cognitive Therapy of Depression*. New York: Guilford Press, 1979.

Beck, A. T., and Weishaar, M. "Cognitive Therapy." In A. Freeman (ed.), *Comprehensive Handbook of Cognitive Therapy* (pp. 21–36). New York: Plenum Press, 1989.

Bradford, L. P., and Harvey, J. B. "Dealing with Dysfunctional Organization Myths." In W. W. Burke and H. A. Hornstein (eds.), *The Social Technology of Organization Development* (pp. 244–254). Fairfax, Va.: Learning Resources Corporation, 1972.

Criddle, W. D., and Tracy, J. "Rational Skills for Business People." In J. L. Wolf and E. Brand (eds.), *Twenty Years of Rational Therapy: Proceedings of the First National Conference on Rational Psychotherapy*. New York: Institute for Rational Living, 1977.

Ellis, A. *Reason and Emotion in Psychotherapy*. New York: Lyle Stuart, 1962.

Ellis, A. *Executive Leadership: A Rational Approach*. Secaucus, N.J.: Citadel Press, 1972a.

Ellis, A. "Psychotherapy Without Tears." In A. Burton (ed.), *Twelve Therapists: How They Live and Actualize Themselves* (pp. 103–126). San Francisco: Jossey-Bass, 1972b.

Ellis, A. "The Biological Basis of Human Irrationality." *Journal of Individual Psychology*, 1976, *32*, 145–168.

Ellis, A. "The Basic Clinical Theory of Rational-Emotive Therapy." In A. Ellis and R. Grieger (eds.), *Handbook of Rational-Emotive Therapy* (pp. 3–34). New York: Springer, 1977.

Ellis, A. "Rational-Emotive Therapy and Cognitive Behavior Therapy: Similarities and Differences." *Cognitive Therapy and Research*, 1980, *4*(4), 325–340.

Ellis, A. "The Impossibility of Achieving Consistently Good Health." *American Psychologist*, Apr. 1987, *42*(4), 364–375.

Ellis, A. "The General Theory of RET." In W. Dryden (ed.), *The Essential Writings of Albert Ellis: Seminal Writings on Psychotherapy* (pp. 3–30). New York: Springer, 1990.

Ellis, A. "My Life in Clinical Psychology." In C. E. Walker (ed.), *The History of Clinical Psychology in Autobiography* (Vol. 1, pp. 1–37). Pacific Grove, Calif.: Brooks/Cole, 1991.

Ellis, A. "Rational-Emotive Approaches to Peace." *Journal of Cognitive Psychotherapy: An International Quarterly*, 1992, *6*(2), 79–104.

Ellis, A. "Changing Rational-Emotive Therapy (RET) to Rational Emotive Behavior (REBT)." *The Behavior Therapist*, 1993a, *16*(10), 257–258.

Ellis, A. "Fundamentals of Rational-Emotive Therapy for the 1990s." In W. Dryden and L. Hill (eds.), *Innovations in Rational Emotive Therapy* (pp. 1–32). Newbury Park, Calif.: Sage, 1993b.

Ellis, A. "Rational-Emotive Imagery: RET Version." In M. Bernard and J. Wolfe (eds.), *The RET Resource Book for Practitioners*. New York: Institute for Rational-Emotive Therapy, 1993c.

Ellis, A., and Abrahams, E. *Brief Psychotherapy in Medical and Health Practice*. New York: Springer, 1978.

Ellis, A., and Whiteley, J. *Theoretical and Empirical Foundations of Rational-Emotive Therapy*. Pacific Grove, Calif.: Brooks/Cole, 1979.

Marshak, R. J. "Managing the Metaphors of Change." *Organizational Dynamics*, Summer 1993, *22*(1), 44–56.

Marshak, R. J., and Katz, J. H. "Covert Processes at Work." *Chesapeake Bay Organization Development Network Newsletter*, May 1991, *6*(2), 1–5.

Marshak, R. J., and Katz, J. H. "The Symbolic Side of OD." *OD Practitioner*, June 1992, *24*(2), 1–5.

Marshak, R. J., and Katz, J. H. *The Covert Processes Workbook: Dealing with the Hidden Dimensions of Individuals, Groups, and Organizations*. Unpublished workbook, 1994.

Morgan, G. *Images of Organization*. Newbury Park, Calif.: Sage, 1986.

Rainey, M. "Appreciative Inquiry: A Guide to Theory and Practice." Photocopy privately printed, copyright 1990.

Srivastva, S., and Barrett, F. "Appreciative Organizing: Implications for Executive Functioning." In S. Srivastva, D. Cooperider, and Associates (eds.), *Appreciative Management and Leadership: The Power of Positive Thought and Action in Organizations*. San Francisco: Jossey-Bass, 1990.

Weinrach, S. "Cognitive Therapist: A Dialogue with Aaron Beck." *Journal of Counseling and Development*, 1988, *67*(3), 159–164.

Weishaar, M. E. *Aaron T. Beck*. Newbury Park, Calif.: Sage, 1993.

Wessler, R. A. "Alternative Conceptions of Rational-Emotive Therapy: Toward a Philosophically Neutral Psychotherapy." In M. A. Reda and M. J. Mahoney (eds.), *Cognitive Psychotherapies: Recent Developments in Theory, Research, and Practice* (pp. 65–79). Cambridge, Mass.: Ballinger, 1984.

Wessler, R. A., and Wessler, R. L. *The Principles and Practice of Rational-Emotive Therapy*. San Francisco: Jossey-Bass, 1980.

Wexler, D. A., and Rice, L. N. *Innovations in Client-Centered Therapy*. New York: Wiley, 1974.

Chapter Five

Carl Rogers
The Power of Feelings

Why Carl Rogers? An Overview of Organizational Applications

Rogers's theory illustrates how consultants and their clients have an inborn capacity to solve problems and work creatively and effectively. His point of influence identifies the *intrapersonal* drive behind this capacity and also defines the contours of the *interpersonal* relationships that help it unfold.

Rogers's Theory as an Organizational Image or Metaphor

Rogers describes three attitudes or conditions of a helping relationship: congruence, unconditional positive regard, and empathic understanding. *Congruence* is being genuine and real, and consistent in thought, behavior, and feelings. *Unconditional positive regard* is acceptance. The person is valued without conditions. *Empathic understanding* is the ability to step into the other person's world, in effect, feeling with the other person. All three conditions can be used as metaphor at the organizational level. Organizations can be viewed as internally congruent or incongruent in values, norms, policies, and so on. Unconditional positive regard or a lack of it can become a metaphor to describe how the organization treats its members, clients, and others. Empathic understanding or its absence can also be used to symbolize norms, values, and attitudes in an organization.

Rogers's Theory as a Point of Influence for Dealing with Psychological Growth

Rogers's theory is based upon the premise that all individuals have within themselves the ability to guide their own lives in a manner that is both personally satisfying and socially constructive. Rogers's definition of a particular type of helping relationship frees individuals to find their inner wisdom and confidence so that they will make "healthier and more constructive choices" (Kirschenbaum and Henderson, 1989, p. xiv).The combination of Rogers's optimistic assumptions about human nature and the effectiveness of his helping relationship to release the basic drive for actualization make his theory particularly effective for encouraging psychological growth.

Rogers's Theory as a Point of Influence for Dealing with Organizational Conflict

Empathic listening is an essential aspect of Rogers's theory. His classic *Harvard Business Review* article, which outlined a specific method by which individuals and even leaders of nation-states could escape from sustained conflict by listening to each other, is both a profoundly theoretical and a profoundly practical approach to dealing with conflict (Rogers and Roethlisberger, [1952] 1991, pp. 105–111). Rogers's identification of the quality of being congruous and the attitude of unconditional positive regard can also make significant contributions to managing conflict.

Rogers's Theory as a Point of Influence for Dealing with the Dilemmas of Joining

The degree to which an individual commits to a group or organization is expressed through feelings. Rogers's theory and approach surfaces blocked or denied feelings, which helps the individual to increase awareness of his or her motivation to commit to a group or organization. If it is listened to, this information can also help the group or organization to understand what it must do to gain that commitment. Rogers's theory helps groups and organizations to gain their own commitment to participation.

Rogers's Theory as a Basis for Other Organizationally Relevant Theories

Rogers's theory has been more notable for stimulating applications in nonclinical settings than for prompting the development of new theories. His client-centered approach has encouraged the spread of professional counseling and psychotherapy in psychology, social work, education, the ministry, lay therapy, and other areas (Kirschenbaum and Henderson, 1989, p. xi). His principles of congruence, unconditional positive regard, and empathic understanding have been applied in education, organizational training, and conflict resolution. Roger's theory has also spawned several other theoretical approaches, of which some highlight the bodily and feeling responses (Gendlin, 1984) and others emphasize the cognitive aspect of his concepts (Wexler, 1974).

Limitations of Rogers's Theory for Use in Organizations

Rogers's theory is one of individual psychotherapy and change. As such, it does not offer explanations or strategies for the full range of problems faced by organizations. At the same time, his general approach to individual functioning adds value to most individual, group, and organizational interventions.

Another limitation of Rogers's theory grows out of its apparent simplicity. This seeming simplicity lends itself to misuse and even caricature. For example, practitioners who are training managers in listening skills have to be prepared to face the initial misunderstanding that Rogers's approach to listening simply means parroting back the last few phrases one has heard. To offset this tendency, this chapter emphasizes the importance of the underlying personal qualities and attitudes that Rogers designates as essential to the process of change.

The quality of apparent simplicity can also be a strength. Rogers's theory draws on the fundamental and verifiable human tendency for actualization. This approach makes sense to many and has helped Rogers and others to apply his theory in many areas outside of clinical psychology.

❧

How Rogers Developed His Theory

Carl Rogers was born and raised in Illinois, and his formative years were spent on a farm. His family was close-knit and religious—what he describes as "almost fundamentalist"—with no drinking, dancing, movies, parties, or expressions of interest in the opposite sex. His family strongly emphasized hard work, and in the rural atmosphere, Rogers developed what came to be a lifelong interest in plants and wildlife.

In 1919, Rogers started his undergraduate study at the University of Wisconsin. His first major was agriculture, but he became increasingly interested and involved in religion. By his junior year, his interest and leadership in campus Christian groups led to his being chosen as one of ten U.S. youth delegates to attend the World Student Christian Federation Conference in Peking, China. The trip lasted six months, and young Rogers visited a number of countries throughout the Far East, where he was exposed to many new ideas. As a result of his travels and discussions on the long ocean voyage, his religious views became less fundamental, with less emphasis on strict doctrine and more on reason and good works. When he returned, he changed his major to history to better prepare himself for the ministry (Kirschenbaum, 1979, pp. 22–25).

Rogers's new view of the ministry was more liberal than the fundamental views that he grew up with. His new orientation was reflected in his decision to attend the Union Theological Seminary, at that time the most liberal theological school in the country. He also married prior to enrolling in graduate school, which was an unusual sequence of life events at the time.

At that time, Union Theological Seminary was deeply committed to freedom of philosophical inquiry, whether that led into or away from the church. In Rogers's case, it led him across the street to Columbia Graduate School (Rogers, 1959, p. 186). His views continued to evolve at the seminary, and in 1926 he decided that he would have to enter a field in which he "could be sure [his] freedom of thought would not be limited" (Kirschenbaum, 1979, p. 52). He then transferred to Teachers College, Columbia University, where he earned a doctorate in educational and clinical psychology.

Rogers spent the first twelve years of his professional life at the Rochester Society for the Prevention of Cruelty to Children. This was a crucial formative time for the development of his ideas. He had been trained in testing and measurement and the then-prevailing doctrine of Freudian psychodynamics. His practice called upon him to assess and make written recommendations about a wide variety of troubled children and families. During this time he experimented with a number of approaches, even devising a "component factor method" that included eight of the internal and external factors that were then considered important in diagnosing troubled children (Kirschenbaum, 1979, p. 68).

As a clinician he applied a number of approaches, including Freudian methodology. He found that, although he could often come up with a "brilliant" interpretation of a patient's problem, the interpretation did not seem to help the patient or the problem. In 1936 Rogers invited Otto Rank, a former Freud protégé who had broken from Freudian orthodoxy, to deliver a lecture at the Rochester Center. Later Rogers cited Rank as an important influence on the development of his own thought (Kirschenbaum, 1979, p. 95). Others have found evidence of Rank's influence throughout Rogers's career (Kramer, 1995, p. 55).

Rogers's own experience was characteristically more prominent in his awareness than theories based on someone else's experience. He later cited one incident that illustrated how his ideas developed during this period (Rogers, [1967] 1989a, p. 48):

> I had been working with a highly intelligent mother whose boy was something of a hellion. The problem was clearly her early rejection of the boy, but over many interviews I could not help her to this insight. I drew her out, I gently pulled together the evidence she had given, trying to help her see the pattern. But we got nowhere. Finally I gave up. I told her that it seemed that we both had tried, but we had failed, and that we might as well give up our contacts. She agreed. So we concluded the interview, shook hands, and she walked to the door of the office. Then she turned and asked, "Do you ever take adults for counseling here?" When I replied in the affirmative, she said, "Well then, I would like some help." She came back to the chair she had just left and began to pour out her despair about her marriage, her troubled relationship with her husband, her sense of failure and confusion, all very different from the sterile "case history" she had given before. Real therapy began then, and ultimately it was highly successful—for her and for her son.

This incident was one of a number which helped me to experience the fact—only fully realized later—that it was the *client* who knows what hurts, what directions to go, what problems are crucial, what experiences have been deeply buried. It began to occur to me that unless I had a need to demonstrate my own cleverness and learning, I would do better to rely on the client for direction of movement in the process.

From this and similar experiences, Rogers went on to develop a new approach to help and therapy. This approach centered on enabling the individual being helped to set the direction and control the pace of the therapeutic relationship. It was formally introduced in 1942 in *Counseling and Psychotherapy: New Concepts in Practice*. From his theory of how to help individuals, Rogers developed his theory of the human personality. As a therapist, he had noted that individuals respond to a supportive relationship by becoming more aware and accepting of their own experiences. From this insight, Rogers went on to develop a theory of therapy and personality.

For the next four decades Rogers served on a number of university faculties, including that of the University of Chicago, where he "administered" the university counseling center in a participative style consistent with his counseling philosophy (Cain, 1987, p. 486). Rogers continued to refine and extend his basic approach. Succeeding books and articles applied the client-centered approach to education, personal power, encounter groups, communication, conflict resolution, and marriage and couple relationships. During the last fifteen years of his life, Rogers attempted to build an experience base for his ideas in the international arena. He held workshops in a number of world trouble spots, including Northern Ireland, Poland, South Africa, and the Soviet Union. The last such effort was held in Rust, Austria, where fifty leading Latin American figures in government and various areas of thought participated in a four-day workshop. The emphasis in this and in his other workshops was on the person, not the role. Although only limited evidence is available, it suggests that in this workshop, as in others based on Rogers's ideas, the individuals did begin to build trust and improve their ability to hear each other (Solomon, 1990, p. 48). Shortly before he died in 1987, Rogers was nominated for the Nobel Peace Prize.

Rogers's Point of Influence

Rogers emphasizes the *subjective awareness* of individuals and their world. His theory describes how, in the process of development, individuals lose awareness of some of their feelings and experience but regain it in a particular type of relationship. Access to and understanding of these feelings is Rogers's point of influence.

The Basic Human Condition

Rogers has a positive and optimistic view of human nature. He identifies a single overriding human tendency, which is to develop one's capacities in a way that maintains or enhances the person. He views humans as tending toward development, differentiation, and cooperative relationships, and as moving from dependence to independence. To be human for Rogers means to "enter into the complex process of being the most widely sensitive, responsive, creative, and adaptive creature on this planet" (Rogers, [1957] 1989d, p. 405).

Rogers calls this a tendency toward self-actualization. For him, humans have an innate and powerful striving for self-actualization and an innate valuing process that tells them what will help them achieve it. If this self-actualizing tendency is consistent or in harmony with the portion of experience that individuals symbolize as

---

**Preview: When to Use Rogers's
Point of Influence in the Workplace.**

When you wish to use yourself as an instrument of change (pp. 201–202)

When you wish to improve communication or manage conflict
(pp. 202–204)

When you are helping individuals to understand problems or make decisions or are coaching others to do the same (pp. 204–206)

When unexpressed feelings stand in the way of the task (pp. 206–208)

When you are helping to facilitate the process of joining or building a group (pp. 208–209)

When you are designing or implementing a training program
(pp. 209–210)

---

the self, humans have the opportunity to develop in the positive way Rogers describes (Rogers, 1959, p. 196).

Given this description of the basic human condition, we can envision the expression of the self-actualizing tendency in an infant reaching for a toy. Every fiber of that infant's being is striving for the toy. There is no ambivalence—no internal voice saying, "It's wrong to want that toy" or "You don't deserve that toy." The infant's emotion is not just self-feeling, it is also a valuing process, a way of knowing what is right and important for her or him. Stated another way, we can say that there are no distorting mechanisms between feeling and valuing, nor are there any distorting mechanisms between the objective experience and the subjective experience of the person.

In 1948, long before the advent of participative management and self-directed work groups, Rogers identified what holding this view of human nature might mean in an organization. He did so in the form of seven questions that he asked himself when he was in the administrator's role. Rogers later extrapolated the ideas behind these questions into a framework for person-centered administration (Rogers, 1948, pp. 546–548):

1. Do I trust the capacities of the group, and of the individuals in the group, to meet the problems with which we are faced, or do I basically trust only myself?
2. Do I free the group for creative discussion by being willing to understand, accept, and respect *all* attitudes, or do I find myself trying subtly to manipulate group discussion so that it comes out my way?
3. Do I, as leader, participate by honest expression of my own attitudes but without trying to control the attitudes of others?
4. Do I rely upon basic attitudes for motivation, or do I think that surface practices motivate behavior?
5. Am I willing to be responsible for those aspects of action which the group has delegated to me?
6. Do I trust the individual to do his job?
7. When tensions occur, do I try to make it possible for them to be brought out into the open?

Rogers later noted that there was no single right way to implement what he later termed "the person centered approach to administration." At times decisions could be made by the entire group operating in consensus; at other times, authority had to be delegated to one member to act in a crisis. At the bottom for Rogers in his style of administration—as in therapy—was the primacy of feelings (Rogers, 1977, pp. 94–95):

> Often the staff would spend *hours* (or so it seemed) in arguing some trivial issue, until a perceptive member would see and state the feelings underlying the issue—a personal animosity, a feeling of insecurity, a competition between two would-be leaders, or just the resentment of someone who had never really been heard. Once the *feelings* were out in the open, the issue which had seemed so important became a nothing. On the other hand when the staff was in open communication with one another, heavy issues such as the allocation of the budget for the following year . . . might take only minutes to decide.

How We Block or Diminish the Self-Actualizing Tendency

If this were all of Rogers's theory, it would leave little room for human complexity and little likelihood of conflicting emotions. Problems arise because humans have, or soon learn to have, a second powerful striving for emotional closeness with other human beings and for their approval (Rogers, 1959, p. 208). Much of the complexity and conflict center around what Rogers defines as "the self." The self is the organized, consistent, conceptual gestalt of the "I" or "me." Although he was initially skeptical of this concept, Rogers gradually accepted it as he heard more and more of his clients make such statements as "I am not feeling myself" or "I never had a chance to be myself" (Rogers, 1959, p. 201). Much of Rogers's research was based on how the self changed in the process of therapy.

The addition of the self to the developing person creates the possibility of incongruence or lack of consistency between self and experience. Such incongruence can develop anytime throughout life. The pattern often begins very early. Consider a newborn infant, untouched by human interaction and expectations. What the infant perceives is her or his own reality. If it is satisfying to the infant to be picked up at a particular moment, then it is a positive experience. If it is not satisfying to the infant, it is a negative experience.

Thus, what the infant perceives to be reality is, in fact, the infant's reality. Simply because an adult picks up the infant lovingly and tenderly does not automatically mean that the infant will have a loving experience. Even though the adult has no intention of frightening the infant, the child may feel fear for his or her own reasons and act frightened.

As infants grow, they begin to develop the second basic need. In order to feel good, they must reach out to others and become interpersonally involved. This means that sometimes their natural organismic response, such as crying when frightened, must be modified to receive acceptance and positive regard from others. This may be a confusing process. If the infants' natural response to a perceived situation is to cry, but they are told not to cry, they are frustrating their own valuing process—their way of being. The paradox is that because they need positive regard from others, they may stifle their own feelings. They may think that it is not right to feel anger or sorrow or need and therefore reject those feelings. The infants are now developing a sense of self-regard through both their intrapersonal (within themselves) and interpersonal (with others) perceptions of reality.

If this sense of self-regard is conditional, where individuals feel prized in some circumstances but not in others, then they are experiencing what Rogers describes as a "condition of worth." Conditions of worth are values of others that individuals substitute in place of their own—the "shoulds," "oughts," and "musts" of others. Gradually, this conditional attitude can be assimilated into the individual's own self-regard complex, and experiences are evaluated positively or negatively solely on the basis of conditions taken over from others (Rogers, 1959, p. 209).

The Results of Blocking the Self-Actualizing Tendency

Conditions of worth occupy a crucial position in Rogers's theory of development. Because of the need for self-regard, the individual perceives experience selectively, in terms of his or her conditions of worth. Experiences that are in accord with the conditions of worth are perceived and symbolized accurately in awareness, and those that are not are perceived inaccurately, distorted, or in part or whole denied to awareness (Rogers, 1959, p. 226). Because these experiences are considered wrong, they are no longer experienced, expressed, or made a part of conscious awareness.

> A manager's budget is cut, and she has to fire a promising subordinate. Her superior might say, "I can't understand why you are upset. You're experienced enough to know that we can't spend money we don't have." The manager may take this condition of worth to heart and deny her own feelings to gain her superior's approval. She may also have a pattern of doing this and as a result may become unaware that she even has these feelings. She then wonders why she is angry and snappish for three days before the meeting with the soon-to-be-fired employee.

In terms of Rogers's theory, what has happened to the manager is the following:

- The *Person* or *Organism* feels badly about firing the employee.
- The *Self* or core identity of the manager accepts her superior's comments that she shouldn't feel badly about this firing because it's "just business."
- The *Person* reacts to this inner incongruity by behaving in a short-tempered or snappish way with her other colleagues and subordinates for a few days prior to the firing.

The incongruities in this example are:

- What is going on inside the manager and what is being presented to the outside
- What the manager is actually experiencing and her core identity or self, which has accepted "conditions of worth" that cause her to muffle or lose awareness of that experience

On a personal level, think of yourself in your work or learning environment. Are there times when you feel unheard or unaccepted, when it seems impossible to express your feelings? What do you say or do about it, and what—if anything—stops you from expressing yourself? Are you aware of the internal message that says, "You shouldn't feel this way because . . ."? Whatever follows the word *because* involves conditions of worth, which cause an individual to perceive his or her world through the attitudes of others. In order to gain your positive regard, I may have to deny my feelings and push away what feels right, and this may cause confusion and tension.

Reclaiming Individual Experience Through a Particular Kind of Relationship

The solution for Rogers is to help an individual reclaim a point of influence for the feelings that were lost in the process of development. This is done through a particular kind of relationship that gives individuals permission to explore themselves and reexperience previously denied or distorted feelings or experiences. The popular name for this relationship is *active listening,* a term coined by one of Rogers's students, Tom Gordon (1977). Brief, active listening involves paraphrasing what an individual has said, usually with some sense of the speaker's feeling and intended and implicit meaning. This is done to ensure the listener's understanding of what the speaker has said. For the speaker, the impact of feeling heard encourages further exploration of inner experiences.

Whether it is called empathic understanding or active listening, the process involves three crucial elements: congruence, unconditional positive regard, and empathy. When we are directly referring to Rogers's ideas we will use the term *empathic understanding.* When we are referring to Gordon's application of Rogers's ideas we will use *active listening.*

Congruence

Congruence involves being real, genuine, and in touch with yourself and knowing what you feel physically and emotionally. The feelings the listener is experiencing are available to him or her, and he or she is able to live with those feelings, *be* them, and communicate them if it is appropriate (Rogers, 1961, p. 61). Rogers later considered this the most basic of the three attitudes (Rogers and Sanford, 1984, p. 1380). Congruence also involves being aware of one's own values clearly and genuinely, so that when someone shares an issue or problem, the individual is able to forgo judgment and the urge to give advice and to truly accept the other person. That person is then free to be real, genuine, and self-accepting. Congruence and the lack of congruence are thus contagious. If one person is clear and open about what she or he is feeling, it can serve as an invitation for others to do the same, and if one person withholds or is unaware of what she or he is feeling, it makes it difficult for others to be more open and forthcoming.

It is not easy to be congruent. The basic task is to know, understand, and accept oneself, including one's feelings, thoughts, perceptions, and judgments. Not acknowledging one's own experience can be conscious or unconscious. At a conscious level, a person may fear another person's reaction. Unconsciously, the individual may simply be unaware of his or her own feelings.

A manager who is embarrassed by a subordinate's awkward political move may feel, "I am really embarrassed. How can I face my boss when one of my people writes such an angry, ignorant memo?" The manager may try to counsel the subordinate on the political norms of the organization. He has decided that his own feelings of embarrassment are not relevant to the situation, so he tries to explain calmly, objectively, and rationally the political behavior expected in the organization. He either has decided not to express his feelings of embarrassment or is not consciously aware of his feelings. In either case, the manager is not congruent. He is experiencing strong feelings but not expressing them, and the subordinate picks up the incongruence and reacts defensively. In such a situation, it is very difficult for a subordinate to be congruent. Despite the manager's careful and seemingly helpful demeanor, the subordinate may react defensively and argue with the manager.

Gordon suggests that the first step toward congruence is filling one's own cup by taking care of one's own needs. He notes that it is very difficult to be accepting if one does not feel accepting. Incongruence in a helping relationship usually does not work: "If, for whatever reason, you don't feel accepting when a group member shares a problem, the active listening skill will never disguise your true feelings. And if it is not your intention to be understanding, you won't do an accurate job of listening anyway" (Gordon, 1977, p. 73).

Without congruence, as Gordon indicates, it is very hard to be helpful. With congruence alone, however, one can make a difference. For example, a meeting may seem to be going around in circles and no one in the meeting is able to acknowledge the situation, let alone do anything about it. If one person can say, "I don't know about the rest of you, but this is really confusing for me. We seem to be going over the same ground but not getting anywhere," there is a good prospect that others will say, "Well, yes, it seems that way to me too." This is a way of helping others become aware of their own confusion—by simply acknowledging your own. It is the first step toward doing something about the problem.

Unconditional Positive Regard

Unconditional positive regard is a stance toward other people based upon Rogers's assumptions about human nature. It involves totally accepting, caring for, and prizing another person (Rogers, 1961, p. 62). When one individual has this attitude, a nonjudgmental, nonevaluative atmosphere is experienced by others. A relationship built on unconditional positive regard helps people to explore their own feelings, temporarily push aside conditions of worth, and become aware of their true feelings. In personal terms, this means that what I need as an individual in order to grow and change is acceptance from someone I value, someone important to me. This person may not approve of my behavior. For example, an angry child tells her mother, "I hate you." The mother may respond, "You shouldn't talk to me that way" (conditions of worth). Or the mother could say, "It doesn't make me feel good to hear you say that, but I understand your angry feelings." The mother is accepting both her own feelings and her child's, while letting the child know the meaning of her behavior. The manager who is upset about his subordinate's intemperate memo has to accept his feelings before dealing with the subordinate. The manager might well say, "You know, when I read this memo I think I turned three shades of purple, and I still have some of those feelings, but I also realized that no one ever talked to you about how we deal with such things here, so we'd better do that."

   This is unconditional positive regard. It requires empathy, the ability to step into someone else's world, hear what is behind the behavior, and recognize one's underlying feelings. When this process is experienced, the conditions of worth decrease, freeing the person to explore, gain understanding, recognize that choices exist, and evaluate the "shoulds." The integration of internal reactions with environmental pressures is no longer out of balance—

feelings and behavior can be recognized and accepted, and self-regard and self-respect develop. Unconditional positive regard is based on Rogers's conviction that humans have an internal valuing process that urges them to naturally strive for what is best for themselves.

Empathic Understanding

Empathic understanding is the most complex of the three helping processes. Although unconditional positive regard and congruence can have an impact by themselves, empathic understanding can only exist if it is built on a foundation of the other two processes. Rogers defines empathic understanding in these words (Rogers, 1980, p. 116):

> This means that the therapist senses accurately the feelings and personal meanings that the client is experiencing and communicates this understanding to the client. When functioning best, the therapist is so much inside the private world of the other that he or she can clarify not only the meanings of which the client is aware but even those just below the level of awareness. This kind of sensitive, active listening is exceedingly rare in our lives. We think we listen, but very rarely do we listen with real understanding, true empathy. Yet listening, of this very special kind, is one of the most potent forces for change that I know.

It is important to understand the meaning of empathy. Empathy is not sympathy, although the two words are often lumped together as the same thing. Empathy is feeling with a person—stepping into her or his world. Sympathy is feeling sorry for a person. Sympathy by itself may imply a sense of helplessness that may hinder self-exploration and cut off communication. It may promote "war stories," too much self-disclosure, and solutions by the listener. It does not provide an atmosphere in which people can truly express their feelings. Empathy places the responsibility for changing oneself with the person, not the listener. Sympathy tends to bring forth personal conditions of worth in the listener—the "shoulds" of talking to and treating someone with a problem and the emotions the problems trigger in the listener. With sympathy, it is very hard to drop one's personal experiences and genuinely step into another person's frame of reference.

When to Use Rogers's Theory

When You Wish to Use Yourself as an Instrument of Change

The use of the self as an instrument of change is an important concept in organization development and training. Peter Block states, "Authentic behavior with a client means you put into words what you are experiencing with the client as you work" (Block, 1981, p. 31). The notion is that the practitioner's authentic self—thoughts, feelings, even physical reactions—can be an important ingredient in organizational change efforts. What Block termed an *authentic relationship,* Rogers called *congruence,* and he made it a basic cornerstone of his therapy. As early as 1954, Rogers stated in a speech that as a therapist, he must not only be aware of his own feelings but must also be willing to express, "in my words and my behavior, the various feelings and attitudes which exist in me. It is only in this way that the relations can have *reality,* and reality seems deeply important as a first condition. . . . I have found this to be true even when the attitudes are not attitudes with which I am pleased, or attitudes which seem conducive to a good relationship. It seems extremely important to be *real*" (Rogers, 1961, p. 33).

To illustrate, if a consultant is interviewing a CEO, and the CEO repeatedly allows the interview to be interrupted by telephone calls and questions from staff members, the consultant's own feelings and reactions are important data about the priority the CEO may be giving to the change project. In addition, her reactions may provide a clue about how others may be reacting to the CEO. In order to carry out Rogers's principles in an organizational setting the consultant must:

1. Be in touch with her own inner reactions, and her outer behavior must reflect this awareness (the Rogerian principle of *congruence*).
2. Communicate a basic respect for and valuing of the CEO as a person, thus making it more likely that the CEO will hear her comments (the Rogerian principle of *unconditional positive regard*).
3. Demonstrate that she is listening to the CEO, for this will make it more likely that the CEO will listen to her (the Rogerian principle of *empathy*).

Following is an example of the use of self within the context of Rogers's principles.

> "I notice that when we meet, interruptions are okay for you. When this happens, I lose my train of thought and begin to feel less involved in this project. I also begin to wonder how interested you are."

Rogers's view of *reality* as described above is an overlay, a way of being that adds truth to consulting situations ranging from the most interpersonal team building to system-wide socio-tech or reengineering.

When You Wish to Improve Communication or Manage Conflict

For Rogers, the solution to human problems begins with communication. When Rogers describes the conditions needed for effective psychotherapy, he also describes what would be effective human relations in any context or situation. Good therapy for Rogers is based on good human interaction, and good human interaction *is* therapeutic.

This was illustrated in a 1952 article that Rogers wrote with F. J. Roethlisberger of the Harvard Business School (Rogers and Roethlisberger, 1952). The article, entitled "Barriers and Gateways to Communication," was published in the *Harvard Business Review*. (It was not jointly written but consisted of separate sections by each author.) Although it initially was controversial, the article has been widely reprinted, and in 1991 it was republished as part of a series of *Harvard Business Review* "Classics."

In a retrospective commentary, John Gabarro (1991) identified three enduring insights in the article that transcend institutional and social boundaries. They involve the communication barriers and gateways that can occur between two nations as well as between two individuals. They are as follows:

1. "The greatest barrier to effective communication is the tendency to evaluate what another person is saying and therefore to misunderstand or not really 'hear.'"

Differences in background, perspective, and attitude are a natural source of mishearing and misunderstanding. We hear what we expect to hear depending on our background and experiences. In 1952, Roethlisberger noted the tendency for communication to break down with what we now view as a relatively homogeneous work force. Given today's increasingly diverse work force, Rogers's emphasis on communication is even more important.

    2.   "Checking the natural tendency to judge yields a better understanding of the person with whom you are communicating."

With today's organizations requiring more from their work force both intellectually and emotionally, this second principle is important. If the organization wants individuals to be creative, "think quality," be customer-oriented, or whatever the currently favored maxim is, then the flow of communication must travel both ways. The organization must be equally open to understanding and accepting the individual from whom it hopes to extract this increased effort and productivity. Rogers's theory outlines the conditions that make this two-way communication possible.

    3.   "A better understanding of the other person's point of view in turn helps you to communicate better."

Effective communication is equal parts listening and expression. The clarity of what one says depends upon the clarity of what one hears.

Managing Conflict: A Practical Example of Rogers's Views on Communication

In his section of the *Harvard Business Review* article, Rogers suggested, "The next time you get into an argument with your spouse, friend or small group of friends, stop the discussion for a moment and suggest this rule. Before each person speaks up, he or she must *first* restate the ideas and feelings of the previous speaker accurately and to that speaker's satisfaction" (Rogers and Roethlisberger, [1952] 1991, p. 106). Rogers indicated that using this method was not only difficult but also required courage. Truly hearing the other person might well mean that one's own mind and position could be changed.

Tom Gordon's "no-lose" system of conflict resolution combined Rogers's basic stance with a problem-solving methodology (Gordon, 1977, p. 194):

First, your statement of the problem should be expressed in a way that does not communicate blame or judgment. Sending I-messages is always the most effective way for stating a problem. [I-messages are statements that directly state the speaker's thoughts, values, feelings, or attitudes and what the speaker wishes from the other person. For example, if you have a colleague who frequently interrupts you, instead of saying, "Why do you always interrupt me?" you can say, "I have trouble thinking clearly when I don't finish my sentences. I need you to listen to me until I finish my thought."]

Secondly, after you have stated your feelings, try to verbalize O's side of the conflict. If you don't know what that is, ask O to state his or her position.

Frequently, it will take a while to get the problem or conflict defined accurately. O may need some time to get feelings out. O may initially get angry or defensive. This is the time to use Active Listening. O must have a chance to ventilate feelings; else he or she will not be ready for the remaining steps.

When You Are Helping Individuals to Understand Problems or Make Decisions or Are Coaching Others to Do the Same

In the organizational context, sometimes a blurry line exists between what is work and what is personal. The ability to help another individual to become aware of what he or she wants is a part of effective management. Following is an illustration of this (Athos and Gabarro, 1978, pp. 401–402):

> A senior partner of an accounting firm, who manages one of her firm's large Midwest offices, is approached by one of her most promising junior associates. The associate wished to discuss a "personal but also a business" problem with the manager. The problem the man describes is that his wife's father has recently died, and his wife wants to return to the East Coast to be near her mother. Yet the associate feels that he has just begun an exciting phase of what the manager knows is a promising career in the firm's growing Midwest office. Clearly, the manager would like to keep him.

The preference of most managers in this position would be to think of the company and advise the man to stay in the Midwest office. But if the manager does this, what effect will the wife's discomfort and the employee's possible guilt have on the employee's work? If the manager decides to be altruistic and recommend that the man transfer to the East Coast, what effect will the employee's resentment over lost opportunities have on his relationship with his wife and his work in the East Coast branch? What is the answer? There is no theory, no framework, no formula that can tell the manager *what* to advise in this situation. *The answer lies in the individual himself,* yet at the moment the employee is confused. He is not fully aware of his own feelings in regard to these issues. The process of both understanding the man and helping him understand himself is crucial to any solution that would help the employee or the organization.

In cases like this, a useful option for the manager is to help the individual understand himself better. The key to such help lies in the manager's ability to listen in the deeper way described by Rogers and Gordon. Such listening could help the employee to increase his awareness of his own feelings and values regarding each of the options. This would make the employee more accepting of whatever decision he happens to make. This can be true even in issues that do not have such a clear personal overtone. The capacity to understand why others take a particular position on a substantive question and the ability to help them explore what they do not fully understand about that position is at the very core of effective decision making. In this respect, Rogers's theory, which at first glance seems only applicable to counseling and psychotherapy, is actually essential to a key aspect of managerial work (Athos and Gabarro, 1978, p. 402).

Most managers also face the situation in which two subordinates have such difficulty working with each other that both the quality of their work and their relationship suffer. The feud may easily escalate so that it becomes a matter between departments. In such instances, the ability to listen to both employees and help them realize what is involved is a crucial step in solving the problem so that work can resume.

The division of labor in organizations breeds such situations. To illustrate, consider the traditional differences between Production and Marketing. The organizational task of each department leads to a quite different perspective. These differences can be expressed in an evaluative and judgmental way. Production may characterize

Marketing as caring only about sales and not the product, using such phrases as "huckster," "greedy," and "superficial." Marketing in turn views Production as isolated and not understanding that someone has to buy their products. They use such phrases as "rigid," "technocrat," and "unrealistic," and the feelings and negative images evoked by these judgmental words easily escalate, building on one another until the two departments communicate in only the most formal and limited way. Rogers's approach to listening does not eliminate the natural differences promoted by the two functions. It does, however, help organization members to get beyond the negative images evoked by these comments so that the real differences can be discussed.

When Unexpressed Feelings Stand in the Way of the Task

Inner exploration and deepening personal awareness of feeling are remote from the announced purpose or norms of most organizations. At the same time, the *lack* of feeling awareness can be an organizational problem. Blocked feelings are not only confusing to the individual but can also be costly to the organization. Blocked feelings restrict the joining process, limit individual response to organizational change, and stifle the psychological growth that is now demanded by high-performing organizations. When organizations reach for "excellence," "quality," or whatever is the current goal and place demands on individuals, these individuals react in terms of feelings.

Rogers is clear about his approach to feelings. He focuses on the *individual experience of feeling*, rather than on intellectual understanding. Rogerian process provides an accepting atmosphere and presence so that the individual is able to explore himself or herself through greater awareness of feeling. This exploration results in an ever-deepening awareness of values, meaning, and feeling. For Rogers, before an individual can understand or even apply an identifying label to a feeling, he or she must experience it. Rogers emphasizes experiencing feeling as deeply as possible as a way of understanding it.

The varied effects of feelings in an organization are illustrated in the dilemma faced by Police Officer Hal Ridley and the police department he worked for:

Hal was a combat veteran and was not unfamiliar with shootings and violence, but his new assignment in the Police Narcotics Bureau of a large midwestern city brought up feelings that were very puzzling. Many days he found
himself arresting ten- to twelve-year-old children. These boys and girls were
often younger than his own children, and although they were frightened, they
also viewed him with a degree of contempt, confident that the criminal justice
system would soon have them out on the street, where some of them made as
much money in a day as he made in a week. On other days, he dealt with the
results of gang warfare, and this meant handling the homicides of these same
young people or of innocent victims who happened to be in the wrong place at
the wrong time. Hal believed that he ought to be able to handle the feelings
that his job evoked, but it was not always easy to do so.

As he worked longer in the Narcotics Bureau, it became harder and
harder for Hal to understand his feelings. They combined in odd and unexpected ways—anger with fear and rage with sympathy. He was particularly
puzzled when anger at a nine-year-old suspect turned into sympathy and caring and when rage at the homicide of an elderly pensioner who was just sitting
on his porch at the wrong time turned into anger with his own wife, because
she went to an evening parents' meeting by herself. The feelings would come
to the surface at unexpected times and places. He would dismiss these reactions as part of the job, only to find himself later inappropriately yelling at his
own ten-year-old. What was happening did not make sense to him, and for this
reason he did not know how to deal with it.

A similar phenomenon of puzzling, unexpressed feelings occurred at the
organizational level of the department. It was not consistent with the culture
of the department for individuals to discuss their feelings. If they did so, the
discussion was indirect and often laced with sarcasm. This style spilled over
into the relationship between the various units in the department. The contact
between the Narcotics Bureau and the Patrol Bureau was a good example of
this. Neither unit believed that the other understood the difficulty of their job,
and neither thought that the other supported them as they should. Conse-
quently, the exchange of information between the units was confused and at
times nonexistent. If the uniformed officers worked unusually hard to dig up
some information, it was received with no acknowledgment. If the narcotics
officers took unusual risks in going undercover to make an arrest, they did not
believe that the uniformed officers understood their danger.

On the individual level, active listening could be used to help Hal and other narcotics officers become aware of the feelings that their work evoked. It would be especially helpful to have them become aware of the impact that their unexpressed feelings were having on their families.

On an organizational level, active listening could first help individuals to become aware of the impact of this aspect of their culture on them and their families. As part of an intergroup intervention between the Narcotics and Patrol bureaus, active listening could play a *part* in changing the relationship between the bureaus. An intergroup team-building effort could use active-listening dialogues between pairs of officers as they discussed their daily experiences. As Rogers and Roethlisberger ([1952] 1991) state, active listening would not by itself solve the problems between the two bureaus, but it would be a useful part of an organizational intervention. This scenario is representative of many in which active listening functions as an overlay methodology, combined with other interventions.

When You Are Helping to Facilitate the Process of Joining or Building a Group

While Kurt Lewin and his colleagues were conducting their pioneering experiments in group dynamics in the late 1930s and early 1940s (see Chapter Seven), Rogers was developing his approach to client-centered therapy. Rogers referred to Lewin's work with groups in his 1951 book, *Client-Centered Therapy*. Although the two theorists worked independently of each other, their findings moved in the direction of greater individual and group autonomy. Both of them defined a new relationship of the individual to the group or organization. Lewin's research has been more obviously applicable to organizations because he worked with task- and decision-making groups. However, Rogers, working with individuals in psychotherapy, produced a theory and defined a personal style that has proved basic to the whole thrust for participation in management.

Rogers focused on the inner process (conditions of worth) that inhibits self-direction and autonomous behavior in psychotherapy and on the job. He also identified the conditions in a group (congruence, unconditional positive regard, and empathic understanding) that help to restore that self-direction. Rogers pinpointed the needs of the leader (the urge to take charge when nothing seems to be happening) that can thwart group and individual development. In doing so, he defined a new, nondirective leadership style and demonstrated how it could be effective.

Following are Rogers's seven questions to managers, which were cited earlier, rephrased as principles and regrouped under his three therapeutic principles of congruence, unconditional positive regard, and empathic understanding (Rogers, 1948, pp. 546–548):

1. *Congruence:* The leader only expresses his or her own attitudes and feelings without trying to influence others.
2. *Unconditional positive regard:* The leader trusts the basic capacities of individuals in the group to solve problems and do their job. The leader also relies on the individuals' basic attitudes rather than external threats or rewards for motivation.
3. *Empathic understanding:* The leader works to establish a group atmosphere that is open to understanding, accepting, and respecting all attitudes and—when tensions occur—tries to make it possible for them to be brought into the open.

Lewin's experiments demonstrated how nonauthoritarian leadership can be effective. Rogers, operating from the more personally oriented world of psychotherapy, revealed the personal qualities needed to lead in such a nonauthoritarian way.

When You Are Designing or Implementing a Training Program

Rogers's ideas have also played a significant role in defining a new approach to learning as opposed to teaching. Rogers made the case that congruence, unconditional positive regard, and empathic understanding are the necessary conditions for change in both psychotherapy and education (Rogers, 1951, p. 132). These ideas became an essential pillar in Malcolm Knowles's pioneering definition of andragogy or adult education (Knowles, 1978, pp. 41–42). Training in organizations is, of course, adult education and, through Knowles, Rogers's ideas are frequently part of organizational training. The similarity between Rogers's ideas and effective trainer behavior is illustrated in Exhibit 5.1.

Exhibit 5.1. Rogers's Principles of Learning: Application to Training in an Organization.

Rogers's Principles of Learning	Application to Training in an Organization
Congruence The teacher can be a real person in her relationship with her students. She can be enthusiastic, bored, interested in the students, angry, sensitive, or sympathetic. Because she accepts these feelings as her own, she has no need to impose them on her students. She can like or dislike a student's product without implying that it is good or bad (Rogers, 1983, p. 122).	The trainer who can get her real self in the training situation not only models what can be effective behavior in many organizational situations (performance appraisal, conflict resolution, supervision, and so on) but also provides a level of excitement and interest so that the very way the sessions are conducted maintains the students' interest.
Unconditional Positive Regard The facilitator who has a considerable degree of this attitude can fully accept the fear and hesitation of students as they approach a new problem as well as their satisfaction in achievement. Such a teacher can accept students' occasional apathy and their erratic desires to explore byroads of knowledge, as well as their disciplined efforts to achieve major goals (Rogers, 1983, p. 124).	Much organizational training is designed to encourage new or different behavior. The more the participants can feel accepted as they are at present in the training situation, the more open they will be to attempting new behavior.
Empathic Understanding When the teacher has the ability to understand the student's reactions from the inside and has a sensitive awareness of the way the process of education and learning seems to the student, the likelihood of significant learning is increased (Rogers, 1983, p. 125).	Training programs must be relevant to the participants' experience in the organization. Active listening creates a greater likelihood that they will hear and understand the relevance of what is said in the training session and that participant feedback will be more immediate and honest.

As in the case of group and organizational leadership, Rogers's three concepts of congruence, unconditional positive regard, and empathic understanding focus on the individual's internal process. By doing so, they help practitioners to define the behavior that supports the adult process of learning.

Using Active Listening: Cautions and Guidelines

Active listening is the process of clearing the path and inviting the other person to explore himself or herself. This is why some individuals who are known as "good listeners" naturally and effectively employ active listening without ever having heard of the term or Carl Rogers. The effectiveness of these individuals demonstrates that Rogers built his clinical method on a natural and intrinsic way of relating.

Unlike many therapeutic methods that must be reserved for clinicians, Rogers's methods travel very well from the psychotherapist's office to the environment of daily life. Still, some cautions and guidelines must be observed to make sure that control remains in the hands of the person being helped.

Cautions

Although some individuals are natural listeners, active listening remains a complex and subtle art. The following examples are offered as illustrations of the power and practicality of this method. However, most individuals, even naturals, can benefit from training, practice, and coaching. More detailed information, drills, and practice can be found in Tom Gordon's *Leader Effectiveness Training* (1977); Gerard Egan's *The Skilled Helper* (1986); Robert Carkhuff and Richard Pierce's *The Art of Helping* (1993); and Robert Bolton's *People Skills* (1979).

When using active listening, it is important to have a sense of one's limitations. This is a powerful tool, and its use can bring up feelings and memories that managers or organizational consultants might not be prepared to deal with. They must be prepared to recognize such a situation and refer the person to an appropriate mental health professional.

Guidelines for Finding Your Own Empathic Response

In his 1951 book, *Client-Centered Therapy,* Rogers gave an example of a statement that a therapist might hear and then illustrated a series of nonempathic responses that might have been going through the therapist's mind. He pointed out that none of these responses were necessarily "wrong" or "bad." They were, however, all attempts to "understand about" rather than "understand with." The locus of perceiving in each instance was outside that of the client (Rogers, 1951, pp. 32–33). Following is a similar example in an organizational context.

> "I have to do something but I don't know what to do about Emma. Whenever she challenges me we get into a big argument. I'm her supervisor so it's wrong that she always challenges me, but that's not the whole problem. Its awful to have to keep going through this with her. The other problem is that sometimes I have to involve other people, like Personnel. I really got worried yesterday when I found myself doing something that I knew I shouldn't, just so I wouldn't have to deal with Emma. I just can't stand it when she starts yelling. I don't know how she gets away with it. I always feel so embarrassed when she does it, but it doesn't bother her and then she just goes on as if nothing had happened, and I'm upset for a couple of days. I don't know what I'm going to do. I know I should be more authoritative."

Hearing this statement may trigger a number of reactions in your mind. Note whether these reactions are in your (the listener's) frame of reference or that of the speaker:

> "Maybe she should take some assertiveness training."

> "I wonder if Emma reminds her of her mother."

> "What makes her so embarrassed? I wonder if her mother did that."

> "She must really be repressing these feelings."

> "Maybe she needs to talk more about being embarrassed."

> "I didn't know she called Personnel!"

Following are responses that are more likely to reflect the feelings of the speaker:

> "It seems really hard to be a supervisor."

> "It sounds really frustrating for you to go through this over and over again."

Guidelines to Applying Active Listening in an Organizational Setting

An organizational practitioner can have a relatively long conversation, as would have occurred with the manager who was trying to decide whether to move to the East Coast, or a very short conversation in which the listener begins to identify the real issues behind a statement, with active listening perhaps being combined with an action statement. Unlike clinical situations, which are usually more protracted, sometimes it is necessary for organizational practitioners to merely help an individual to identify the feeling behind a remark and then quickly return to the task.

> Just before a consultant was to present feedback to a group during a team-building session, one person suddenly stood up and said, "I don't really want to be here. I don't like this whole process and I don't know what's on those sheets, and I don't know why you have them hidden [referring to turned-up newsprint sheets], and I don't know if this is going to help us."
>
> The consultant responded: "It sounds like you would rather be back doing your own work. Let's end the mystery, take down these sheets, and get the show on the road." Several group members responded, agreeing: "Yes, let's get on with it."

The consultant here simply reflected the concerns of one individual, which, not untypically, were also concerns of others in the group, and then returned to the task. The group thus became more aware of its feelings. Perhaps a discussion of the process would follow, or perhaps the group would simply get started with the feedback. In either case, the reflection of feelings served the purpose that Rogers described in the *Harvard Business Review* article: it was a *gateway to communication*.

Despite its brevity and link to action, this statement had to be *congruent*. The practitioner had to convey that he or she was not defensive, but was truly listening. The practitioner was also displaying *unconditional positive regard* by respecting the speaker's desire to be out of the session and doing his own work. Finally, the practitioner conveyed *empathic understanding* by responding to the worry or anxiety about what was on the turned-up newsprint sheets.

Conclusion

Rogers's theory is built around a powerful inner tendency to achieve actualization and an intrapersonal relationship that frees and encourages this tendency. Practitioners using Rogers's focus and methodology are able to help their clients to solve their own problems and to work more productively and creatively. The cornerstone of these applications is a special form of communication termed *empathic understanding* by Rogers and *active listening* by Tom Gordon, one of Rogers's early students.

This chapter has described applications of the Rogerian process in a number of organizational areas. The most basic, and the one most unique to Rogers, is that of using oneself as an instrument of change. Although Rogers never used such a phrase or commented upon the organization development field, the chapter has illustrated how his focus on the congruence of the therapist applies to the congruence of the organizational practitioner. An important aspect of such congruence is the ability to be aware of expressed feelings. The chapter has illustrated how Rogers's theory can be applied to both the practitioner and organization members.

Annotated Bibliography
Original Sources: Readable Rogers

Rogers, C. R. *On Becoming a Person: A Therapist's View of Psychotherapy.* Boston: Houghton Mifflin, 1961.
This is the book that helped Carl Rogers to become a significant public figure in the world of counseling and psychology. Rogers had first presented his theory almost twenty years before, but this work, containing both theory and applications and written in Rogers's unique personal style, is *the* book to read to gain a taste of his theory and personality.

Rogers, C. R. *A Way of Being.* Boston: Houghton Mifflin, 1980.
Written in the same personal style as *On Becoming a Person,* this book brings Rogers's theory largely up to date.

Raskin, N. J., and Rogers, C. R. "Person-Centered Therapy." In R. Corsini, D. Wedding, and J. W. McMahon (eds.), *Current Psychotherapies* (4th ed., pp. 155–194). Itasca, Ill.: F. E. Peacock, 1989.
Rogers was working on this article at the time of his death.

Secondary Sources: Books About Rogers and His Theories

Gabarro, J. J. "Retrospective Commentary." In C. R. Rogers and F. J. Roethlisberger, "Barriers and Gateways to Communication." *Harvard Business Review*, Nov.–Dec. 1991, *69*(6), 105–111.

The article itself was first published in 1952 and was Rogers's best-known communication with the organizational world. It contains his application of empathic understanding to conflict resolution and was chosen as one of the *Harvard Business Review*'s all-time classic articles forty years later. Gabarro's comments sum up Rogers's contributions to interpersonal communication in organizations.

Kirschenbaum, H. *On Becoming Carl Rogers*. New York: Delacorte Press, 1979.

This is a well-written and generally laudatory biography, written with the full cooperation of Rogers, who made all of his files available to the author, including those that revealed his foibles and limitations.

Solomon, L. N. "Carl Rogers's Efforts for World Peace." *Person-Centered Review*, 1990, *5*(1), 39–56.

This review in this now-defunct journal addressed Rogers's efforts in various areas of the world to apply his ideas to international and ethnic conflicts.

Organizational Applications

Athos, A., and Gabarro, J. *Interpersonal Behavior: Communication and Understanding in Relationships*. Englewood Cliffs, N.J.: Prentice Hall, 1978.

This text, which is not limited to Rogers's ideas, draws heavily on them. It explains the theory and provides numerous case studies and specific instructions for application.

Carkhuff, R. *The Art of Helping VII*. Amherst, Mass.: Human Resource Development Press, 1993.

This is representative of a large series of works that are based heavily, but not exclusively, on Rogers's ideas. It is not specifically organizationally focused, but it provides directions for helping other individuals in various day-to-day life situations.

Gordon, T. *Leader Effectiveness Training, L.E.T.: The No-Lose Way to Release the Productive Potential of People*. New York: Wyden Books, 1977.

Gordon was a student of Rogers who coined the term *active listening*. This book is patterned after Gordon's earlier and better-known P.E.T—or Parent Effectiveness Training. Gordon takes Rogers's ideas and shows how to apply them in the workplace, including how to become a group-centered or facilitative manager.

Rogers, C. R. "The Rust Workshop." In H. Kirschenbaum and V. L. Henderson (eds.), *The Carl Rogers Reader.* Boston: Houghton Mifflin, 1989. (Originally published 1986.)
This is Rogers's own account of how he applied his ideas in a conference composed of Latin American political leaders.

Bibliography

Athos, A., and Gabarro, J. *Interpersonal Behavior: Communication and Understanding in Relationships.* Englewood Cliffs, N.J.: Prentice Hall, 1978.

Block, P. *Flawless Consulting: A Guide to Getting Your Expertise Used.* Austin, Tex.: Learning Concepts, 1981.

Bolton, R. *People Skills: How to Assert Yourself, Listen to Others, and Resolve Conflicts.* Englewood Cliffs, N.J.: Prentice Hall, 1979.

Cain, D. J. "Carl Rogers's Life in Review." *Person-Centered Review,* Nov. 1987, *2*(4), 476–505.

Carkhuff, R., and Pierce, R. *The Art of Helping: An Introduction to Life Skills, VII.* Amherst, Mass.: Human Resource Development Press, 1993.

Egan, G. *The Skilled Helper: A Systematic Approach to Effective Helping* (3rd ed.). Pacific Grove, Calif.: Brooks/Cole, 1986.

Gabarro, J. J. "Retrospective Commentary." In C. R. Rogers and F. J. Roethlisberger, "Barriers and Gateways to Communication." *Harvard Business Review,* Nov.–Dec. 1991, *69*(6), 105–111.

Gendlin, E. T. "The Client's Client: The Edge of Awareness." In R. F. Levant and J. M. Shlien (eds.), *Client-Centered Therapy and the Person-Centered Approach: New Directions in Theory, Research, and Practice* (pp. 76–107). New York: Praeger, 1984.

Gordon, T. *Leader Effectiveness Training, L.E.T.: The No-Lose Way to Release the Productive Potential of People.* New York: Wyden Books, 1977.

Kirschenbaum, H. *On Becoming Carl Rogers.* New York: Delacorte Press, 1979.

Kirschenbaum, H., and Henderson, V. L. (eds.). *The Carl Rogers Reader.* Boston: Houghton Mifflin, 1989.

Knowles, M. S. *The Adult Learner: A Neglected Species.* (2nd ed.) Houston: Gulf, 1978.

Kramer, R. "The Birth of Client-Centered Therapy: Carl Rogers, Otto Rank, and 'The Beyond.'" *Journal of Humanistic Psychology,* Fall 1995, *35*(4), 54–110.

Levant, R. F., and Shlien, J. M. *Client-Centered Therapy and the Person-Centered Approach: New Directions in Theory, Research, and Practice.* New York: Praeger, 1984.

Rogers, C. R. *Counseling and Psychotherapy: New Concepts in Practice.* Boston: Houghton Mifflin, 1942.

Rogers, C. R. "Some Implications of Client-Centered Counseling for College Personnel Work." *Educational and Psychological Measurement,* 1948, *8,* 540–549.

Rogers, C. R. *Client-Centered Therapy: Its Current Practice, Implications, and Theory.* Boston: Houghton Mifflin, 1951.

Rogers, C. R. "A Theory of Therapy, Personality, and Interpersonal Relationships, as Developed in the Client Centered Framework." In S. Koch (ed.), *Psychology: A Study of a Science* (Vol. 3, pp. 184–256). New York: McGraw-Hill, 1959.

Rogers, C. R. *On Becoming a Person: A Therapist's View of Psychotherapy.* Boston: Houghton Mifflin, 1961.

Rogers, C. R. "My Personal Growth." In A. Burton (ed.), *Twelve Therapists: How They Live and Actualize Themselves.* San Francisco: Jossey-Bass, 1972. (Originally published 1967.)

Rogers, C. R. *Carl Rogers on Personal Power.* New York: Delacorte Press, 1977.

Rogers, C. R. *A Way of Being.* Boston: Houghton Mifflin, 1980.

Rogers, C. R. *Freedom to Learn for the 80's.* Columbus, Ohio: Charles E. Merrill, 1983.

Rogers, C. R. "The Interpersonal Relationship in the Facilitation of Learning." In H. Kirschenbaum and V. L. Henderson (eds.), *The Carl Rogers Reader.* Boston: Houghton Mifflin, 1989a. (Originally published 1967.)

Rogers, C. R. "The Politics of Education." In H. Kirschenbaum and V. L. Henderson (eds.), *The Carl Rogers Reader.* Boston: Houghton Mifflin, 1989b. (Originally published 1977.)

Rogers, C. R. "The Rust Workshop." In H. Kirschenbaum and V. L. Henderson (eds.), *The Carl Rogers Reader.* Boston: Houghton Mifflin, 1989c. (Originally published 1986.)

Rogers, C. R. "A Note on the Nature of Man." In H. Kirschenbaum and V. L. Henderson (eds.), *The Carl Rogers Reader.* Boston: Houghton Mifflin, 1989d. (Originally published 1957.)

Rogers, C. R., and Roethlisberger, F. J. "Barriers and Gateways to Communication." *Harvard Business Review,* Nov–Dec. 1991, *69*(6), 105–111. (Originally published 1952.)

Rogers, C. R., and Sanford, R. C. "Client-Centered Psychotherapy." In H. I. Kaplan and B. J. Sadock (eds.), *Comprehensive Textbook of Psychiatry* (Vol. 4, pp. 1374–1388). Baltimore: Williams & Wilkins, 1984.

Solomon, L. N. "Carl Rogers's Efforts for World Peace." *Person-Centered Review,* 1990, *5*(1), 39–56.

Wexler, D. A. "A Cognitive Theory of Experiencing, Self-Actualization, and Therapeutic Process." In D. A. Wexler and L. N. Rice (eds.), *Innovations in Client-Centered Therapy.* New York: Wiley, 1974.

Part Three

The Individual and the Environment

External Points of Influence

Chapter Six

B. F. Skinner

The Influence of Environment on Behavior

Why B. F. Skinner? An Overview of Organizational Applications

The bottom line for organizations is performance, and Skinner's ideas are a direct route to that end. Skinner is characterized as a radical behaviorist. His theories ignore internal psychic processes and focus on the relationship of behavior to the external environment. For Skinner, behavior is a result of its consequences. This means that the perceived consequences of a behavior determine the degree to which that behavior is likely to reoccur. There is ample documentation that, within the narrow definition Skinner prescribes, his methods are highly effective.

Skinner's Theory as an Organizational Image or Metaphor

Skinner's theory is the least complex in this volume. He states that behavior is determined by its consequences. His work does not produce the rich poetic allusions of a more complex theory like Jung's. Rather, Skinner's straightforward model engenders the simple but useful image or metaphor of a machine or organism that reinforces behavior. This image is a powerful reminder to focus upon the organization's important but often hidden messages of reinforcement.

Skinner's Theory as a Point of Influence for Dealing with Conflict

Unlike other theories in this volume that focus upon the feelings or the inner experience of individuals in conflict, Skinner's theory focuses upon the external conditions that elicit conflict. In many conflict situations, both parties view the situation in win-lose terms, believing that the inevitable result of someone else's gain is their loss. Skinner's theory serves as a framework for identifying conditions in which all parties' interests can be supported (reinforced). Skinner's theory thus deals with conflict by defining the conditions in which it can be prevented.

Skinner's Theory as a Point of Influence for Dealing with Psychological Growth

Skinner defines growth in terms of changes in behavior and treats concepts such as "inner desire" as mental fictions. In highlighting the experience of the individual organism (Fallon, 1992, p. 1436), Skinner encourages personal awareness by establishing procedures for individuals to monitor their own behavior. For example, for a specified time, an individual would keep accurate track, without judgment, of the number of times that he or she smoked a cigarette, ate candy, spent money, or whatever happened to be the specific behavior he or she wished to change. This encourages personal awareness, which is an important aspect of psychological growth. Skinner also strongly rejects punishment as a means of influencing behavior; this position is also consistent with a humanistic process of personal growth.

Skinner's Theory as a Point of Influence for Dealing with the Dilemmas of Joining

Skinnerian methodology excels in providing relevant goals and feedback for an individual or group performing a task. To the extent that one views an organization as a collection of individuals or groups performing a task, Skinner's framework can help individuals to perform their tasks more effectively and with more satisfaction. In this context Skinner's theory can be applied to the overall relationship of the individual to the organization.

Skinner's Theory as a Basis for Other Relevant Theories

Skinner is often described as a "radical behaviorist," meaning that he chooses to focus on reinforcement from the environment alone as a way of understanding human behavior. Given the fixed nature of this theory, we are unlikely to find Skinner supporting variations in it. Others such as Albert Bandura, however, have found Skinner's pure version of behaviorism as a useful ingredient in creating their own theory. Bandura combines Skinner's view of behavior with his own focus on modeling or imitation to develop his theory of the social origins of behavior. Albert Ellis and Aaron Beck have combined Skinner's behavioral emphasis with their own cognitive view to develop a cognitive behavioral theory.

Limitations of Skinner's Theory for Use in Organizations

Skinner's theory is so clearly defined that its limitations also lead to corresponding strengths. For example, the theory is often criticized as being narrow. It is hard to use the theory to understand sweeping transformations in organizational culture or links to spirituality or higher purpose. However, this narrow focus on reinforcement of specific behavior is a useful supplement to other, more sweeping, theories. Similarly, Skinner's exclusive focus on the measurable aspects of behavior is not appealing to practitioners who are value-oriented or concerned with spirituality, but this same focus appeals to scientist and engineer clients who are more accustomed to dealing only with what can be observed and counted.

Skinner's ideas have also been associated with electric shock, Fascism, totalitarianism, and other forms of manipulation and aversive control. Although it is lacking in foundation, this association is still widespread, and in using Skinner's theories practitioners might have to take steps to clarify their intentions (Todd and Morris, 1992, p. 1444; Dinsmoor, 1992).

How Skinner Developed His Theory

Burrhus Frederic Skinner was born in Susquehanna, Pennsylvania, in 1904. In his three-volume autobiography he characteristically emphasizes the tangible physical aspects of his early years. It was not a coincidence that the first volume of that autobiography was entitled *The Particulars of My Life* (Skinner, 1976a). He notes that his mother, a local beauty with a strong will and clear values, set high standards for the family. His father, an attorney, was a strict but loving parent. Throughout his life, Skinner maintained that the small-town environment shaped his life and offered the best explanation for his contribution to behavioral science. He blossomed academically under the personal attention of his teachers in small classes and later credited this experience with giving him the idea for his teaching machines. His outside environment was even more influential. The small town offered a closeness to nature that rewarded and reinforced him every time he turned over a stone or watched a wild animal.

Skinner also loved to build machines and gadgets, a quality that stayed with him for life. He cites an early incident in which his strong-willed mother embarked on a campaign to get him to hang up his pajamas. Each morning at breakfast she called him back to his room to hang them up. Finally, young Skinner built a device that displayed a sign saying "Hang Up Your Pajamas." When the pajamas were hung on a connecting hook, the sign disappeared (an early example of what Skinner later termed *negative reinforcement*).

Skinner attended Hamilton College and, after encouragement from the poet Robert Frost, decided to embark on a literary career. But after a disappointing stint in Greenwich Village and a year at home, he decided, as he expressed it in his own words, that he had "nothing to say." He then concluded that if he could not understand humans and life through literature, he would attempt to do so scientifically; thus he enrolled in a doctoral program at Harvard University. His early literary experience, however, never left him. He is the only major psychologist to have written a popular Utopian novel, *Walden Two* ([1948] 1976b), and his other works frequently contain literary and philosophical examples. At Harvard, Skinner specialized in animal and physiological psychology, and the path was set for the development of his ideas. Three earlier psychologists formed the basis for his ideas: E. M. Thorndike, Ivan Pavlov, and John Watson.

Thorndike attempted to answer the question of whether animals "thought" in the same way as humans. His experiments revealed that learning for animals started with random behavior and that behavior with a satisfactory outcome tended to be repeated. Thorndike called this the "law of effect." This was his way of explaining what others might view as the inner psychic process of thinking. Skinner credited Thorndike with pointing the way toward his own focus on the consequences of behavior (Kazdin, 1978).

Pavlov (1849–1936), a Russian psychologist, identified the process of *respondent conditioning*. Respondent conditioning refers to the process in which the organism (human or animal) associates a behavioral response with a stimulus, thereby allowing an individual who can produce a stimulus to also produce the behavior. The classic experiment in which Pavlov demonstrated this involved a hungry dog that salivated when presented with food. Pavlov accompanied the food with the ringing of a bell, and before long the dog was conditioned to salivate at the mere ringing of the bell, without receiving any food (Kazdin, 1978, p. 56).

The same principle was illustrated in a popular film of the 1970s, *A Clockwork Orange,* in which adolescents with a propensity for violence were conditioned to associate violent behavior with extreme nausea. This conditioning reduced their desire for violence. Skinner's ideas were gaining considerable popularity at the time of the film's release, and his theories were often associated with Pavlov's experiment and the frightening way it was applied in the film. Neither Pavlov's salivating dog nor the unfortunate adolescents in *A Clockwork Orange* were involved in an application of Skinner's theory, but this distinction was not widely known, and in the popular mind Skinner's ideas became associated with equating humans to animals and authoritarian control of human behavior.

Skinner also built upon the work of John B. Watson (1878–1958), who published his main works in the early twentieth century. Watson applied Pavlov's respondent conditioning to humans, and from that experience he developed the philosophy of behaviorism (Hilgard, 1956, pp. 48–53). By today's standards, and perhaps even by the standards of the 1920s, Watson was amazingly insensitive to the ethics and values involved in dealing with human subjects. The most dramatic example of this is an experiment in which he conditioned an infant to fear a white rat by pairing the presence of the rat with a loud noise that the infant was afraid of. The infant soon became afraid of the white rat, establishing the fact that human emotional reactions could be controlled. The later impact on the infant is not known, but Watson's approach helped to link behaviorism in the public mind with the callous treatment of human subjects.

Although they are accurate as far as they go, Pavlov's and Watson's theories have limited application. Only a small part of our behavior is the result of antecedents. Respondent conditioning was too thin a reed to support the full-blown philosophy of science that Watson espoused. If behavior was to be the basis for a science, a more fully developed theory would have to be created, and this was Skinner's major contribution: the concept of operant conditioning.

This concept was Skinner's lifework. He conducted basic research to examine and verify it and elaborated on the philosophy of science on which his work was based. He applied his findings to education and to the development of a pioneering teaching machine and achieved both fame and notoriety with *Walden Two*. Skinner also applied these same principles to the latter part of his life, in *Enjoy Old Age* (Skinner and Vaughan, 1983). He remained productive to the end and died of leukemia in 1990.

Skinner's Point of Influence and Theory of Behavior

Skinner's point of influence is the human tendency to repeat a behavior the organism experiences as being *reinforced* by the environment. His unique contribution is to look at the influences and

Preview: When to Use Skinner's Point of Influence in the Workplace.

relationships between the environment, the psyche, and behavior. Other theorists trace the chain of causation from the inside out. Something is presumed to happen internally, triggered either by the environment or, more likely, by the psyche itself. From this internal origin, some external behavior occurs. Skinner reverses the process. He starts from the premise that organisms—human and animal—emit behavior. By "emit" he means that behavior just occurs, and he does not try to explain its origin. This behavior is observable and measurable and is the starting point for a scientific study of human activity. Unlike other theorists who focus on the structure and operation of the psyche, Skinner focuses on *behavior* and treats the psyche as a neutral receptacle for the individual's behavioral history. This history is what makes it more or less likely that the behavior will occur again. For Skinner, behavior *operates* on the environment, hence the term *operant behavior* or *operant conditioning* (Skinner, 1953, pp. 59–90). What this behavior does to the environment is what makes it more or less likely that the behavior will occur again.

The following example illustrates the Skinnerian sequence: a manager asks a subordinate for a report, the subordinate turns in the report to the manager, and the manager compliments the subordinate on the report. This transaction represents the three elements in Skinner's analysis of behavior:

Antecedent	Response	Consequence
Manager requests report	Subordinate turns in report	Manager compliments subordinate

The request for the report is an antecedent. It functions as a cue or trigger for the behavior. Antecedents are important but are not Skinner's principal focus. In organizations, antecedents such as job descriptions and statements of goals communicate basic job expectations. Resources, tools, training, instructions, directions, and the actions of other people are all antecedents that prompt behavior. Antecedents provide information, but this cue alone does not always govern whether the behavior will occur. To be effective, antecedents must be paired with consequences. This is especially true in organizations in which requests for behavior or performance can come from many sources, with a wide range of implicit and explicit effects.

Antecedents thus create immediate reactions but will not maintain performance (Daniels, 1989, p. 16). The manager in the previous example might have called upon a wide array of antecedents (requesting, writing memos, making signs, threatening, begging, cajoling, and so on), but his or her effect on behavior would have been limited. The larger implication is that traditional management training overemphasizes antecedents. Managers are trained to plan, set objectives, and otherwise tell people what to do. They are not trained to provide consequences, particularly the positive consequences that Skinner believes influence behavior (Daniels, 1989, p. 17).

Note that this explanation says nothing about the inner psyche of either the manager or the subordinate. Skinner is not saying that the manager and the subordinate do not have feelings about their own inner reactions to this exchange. Skinner would not deny that each of these individuals might have their own internal reactions to this incident. The crucial point is that Skinner views such inner reactions as the *result* of external events, not the *cause*. Skinner thus ignores what he terms *mentalism* or the so-called inner life of humans.

How Operant Conditioning Works in Organizations: The Range of Behavioral Interventions

To illustrate how operant conditioning functions in a wider organizational setting, we will examine the efforts of the safety office in Central States Power, a midwestern public utility:

The crew in the Central States Power generating station worked in an area with a continuous, high noise level. Quite commonly, individuals who had worked ten or more years in such an environment had lost much of their hearing. A standard joke in Central States Power was, "You can always tell a station man, but it won't do any good because he can't hear you." As part of an Occupational Safety and Health Administration campaign against industrial deafness, the company began supplying earplugs and ear mufflers. The program, however, met only limited success. Employees had become used to shouting above the level of the generators, and most of them only wore the safety devices when a supervisor was watching.

The problem and the steps the company took to manage it illustrate a continuum of behavioral principles and strategies.

Simple Reflex Behavior

Simple reflex behavior did not work to prevent long-term hearing loss (Skinner, 1953, p. 47). If the high noise levels had created the sensation of burning, pinching, or some other painful reaction, the employees would have automatically withdrawn. This, however, was not the case. The damage to the employees' hearing was indisputable, but it was painless and took place slowly over years; employees simply got used to it and shouted over the commotion.

Conditioned Reflex Behavior: The Use of Antecedents

The first step the company took was an education and training program about noise-induced deafness. In Skinnerian terms, antecedents were presented that suggested that when individuals entered a high-noise area they should put on earplugs. The program included straightforward information about the effects of exposure to continuous, loud noise. This basically cerebral approach had a limited effect. The use of earplugs went up, but only slightly.

Next, the company posted a number of signs in the areas in which employees should be wearing protective devices. These signs reminded employees to wear the earplugs. In Skinnerian terms, these were *prompts* or cues for the desired behavior. The prompts encouraged employees to initiate some of the desired behavior, but, again, the employees were not using the earplugs to the extent that the company desired.

The next effort was to use a more *generalized antecedent.* The company had an ongoing safety program that utilized cartoon characters who appeared in posters, short videos, and cartoons in the company newspaper. One cartoon character followed the safety procedure and the other did not. The one who followed safe procedures avoided the comical and sometimes unfortunate mishaps that the other character experienced. The series was professionally done and had been well accepted by the power plant staff. At this point the company added the inducement of wearing hearing protection to the other safe practices promoted in the series. The prompts to follow other safe practices, such as wearing goggles and safety shoes, were now *generalized* to hearing devices.

In this campaign the company also made use of *discriminating stimuli* or *antecedents*. Not every hearing device was appropriate for every situation. Noise levels varied, and in some instances it was unsafe for the employees to block their hearing, because it was important for them to hear certain sounds. The company then color-coded the various hearing environments and used the cartoon characters to illustrate the various degrees of hearing protection needed in each environment. The stimulus in the video thus discriminated between the responses that were needed in the different environments. The most effective part of this program was a video that simulated the world of a hearing-impaired person. In this instance the stimulus of not wearing a hearing protection device was combined with the distorted and fragmentary cues to which a hearing-impaired person responded. The confusion and embarrassment that the cartoon character experienced were paired with the behavior of not protecting one's hearing. The clarity and success that the other character experienced were paired with preserving one's hearing by wearing earplugs. In this respect, the company's effort was similar to that of some governments, in which a symbol, such as a flag, an enemy soldier committing atrocities, or a song is paired with a particular type of desired or undesired behavior.

Both of these methods were examples of *conditioning* an antecedent. A poster with the cartoon character who had lost a significant part of his hearing was paired with prompting of the behavior of putting on the protective hearing equipment. This illustrated two of Skinner's principles. The color-coding to signal when to wear a hearing protection device is an example of *a discriminating stimulus*. The pairing with a cartoon character is an example of *conditioning a response*.

These measures persuaded more employees to wear hearing protection devices, but the effect was not sustained. After the training session and the showing of videos, employees put on the devices, but they did not keep wearing them. The company now turned from dealing with *antecedents* to dealing with *consequences*.

Operant Behavior

In operant behavior, a behavior does something to the environment that makes that behavior more or less likely to occur in the future. Since humans can and do control parts of the environment, this can be a powerful point of influence. In this instance, Central States finally found the actions that would bring about the desired behavior on a sustained basis. They moved from controlling the antecedent of the behavior to developing a consequence. Employees in the power plant were given regular hearing checks so that they could receive direct and specific feedback regarding the consequences of wearing or not wearing devices to protect their hearing. All of the previous measures had some effect, but this measure was the most powerful. The use of hearing protection devices finally reached the level the company was seeking. The new measures were particularly successful with the younger employees, who now had immediate evidence of the effect of not protecting their hearing and who also had not lost so much hearing that they felt it was too late to take preventive action.

This power company's experience illustrates Skinner's basic principle, which he eventually applied to entire societies: *the environment reinforces, thereby controlling human behavior, but it is possible for humans to control the environment* (Skinner, [1948] 1976b, pp. v–xvi). This experience also illustrates an important change that takes place when Skinner's ideas are applied to humans. Skinner developed his behavioral principles by working with pigeons and rats. He had to discover what served as a reinforcer through trial and error and observation. The managers of the safety program at the power company could ask the employees what would encourage them to wear earplugs. The application of Skinner's ideas to humans thus includes a degree of involvement and participation that was not possible for Skinner.

When You Want to Influence the Consequences of Behavior

To implement Skinner's principle in an organizational setting, the practitioner needs additional guidelines and methods. We will explore these methods as we examine the experience of a family restaurant attempting to change the behavior of its employees:

> A family restaurant was experiencing a decline in revenue (Johnson and Masotti, 1990). Because the restaurant did not have funds available for an advertising program, the management decided to increase sales per customer

by increasing the sale of high-profit food items such as wine, cocktails, appe-
tizers, and desserts. The first step was to identify the behaviors that would increase such sales. The managers determined that regularly greeting the
customers, smiling, and suggesting various items would increase sales. Such
behavior also increased the tips, which were based on sales. Presumably, this
would be enough inducement for the wait staff, but it was not sufficient to
change their behavior in a consistent manner.

The management had to find other ways to reinforce behavior
that would increase sales so that it would occur on a regular basis.
The management decided on three techniques: *goal setting, feedback,* and *selected reinforcers.*

Goal Setting

Skinner's use of goals is consistent with his practice of avoiding
inner mental concepts. His theory views goals in terms of the individual's past behavioral history rather than her or his "future aspirations," a term that Skinner would describe as "mentalistic."
Instead of saying that an individual behaves because of an inner
belief about the future, we say that the person behaves because of
the consequences that have followed similar behavior in the past.
This is the *law of effect,* or *operant conditioning* (Skinner, 1953, p. 87).
To illustrate the two perspectives, we could say that a waitperson
who asks if a customer is interested in a dessert is "hopeful" of selling that customer a dessert—this Skinner would not do. On the
other hand, in the language of operant conditioning, we could
state that the waitperson who in the past had asked customers
about ordering dessert had found that asking someone if they
wanted to order dessert increased the likelihood that some of them
would say yes.

This version of goal setting has become very important in the
organizational application of Skinner's ideas, and it was an important part of the family restaurant's effort to increase sales of
food items. Goals were set with the wait staff on a group basis, and
an effort was made to make the goals challenging but attainable.
When a waitperson achieved a goal, the goal itself became a reinforcer for the next series of behaviors. This occurred when a supervisor and waitperson agreed on a goal, such as selling dessert,
an appetizer, or drinks to one out of three customers. That goal

was indicated by a dark line on a chart next to the waitperson's name. When the individual met or exceeded that goal, the supervisors praised the accomplishment. The consequence of the behavior was now paired with the praise. The goal now functioned as an *antecedent* or *discriminating stimulus* (Fellner and Sulzer-Azaroff, 1984, p. 35).

The use of a goal as a motivator requires a particular set of methods. These include recording what was done in the past as a baseline, developing goals from that baseline, and then keeping accurate track of how the behavior changed from the baseline. Keeping track of current behavior and comparing it with a baseline leads to the second major method used by the restaurant management: *feedback*.

Feedback

Feedback provides opportunities for two powerful types of reinforcement. When people receive feedback, they may react to it by saying, "I'm doing pretty well" or "This is what I should be doing," or they may hear from a supervisor or employer that they are doing a good job (Daniels, 1989). Feedback thus is the antecedent for a positive reinforcement.

In Skinner's framework, feedback sets the stage for a consequence that can influence the future probability that a behavior will reoccur. Not all feedback, however, has this positive impact. For feedback systems to work, it is important that there be no penalty for reporting negative performance. If a supervisor or a system punishes people for reporting unfavorable data, the likelihood of false reports increases. To guard against this, feedback systems should reward or reinforce the reporting of accurate information whether it is favorable or unfavorable. This was done in the family restaurant. Employees who did not achieve their goal received a positive response for any improvement they had made and encouragement to build on the initial change.

The feedback system in the restaurant also involved mutual goal setting and personal record keeping. Goals were set by the groups on each shift, with minimal direction from the supervisors. The supervisors urged them to set goals that were challenging but attainable. In addition, the restaurant established a program of public written feedback. The staff were grouped by shifts to avoid some of the negative aspects of individual comparisons and competition, but a chart was prepared that demonstrated how each shift met its goals. In this way, feedback became a conditioned reinforcer. Receipt of the feedback by each individual was coupled with praise for progress in meeting the shift's goal; thus the whole feedback process reinforced the desired behavior.

Although the data were publicly posted, each individual also kept track of his or her own record, comparing it to a baseline figure each day. Such self-management systems have been widely used for changing personal habits and behavior patterns in areas such as weight control and budgeting. They have also been effective in work settings as a part of a more comprehensive change strategy.

Other Reinforcers

Skinner's theory does not include a list of reinforcers. He decides on a reinforcer on the basis of what he calls *functional analysis*. A particular act is not assumed to have a uniform impact in every circumstance, and particular reinforcements can function in different ways. For example, giving someone prominent attention for performing in a specific way can *function* to encourage or discourage that behavior. Attention may be experienced positively or it may be experienced as an embarrassment. Skinner, working with animals, relied on observation to determine how a particular action functioned to reinforce behavior. If the behavior increased in frequency after the consequence, it was a reinforcer. If it did not increase, the action was not a reinforcer. It is possible to observe humans the same way, but managers can also involve their employees in a way that Skinner could not do with his pigeons. Humans can be asked how they would experience a particular action. This was done in the restaurant, and a variety of relatively low-cost benefits, such as free games in a nearby bowling alley, were given to wait staff who achieved their goal.

Those who apply Skinner's principles in management situations also make the distinction between rewards and reinforcement. Rewards are given for one-time behavior; reinforcements are given for behavior that we wish to occur again. For example, a reward might be given to an employee who displayed unusual personal bravery in foiling a holdup. A reinforcement would be given to a waitperson who exceeded the goal in selling desserts.

Negative Reinforcement

Negative feedback means the removal of something that was considered aversive (Skinner, 1953, p. 73). For example, factory workers who dislike having to punch time clocks would no longer be required to do this if their attendance record reached a certain point. The waitpersons in the family restaurant were all under twenty-five years of age and disliked having to work holiday weekends. As a reinforcement (reward), a waitperson no longer had to work on three-day holidays such as the July Fourth weekend. Working these holiday shifts was considered to be aversive, or punishment, and the *removal* of the punishment was thus a negative reinforcement. Negative reinforcement can be very effective. In this instance, so many individuals met or exceeded their goals that no staff were available for the holiday weekends.

Several behavioral techniques exist that the restaurant management could have used but did not.

Punishment

In Skinnerian theory, punishment is not an effective way to influence behavior. Punishment reinforces the punisher (Skinner, 1953, pp. 190–191). The individual being punished is not predictable; Skinner cites this unpredictability rather than a moral stance as a reason for avoiding punishment. Except for achieving very short-term goals, punishment usually does not work. Skinner notes that punishment encourages all sorts of avoidance or retaliatory behavior, including absenteeism, tardiness, forgetting, mistakes, destruction of property, and all manner of mischief. The individual being punished attempts to avoid the situation and thus does not necessarily behave in the way the punisher is attempting to encourage. If, for example, a child is punished for teasing a younger sibling, the child could stop teasing the sibling, tease the sibling more in defiance, tease the sibling in a less visible way, or even avoid situations in which the sibling or other members of the family are present.

Ironically, it is the *punisher* who is reinforced to punish again. If, for example, a waitperson in the family restaurant was punished or fined for not selling sufficient amounts of the targeted items, we might expect that person to try to avoid such a situation in the future. This could mean selling more desserts, but it could also mean resigning, showing up late, trying to manipulate the supervisor or a host, or exhibiting other nonproductive behaviors. In contrast, the supervisor who is doing the punishing would be reinforced, because every punishment would have some immediate and visible impact on the other person's behavior.

Punishment, like positive reinforcement, is also in the eyes of the beholder. If a salesperson meets or exceeds a quota and then is given public congratulations, what management perceives as an incentive may be experienced by the salesperson as embarrassment. Instead of categorizing actions as inherently punishing or rewarding, Skinner suggests that we delay the decision until we see the consequences of the action.

Extinction

In Skinnerian theory, the way to get rid of a behavior is to stop reinforcing it (Skinner, 1953, pp. 69–72). Although this may seem to be simplistic, it has very practical implications. The Skinnerian framework helps us to become aware of the times when we are unknowingly or inadvertently reinforcing behavior we are trying to get rid of. In his autobiography, Skinner quotes Henry Kissinger, who described a telling incident in which President Richard Nixon failed to use extinction. Nixon had a dog that frequently chewed the carpet. When it did so, Nixon threw the dog a biscuit. One evening, when this happened, Kissinger said, "'Mr. President, you have just taught your dog to chew carpets'" (Skinner, 1983, p. 152).

The most effective strategy for eliminating behavior, when it is difficult to continue to ignore it, is to reinforce an incompatible behavior. This will be discussed in the following section.

Shaping

Skinner and his followers achieved impressive results with animals, and later with children and retarded adults, dealing with behavior that at some point seemed far beyond the capacity of the individuals involved. The most dramatic examples of these results utilized the process of *shaping*. In shaping, individuals are reinforced for successive small steps toward a larger goal (Skinner, 1953, pp. 91–98). Shaping is used to help individuals perform a task that they have not been able to accomplish or believe that they cannot perform. An example in organizational work could be to reinforce successive small steps toward assertive behavior so that individuals eventually find themselves far more assertive than they could have imagined. The desired changes in the wait staff's behavior did not involve the performance of new or difficult tasks; they were asked to behave in a way that was within their capabilities. For this reason, shaping was not used.

When You Need to Fine-Tune Consequences: Schedules of Reinforcement

Reinforcement does not need to be offered each and every time a behavior occurs. The strategies for repeating reinforcements are called schedules of reinforcement. Schedules of reinforcement vary in two basic ways: by ratio and by interval. *Ratio* refers to the number of performances required before reinforcement. This number can be fixed, as in offering one bonus for each sale, or it can be variable, as in offering one bonus for a changing number of sales. *Interval* refers to the amount of time between reinforcements. Bonuses can be given each month or they can be variable, coming at various times of the year.

Not all schedules of reinforcement have the same impact. Table 6.1, constructed from Daniels's *Performance Management*, summarizes the basic characteristics of each strategy. This table reveals several useful generalizations about schedules of reinforcement. Continuous ratio reinforcement is effective while it is taking place, but if the reinforcement ceases, the behavior also extinguishes rapidly. This means that continuous reinforcement is most useful for *establishing* a behavior; however, once the behavior is established, it is a good idea to gradually replace it with intermittent reinforcement.

For example, vending machines are usually set up on the basis of continuous reinforcement: put in the coins and you receive a soft drink. However, once a vending machine ceases to work, perhaps even after the first failure to deliver a soft drink, individuals stop putting in coins. In contrast, a gambling machine, which is set up on the basis of intermittent reinforcement (sometimes you win and sometimes you don't), continues to evoke behavior long after it stops the reinforcement (paying off). Intermittent reinforcement can thus be very powerful. For example, one organization utilized the uncertainty generated by a variable ratio as a means to cut

Table 6.1. Summary of Reinforcement Schedules.

Schedule	Description	Example	What It Does to Performance	What It Does During Extinction	When to Use It
Fixed Ratio	Fixed no. of responses must occur before R	Piece rate or commission work	High and steady response	Performance weakens rapidly if R withheld	If you need high rates
Fixed Ratio 1:1	R for every response		High and steady performance if R maintained	Weakens rapidly if R is lowered	New employees or new skills
Variable Ratio	Varying or random responses before R	Gambling	A lot of performance for minimal R	Responds longer than fixed ratio	If need high performance, tolerance for delays in R
Fixed Interval	Fixed amount of time must pass before each R	Salary, end-of-month quotas	Uneven impact, high before R, drops after R	Responses gradually fade	If R not possible for all performance; if you need medium performance
Variable Interval	R after varying or random performance	Pop quizzes, surprise bonuses	Low-to-moderate but consistent performance	Takes longest to extinguish	Best for stable performance over a long period

Note: R = reinforcement.

Source: Adapted from Daniels, 1989, pp. 95–107.

down on absenteeism. It did so by awarding a playing card to each employee with a month of no absences. At the end of five months, the employee with the highest poker hand won a bonus. A caution in using such strategies is that variable ratios or intervals cannot be changed arbitrarily. Change should include employee involvement or some clear rules (like the poker hand) that make sense to the employees. The gambling phenomenon is not the answer to every problem. If every performance cannot be reinforced, then fixed-interval reinforcement, such as a salary, does produce steady but moderate performance.

The final generalization is that the fixed-ratio schedule produces a letdown in behavior immediately after the payoff. An illustration of this phenomenon is the behavior of employees working on the piecework system. When they receive a reward or reinforcement, say, after every fifteen items, they usually experience a letdown in effort. In contrast, a variable ratio of reinforcement approximates the conditions of the real world, creating excitement and enthusiasm. Workers do not know when a reinforcement will appear (although they are certain that it will), so effort is more likely to be maintained at a steady rate.

When You Want to Combine Tools of Reinforcement

Positive reinforcement, negative reinforcement, punishment, and extinction can be used separately, but certain ways of combining them increase their effectiveness.

Replacement and Positive Reinforcement

Extinction is the basic method used to end a behavior, but it can sometimes be very slow and hard to sustain. The example of a young child who misbehaves in order to gain attention dramatically illustrates this point. The parent attempts to follow Skinner's advice and stop the behavior by ignoring it (extinction). The parent is successful in ignoring the child for a while, but finally her or his patience wears thin and the parent becomes angry, giving the child a good deal of notice and thus reinforcing the attention-getting behavior and negating the efforts toward extinction. In Skinner's terms, this process sets up a schedule of variable reinforcement, which will then be even harder to extinguish.

One alternative to this discouraging sequence is to positively reinforce incompatible behavior. Some other behavior is identified, such as playing with a toy or game, and this behavior is positively reinforced. Parents, of course, do this instinctively, but they often do not think of this strategy when dealing with behavioral problems in other settings. An example of this strategy in organizations would be to ignore tardy behavior but positively reinforce individuals who are consistently on time. For example, in the family restaurant, if the problem was that the wait staff was spending too much time kibitzing in the kitchen, rather than punishing the kibitzers the management might have identified a counterbehavior they wished to reinforce. This could be to have the staff check with each customer midway through the meal.

Extinction and Positive Reinforcement

If it is difficult to identify behavior that is clearly incompatible, one alternative would be to simultaneously ignore (extinguish) the undesirable behavior and reinforce behavior that could replace it. This combination can be used as a means of what is commonly referred to as *empowerment*. If, for example, a regional sales manager had a salesperson who exhibited a good deal of dependent behavior, asking permission for things that required no permission, giving detailed reports, and seeking approval for minor items, the sales manager could ignore that behavior but praise and otherwise pay a good deal of attention to any fragment of behavior that exhibited self-direction, assertiveness, or risk taking.

Punishment and Positive Reinforcement

Within the strict Skinnerian framework, punishment is strongly discouraged. Punishment can have an immediate, if short-lived, influence on behavior. Sometimes, as when individuals are committing dangerous acts, the short-term benefits outweigh the long-term costs. In these cases it is useful to combine punishment with positive reinforcement of incompatible behavior. For example, construction workers could be fined for not wearing a hard hat in unsafe areas and at the same time encouraged to decorate their own hat with symbols that are significant for them, such as the logos of professional athletic teams.

When You Need a Formula for Changing Individual, Group, or Unit Behavior

Skinner's ideas have been applied at both the organizational and individual levels. Both applications follow the pattern of:

1. Identifying a behavior
2. Establishing a baseline or frequency at which the behavior occurs without intervention
3. Analyzing the context (antecedent and consequences) in which that behavior occurs
4. Selecting some antecedent or consequences to make that behavior occur more or less frequently

Two versions of this sequence are currently widely used in organizations. Luthans and Kreitner (1985, pp. 77–82) illustrate the first, which is a basic model for applying the theory in entire units or organizations. In this model a manager or consultant typically is attempting to change a behavior, such as absenteeism, for a number of employees. The second version comes from *Putting the One Minute Manager to Work* (Blanchard and Lorber, 1984), which takes a more personal and participative approach. Blanchard and Lorber's approach includes paying attention to feelings, which is not included in strict Skinnerian strategy. Table 6.2 illustrates both versions.

Changing Organizational Behavior

Lee Frederiksen (1982) identified several applications at the group and organizational levels.

Production Task Completion

Production task completion includes using performance feedback and supervisor praise to improve factory workers' output (Chandler, 1977; Emmert, 1978); financial incentives to increase planting of seedlings in the forest products industry (Yukl and Latham, 1975; Yukl, Latham, and Pursell, 1976); social praise and mental reinforcement to improve task completion in human service settings (Montegar, Reid, Madsen, and Ewell, 1977; Hollander and Plutchik, 1972; Pommer and Streedbeck, 1974); and the impact of

Table 6.2. Two Frameworks for Changing Individual Behavior.

Group or Unit Approach Luthans and Kreitner The Organizational Behavior Model	Individual Approach Blanchard and Lorber The PRICE Model
1. *Identify performance-related behavioral events.* Such behaviors must be observable, countable, and clearly related to performance. They should be considered in the context of variables such as ability, training, and performance standards, which are beyond the control of the employee.	1. *Pinpoint.* Define key performance areas in terms of observable, measurable behavior.
2. *Measure the frequency of the behavior.* This establishes a graphic baseline as a basis for later comparison; it is best to figure out existing data so that measurement is unobtrusive. In establishing a baseline, you may discover that a problem is smaller or larger than was believed.	2. *Record.* Measure the frequency of that behavior at the current time, preferably on a graph.
3. *Identify existing contingencies through functional analysis.* Notice what happens before and after the behavior; it is possible to design a strategy to change the behavior.	3. *Involve.* Involve the employee in a supportive way. Discuss the results on the graph, soliciting antecedents and consequences that would change the frequency of the behavior in the desired fashion. The goal should be moderately difficult but attainable.
4. *Use intervention strategies.* While measurement continues, select from positive and negative reinforcement, extinction, punishment, or a combination of these strategies a way of altering behavior by altering contingencies.	4. *Coach.* Observe behavior and give feedback on results. Find out how the individual would like to receive feedback and be helped; negotiate a process that suits both of your needs. Approach difficult goals as a series of small steps (shaping) and encourage the individual to record his or her own performance.
5. *Evaluate.* In addition to charting changes in behavior, consider reactions, changes in job performance, and the degree to which the manager and/or employees understand and can generalize the change.	5. *Evaluate.* Redirect before reprimanding; consequences can be jointly or unilaterally agreed upon. In neither case should you manage the consequences. Gradually turn more and more control over to the individual.

Note: Adapted from Blanchard and Lorber, 1984, p. 84.

performance posting for individuals performing cleaning tasks (Anderson, Crowell, Hantula, and Siroky, 1988).

Absenteeism and Tardiness

Being present on time is the kind of discrete behavior that is well suited for Skinnerian application. A number of creative applications of Skinnerian theory have been used to accomplish this goal. The simplest application has been that of small monetary bonuses (Hermann and others, 1973). Pedalino and Gamboa (1974) applied the notion of schedules of reinforcement in a lottery incentive system to increase attendance. Kempen and Hall (1977) combined disciplinary action for excessive absences with a creative use of negative reinforcement. Workers who compiled a good attendance record were freed from the aversive experience of punching the time clock. Deluga and Andrews (1985) demonstrated that operant learning principles could be used to reduce dysfunctional behaviors in a clerical training program.

Sales Training

Improving the effectiveness of salespeople is also a natural area for the application of Skinner's ideas. Salespeople become part of the environment of their prospective customers, and they influence their customers' behavior accordingly. Sales work involves similar behavior in a succession of settings. Skinnerian principles used in sales training can help salespeople focus on specific targeted behavior, such as approaching customers, greeting them, being courteous under adverse conditions, suggesting a purchase, and closing the sale. In addition, since salespeople are often compensated on a commission basis, the research on schedules of reinforcement is relevant to developing incentive systems for them (Mirman, 1982; Luthans, Paul and Taylor, 1985; Ralis and O'Brien, 1986).

Changing Individual Behavior Through the One Minute Manager, Teaching Machines, and Social Learning

The One Minute Manager

Two books in the One Minute Manager series, *The One Minute Manager* and *Putting the One Minute Manager to Work*, illustrate how to use Skinnerian reinforcement, along with a dash of Rogerian acceptance, to encourage new behavior. *The One Minute Manager* (Blanchard and Johnson, 1982) applied Skinner's ideas (shown in italics) to the day-to-day activities of managers working with individual employees. This application centered on three activities, *one-minute goals, one-minute praising,* and *one-minute reprimands.*

One-Minute Goals. In Skinnerian terms, frequent feedback on performance is a powerful reinforcer, but it is impossible to have such feedback without simple, precise, and frequently consulted goals. One-minute goals are brief statements (fewer than 250 words) in behavioral terms on single sheets of paper that can be frequently read and matched with performance (p. 44).

One-Minute Praising. Skinner emphasizes positive reinforcement as the single best way to increase the likelihood of a behavior reoccurring. Skinner also identifies shaping as an effective way to teach new or difficult tasks. The emphasis on feelings is a Rogerian addition. One-minute praising includes specific comments about good performance. They occur close to the event and are followed by a statement of how the speaker feels about the behavior, a moment of silence for the feeling to sink in, encouragement to do more of the same, and, if appropriate, a handshake or touch. The slogan "Catch them doing something right" is a lively and compelling way to remind managers of the importance of positive reinforcement (p. 44).

One-Minute Reprimands. Skinner recommends immediacy in any method of behavioral change. Carl Rogers emphasizes the feeling aspect of all communications, including reprimands, and the importance of separating behavior from one's overall reaction to an individual. The one-minute reprimand involves telling someone immediately and clearly what she or he did wrong. This is followed by sharing one's feelings and allowing a pause for the feelings to sink in. The final step is affirming that it is the behavior rather than the person that is causing the reprimand. The goal is to state the reprimand in such a way that when the discussion is finished, the matter is resolved, with a minimum chance for lingering feelings of resentment or guilt (p. 59).

In *Putting the One Minute Manager to Work,* Blanchard and Lorber (1984) present their version of the full-blown Skinnerian formula (the PRICE model in Table 6.2) for measuring and changing behavior.

Programmed Learning

Organizational change usually also involves a need for new skills. Learning such skills can be difficult for adults who are long removed from the classroom environment. In the early 1950s, Skinner developed a teaching machine that has proved very effective for adult learners. Skinner's teaching machine presents small segments of material of increasing difficulty followed by a question or application. If the learner offers the correct answer, the machine reinforces the answer with a positive comment and the pleasure and challenge of moving on to the next segment. If the learner offers an incorrect answer, the machine does not punish but offers the correct information and encourages the individual to try again. The machine is based on the principles of operant conditioning in that the individual's answer operates on the environment (the machine), which presents a consequence (praise or correction) that makes the desired behavior (a correct answer) more likely to occur in the future.

Programmed learning and teaching machines are now widely used in industry for training in specific skills, such as basic electronics, statistics, sales procedures, office procedures, and product knowledge (Babb and Kopp, 1978). Using the principles of operant conditioning, teaching machines allow the learner to progress at his or her own pace in remote locations without an instructor or trainer. Skinner's early machines operated on a mechanical basis with keypunch cards or disks. Computer-assisted learning, which adds the power of the computer to Skinner's original principles of behavior, allows the teaching machine to teach more than basic skills and can be more interactive with the learner, altering and improving the instruction based on the student's response (Poppen and Poppen, 1988).

Social Skills

Skinner's theory can also be used to train individuals in social skills, but to do so it has been necessary to combine Skinner's approach with that of another theorist: Albert Bandura (1963). Social skills training for managers includes teaching how to conduct counseling, selection, and appraisal interviews and the varied skills involved in negotiation, supervision, and leadership. For effective training in this area, Bandura expanded Skinner's foundation of learning through operant behavior to include learning through vicarious processes, covert cognitive processes (modeling), and the self-control of the individual in producing her or his own consequences (Luthans and Kreitner, 1985, p. 33). Social skills training combines role playing, modeling of effective behavior, and practice, followed by feedback and reinforcement. It departs from a straight Skinnerian approach in that it acknowledges that the individual learns by observing, vicariously experiencing, and then cognitively digesting the behavior of others. It is Skinnerian in that the base of learning is behavior rather than cognitive understanding and that learning is promoted through feedback and other reinforcements.

Conclusion

Skinner's theory provides a useful, specialized tool for the organizational practitioner. In situations in which a specific behavior is identified or the practitioner can coach the client to identify a specific behavioral objective, Skinner's operant conditioning is the best means to ensure that this behavior is likely to reoccur. It is also useful to use a prompt such as "Think behaviorally" and to turn fuzzy goals such as "a change in attitudes" to behavioral specifics such as "thanking each customer."

The narrow and focused nature of Skinner's theory also helps it to serve as a part of the three broad psychological tasks of *joining* an organization, *growing psychologically,* and dealing with *conflict.* In each instance, no aspect of the theory comprehensively addresses the full psychological task; however, understanding how to encourage specific behaviors helps a practitioner to work with all three tasks. Encouraging task satisfaction is an important aspect of joining or becoming a part of an organization; finding an objective way for all parties to a conflict to gain satisfaction and achieve their goals is one way to deal with conflict; and the self-observation and awareness that are part of behavioral change comprise an important aspect of psychological growth.

Skinner's theory lacks the rich complexity and spiritual aspects of Carl Jung's theory. It also lacks the overtones of personal warmth of Carl Rogers's theory. It is straightforward and has a somewhat mechanical connotation. For this reason it might appeal more to scientist, engineer, and manager clients than practitioners who are oriented toward feelings or spirituality, and it therefore should be a part of each practitioner's theoretical tools.

Annotated Bibliography
Original Sources: Readable Skinner

Skinner, B. F. *Beyond Freedom and Dignity*. New York: Knopf, 1971.
This book is a good exposition of Skinner's views; it is very readable and is written in a persuasive style.

Skinner, B. F. *The Particulars of My Life*. New York: Knopf, 1976.
Skinner, B. F. *Shaping of a Behaviorist: Part Two of an Autobiography*. New York: Knopf, 1979.
Skinner, B. F. *A Matter of Consequences: Part Three of an Autobiography*. New York: Knopf, 1983.
Skinner's three-volume autobiography is as specific as Jung's is spiritual. Skinner gave the public appearance of being relatively reserved but he was quite open and surprisingly frank about his life, both personally and professionally. Each of the three volumes can be read independently.

Skinner, B. F. *Walden Two*. New York: Macmillan, 1976. (Originally published 1948.)
This is a Utopian novel in which the characters represent Skinner's views and the opposite views regarding the cause of or motivation for human behavior. It presents a view of what the world might look like if it were run on Skinnerian principles and includes a 1976 essay by Skinner containing his thoughts twenty-eight years later.

Secondary Sources: Books About Skinner and His Theories

Nye, R. *What is B. F. Skinner Really Saying?* Englewood Cliffs, N.J.: Prentice Hall, 1979.
This book contains an excellent and convincing exposition of Skinner's ideas.

Organizational Applications

Blanchard, K., and Johnson, S. *The One Minute Manager*. New York: William Morrow, 1982.
Blanchard, K., and Lorber, R. *Putting the One Minute Manager to Work*. New York: William Morrow, 1984.
These two books, written in the style of children's books, were best-sellers about management in the early 1980s. They are based mostly on Skinner's ideas but converted the terminology into everyday language.

Daniels, A. *Performance Management: Improving Quality and Productivity Through Positive Reinforcement*. (3rd ed.) Tucker, Ga.: Performance Management Publications, 1989.

This is an excellent application of Skinner's ideas, with a useful "ABC" framework for analyzing and then intervening in behavioral problems.

Frederiksen, L. "Organization Behavior Management: An Overview." In L. Frederiksen (ed.), *Handbook of Organizational Behavior Management*. New York: Wiley, 1982.
This is a comprehensive review of the application of Skinner's ideas in organizations to that date. The articles cover a wide variety of specific applications.

Luthans, F., and Kreitner, R. *Organization Behavior Modification and Beyond.* Glenview, Ill.: Scott, Foresman, 1985.
This small text outlines Skinnerian applications in organizations. "Beyond" refers to a useful last chapter applying Albert Bandura's theory of social modeling to work in organizations.

Bibliography

Anderson, D. C., Crowell, C. R., Hantula, D. A., and Siroky, L. M. "Task Clarification and Individual Performance Posting for Improving Cleaning in a Student-Managed University Bar." *Journal of Organizational Behavior Management,* 1988, *9*(2), 73–90.

Babb, H. W., and Kopp, D. G. "Applications of Behavior Modification in Organizations: A Review and Critique." *Academy of Management Review,* 1978, *3,* 281–292.

Bandura, A. "Behavior Theory and Identificatory Learning." *American Journal of Orthopsychiatry,* 1963, *33,* 591–601.

Blanchard, K., and Johnson, S. *The One Minute Manager.* New York: William Morrow, 1982.

Blanchard, K., and Lorber, R. *Putting the One Minute Manager to Work.* New York: William Morrow, 1984.

Bolton, R. *People Skills: How to Assert Yourself, Listen to Others, and Resolve Conflicts.* New York: Simon & Schuster, 1979.

Chandler, A. B. "Decreasing Negative Comments and Increasing Performance of a Shift Supervisor." *Journal of Organizational Behavior Management,* 1977, *1,* 99–103.

Daniels, A. *Performance Management: Improving Quality and Productivity Through Positive Reinforcement.* (3rd ed.) Tucker, Ga.: Performance Management Publications, 1989.

Deluga, R. J., and Andrews, M. H. "A Case Study Investigating the Effects of a Low-Cost Intervention to Reduce Three Attendance Behavior Problems in a Clerical Training Program." *Journal of Organizational Behavior Management,* Fall–Winter 1985, *7*(3–4), 115–125.

Dinsmoor, J. A. "Setting the Record Straight: The Social Views of B. F. Skinner." *American Psychologist,* 1992, *47*(11), 1454–1463.

Emmert, G. D. "Measuring the Impact of Group Performance Feedback vs. Individual Performance Feedback in an Industrial Setting." *Journal of Organizational Behavior Management,* 1978, *1,* 134–141.

Fallon, D. "An Existential Look at B. F. Skinner." *American Psychologist,* Nov. 1992, *47*(11), 1433–1440.

Fellner, D. J., and Sulzer-Azaroff, B. "A Behavioral Analysis of Goal Setting." *Journal of Organizational Behavior Management,* Spring 1984, *6*(1), 33–51.

Ferster, C. B. *Schedules of Reinforcement.* New York: Appleton-Century-Crofts, 1957.

Frederiksen, L. "Organizational Behavior Management: An Overview." In L. Frederiksen (ed.), *Handbook of Organizational Behavior Management.* New York: Wiley, 1982.

Hermann, J. A., and others. "Effects of Bonuses for Punctuality on the Tardiness of Industrial Workers." *Journal of Applied Behavior Analysis,* 1973, *6,* 563–570.

Hilgard, E. R. *Theories of Learning.* (2nd ed.) Englewood Cliffs, N.J.: Appleton-Century-Crofts, 1956.

Hollander, M. A., and Plutchik, R. "A Reinforcement Program for Psychiatric Attendants." *Journal of Behavior Therapy and Experimental Psychiatry,* 1972, *3,* 297–300.

Johnson, C., and Masotti, R. "Suggestive Selling by Waitstaff in Family-Style Restaurants: An Experiment and Multisetting Observations." *Journal of Organizational Behavior Management,* 1990, *11*(1), 35–54.

Kazdin, A. E. *Behavior Modification in Applied Settings.* Chicago: Dorsey Press, 1975.

Kazdin, A. E. *History of Behavior Modification: Experimental Foundations of Contemporary Research.* Baltimore, Md.: University Park Press, 1978.

Kempen, R. W., and Hall, R. V. "Reduction of Industrial Absenteeism: Results of a Behavioral Approach." *Journal of Organizational Behavior Management,* 1977, *1,* 1–21.

Luthans, F., and Kreitner, R. *Organization Behavior Modification and Beyond.* Glenview, Ill.: Scott, Foresman, 1985.

Luthans, F., Paul, R., and Taylor, L. "The Impact of Contingent Reinforcement on Retail Salespersons' Performance Behaviors: A Replicated Field Experiment." *Journal of Organizational Behavior Management,* 1985, *7,* 25–35.

Luthans, F., and Schweizer, J. "O. D. Mod. in a Small Factory: How Behavior Modification Techniques Improve Total Organizational Performance." *Management Review,* Sept. 1979, *68,* 43–50.

Mirman, R. "Performance Management in Sales Organizations." In L. Frederiksen (ed.), *Handbook of Organizational Behavior Management.* New York: Wiley, 1982.

Montegar, C. A., Reid, D. H., Madsen, C. H., and Ewell, M. D. "Increasing Institutional Staff-to-Resident Interactions Through In-Service Training and Supervisor Approval." *Behavior Therapy,* 1977, *8,* 533–540.

Pedalino, E., and Gamboa, V. U. "Behavior Modification and Absenteeism: Intervention in One Industrial Setting." *Journal of Applied Psychology,* 1974, *59,* 694–698.

Pommer, D. A., and Streedbeck, D. "Motivating Staff Performance in an Operant Learning Program for Children." *Journal of Applied Behavior Analysis,* 1974, *7,* 217–221.

Poppen, L., and Poppen, R. "The Use of Behavioral Principles in Educational Software." *Educational Technology,* Feb. 1988, *28*(2), 37–41.

Ralis, M., and O'Brien, R. "Prompts, Goal Setting and Feedback to Increase Suggestive Selling." *Journal of Organizational Behavior Management,* 1986, *8*(1), 5–18.

Skinner, B. F. *Science and Human Behavior.* New York: Macmillan, 1953.

Skinner, B. F. *The Particulars of My Life.* New York: Knopf, 1976a.

Skinner, B. F. *Walden Two.* New York: Macmillan, 1976b. (Originally published in 1948.)

Skinner, B. F. *A Matter of Consequences: Part Three of an Autobiography.* New York: Random House, 1983.

Skinner, B. F., and Vaughan, M. E. *Enjoy Old Age: A Program of Self-Management.* New York: W. W. Norton, 1983.

Smith, J. M., and Chase, P. N. "Using the Vantage Analysis Chart to Solve Organization-Wide Problems." *Journal of Organizational Behavior Management,* 1990, *11*(1), 127–148.

Todd, J. T., and Morris, E. K. "Case Histories in the Great Power of Steady Misrepresentation." *American Psychologist,* Nov. 1992, *47*(11), 1441–1453.

Yukl, G. A., and Latham, G. P. "Consequences of Reinforcement Schedules and Incentive Magnitudes for Employee Performance: Problems Encountered in an Industrial Setting." *Journal of Applied Psychology,* 1975, *60*(3), 294–298.

Yukl, G. A., Latham, G. P. and Pursell, E. D. "The Effectiveness of Performance Incentives Under Continuous and Variable Ratio Schedules of Reinforcement." *Personnel Psychology,* 1976, *29,* 221–231.

Chapter Seven

Kurt Lewin

Individual Perception and the Environment

Why Kurt Lewin? An Overview of Organizational Applications

Kurt Lewin first demonstrated the basic psychological relationships that became the foundation for the field of organization development. The processes he demonstrated are fundamental to many current efforts to change behavior at the individual, group, and organizational levels.

Lewin's Theory as an Organizational Image or Metaphor

Lewin was the most visual of the theorists in this volume. His field theory enables practitioners to view individuals, groups, and organizations as entities within a field of forces. Lewin's concepts lend themselves to visual demonstration and he used diagrams and graphics to develop and present his theory. His followers developed a visual application termed "force-field analysis" that enabled practitioners and clients to apply his ideas to a wide array of organizational problems.

Lewin's Theory as a Point of Influence for Dealing with Conflict

Both Lewin's theory and his life experiences helped to foster a strong interest in dealing with conflict. Field theory portrays human experience in terms of a balance of conflicting forces acting upon individuals, groups, and organizations. Lewin's own life involved close and tragic association with the forces of Nazism and anti-Semitism.

The Lewinian approach to conflict is to unblock gridlock by creating a new balance among the forces at work in the field. Lewin also developed ways of refocusing struggles from a win-lose orientation to a win-win one. His most concrete approach to managing conflict is action research, a method that empowers parties to a conflict to deal with their differences by jointly researching their own attitudes and behavior.

Lewin's Theory as a Point of Influence for Dealing with Psychological Growth

Lewin's three-step theory of unfreezing, change, and refreezing is the underlying approach in many organizational workshops and training sessions. This method evolved from Lewin's field theory, in which the individual identifies the current equilibrium of forces operating on an identity and then pinpoints the particular forces most amenable to change. The idea of unfreezing came from Lewin's observation that individuals were most amenable to change when they were relaxed and not feeling defensive. Refreezing evolved as Lewin realized the necessity of anchoring change in the individual's ongoing methods of operation. In organizational work, we often find Lewin's theory combined with other theories. This is because his theory can function as a framework that leaves open the specific content and processes of the internal psyche. This allows the practitioner to draw upon the concepts of other theorists.

Lewin's Theory as a Point of Influence for Dealing with the Dilemmas of Joining

Lewin's experience with anti-Semitism in Nazi Germany and the United States motivated him to be concerned with the importance of group membership. His field theory gave him the tools to do this. His research on food habits demonstrated the importance of group affiliation in determining and changing behavior, and his identification of the process of group dynamics, in which members learn about their own behavior, supplied another tool with which individuals could examine the process in which an individual becomes part of a larger entity.

Limitations of Lewin's Theory for Use in Organizations

Lewin's theories are widely applied in the field of organization development. Action research has a strong record of results as does Lewin's unfreezing, change, and refreezing methods of change. Their limitations come not from the theories themselves but from others' less-than-judicious application of them. Lewin's theories lead to application so quickly that they can be treated as all-purpose remedies without any knowledge of why and how they work. This problem is exacerbated by the fact that his writings, although they are influential for other scholars, are cumbersome for practitioners. Thus, few practitioners who use or quote Lewin have read his original formulations. This makes Lewin's work more open to misunderstanding and misapplication.

How Lewin Developed His Ideas

Kurt Lewin was born in 1890 in the former Prussian province of Posen, now a part of Poland. Much of German society was closed to Jews, who had been freed from physical incarceration in ghettos less than a hundred years earlier. The many instances of legal discrimination and social abuse to which Lewin was subjected throughout his life in Germany had a powerful influence on his later work (M. Lewin, 1992).

When Lewin was fifteen, his family relocated to Berlin so that the children could have the advantage of a first-rate education. Here young Kurt received a classical education, including a thorough grounding in science and mathematics. In 1910, he enrolled in the University of Berlin to complete a doctorate in philosophy. Lewin's particular area of interest was the theory and methodology of science. German psychology at that time focused on measurable physiological phenomena like visual perception, excluding as topics for research such "poetic" or intangible forms of mental activity as motivation, emotions, and creativity. Lewin's mentor, his professor Ernst Cassirer, taught that breakthroughs in any branch of science required discarding the prevalent conceptual and methodological restrictions. New insights could only be discovered by investigating areas and using techniques of research that conventional wisdom considered beyond the bounds of legitimate inquiry. This iconoclastic philosophy made a lifelong impression on Lewin, and he adopted it as his personal scientific credo (Marrow, [1969] 1984, p. 9).

Lewin chose a career as a university instructor at a time when the chances of a Jew ever being awarded tenure or a well-paid post were remote. Something about the subject matter and the setting must have been very compelling for him. One factor that surely influenced his decision was the emergence during this period of an exciting new approach to psychology, which later came to be called the Gestalt school. Gestalt psychology focused upon the learning and perception of the total situation and relegitimized research on "intangible" mental processes such as motivation and personality.

In 1914, Europe erupted in war. Lewin enlisted in the German army as a private, completing his doctoral examination while on furlough. During four years of active duty in France and Russia, he rose to the rank of lieutenant, then was wounded and sent back to Germany to convalesce. While recuperating, Lewin wrote his first professional publication, which was based on his military experiences. This article, entitled "The War Landscape," prefigured Lewin's notion of psychological field that would later be such an important part of his work. Another article, published while Lewin was establishing himself as a lecturer at the University of Berlin, proposed ways in which psychologists could collaborate with farm laborers and industrial workers to increase job satisfaction and efficiency.

Lewin and his students fanned out to farms, schools, and factories to investigate larger questions of human motivation and behavior in their natural settings. They often gathered at cafés or at Lewin's home to share the results of their research in long, freewheeling discussions. Lewin was not the stereotypical authoritarian German professor. His collaborative style modeled the relationship that, later, many organization development consultants would try to establish with their clients. Psychiatrist Jerome Frank, an American student of Lewin's in Berlin, recalled his teacher many years later (Frank, 1978, pp. 223–224):

He was a little man with an apparently inexhaustible supply of energy and a ruddy complexion that suggested vigorous health. Although he must often have been seated in my presence, in my memories he is almost always in motion. . . . Although supremely self-confident, he was devoid of any trace of arrogance. Rather, he was friendly and unpretentious; he urged even the lowliest of his students to call him by his first name. Metaphorically speaking, he would get down on the floor and wrestle intellectually with anyone, from the most junior student to a prestigious colleague. He would pull no punches in an argument, which made you feel that you were being taken seriously. Arguments were never personal, and afterward he would be as friendly as ever. . . . [A]lthough ultimately his hold on his students depended on the vigor, creativity, clarity, and discipline of his thinking, it was enhanced by his magnetic personal qualities.

Vera Mahler, another student, remembered how Lewin's important notion of life space was presented in one of his child psychology classes (Marrow, [1969] 1984, pp. 22):

[He] would interrupt his lectures about some aspect of child psychology, for example, and begin to draw funny little "eggs" on the blackboard. These he called the "total psychological field" or "life space" of the child's world. These little ovals would in turn contain smaller circles representing the child himself and containing plus and minus signs; arrows would appear to indicate the direction of various field forces; thick lines represented the barriers. Quickly we were in the midst of a conflict in the child's life or a situation representing reward and punishment. All this was graphic, all was made clear, in Lewin's little drawings on the blackboard.

By the end of the decade, the Lewin group at the Berlin Psychological Institute began to attract international attention for their ground-breaking studies of psychological phenomena. Discontent about the anti-Semitic system that barred Lewin from a permanent, financially secure appointment at the university escalated to alarm when the depression swept Hitler's Nazi party into national prominence. Anti-Jewish riots erupted on campus, leading to at least one murder. Conditions worsened over the next several years, making Lewin's position at the Institute very difficult. Temporary relief came in the form of an invitation from Stanford University in California to teach for a semester as a visiting professor in psychology in 1932. While traveling back to Germany, Lewin learned of Hitler's elevation to chancellor. As his train crossed Europe, he determined to leave Germany. As soon as he arrived back home, he wired

American acquaintances in code, asking them to help him find a teaching position. It was a race against time; the Nazis were passing new laws restricting the rights and freedom of movement of Jews on an almost daily basis. Depression-era America was hostile to immigrants and required that they have a job and a sponsor before entering the country. Despite this uncertainty, Lewin resigned from the Psychological Institute in protest against the new regime.

Lewin left Germany in the summer of 1933 to accept a two-year appointment in the Home Economics Department at Cornell University on the basis of his past studies of early childhood development (M. Lewin, 1992). During this period, he concentrated on getting his ideas published in English with the assistance of American colleagues. His first two books, *A Dynamic Theory of Personality* (1935) and *Principles of Topological Psychology* (Lewin, Heider, and Heider, 1936), contained the basic elements of his theory.

In 1935, Lewin received an offer of a research professorship from the Child Welfare Research Station at the University of Iowa. Here his stimulating intelligence and openness again drew a number of students into his sphere, while his publications attracted others to the campus for the express purpose of studying with him. They met in the classroom, at Lewin's home, and at regular Tuesday afternoon discussion sessions at a local restaurant. Lewin peppered these discussions with original ideas in his heavily accented English, but he was quite content for his students to develop and expand on these concepts in their own research. Rather than attempting to protect his ideas from "deviation," he encouraged his students to challenge and disprove them if they could.

Lewin inspired rather than dominated, and the results of this unique teaching style were extraordinary. His students included some of the most distinguished psychologists of the next generation, including Dorwin Cartwright, Alvin Zander, Ronald Lippitt, Leon Festinger, Beatrice Wright, and John French. Social scientists from across America, including Margaret Mead, Gordon Allport, and Abraham Maslow, stopped in Iowa City and were absorbed into the ferment of ideas, conversation, and music that ceaselessly swirled around the extended Lewin household (Marrow, [1969] 1984, pp. 88–93).

The worldwide economic collapse of the 1930s led many thoughtful commentators to question whether Western democratic institutions were capable of withstanding the brutal competition of emerging fascism. Lewin was disturbed by manifestations of anti-Semitism and racism in his adopted country and by its denial of the threat posed by the rising tide of intolerance. He remained deeply involved with the horrors going on in Europe and managed to get several close relatives out before it was too late. These concerns, born of his personal experience of persecution, guided Lewin toward applying field theory in a variety of group and organizational situations.

Throughout these years Lewin divided his time between researching and writing at the university, promoting topological psychology among a growing network of colleagues across America, and supporting Zionist activity. He believed that the establishment of a Jewish homeland was essential for the psychological well-being of all Jews, who would otherwise be permanently relegated to a restrictive minority status among other nations—a situation with which he was all too familiar. He was constantly upset by his unsuccessful efforts to get his mother out of Europe. She had fled Germany to the Netherlands, but the U.S. State Department routinely blocked most attempts to obtain visas for refugees. When the Nazis occupied Holland in 1943, Recha Lewin was deported to an extermination camp in Poland. Although he did not receive confirmation of her death until after the war, enough was known about the genocide in progress for Lewin to feel tormented by helplessness (M. Lewin, 1992).

By 1944, Lewin was looking beyond Iowa, where his many outside activities had aroused resentment in some quarters. He envisioned the creation of a psychological research center that would specialize in the study and solution of pressing social problems. Lewin wanted it to be a place where social scientists with an interest in real-life issues could work directly in the community to perfect their methods and understanding. Lewin approached potential sponsors about this idea and was able to found the Research Center for Group Dynamics at Massachusetts Institute of Technology, the first formal center ever established for this area of study.

Lewin died in 1947, involved to the last day of his life in a whirlwind of talk and travel to promote the activities of the institutions and causes he so ardently supported.

Lewin's Point of Influence

Lewin's point of influence is a figurative glass bubble around each individual, group, or organization that includes all that influences that entity's behavior at a given moment. Lewin called this *life space,* and it included factors such as goal regions, paths to goals, barriers, threats, and social relationships (Deutsch, 1968, p. 414). As is befitting a thinker identified with the saying, "There is nothing as practical as a good theory," Lewin's concept of the psychological field is both abstract and practical. It is abstract in that it is a field theory in which the field is an intangible area that is each individual or entity's life space. It is practical in that the concept of life space allows the practitioner to focus on all that is influencing an individual at a given moment. This focus triggers action.

Lewin expressed this as $B = F(P, E)$: behavior (B) is a function (F) of the combined personal (P) and environmental (E) factors that make up an individual's life space *at a particular moment in time* (K. Lewin, 1951a, p. 239). The concept of life space can be applied at all levels of human activity including the individual, group, departmental, or organizational levels, or even the societal level. Field theory is a metatheory, a theory of theories, and it can be combined with a number of other theoretical concepts. For example, Chapter Two of this book includes a discussion on how to use action research to examine the Jungian shadow of a group.

Preview: When to Use Lewin's
Point of Influence in the Workplace.

When you are interested in increasing participation and increasing democratic leadership (pp. 274–276)

When you wish to influence individual behavior (pp. 276–277)

When you wish to influence motivation and goals (pp. 277–279)

When you wish to influence behavior in a large system (pp. 279–281)

When you wish to promote individual awareness and change (p. 281)

When you are concerned with managing conflict (pp. 282–284)

When you wish to influence cohesion within a group or organization (pp. 284–285)

When you wish to influence psychological growth (p. 285)

The Importance of Knowing Why Lewin's Theories Work

Lewin's ideas, such as force-field analysis, are so practical that it's possible to apply them without really understanding *why* they work as well as they do. Knowing why, however, has its advantages. Understanding the internal psychological process that occurs when Lewin's theories are applied enables the practitioner to fine-tune applications, vary them according to the situation, and use Lewin's ideas with more confidence, skill, and impact. We now focus on the underlying theory behind Lewin's work. The interventions themselves are in the next section.

The Gestalt Learning Background to Lewin's Theory

The German word *Gestalt* has no direct English counterpart, the closest equivalent perhaps being "configuration," "pattern," or "shape." Gestalt psychology challenged the dominant nineteenth-century view that humans learn by associating isolated bits of experience. In the traditional view, a manager's perception of a subordinate would be the result of a "bundle of sensations" bound together by associations (Bower and Hilgard, 1981, p. 302).

Beginning in 1910, Max Wertheimer, Kurt Koffka, and Wolfgang Kohler, a trio of young psychologists at the University of Berlin, conducted a series of experiments that proved that this same pattern-forming phenomenon operated in visual perception and many other areas of mental activity. This can be illustrated by a well-known optical illusion consisting of five forty-five-degree angles, or V's, arranged with their open ends clustered around a common center but with no pair actually touching another pair. When asked to describe the resulting image, most observers say that it is a five-pointed star, even though the five angles are visibly separated. The psychological Gestalt "star" is stronger than the visual fact of five unconnected angles. The mind, rather than the eye, controls what we see, and the mind registers Gestalts rather than items.

Wertheimer and his colleagues proved that people perceive the world around them in meaningful wholes, not as isolated experiences strung together through an additive process of association. A Gestalt is thus a pattern of relationship among various elements, where the meaningful unit is the pattern rather than the separate elements of which it is composed. For example, when we transpose a musical melody from one key to another, the melody itself is recognizably the same even though every individual sound is different. The melody is a Gestalt, a distinctive pattern of relationship with an identity of its own.

Having demonstrated this basic point, the Gestalt psychologists wanted to identify the underlying principles that govern the way in which the mind organizes such patterns of relationship. Of the 114 "laws of Gestalten" they eventually discovered, three concepts were particularly influential in shaping Lewin's work: closure, insight, and the figure-ground relationship.

Closure

Closure is the principle that accounts for our earlier example of the five-pointed star illusion. People tend to seek familiar and complete patterns. Given a few cues to work with, they will "fill in the blanks" to see complete or meaningful patterns even where none exist. Lack of closure, such as failing to reach a goal, gives rise to psychological tension. People relieve this tension whenever possible by attempting to achieve closure, either directly (by trying again to reach the goal) or through substitution (forming fantasies in which the goal is reached). Lewin adopted and expanded on this Gestalt model of the mind as a system under tension seeking release.

Current efforts to restructure tasks so that individuals or teams turn out complete products are a good example of how organizations draw upon the Gestalt principle of closure.

Insight

Insight is a sudden restructuring of the psychological environment that creates a new Gestalt. Kohler first demonstrated this phenomenon in experiments with chimpanzees. He placed food outside the bars of their cages or suspended it above their reach. Then he provided objects that could be used to reach the food but only in combination (for example, barrels that could be stacked together or hollow sticks that could be assembled into poles). The chimpanzees initially displayed angry frustration at their inability to reach the food unaided or with the help of a single object. Then they seemed to withdraw from the situation, sitting passively or idly playing with the objects. Eventually they rushed to the equipment, stacking up the barrels or assembling the sticks, moving them to the proper position, and getting the food.

This was not an incremental trial-and-error method of problem solving. When the insight came, it was sudden and complete. In many cases, the steps between the apparent withdrawal from the problem and the implementation of the solution were entirely mental: the chimpanzees developed the complete answer by envisioning the intermediate actions without physically performing them. Having once hit on this solution, Kohler's chimpanzees were able to generalize from it to other experimental situations, using various types of objects to achieve the same goal. The initial burst of insight permanently restructured the chimpanzees' perception of the boundaries of their environment and the uses of the objects in it. Later experiments confirmed that human beings experience substantially the same phenomenon. Moments of insight can profoundly alter our psychological environment, changing the way we look at people, problems, and situations. In Lewinian terms, insight can restructure our life space (Hunt, 1993, pp. 292–299).

The technique of "brainstorming," in which individuals are asked to voice spontaneous ideas that are then posted for group viewing, is a good example of encouraging such insight. Looking at randomly listed ideas commonly triggers creative new insights.

The Figure-Ground Relationship

Out of the mass of sensory and mental data our brains process at any given moment, we select certain elements for concentrated, detailed attention. These elements are *figural.* By contrast, the rest of the thoughts and sensations we experience at that same moment recede into the background, or *ground.* We focus on the Gestalt that is most meaningful to us right now, and the rest of the information that constitutes our experience remains in the background without reaching the level of conscious awareness. Figure and ground are interdependent: each defines the other. In 1915, the Gestalt psychologist Edgar Rubin developed the illustration shown in Figure 7.1 to demonstrate this principle.

Merla Robbins was one of the first African-Americans to be employed in the management training program of a large Rocky Mountain bank. Whenever she entered a meeting, her first focus of attention was whether there were any other African-Americans in the group. This was figural *for her. In most situations, it was not figural for other trainees at the meeting. Sometimes when Merla felt particularly isolated, it was hard for her to shift her focus so that other aspects of the meeting became figural.*

Figure 7.1. Figure and Ground: Vase and Profiles.

If you concentrate on the white outline, it appears to be a vase or chalice set against a solid black background. If you concentrate on the black outline, you can see the figure of two profiles facing each other across a featureless white space. The visual elements of both images are continuously present on the page, yet it is difficult to see both of them at the same time. A shift of attention determines which one is figural and which fades into the undifferentiated background. In the case of Rubin's vase, we can cause the figure-ground relationship to reverse itself at will.

How Lewin Extended Gestalt Learning Theory

Gestalt learning psychologists stopped at this point, content to establish a new way of understanding human learning, which was no small achievement. In his early years in Germany, Lewin built on Gestalt *learning* to develop his field theory of human behavior.

Lewin diagrammed the forces acting upon an individual or group at a given time as regions within the individual's or group's life space or personal world. Each region possessed a greater or lesser degree of attraction or repulsion for the individual. Lewin maintained that if you know what forces are uppermost in a person's awareness and the intensity with which each force attracts or repels that individual, you can predict—and even influence—how that person will behave.

At this early stage, Lewin was laying the foundation for the idea that *what exists psychologically is what is real for the person being studied* (Deutsch, 1968, p. 416). Later, second- and third-generation Lewinians would build on this focus to develop a cluster of group and organizational interventions that formed the core of organization development (French and Bell, 1984, pp. 20–23). Focusing on the individual rather than on groups or organizations, Fritz and Laura Perls would extend Lewin's work with Gestalt into a new approach to psychotherapy (see Chapter Eight).

Lewin noted that people try to maintain a dynamic state of equilibrium by moving toward the regions of their life space that will enable them to satisfy their needs. To illustrate, a sensation of hunger creates a condition of psychological tension within the individual. A nearby restaurant, which might have been a neutral feature of the psychological environment a short time earlier, begins to acquire a positive attraction in the individual's life space. Entering the restaurant and eating a meal enables the person to "discharge" the tension and restore a state of psychological equilibrium. When the need to eat has been satisfied, the attraction of the restaurant diminishes, and awareness of the restaurant fades to the background of the person's life space.

As people mature, their life space becomes increasingly differentiated, acquiring more regions and a greater number of potential pathways among the regions. The hungry individual in our example might be near a restaurant, but barriers could exist in his or her life space that would make it difficult to move toward the restaurant. Perhaps the person is a vegetarian or will only eat at kosher restaurants or is trying to lose weight. Such concerns are related to regions of personal identity in the life space that may exert a force greater than the prospect of relief from hunger offered by the restaurant. Perhaps the restaurant looks too crowded, or a group loitering by its entrance seems threatening, or the restaurant's prices are too high. These repellent external influences in the life space might be stronger than the tension caused by hunger. Faced with such barriers, the hungry person might actually turn away from the nearby restaurant in order to find a source of food less encumbered by psychological conflict. For Lewin, the ability to create alternative pathways around barriers in order to reach a goal was the defining characteristic of psychological growth.

In Lewin's model, individual personality is less a stable structure than a sense of continuity ("genidentity") imposed on a changing constellation of behaviors, attitudes, and affiliations (Back, 1986). Who you are is very much a function of what is present in your life space at a given moment. One major determinant in this regard is group membership. We all behave differently in different group settings: at a family reunion, in a business meeting, at a concert, or in a classroom. Lewin conducted a number of experiments that demonstrated the remarkable power of groups to alter individual attitudes and behavior. He used this insight to explore group-based methods for social change from the base of Gestalt learning theory. Lewin's conceptualization of forces that influence behavior would later form the basis for an exceptionally useful and fertile tool of group and organizational problem solving: force-field analysis (Weisbord, 1987, pp. 78–79). Lewin's basic theoretical formulations yielded so many applications because he demonstrated that perceptions are not only the basis for learning but ultimately the basis for attitudes and feelings and therefore for behavior.

Lewin typically viewed each new scientific finding as a springboard for further exploration. If the process that the Gestaltists discovered could alter the way we view an object, could it not also alter how different regions of the life space move in and out of prominence? Lewin suspected that it could, and he spent the rest of his life exploring this process.

The first step in this exploration came from Lewin's personal experience before he was established as a professional. As a soldier in the First World War, Lewin observed that the landscape changes in the soldier's perception as he moves toward or away from the area of combat. A "peace landscape" is omnidirectional, whereas the "war landscape" is experienced as having a front and a back, defined by the location of the fighting. In the peace landscape, objects such as church steeples or haystacks have familiar connotations, but in a war landscape they are seen as possible points of defense or potential threats. In the battle zone, using domestic objects for their peacetime purposes rather than their military potential seems incongruous. This phenomenon strengthens as one moves closer to the zone of active combat and diffuses as one moves away from it (Marrow, [1969] 1984, p. 11).

In 1920, Lewin expanded on his view of the psychological field in a critique of the "scientific management" principles of the American engineer Frederick Winslow Taylor. Lewin observed that work has a psychological "life value" for the worker in addition to its physical dimensions. He suggested that means of production that result from overspecialization and devaluation of the meaningfulness of the work eventually damage both the individual and the enterprise. Lewin proposed that psychologists, workers, and efficiency experts combine their expertise to create ways of working that would increase both productivity and job satisfaction. The essence of field theory had been laid. In the next decade Lewin would develop this theory, and nearly twenty-five years later he would get the opportunity to put these proposals to the test in the workplace (Weisbord, 1987, pp. 76–81).

Topology: The Foundation of Lewin's Thought

Lewin moved continuously between theory and experience, and in 1936 he began to develop a formal theory. His goal was to create a language that would be capable of depicting the important distinctions and interrelationships unique to the field of psychology. Unlike some of the "single-cause" theories then prevalent, topology accounts for multiple causation, sudden changes, and reversals and shifts in insight and perspective. It is adaptable to presenting problems in a form that corresponds with our commonsense experience of turmoil and uncertainty. Kurt Back later likened Lewin's formulations to contemporary catastrophe theory, which attempts to account for major variations by attributing them to changes in minor and unpredictable variables—for example, the shift of a few votes in one precinct may change an election (Back, 1992, p. 59).

In retrospect, it appears that although the theory of topology was too cumbersome even for academic researchers, in scope and theoretical vision it was ahead of its time, because it encompassed the complexity and chaos of the real world. This austere and somewhat unwieldy theory provided the appropriate point of view for major gains in the emerging academic subfield of social psychology and the creation of the applied field of organization development.

Lewin's basic formulations that provided the base for all of this thinking were an offshoot of geometry, which addresses relationships of position rather than quantitative properties. Topological egg-shaped diagrams and equations enabled Lewin to express psychological events in terms of movement between regions in the psychological field (Lewin, 1936).

Lewin theorized that a person could be portrayed as a field of psychological energy divided into various shifting regions, with each region representing some force in his or her perceived environment. The psychological field (the life space) is dynamic rather than static, and its regions expand, shrink, or merge, growing more or less differentiated as the balance of forces changes over time. The source of energy for this mental activity is psychological tension. "Tension" in this usage does not mean anxiety, but rather the energy aroused in a system as a result of a goal or need. Tension in the psychological field gives rise to the urge to achieve closure and restore equilibrium, a state in which the tensions within the field are in balance, like the girders and trusses that allow a building to flex under stress. When psychological tension activates this innate desire for equilibrium, the result is movement from one region of the life space to another.

Lewin posited two different sources for this psychological tension: *needs* and *quasi-needs*. Needs are basic and often have a physiological source, such as hunger, thirst, or feeling cold. Quasi-needs are goals or intentions, such as getting a good grade in a course or completing a project. Quasi-needs arise more often than basic needs, but they are less persistent. A basic need must be satisfied directly—for example, by eating or drinking. Quasi-needs can sometimes be relieved through substitute satisfactions, such as fantasies of the desired outcome. These needs and quasi-needs can maintain their tension independently of each other, so contradictory forces may operate simultaneously in the life space (K. Lewin, 1951a, pp. 273–280).

Using Topology to Capture One Person's Psychological Field

Consider the life space of Mike, an engineer waiting to present a proposal for a new project at a management meeting. If Lewin were to draw an "egg" illustrating the forces at work in Mike's psychological field, he might include the factors shown in Figure 7.2.

Mike's Psychological Field

The area designated C1 represents Mike's career *goal*. This is a prominent region in Mike's life space at this meeting because if his presentation is successful, he may get to manage the project, an outcome he greatly desires. This goal, a quasi-need, is the dominant source of tension in his psychological field at the moment. However, other forces are at work in the field that may also affect Mike's behavior.

Area C2 represents Mike's career *worries*. He's heard rumors that the company may soon be downsizing the division in which he works. Management approval of this new project may mean the difference between keeping or losing his job in the near future.

**Figure 7.2. Illustration of the Forces
at Work in a Psychological Field.**

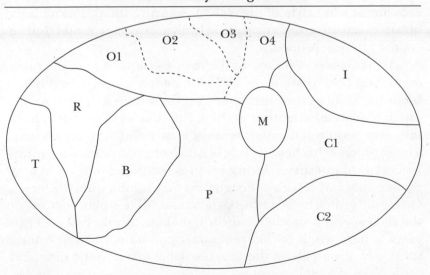

Mike's awareness of this is another source of tension as he waits to make his presentation.

Area I represents an urgent *interrupted task* back in Mike's work area that he had to leave in order to attend this meeting. Mike has been absorbed in this task for several days now, and his boss expects to review Mike's results by the end of the week. Mike occasionally finds his attention withdrawing from the meeting and drifting back to the interrupted task.

Area P represents the *presentation* Mike has prepared to support his proposal. Mike doesn't often make presentations to management, so he is feeling some anxiety. While other people at the meeting speak about different topics on the agenda, Mike mentally reviews the key points he intends to make. He is far more aware of what is about to happen (his presentation) than of what is happening (other people's presentations). The hopes and fears Mike has tied up in his presentation make it a powerful force in his life space right now.

Area B represents Mike's *boss,* another influential force in his psychological field. Mike's boss will make the final decision to approve or disapprove the proposed project. Mike has tailored his presentation to appeal to his boss's priorities. As Mike's turn on the agenda draws closer, he starts to notice every twitch, grimace, and remark that his boss makes. This heightened awareness has a narrow focus: Mike could not tell you exactly what color his boss's eyes are or what style of dress she is wearing today, but he is exquisitely sensitive to any possible indicator of her mood and receptivity to new proposals.

Areas O1 to O4 represent the *other people* present at the meeting in addition to Mike's boss. These people come in and out of focus for Mike as they speak, but on the whole he is not paying much individual attention to them. In Mike's current life space, the other people at the meeting exist as an undifferentiated group. They influence his field mainly because of their potential for raising awkward questions during his presentation. Were we to draw the life space of Mike's colleagues, it might look quite different. One colleague who is enthusiastic about Mike's plan focuses on the final agenda; another, concerned about another type of program of her own, picks out potential opponents and allies; and a third, concerned about the support being given to the new planning director, notices how many other executives have come to the meeting.

Area T represents Mike's *craving for tobacco*. He is trying to quit smoking, but he still experiences a strong desire for cigarettes whenever he is in a stressful situation. Right now he badly wants a cigarette, although he would have to leave the meeting room to smoke it. Earlier resolutions Mike made about his health have lost their force in the present situation. However, Mike knows that his boss, a nonsmoker, would disapprove of his leaving the meeting for that purpose. It would be smarter to wait until after the meeting to smoke, but this knowledge does not help Mike's growing distress.

Area R represents Mike's awareness of the *poor ventilation* in the meeting room. This environmental factor contributes to Mike's physical discomfort. He can see it affecting others as the meeting proceeds. People are beginning to fidget, and their overall level of energy appears to be waning. Mike is concerned that the stuffy climate will detract from his presentation. He wonders whether he should get up and open the door. He's uncertain about whether the managers prefer a closed meeting room, and he does not want to do anything inappropriate.

Mike's career goal, his worries, his interrupted task, his presentation, his boss, the other people, his craving for tobacco, and the poor ventilation summarize his *psychological field*—or the personal needs and environmental influences uppermost in his awareness at a particular moment. The next step is to find out their relative influence on his behavior.

Action (Locomotion) in Mike's Field

Lewin taught that each region in a person's life space possesses a particular value for that individual. His term for this perceived value was *valence*. The valence of a particular region can be positive (attractive) or negative (repellent) in character. Movement toward a region with a positive valence releases psychological tension, whereas movement toward a region with negative valence increases tension. As the early Gestalt researchers showed, the need to release tension by achieving closure is a basic psychological trait. In Mike's case, his career goal (area C1) has a positive valence: the tension it creates in his life space can be relieved by behavior aimed at moving closer to its realization. Mike's career worries (area C2) have a negative valence: they create tension that can best be relieved through behavior intended to avoid or negate them.

In field theory, the movement of a person from one region to another within the life space is known as *locomotion*. Locomotion can take the form of observable physical behavior, or it may be psychological in nature. When Mike's attention strays from the events of the meeting to the interrupted task back on his desk, he is "moving" to another psychological location. Locomotion also occurs at different levels of reality. When Mike actually makes his presentation, his locomotion to that region of his life space will be wholly in reality. His mental rehearsals before the actual event are also a form of locomotion to the same region, but they take place at a lower order of reality. If Mike were to imagine the possible consequences of his presentation as either an unconditional triumph or a total disaster, this fantasy would be locomotion as well, though at a still lesser degree of reality (K. Lewin, 1951a, p. 245).

Any region in the life space that possesses a strong positive or negative valence sets up a tension system that impels an individual to some form of locomotion. This tension system operates on the person like a force that has a specific direction, either toward or away from the valence region. Lewin called this directional force a *vector*. Mike's craving for a cigarette is a vector influencing him in the direction of leaving the meeting room. At the same time, his need for his boss's approval is a vector pointing in the direction of staying in the meeting. These opposed vectors can exist side by side in Mike's life space because they derive from independent tension systems, each organized around a particular psychological fact with its own valence. If the vector of Mike's tobacco withdrawal is substantially stronger than the vector of his need for his boss's approval, he will probably leave the meeting room.

Boundaries in the Psychological Field

Another important factor in Lewin's theory is the *permeability of boundaries* in the psychological field. Life spaces are constantly changing because they are open to the introduction of new facts from the person and the environment. However, some regions of the life space are more readily influenced than others. Behavior in a specific situation is partially determined by where in the life space tension can most readily move toward closure. In our earlier example of the hungry individual, several factors were cited in which the vector of hunger might direct the person away from, rather than toward, the closest restaurant. Assume for a moment that the constraining factor is vegetarianism that is founded on strong religious convictions. Important aspects of the individual's personal identity are connected to this set of beliefs, including self-esteem, morality, and group affiliation. This region of the life space is central to this person's sense of continuity of self: its boundaries are relatively rigid and persistent over time. Therefore, the vector of hunger is diverted toward more distant food sources that offer meatless fare. It is easier to release the tension of the need by locomoting through regions of the life space whose borders are more fluid and permeable.

From Topology to the World of Work: How Lewin's Theories Became Practical

Lewin's approach set him apart from the prevailing schools of psychology of his day and established what has come to be the prevailing "here-and-now" stance of the organization development practitioner. Unlike the Freudian psychoanalytic system, Lewin's approach did not assume the existence of lifelong unconscious forces operating independent of the reasoning will. Lewin recognized that certain tension systems could persist below the threshold of conscious awareness for many years, but he asserted that they affected behavior only when they were reactivated to the level of perceived needs in the current life space. Similarly, the prevailing stance in organization development is to avoid probing for underlying motives but instead to work with what is available from heightened consciousness.

Field theory differed from behaviorist psychology as well, notably by ascribing behavior to inner personal motives that were not dependent on reinforcement from the environment for their existence. Similarly, organization development has focused, and continues to focus, on consciously held feelings, attitudes, and values.

With field theory as a framework, Lewin's students were able to do pioneering work in social psychology and investigate topics that had been considered too intangible for scientific research. Although these studies did not take place in organizations, they provide valuable insights that have formed much of our current understanding of the motivation for work. They included responses to frustration (Dembo, [1931] 1976), the effects of success and failure on motivation (Hoppe, [1930] 1976), and satiation resulting from repetition (Karsten, [1928] 1976).

The best-known example of Lewin's collaborative approach to the work of his students occurred when several of them met at a local café to discuss their work. When they had finished numerous rounds of coffee and pastries, the waiter presented each person with an itemized bill, which he had accumulated and tallied entirely by memory. After the students paid, their conversation unexpectedly resumed and more food was consumed. When Lewin asked the waiter for a second accounting of the original bill, he indignantly replied that he could not be expected to remember their earlier total after it was paid. Lewin suggested to his colleagues that this incident demonstrated that the tension aroused by a quasi-need (the waiter's intention to remember what each diner ate and owed) is sustained only until the goal is reached.

Bluma Zeigarnik, a Russian graduate student, made this observation the subject of her dissertation. Over the next two years she conducted a series of controlled experiments that proved that people perform and remember interrupted tasks better than those that have already been completed. This phenomenon, now known as the Zeigarnik effect, confirmed Lewin's hypothesis regarding the arousal and discharge of tension systems. In this instance the research demonstrated how memory itself is a product of the psychological field (Marrow, [1969] 1984, pp. 42–43).

This is the logic behind starting training or team-building programs with a short evening session that initiates, but does not draw closure on, a process. Participants then are more likely to remember and think about the session overnight and start in the morning already "warmed up."

It was typical of Lewin to perceive the outlines of a basic psychological principle in a passing incident in a café. The science that fascinated him was the science that would explain and alter behavior in ordinary domestic settings, not just the laboratory. The young idealist who wanted psychologists to go out into the fields and collaborate with farm workers on the improvement of their labors was still discernible at the core of the self-assured university instructor.

When Lewin moved to Iowa, he continued to broaden the area in which he focused on life space as a framework for understanding human behavior. He collaborated with Dembo and Roger Barker on a study of frustration and regression in children. They allowed children to play with a variety of interesting toys for a period of time. Then an observer partitioned the play area so that some of the toys were visible but inaccessible. Frustrated in their attempts to reach the sequestered toys, the subjects reacted by exhibiting behavior typical of children several years younger than their actual ages. Their ability to engage in constructive or cooperative play dropped off significantly, and they displayed a loss of emotional control. They also showed a marked increase in aggressive behavior: in some cases children would team up to attack the observer (Marrow, [1969] 1984, pp. 12–13)! In terms of Lewin's theory, frustration had the effect of de-differentiating (breaking down the boundaries of) life space. In other words, the unreleased tension overwhelmed the more recent and sophisticated social behaviors the children had learned, restructuring their life spaces into a form with fewer available distinctions and pathways.

Anyone who has ever witnessed an organization in the throes of a downsizing or cutback crisis will recognize that the regression Lewin identified is not restricted to psychology experiments.

Lewin also broadened his focus on the psychological field from the individual to a large social group in a comparative study of the differences in social upbringing between German and American children. His primary conclusion was that from childhood, the life space of Americans included a broader "area of free movement," with more permeable boundaries. Germans were, by contrast, taught to be more rigid and restricted in their interactions with others, maintaining a greater "social distance." This reduced the number of pathways available to them for reducing tension in social settings (Marrow, [1969] 1984, pp. 98–100). Lewin employed this same concept of a reduced area of free movement to explain the destructive effects of discrimination on members of stigmatized groups, a subject to which he devoted several articles. His interest in the psychological impact of prejudice on personality development in minority groups was a theme to which he returned at intervals for the rest of his life (M. Lewin, [1974] 1976).

These studies of minority groups led Lewin to place an increased emphasis on the importance of group membership as a factor in the psychological environment. He stated that identification with a group is one of the core elements of the person, shaping self-esteem, values, morality, and goals. People participate in many different groups over a lifetime: families, fraternities, ethnic groups, professional groups, and so on. Only a few such affiliations are likely to be active in a person's life space at any particular moment, but Lewin suggested that these few would be important factors in determining the course of the individual's behavior.

Organizational Applications of Field Theory

Lewin's field theory highlights how individual behavior is the product of the person in her or his *perceived* environment. Given this context it is possible to create groupings or structures that redefine an individual's or group's perceived environment. This is the process behind such classic organization development interventions as the intergroup exercise and team building. Lewin did not live to see the birth and evolution of organization development, but the intellectual base of both organization development and modern participative management can be found in the following eight practical experiments conducted by Lewin and his students.

When You Are Interested in Increasing
Participation and Democratic Leadership

A study that Lewin conducted with Ron Lippitt and Ralph White was especially important in establishing a rationale for a participative style of leadership. In this study, the researchers examined the effects of different leadership styles (or "social climates") on groups of eleven-year-old boys who were organized into clubs to work on projects. Some of the clubs began with an autocratic adult leader who gave detailed instructions for every activity and closely supervised the boys. Other clubs started out with an adult leader who kept aloof from the boys, offering neither interference nor assistance. Lewin called this passive leadership condition "laissez-faire." He later identified such passive leadership, which simply fosters "individualistic freedom," as one of the root problems of Germany in the 1930s and 1940s (K. Lewin, 1948b, pp. 34–42). A third type of group had an adult leader who worked with the boys, offering them encouragement and guidance whenever necessary while letting them manage their own tasks.

The results of these experiments showed that the groups that operated under "democratic" leadership conditions were consistently more productive than their autocratic or laissez-faire counterparts. Members of these groups also cooperated with each other on tasks and continued working on their own initiative when the adult leader left the room. Horseplay and humor, but little active aggression or scapegoating, were observed among the members of the democratic groups. When questioned, they rated the team and their participation in it positively.

Things were less satisfactory for the laissez-faire groups. They had more difficulty organizing themselves to work on their projects and accomplished less. A great deal of aimless activity and horseplay occurred in these groups, distracting even the individuals who were intent on their own tasks. Cooperation among the boys was infrequent. When the adult leader left the room, things deteriorated even further, with scuffles breaking out and goal-directed activity slowly grinding to a halt. The boys in these groups seldom spoke positively of their group or their membership in it.

The boys in groups with an autocratic adult leader were the least productive among the three experimental conditions. After each stage of a task, they would stop working to get approval and directions from the leader. They displayed little independent initiative and seldom spoke to each other while they were working. When the leader left the room, they stopped working almost immediately. During these leaderless intervals, fights and other displays of aggression were common. Many of the autocratic groups cast one or more of their members in the role of the scapegoat, eventually driving these people out of the group. Then someone else would be forced into the same role to repeat the cycle. The boys in the groups with autocratic leadership professed mild approval at best for their club.

In a series of follow-up studies, Lewin and his colleagues demonstrated that the same boys, given a different set of leadership styles,

would alter their behavior accordingly. Boys who had been cooperative and creative in a democratic group were placed under an autocratic leader. They soon became sullen and submissive, and their
productivity dropped off. When clubs that had formerly operated
under autocratic or laissez-faire conditions gained democratic leaders, the boys learned to discard their aggression. They became more
productive, began to exercise independent judgment, and cooperated on tasks (Lewin, Lippitt, and White, 1939). Noting that it took
longer to switch from autocracy to democracy than the reverse,
Lewin concluded: "Autocracy is imposed on the individual. Democracy he has to learn!" (Marrow, [1969] 1984, p. 127).

When You Wish to Influence Individual Behavior

By 1940, open warfare engulfed Europe and loomed on the American horizon. Lewin wanted to establish with scientific irrefutability
that democracy could and would compete successfully with more
repressive systems of governance. Another study that eventually led
to the importance of the small group as a point of influence for
changing individual behavior was conducted with anthropologist
Margaret Mead on behalf of the U.S. government. Rationing of
some types of foods had been introduced following America's entry
into World War II, with only indifferent public acceptance. Mead
and Lewin accepted a commission to discover how to change the
eating and food-purchasing habits of families. In the course of this
study, they discovered two important facts. First, while the husband
generally stated that his wife cooked to satisfy her family's tastes,
in fact most housewives bought and prepared food that appealed
to their own preferences (K. Lewin, 1951c, p. 177). Therefore, to
change a family's eating habits, it was necessary to persuade the
housewife. She performed a function at the boundary between the
family group and the larger social environment that Lewin designated *gatekeeping*. If you could convince the gatekeeper to change,
the rest of the group would follow.

The second major finding in this study closely followed the
first. How could the gatekeeper be persuaded to change her
habits? Lewin and Mead found that lectures on the nutritional
virtues of alternative foods had little effect on the purchasing behavior of their subjects. Yet when the participants in their study
groups discussed their experiments with unfamiliar foods, shared

their recipes, and exchanged information about the problems they found in making the adjustment, they showed a measurable difference in what they bought (K. Lewin, 1951b, pp. 229–233). This observation dovetailed neatly with the results of Lewin's autocracy-versus-democracy studies. Lasting behavioral change is most likely to occur when people are able to get valid information, define the problem for themselves, and develop their own solutions in a group.

Membership in a group with a strong positive valence has come to be an essential part of many overall organizational change efforts, such as Social Technical Change and Total Quality Management.

When You Wish to Influence Motivation and Goals

In 1939, Lewin was approached by Alfred Marrow, a former student and an officer in his family business, the Harwood Manufacturing Company. This led to one of Lewin's few excursions into a business organization. Harwood's latest apparel factory was located in rural Virginia. The work force, mainly women without previous industrial experience, seemed unable to produce at the same level of output as Harwood employees in other parts of the country. Marrow asked Lewin to consult with his managers on-site and provide an assessment of the problem. From this simple request a research project grew that lasted almost a decade and changed the definition of good management (Marrow, [1969] 1984, p. 141).

By this time, Lewin had conducted several important experiments at the group level, and his initial visits to Harwood convinced him that it would be more effective to work with the employees in small groups rather than individually. He also suggested that employees be given more control over their own work and production quotas. This strategy was based on what his research had shown regarding the power of participatory groups to bring about change. Lewin convinced management to hire one of his graduate students, Alex Bavelas, to study methods for improving the way the company worked with people. Lewin, Bavelas, and their associates discovered many principles during their years at Harwood that are still used in contemporary organizations. Among them were the following.

First, groups that reached decisions together about their goals were usually able to achieve them, in contrast to groups that discussed issues without arriving at a specific agreement. In terms of field theory, an expression of interest is not a sufficient force to bring about a lasting change in behavior, whereas a decision is powerful enough to influence action.

Second, supervisors who received training in human relations and leadership skills were more effective in the workplace than those with exclusively technical skills. The need for this type of management training is virtually taken for granted today, but when it was introduced at Harwood, it was unheard of (Marrow, [1969] 1984, p. 46).

Third, most Harwood managers held the belief that older workers were too slow and caused problems. John French, Bavelas's successor, encouraged a committee of managers to conduct their own research project to determine whether this stereotype was true. The managers were startled to learn that older employees were among the most productive and dependable in the work force. The committee advocated hiring additional older workers, only to encounter resistance from colleagues who clung to the old beliefs despite the committee's research findings. From this experience, French concluded that although the action of group research is powerful enough to dislodge the prejudices of those who participate in it, simple information about the results does not have an equivalent impact on others. Direct involvement is the key to changing attitudes (Marrow and French, 1945, pp. 33–37).

Fourth, whenever it became necessary to change the clothing lines or manufacturing processes at Harwood, a period of low productivity and disciplinary problems followed. The employees, who were paid by the piece, resented having to periodically start over after having attained a consistent level of production. Coch and French (1948) used Lewin's experimental approach to set up three groups at a time when the plant was being retooled for a new season. Workers in the first group were simply told what they would be expected to do and how they would be paid following the changes. Workers in the second group elected representatives who met with management before the changes were implemented to discuss employee concerns and make suggestions regarding the new setup. In the third group, all the members of the work team met with management to discuss and help plan every aspect of the forthcoming changes.

After the changes were implemented, the productivity of the first (nonparticipatory) group dropped an average of 20 percent and never regained previous levels. Employee turnover increased, and numerous disciplinary incidents were recorded. The second (elected-representative) group regained its earlier level of productivity within two weeks of the change. They had no turnover and little disruptive behavior. The third (full-participation) group recovered its previous level of productivity within two days of the change and soon surpassed it by a considerable margin. They had no turnover, and no disciplinary incidents occurred in this group. This study clearly demonstrated that learning and performance thrive in conditions of high participation, whereas lack of participation increases hostility and resistance to change (Coch and French, 1948).

When You Wish to Influence Behavior in a Large System

Lewin's work in field theory also provided many of the basic concepts for the new discipline of group dynamics. The influence of group affiliation had always been an important facet of individual psychology in Lewin's system. Now he proposed to apply similar principles to the study of the behavior of groups. A group, no less than an individual, can be described in terms of the interplay of forces and tension systems in a psychological field. The stronger the valence of the group, the better able it is to influence the behavior of its members. Change can more readily be effected by shifting the whole social climate that supports existing behavior than by focusing on the actions of individuals in isolation. When the array of forces in the group changes, the life space of the individual group members must necessarily change as well.

The Research Center for Group Dynamics at MIT was just one of Lewin's commitments in the mid 1940s. He also organized the Commission on Community Interrelations (CCI) for the American Jewish Congress. The purpose of the CCI was to study and intervene scientifically in problems of intergroup prejudice. Not surprisingly, both the Center and the CCI were staffed in large part by Lewin's former students and colleagues, many of whom were now eminent psychologists in their own right. The chief research approach favored by both organizations was a method Lewin had

termed *action research*. The action research method involved studying a social system by attempting to change its operations, usually
working in active collaboration with its members. This was a radical departure from the tradition of controlled experimental studies. Lewin's experiences at Iowa and Harwood had convinced him
that the behavior of people in groups could best be changed by involving the group members themselves in the process of identifying and solving the problem.

In action research, a consultant interviews a group, usually on
an individual basis, and then collectively and publicly "feeds back"
the data to the group for their own interpretation. This process
typically involves publicly posting the raw data (answers to interview questions without personal attribution) on newsprint or
poster paper. The impact comes from the interaction that takes
place when participants read, react to, and discuss their own interview responses.

With this new methodology, Lewin's new psychology laboratories would be real schools, factories, and communities. Action research was a natural outgrowth of Lewin's collaborative style and
penchant for seeing every aspect of life as a demonstration of psychological forces at work. Other researchers who learned to apply
his methods at the Center and the CCI found them to be excep-
tional tools for managing change in human systems. Under Lewin's
direction, the CCI staff conducted action research projects that included reducing violence between ethnic youth gangs, changing
store owners' attitudes about hiring African-American salespeople,
creating community acceptance for integrated housing, and reconciling community groups in the wake of an urban riot (Marrow,
[1969] 1984, pp. 201–210).

Today Lewin's influence is also felt in such systemic change
strategies as the Future Search. In a Future Search the psychological field is widened to include many who may have had a stake in
the future of a system, but who have not been included in the planning. This can include representatives from the workers, management, customers, suppliers, the community—anybody who might
have a stake in the future of the organization. These individuals
spend three days in a systematic search for common ground. The
"whole system" comes together in the room in a Lewinian process,
to assume responsibility for something that is important to them

and to study their organization or community in order to change it (Weisbord and Janoff, 1995, p. 57).

When You Wish to Promote Individual Awareness and Change

An especially notable outcome of this period was the development of the laboratory training group in human relations (sometimes called a T group or encounter group). In 1946, Lewin was approached by the Connecticut State Interracial Commission to train local community leaders to battle bigotry. As was his wont, Lewin contrived a way to make the event both a workshop to fulfill the original request and an experiment for studying how the training brought about change in the participants (K. Lewin, 1948a, p. 210). He assembled a staff of educators and researchers to work together on the project, headed by Kenneth Benne and Leland Bradford. The participants and staff members mingled as peers, addressing topics such as how best to change prejudicial attitudes. The participants then practiced communication skills in groups, observed by the trainers and researchers. In the evening the staff met to discuss their impressions of the day's events.

Some of the participants who were staying at the conference site asked to be allowed to listen in on this discussion. The researchers were reluctant to allow this, fearing that it might unduly influence the group's subsequent behavior, but Lewin encouraged the participants to join them. Before long, the participants were actively engaged in reviewing critical incidents from the workshop and exchanging points of view with the staff. The resulting feedback was so useful for everyone concerned that similar discussions were incorporated as a regular feature for the remainder of the two-week workshop.

In this almost accidental fashion, Lewin and his associates discovered that a dialogue based on specific feedback regarding real-time incidents in a workshop setting could precipitate behavioral change in both individuals and groups. Today this T-group method of education, which uses feedback and group dynamics to restructure the life spaces of the participants, is in wide use. Another direct outgrowth of this event was the foundation in 1947 of the National Training Laboratories, an organization that still sponsors research and experiential education in applied behavioral sciences (Marrow, [1969] 1984, pp. 210–214).

When You Are Concerned with Managing Conflict

Field theory portrays conflict as a situation in which forces of approximately equal strength are acting on a person or group in opposite directions. These may be driving forces, impelling the person or group to move, or constraining forces, which impede movement in a particular direction. In other words, conflict is the result of strong tension systems in the life space that prevent each other from achieving release. With this framework in mind, it is possible for a practitioner to initiate a process that will change these forces.

Lewin describes a solution to a chronic conflict in an apparel factory. Often more than one machine broke down at a time, resulting in competing demands upon the single mechanic. The mechanic's inability to meet these demands led to a continual series of interpersonal confrontations and misunderstandings. The Lewinian solution was to refocus the psychological field of the protagonists away from the relative power and privilege of each machine operator to a process of joint problem solving. The machine operators who were the most involved met and the psychologist let the objective facts (one repair person serving too many machines) emerge from that discussion. With this new focus, the machine operators acknowledged the problem of multiple demands and took responsibility for ranking the order in which the machines would be repaired (K. Lewin, 1948c, p. 133).

Shifting the emphasis from stating positions to describing needs has become a commonplace principle of conflict resolution. Fisher and Ury's popular book, *Getting to Yes* (1981) is based on this premise. Lewin's formulations are seldom cited as a source for this process, but this approach was not common practice when Lewin first wrote about it.

At the organizational level, such conflict frequently results from a lack of agreement regarding direction. Complex organizations have many differentiated functions going on simultaneously, each with its own imperative. From the perspective of Finance, the most urgent order of current business may be to increase cash flow. Research and Development may see a need to fund a major new technological advance in order to stay competitive in the future. Assembly-line employees may be most concerned about new policies that change the conditions under which they do their jobs.

None of these priorities is wrong, but in combination they may make it difficult for the organization to move at all.

The Lewinian approach to conflict is to unblock the gridlock by creating a new balance among the forces at work in the field. This can be accomplished by weakening the constraining forces, strengthening the driving forces, or both. A certain level of agreement regarding goals is required in order to bring this about at the organizational level. An entire technology has come into being for this purpose, including the formulation of mission statements, futures conferences, and strategic intent campaigns. All of these tools have a similar aim: to create an overarching purpose and a vision for the future that has a strong positive valence. Such a purpose should be broad enough to encompass the many specialized interests of the organizational subunits but explicit enough to provide a clear direction for productive action. This common goal, then, constitutes a vector that can overpower the constraints of more parochial concerns.

Of course, the mere statement of a common goal will not reconcile a basic structural conflict. The process by which such a goal is formulated and implemented is critical to its success. Detailed analysis and problem solving must accompany the creation of an overarching goal. Lewin's emphasis on participatory process increases the likelihood that the result will be accepted and acted upon. If people are simply handed a goal or mission and told that it is theirs, they may well tuck it into a bottom drawer and never look at it again. In conflict, as in much else, Lewin believed that the most effective intervention was the one that gave a person or group a greater area of free movement. Remove the barriers and people will move forward with the momentum of their own need to grow.

A more recent example of Lewinian conflict management in a cross-cultural setting has been a series of conflict workshops in the Jewish-Arab village of Neve Shalom. Here Arab and Jewish settlers used Lewin's three-step change process of unfreezing, change, and refreezing. This process also involved "a cultural island and action research" (Bargal and Bar, 1992, p. 146). The model followed the classic sequence of differentiation and integration for an intergroup exercise. Arabs and Jews first met separately to explore their own group identity and then met together to share information.

Interestingly, the readiness of Arab participants to maintain contact with their Israeli counterparts and live with the stress of conflict in order to find a solution *increased* in 1988. This was the first year of the Intifada (uprising), the very time when such readiness was *decreasing* elsewhere. This was substantiated by the decreased scores of an Arab control group that did not attend the workshops (Bargal and Bar, 1992, p. 131).

When You Wish to Influence Cohesion Within a Group or Organization

Group affiliation is a critical element in Lewin's system. The groups we belong to help to determine who we are and what we will or will not do. In his study of group affiliation, Lewin defined several variables that remain important today in our focus on both work groups and groups of origin (race, gender, ethnicity, and so on).

Writing about minority groups, Lewin focused on identity. He asked why an individual might identify so closely with a group that he or she could not respond freely and naturally to a situation. He also focused on underidentification, citing the example of what he termed the *self-hating Jews,* who are members of a group they think of as low-status and therefore might like to leave but cannot. Instead of directing hostility toward the powerful majority that is limiting movement, the minority group members direct that negative feeling toward the group or toward themselves. Lewin pointed out that this process is not limited to Jews but takes place in many minority groups (M. Lewin, [1974] 1976, p. 131). One result of such ambivalence is marginality: a person has one foot in each of several camps but belongs to none. Lewin likened such marginality to adolescence, when the uncertainty of the ground he or she stands on makes the adolescent loud and restless and alternately timid and aggressive. This behavior pattern includes being oversensitive and tending to go to extremes—for example, being overcritical of others and oneself (M. Lewin, [1974] 1976, p. 131).

Lewin also focused on work groups and decision-making groups. His research on food habits illustrated the way group membership affects the goals we set for ourselves, how we act toward other people, and how we expect them to act toward us. The more highly we prize our membership in a particular group, the more likely we are to modify our actions to conform to the group's perceived expectations. For this reason, Lewin saw groups as both targets and vehicles for change.

Lewin used the term *cohesion* to describe the array of internal forces that keep a group together. Members of more cohesive groups are more likely to conform to its standards. Military organizations are an interesting case in point. The forces at work in a military unit include coercion, functional interdependence, personal attachments, esprit de corps, a clear mission, and explicit standards of conduct for nearly every situation. This combination of influences is capable of creating a group so cohesive that its members will deliberately walk into deadly danger rather than violate the collective code of conduct. Other groups, such as fire fighters, share a similar ethos.

Once a cohesive group begins to change direction, even the most recalcitrant members make some effort to follow in its wake.

When You Wish to Influence Psychological Growth

Lewin saw growth as a dynamic, lifelong process of expanding and differentiating one's life space. For this movement to occur, it is necessary for existing configurations of psychological forces and facts to change. Late in his career, Lewin formalized a three-stage model describing the underlying mechanism of this process of change. This model applies equally to change on the individual, group, and organizational levels of systems. The first stage of change is to unfreeze the existing constellation of forces. Lewin developed a tool for assessing the state of the current field, known as a *force-field analysis* (see Figure 7.3). The force-field analysis is based on Lewin's topology. It is a deceptively simple instrument consisting of a straight line that represents the existing equilibrium of forces. On one side of the line, the known restraining forces in the field (those that inhibit a change) are listed and their relative strengths are estimated. On the opposite side of the central line, the driving forces (those that are moving toward change) are listed and their respective strengths assessed. The result is an elementary map of the existing psychological field (Deutsch, 1973, p. 441).

The first stage is to unfreeze the status quo; by focusing on the specific driving and constraining forces, it is possible to identify what can most readily be changed. In Lewin's view, it is usually easier to *decrease* the restraining forces rather than to *increase* the

Figure 7.3. Example of a Force Field.

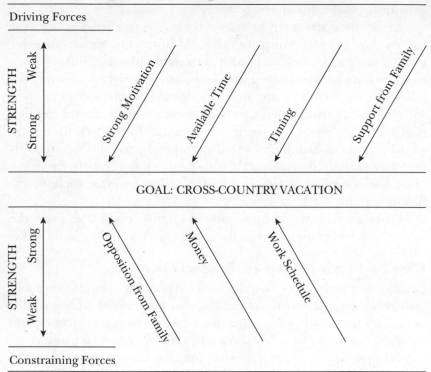

Driving Forces

GOAL: CROSS-COUNTRY VACATION

Constraining Forces

enabling forces. Decreasing the restraining forces lowers tension in the group, and increasing the enabling forces adds tension (K. Lewin, 1951b, p. 217).

In Figure 7.3, your goal is to take the family on a cross-country tour this summer instead of spending the usual two weeks at the rented beach house. Constraining forces include (1) opposition from other family members (your teenage daughter wants to hang out at the beach with her school friends), (2) money (a cross-country trip will be more expensive), and (3) uncertainty about work schedule (you may not be able to arrange your work schedule to get away from the office for the necessary three weeks). Of these, the opposition from other family members is the strongest barrier because three weeks in a car with a sulking teenager will be "hell on wheels". The driving forces are (1) strong motivation (you have wanted to make this trip for years), (2) availability of time (you have finally qualified for three weeks of annual leave), (3) timing (your youngest child is now old enough to tolerate long days of travel), and (4) support from family members (everyone except your daughter is willing to go).

This force field suggests several possible interventions. You can probably rearrange your work schedule if you make a point of it. The money constraint can be overcome if you are willing to cash in some bonds or finance part of the trip on your credit cards. The biggest obstacle to change is your daughter. Perhaps you can invite one of her friends to accompany your family on the trip. Perhaps the family of one of her friends would be willing to have her stay with them at the beach while you are gone. Or you might put her in charge of some aspect of trip planning, with an emphasis on colorful beach brochures. Once you remove or weaken the constraining forces, the driving forces should take you where you want to go.

The second stage of the change process is movement. This is a period of transition during which the field is fundamentally restructured. The boundaries of various regions within the psychological field undergo change. Regions become more or less permeable, or more or less differentiated. New facts gain prominence as old facts lose their previous valence. This is likely to be a time of emotional excitability and some confusion as new behaviors are tested.

The final stage of the change process is the refreezing of the forces in the field in a new equilibrium. It should be noted that Lewin never intended refreezing or equilibrium to imply finality. The term he actually used was *quasi-stationary equilibrium,* for he realized that change was the true constant underlying the appearance of continuity in the psychological field. Lewin's model of human behavior and psychological growth was profoundly dynamic.

Conclusion

Lewin's theory is not the answer to every organizational question, but it is essential in making most other theories and most other answers relevant to work in organizations. This is because Lewin's theory provides a framework that both includes other concepts and turns those concepts into triggers for action. In this chapter, we described the action research method, which could be used to help a group become more aware of (1) what reinforces its behavior (Skinner); (2) its own thought processes (Ellis and Beck); (3) its image of its Shadow (Jung); (4) its gender association (Horney); and (5) its image of the ideal and real selves (Horney).

Although it is abstract, Lewin's theory is not remote. It forms the basis of numerous other approaches that practitioners can use to deal with the conscious experience of individuals in organizations. For example, his basic equation, B = F(P, E), or behavior is a function of the person and the environment, is the starting point practitioners must accept if they are to work within the conscious experience of individuals and the norms of most organizations.

Lewin's theories are also practical because they have a quality of instantaneous and unavoidable application. If a practitioner defines an individual's, group's, or organization's psychological field, the definition is only valid for that moment. It must constantly be redefined; Lewinian practitioners can never become imprisoned in stale or irrelevant theories. They are continually forced to gather fresh data in order to remain applicable. Nor can those data be abstract. Lewin's emphasis on the *personal world* of each person, group, or organization ensures that practitioners will continually return to the individual's personal experience for valid information. Using Lewin's theory, practitioners must stay closely in touch with the individual and his or her environment.

Annotated Bibliography
Original Sources: Readable Lewin

Lewin, K. *Resolving Social Conflicts: Selected Papers on Group Dynamics.* New York: HarperCollins, 1948.
This is Lewin's most readable and socially concerned work. In it, he deals with his comparisons of German and U.S. society, group membership, and, as the title indicates, resolving social conflicts.

Secondary Sources: Books About Lewin and His Theories

Deutsch, M. "Field Theory in Social Psychology." In G. Lindzey and E. Aronson (eds.), *Handbook of Social Psychology* (Vol. 1, 2nd ed., pp. 412–487). Reading, Mass.: Addison-Wesley, 1968.
This classic essay by one of Lewin's students is one of the clearest explanations of his overall theory.

Lewin, M. "Psychological Aspects of Minority Group Membership: The Concepts of Kurt Lewin." In T. Blass (ed.), *Contemporary Social Psychology: Representative Readings* (pp. 128–137). Itasca, Ill.: F. E. Peacock, 1976. (Originally published 1974.)

Lewin, M. "The Impact of Kurt Lewin's Life on the Place of Social Issues in His Work." *Journal of Social Issues,* Summer 1992, *48*(2), 15–29.

Miriam Lewin is Kurt Lewin's daughter and a psychologist at Manhattanville College. In these two articles, she places her father's work in a social and historical context and supplies many heretofore unknown biographical details.

Marrow, A. J. *The Practical Theorist: The Life and Work of Kurt Lewin.* Annapolis, Md.: BDR Learning Products, 1984. (Originally published 1969.)

This is the first and thus far the only biography about Lewin. Alfred Marrow was one of his students. The book combines Lewin's work and theory with an account of his short but dramatic and productive life.

Organizational Applications

French, W., and Bell, C. *Organization Development: Behavioral Science Interventions for Organization Improvement.* Englewood Cliffs, N.J.: Prentice Hall, 1984.

This is the first and one of the most widely used texts covering organization development. The chapter on history traces Lewin's contribution to the development of the field.

Weisbord, M. R. *Productive Workplaces: Organizing and Managing for Dignity, Meaning, and Community.* San Francisco: Jossey-Bass, 1987.

This book traces the beginning of the contemporary field of organizational change trough the life and work of Lewin and other pioneer thinkers, including Frederick Winslow Taylor, Douglas McGregor, and Fred Emery and Eric Trist. It is my personal choice as the single best book in the organizational field that shows us how the field reached its present state of development.

Bibliography

Back, K. W. "Lewin and Current Developmental Theory." In E. Stivers and S. Wheelan (eds.), *The Lewin Legacy: Field Theory in Current Practice* (pp. 52–64). New York: Springer-Verlag, 1986.

Back, K. W. "This Business of Topology." *Journal of Social Issues,* 1992, *48*(2), 51–66.

Bargal, D., and Bar, H. A. "A Lewinian Approach to Intergroup Workshops for Arab-Palestinian and Jewish Youth." *Journal of Social Issues,* 1992, *48*(2), 139–154.

Bower, G. H., and Hilgard, E. R. *Theories of Learning.* (5th ed.) Englewood Cliffs, N.J.: Prentice Hall, l981.

Burke, W. *Organization Development: Principles and Practices.* Boston: Little, Brown, 1982.

Coch, L., and French, R. P., Jr. "Overcoming Resistance to Change." *Human Relations,* 1948, *1,* 512–532.

Dembo, T. "Der Aerger als dynamisches Problem" [The Dynamics of Anger]. In J. de Rivera (ed.), *Field Theory as Human-Science: Contributions of Lewin's Berlin Group.* New York: Gardner Press, 1976. (Originally published 1931.)

Deutsch, M. "Field Theory in Social Psychology." In G. Lindzey and E. Aronson (eds.), *Handbook of Social Psychology* (Vol. 1, 2nd ed., pp. 412–487). Reading, Mass.: Addison-Wesley, 1968.

Deutsch, M. *The Resolution of Conflict: Constructive and Destructive Processes.* New Haven, Conn.: Yale University Press, 1973.

Fisher, R., and Ury, W. *Getting to Yes: Negotiating Agreement Without Giving in.* Boston: Houghton Mifflin, 1981.

Frank, J. "Kurt Lewin in Retrospect: A Psychiatrist's View." *Journal of the History of the Behavioral Sciences,* 1978, *14,* 223–227.

French, W., and Bell, C. *Organization Development: Behavioral Science Interventions for Organization Improvement.* Englewood Cliffs, N.J.: Prentice Hall, 1984.

Hoppe, F. "Erfolg und Misserfolg" [Success and Failure]. In J. de Rivera (ed.), *Field Theory as Human-Science: Contributions of Lewin's Berlin Group* (pp. 454–492). New York: Gardner Press, 1976. (Originally published 1930.)

Hunt, M. *The Story of Psychology.* New York: Doubleday, 1993.

Karsten, A. "Psychische Saettigung" [Mental Satiation]. In J. de Rivera (ed.), *Field Theory as Human-Science: Contributions of Lewin's Berlin Group* (pp. 151–207). New York: Gardner Press, 1976. (Originally published 1928.)

Koffka, K. *Principles of Gestalt Psychology.* Orlando, Fla.: Harcourt Brace, 1935.

Kohler, W. *The Mentality of Apes.* (E. Winter, trans.). Orlando, Fla.: Harcourt Brace, 1925.

Lewin, K. *A Dynamic Theory of Personality.* (D. Adams and K. Zener, trans.). New York: McGraw-Hill, 1935.

Lewin, K. *Principles of Topological Psychology.* (F. Heider and G. Heider, trans.). New York: McGraw-Hill, 1936.

Lewin, K. "Field Theory and Experiment in Social Psychology: Concepts and Methods." *American Journal of Sociology,* March 1939, *44,* 868–896.

Lewin, K. "Action Research and Minority Problems." In G. Lewin (ed.), *Resolving Social Conflicts: Selected Papers on Group Dynamics* (pp. 201–216). New York: HarperCollins, 1948a.

Lewin, K. "Cultural Reconstruction." In G. Lewin (ed.), *Resolving Social Conflicts: Selected Papers on Group Dynamics* (pp. 34–42). New York: HarperCollins, 1948b.

Lewin, K. "The Solution of a Chronic Conflict in Industry." In G. Lewin (ed.), *Resolving Social Conflicts: Selected Papers on Group Dynamics* (pp. 125–141). New York: HarperCollins, 1948c.

Lewin, K. "Behavior and Development as a Function of the Total Situation." In D. Cartwright (ed.), *Field Theory in Social Science: Selected Theoretical Papers* (pp. 238–304). New York: HarperCollins, 1951a.

Lewin, K. "Frontiers in Group Dynamics." In D. Cartwright (ed.), *Field Theory in Social Science: Selected Theoretical Papers* (pp. 188–237). New York: HarperCollins, 1951b.

Lewin, K. "Psychological Ecology." In D. Cartwright (ed.), *Field Theory in Social Science: Selected Theoretical Papers* (pp. 170–187). New York: HarperCollins, 1951c.

Lewin, K., Heider, F., and Heider, G. M. *Principles of Topological Psychology.* New York: McGraw-Hill, 1936.

Lewin, K., Lippitt, R., and White, R. "Patterns of Aggressive Behavior in Experimentally Created 'Social Climates.'" *Journal of Social Psychology,* 1939, *10,* 271–279.

Lewin, M. "Psychological Aspects of Minority Group Membership: The Concepts of Kurt Lewin." In T. Blass (ed.), *Contemporary Social Psychology: Representative Readings* (pp. 128–137). Itasca, Ill.: F. E. Peacock, 1976. (Originally published 1974.)

Lewin, M. "The Impact of Kurt Lewin's Life on the Place of Social Issues in His Work." *Journal of Social Issues,* Summer 1992, *48*(2), 15–29.

Marrow, A. J. *The Practical Theorist: The Life and Work of Kurt Lewin.* Annapolis, Md.: BDR Learning Products, 1984. (Originally published 1969.)

Marrow, A. J., and French, J. "Changing a Stereotype in Industry." *Journal of Social Issues,* 1945, *1,* 33–37.

Weisbord, M. R. *Productive Workplaces: Organizing and Managing for Dignity, Meaning, and Community.* San Francisco: Jossey-Bass, 1987.

Weisbord, M., and Janoff, S. *Future Search: An Action Guide to Finding Common Ground in Organizations and Communities.* San Francisco: Berrett-Koehler, 1995.

Wertheimer, M. "Laws of Organization in Perceptual Forms." In W. D. Ellis (ed.), *A Source Book of Gestalt Psychology* (pp. 71–88). Orlando, Fla.: Harcourt Brace, 1938.

Chapter Eight

Fritz and Laura Perls
The Gestalt of Experience and Behavior

Why the Perls? An Overview of Gestalt Applications in Organizations

Fritz and Laura Perls's evolved framework is a valuable basis for viewing individuals, groups, and organizations as whole systems. These systems meet their needs by reacting to their environment through a Cycle of Experience. Understanding this cycle helps the practitioner to identify where, when, and how to influence the system.

The emphasis on whole systems helps practitioners to focus on multiple levels of action or behavior, for example, seeing the system-wide effects of what may appear to be a problem between two individuals. The focus on how the system meets its own needs helps the practitioner to understand how to help that process when it is blocked. Gestalt theory shows practitioners how to do this by tapping into their own energy as well as the energy of the system.

Gestalt Theory as an Organizational Image or Metaphor

The Gestalt image of the individual, group, or organization as a system reflects the interconnections of past and present, body and mind, organism and environment. These important connections are often not obvious to those who are directly involved in a system. The

Note: The author gratefully acknowledges the assistance of Washington, D.C., consultant Al Templeton for examples of the application of Gestalt principles to work in organizations.

image of whole systems in Gestalt theory helps practitioners to illustrate these linkages.

Gestalt Theory as a Point of Influence for Dealing with Conflict

Gestalt theory makes several contributions to dealing with conflict. Gestalt's focus on the senses brings submerged emotion to awareness, expression, and catharsis. The framework of the cycle of experience brings to light unfinished business in individuals, groups, and organizations.

Gestalt Theory as a Point of Influence for Dealing with Psychological Growth

Gestalt theory assumes growth as a natural function of the human organism, identifies obstacles to this growth, and defines steps that can be taken to minimize these obstacles. The emphasis on internal feedback and awareness helps to surface otherwise hidden feelings and reactions. This process encourages individual responsibility, autonomy, responsibility, and initiative.

Gestalt Theory as a Point of Influence for Dealing with the Dilemmas of Joining

Gestalt theory helps the practitioner to penetrate the various layers that envelop the core of human motivation. This process helps the practitioner to deal with the real reason an individual may or may not be committed to a project or an organization. The theory also emphasizes the impact of self-defined boundaries that lie within and between all aspects of human activity. The notion of boundaries helps practitioners to identify and influence the way individuals become committed to organizations.

Gestalt Theory as a Basis for Other Organizationally Relevant Theories

The Gestalt theory of psychotherapy is adapted and applied to groups and organizations in an ongoing training program at the Cleveland Institute of Gestalt. With this institutional base, Gestalt theory continues to be refined and applied to multiple levels of systems.

Limitations of Gestalt Theory for Use in Organizations

Gestalt theory's emphasis on presence is a strength and a potential limitation. To be effective in using their presence, practitioners need an awareness and knowledge of self, qualities that come to most individuals only through concerted effort. Gestalt theory and its methodology evoke an excitement, a playfulness, and a high level of energy that are not a part of other approaches. Practitioners need both self-awareness and knowledge of systems to introduce these elements into organizations.

How Gestalt Theory Developed

Most other theories of personality in this volume are easily identified as the product of one person. Carl Jung is clearly the creator or synthesizer of the notion of archetypes. Similarly, few dispute that Sigmund Freud, Carl Rogers, and others are the creators or synthesizers of the concepts linked with their names. In the case of Gestalt therapy, however, establishing parentage is more complicated. Fritz Perls is generally associated with the development and dissemination of Gestalt therapy, and ample justification can be found for this connection. Without Fritz Perls, Gestalt therapy would not exist (Wheeler, 1991, p. 4). At the same time, others were involved in the development of Gestalt therapy in very significant ways. Perls's wife Lore (later Laura) had studied with Max Wertheimer, one of the founders of Gestalt psychology (Latner, 1992, p. 14), and was more familiar with these concepts than Fritz. Fritz had been briefly exposed to these concepts but gained much of his understanding from her. In an interview with Dan Rosenblatt (1991, p. 12), Laura stated that she had written two chapters of *Ego Hunger and Aggression* (Perls, 1969a), the first book on the early development of the theory. Laura Perls continued to be an important force in Gestalt therapy as a therapist and a trainer of other therapists (Rosenblatt, 1980, p. 7) until her death in 1990.

Paul Goodman, social critic, writer, and educational theorist, wrote the theoretical foundation of Gestalt therapy from a manuscript Fritz Perls had produced in 1950 (Stoehr, 1994, pp. 81–98). The book is one physical volume, but the table of contents divides the book into two parts, with the first volume composed of aware-ness exercises that Professor Ralph Hefferline of Columbia Uni-versity had performed with his students. Perls and Goodman wrote the important second volume of theory, but there is no way of knowing the precise contributions of each. From the prior and later writings of each of them, however, it is clear that Goodman made a substantial contribution to clarifying the relationship of the individual to social systems and the environment (L. Perls, 1990). Goodman later became a Gestalt therapist, authoring nu-merous books and plays including his classic description of disaf-fected youth, *Growing Up Absurd* (Goodman, 1956).

In 1954 a group of students and therapists who had been study-ing with Fritz Perls, Laura Perls, Isadore From, and Paul Goodman founded the Cleveland Gestalt Institute. Similar institutes were formed in other major cities, and members of these institutes also made further contributions to the theory. The Cleveland group, however, has distinguished itself with a number of important ex-tensions and modifications of Perls and Goodman's theory, apply-ing it to groups, couples, and, eventually, organizations (Wheeler, 1991, pp. 84–109).

Because of the mixed parentage of modern Gestalt therapy, this chapter departs from the pattern of identifying a theory with one individual. The chapter title places the focus on Fritz and Laura Perls; when the focus is on the combined work of the Perls's successors, we refer to Gestalt theory. Fritz Perls's pioneering con-tribution, however, should not be ignored. We now outline his life and personality in order to experience the flavor, excitement, and appeal of his original contribution to Gestalt therapy.

This passage from Perls's autobiography, *In and Out of the Garbage Pail* (1969c), captures some of his unique personality as well as the force behind his life and work:

> I am becoming a public figure. From an obscure lower middle class Jewish boy to a mediocre psychoanalyst to the possible creator of a "new" method of treatment and the exponent of a viable philoso-phy which could do something for mankind.
>
> Does this mean that I am a do-gooder or that I want to serve mankind? The fact that I formulate the question shows my doubts. I believe that I do what I do for myself, for my interest in solving problems, and most of all for my vanity.

I feel best when I can be a prima donna and can show off my skill of getting rapidly in touch with the essence of a person and his plight. However, there must be another side to me. Whenever something *real* happens, I am deeply moved, and whenever I get deeply involved in an encounter with a patient, I forget my audience and their possible admiration completely and I am *all there* [Perls, 1969c, pp. 1–2].

Perls was born in a Jewish ghetto on the outskirts of Berlin in 1893. He was a rebel against his family and most other forms of authority but still served in the German army in World War I, earning a medal for bravery, and attained a medical degree at a relatively young age. In the early 1920s, attempting to deal with the turmoil in his own life, he entered psychoanalysis with Karen Horney, a young analyst who had already established a reputation as an innovator. Perls then went on to become an analyst himself, and his analytic training and early work were valuable building blocks for his later theories.

Perls's style as a theory builder was to take concepts from a wide array of sources and then bring them together as a single unified whole. Gestalt itself is a theory that emphasizes single unified wholes, and Perls demonstrated that process in his development of the theory. Earlier, he had studied theater with famed director Max Reinhardt and creative dance and movement with expressionist dancer Palucca. After leaving Karen Horney, Perls continued analysis with Wilhelm Reich, who gave him an understanding of the crucial linkage of the body to the psyche.

An influence for Perls's later development of Gestalt therapy was Gestalt psychology. (For background on Gestalt psychology, see Chapter Seven.) Perls briefly served as an assistant to Kurt Goldstein, who worked with brain-damaged soldiers and applied the perceptual theories of Gestalt psychology to overall human functioning. While working with Goldstein, Perls met Lore Posner. They became friends, then lovers, and eventually they married. Lore Perls was a talented and hardworking academic and later a gifted therapist and a student of Gestalt and existential psychology. She played a key role in Fritz Perls's intellectual development and was later a cofounder of Gestalt therapy (Clarkson and Mackewn, 1993, p. 10).

Although the early Gestaltists demonstrated that humans perceive in wholes rather than atomistic particles, they limited their research to the area of visual perception. They did not investigate why individuals perceive one figure rather than another or how these differences in perception influence general functioning. Gestalt psychology might have remained an important but narrowly applied area of academic psychology had not Goldstein, Abraham Maslow, Kurt Lewin, and, later, Fritz Perls attempted to answer these questions by applying the Gestalt learning process to the larger area of human motivation and behavior.

Lewin had demonstrated that what an individual perceives in a given situation is related to her or his needs at that time. From this notion he conceptualized a tension system within each individual that influences what that person perceives. Later, in *Ego, Hunger and Aggression* (1969a), Perls attributed the work of Lewin's students Bluma Zeigarnik and Maria Ovsiankina to Lewin himself and noted that unsolved problems were better remembered than those that were solved (Perls, 1969a, p. 101). Eventually this reaction evolved into Perls's notion of "unfinished business," the idea that unfinished emotional tasks remain as an influence on current behavior that is beyond awareness. Perls went on to devise therapeutic interventions that helped individuals attempt to finish unfinished business. *Ego, Hunger and Aggression* is also Perls's first description of the systems view that later became so important in Gestalt organizational consulting. Perls touches on linkages between the individual organism and the environment. This relationship was later developed by practitioners at the Cleveland Institute of Gestalt.

Kurt Goldstein went one step further than Lewin in offering evidence that what an individual perceives as figural or important is related to the individual's current level of functioning. Perls later turned Goldstein's concept into a practical tool for change by showing how we can understand an individual's *inner* perceptual process by observing what is taking place at the boundary between the senses and the environment. For Perls, the senses reach out and literally *make sense* of what is going on.

Perls continued to practice as a psychoanalyst, but his natural inclination to rebel and his early exposure to Wilhelm Reich, Gestalt psychology, and other nontraditional ways of thinking made it difficult for him to adhere to established Freudian doctrine.

Fleeing Nazi Germany in 1933, Perls and his new wife, Laura, became the first psychoanalysts in South Africa. Hoping to revise some analytic concepts, Perls presented a paper in 1936 at an international psychoanalytic meeting in Czechoslovakia. The paper emphasized the importance of hunger as a basic human drive and eating habits as an indicator and determinant of personality. It was not well received, and during the same visit, Perls had a frustrating four-minute visit with Sigmund Freud himself. These two experiences helped to alienate Perls further from psychoanalytic thinking. The result was his first book, *Ego, Hunger and Aggression,* which contained the framework for later Gestalt therapy: the conception of humans as organisms with many drives, the application of Gestalt psychology to overall functioning, the importance of the senses and the present moment, and the changed role of the analyst from a neutral projection screen to a full and available human being.

Perls emigrated to the United States in 1946, and in the following twenty-year period he became, in the words of his then-estranged wife, "part prophet, part bum." These were difficult years for Perls as he wandered the country building a practice and starting an institute, only to move on before he could become settled and comfortable. All the while he was developing Gestalt therapy as a separate modality, and in doing so he freely borrowed concepts and techniques from other therapists, for example, psychodramatic role playing, borrowed from J. L. Moreno. In 1951, with social critic Paul Goodman and Columbia University professor Ralph Hefferline, he published *Gestalt Therapy;* however, the book was not widely read at the time. The Cleveland Gestalt Institute, founded in 1954, lists Perls as one of its thirteen founders. Perls occasionally taught there but did not play an active role in the Institute's development.

In the early 1960s, when Perls was approaching seventy, recognition and fame finally came to both Perls and Gestalt therapy. It came at the Esalen Institute at Big Sur, California, where Perls took up residence, taught, offered workshops, and became something of a symbol of what was termed the "human potential movement." Perls died in 1970 after founding what was to be the first Gestalt therapeutic community on Vancouver Island in Canada (Shepard, 1975, p. 191). Perls's last words were to a hospital nurse, who said, "You must lie down." He looked her in the eye and said, "Don't tell me what to do," fell back, and died (Shepard, 1975, p. 192).

Preview: Applications of the
Gestalt Point of Influence in the Workplace.

The Gestalt Point of Influence

Gestalt's point of influence is the *unity* and *self-regulating nature* of life. This sounds like a lofty abstraction rather than a way to influence human behavior; however, it is both. In the Gestalt view, humans are whole, self-regulating systems that are parts of other whole systems. Thought, feeling, and body, past and present, are tied together in each individual system, as individuals are tied together with their environment and with each other.

We will examine Gestalt theory in terms of five clusters of concepts, adapted from Clarkson and Mackewn (1993, p. 34):

Cluster One: Holism

Cluster Two: Field theory

Cluster Three: The cycle of experience
Cluster Four: Contact
Cluster Five: Interruptions to contact

Cluster One: Holism

In his early theoretical works, Perls made the case that a number of aspects of human existence that are customarily considered as separate or opposites are in fact unitary or wholes. These include:

- *Mind and body:* Perls pointed out the interconnection of the human organism: "No emotion like rage, sadness, shame, or disgust occurs without its physiological as well as its psychological components coming into play" (Perls, 1969a, p. 33).
- *Past and present:* The early Gestalt theorists pointed out that the past exists within the present. Memory and prospects are *present* imaginations (Perls, Hefferline, and Goodman, 1951, p. 290).
- *Individual and environment:* "To consider an organism by itself amounts to looking upon it as an artificially isolated unit" (Perls, 1969a, p. 38). We cannot define "a breather without air, a walker without gravity and ground, an irascible without obstacles" (Perls, Hefferline, and Goodman, 1951, p. 256).

These unitary assumptions are the basis for a theory based on psychological fields.

Cluster Two: Field Theory

Mind and body as a whole can be described as an *organism*. The individual organism in its environment with its past embodied in its present gives us a *psychological field*. Within the psychological field or personal realm is all that is relevant to the individual at that moment. Gestalt therapy builds on the notion of such a field or of a field theory as envisioned earlier by Kurt Lewin and Kurt Goldstein and later by other Gestaltists. It's difficult, if not impossible, to be an impartial bystander to a psychological field. In psychotherapy, the therapist is part of the individual's or group's field; in organizational work the practitioner is part of the organization's field. Within the context of the psychological field are the notions of the *self-regulation* of the organism, *polarities,* and the formation of *figures* from a *ground*.

Self-regulation refers to the tendency of organisms to take steps to meet their own needs. The concept builds upon a philosophical tradition going back to Heraclitus in ancient Greece, who described organisms that are in constant flux as adapting to changing conditions (Clarkson and Mackewn, 1993, p. 54). Numerous examples of such adaptation exist in daily life: a hungry person seeks food; a lonely person seeks companionship. However, not every effort at self-regulation is successful. At times the environment is impoverished in food, emotional support, or whatever the organism needs. And the environment is not the only obstacle to self-regulation. At times the obstacle is within the organism itself in terms of an unsuccessful integration of polarities.

Polarities refers to the Gestalt perspective that, within each individual, feelings and reactions are paired with their opposite. As an individual becomes aware of a characteristic, then inevitably its antithesis is in the background. If the individual recognizes and supports the opposite force, allowing it to make its statement, the self-developing nature of the organism will work for integration (Polster and Polster, 1973, p. 61). If the individual ignores or suppresses the opposite side, it goes underground, using the time-tested methods of underground fighting: "guilt, foot-dragging, playing dumb, and depleting energy" (Polster and Polster, 1973, p. 247).

Perls offered the top dog and the underdog as an example of a generic polarity within the human personality. The top dog knows what is right and exhorts the underdog to obey; the underdog is quite unsure and promises to "do my best" and to "do it tomorrow." The underdog usually has its way (Perls, 1970, p. 21). One way to discover the power of the underdog to sabotage the best intentions of the top dog is to thoughtlessly embrace or accept the wishes of the top dog. The Polsters give a specific example of this (Polster and Polster, 1973, p. 63):

> A woman acts helpless because she fears the power of her anger. Recognizing and accepting her anger (one side of the polarity) helps her to accept and modify the other side of the polarity, her helplessness.

Figure and *ground* describe the process by which polarities come into awareness and attention becomes focused. At any given moment within the psychological field, something figural or prominent emerges from the ground. This emergence is not coincidental. It is a reflection of what is of interest to the organism at that moment

(Perls, Hefferline, and Goodman, 1951, p. 231). The ground replaces what is termed the unconscious in other frameworks, but without the negative connotations described by Freud. The background is always present and always available for framing and supporting our present experience (Latner, 1992, p. 27).

> Eight government scientists from around the country have been brought together to deal with a new problem of soil contamination. Most of them do not know each other, and the meeting starts with the scientists going around and introducing themselves. The first three scientists state simple biographical information that mostly is relevant to their work with soil contamination. The fourth scientist, anxious about inclusion in the group, offers an elaborate description of his degrees and achievements. The remaining three scientists follow suit. At the start of the introductions, the task of soil contamination was figural in the group. The fourth scientist touched on the status and inclusion needs that had been part of the background but that then became figural.

All configurations of figure and ground are not the same. Just as the figures in the visual configurations the Gestalt psychologists identified differed in terms of good organization, definite outlines, satisfying (good) form, closure, stability, balance, and proportion, so too do the figures individuals develop to make sense of their personal environment or field. Gestalt therapists speak of figures that have "power, liveliness, vigor, unity, and clarity"—figures that are rich, compelling, satisfying, and complete. Good figures have these qualities in abundance; bad figures have less, and at some point the dearth of these characteristics turns poor figures into nonexistent ones (Latner, 1992, p. 29). The figure of the task of solving the problem of soil contamination in the previous example did not have the power, liveliness, and vigor to sustain itself over the figure of group inclusion.

The process of forming new figures from a ground is continual. What may be a slight stirring in the ground, such as a nervous tic or reaction, can rapidly emerge as a figure.

> At a meeting of sales managers for modular phones, two female sales managers had been making suggestions that were ignored until the same suggestions were made by a male, at which point the suggestions were considered. When this happened, several women and one man in the group gave each other knowing glances. These glances, however, remained in the background

of what was occurring in the group. The process continued for some time until one of the suggestions was considered to be creative and exciting enough to be named after its presumed male initiator—"The Brandon Plan"—at which point one female member of the team pointed out that the idea was originally suggested, not by Brandon, but by a female colleague fifteen minutes before. A lively discussion ensued. The feeling behind the glances suddenly became figural in the group.

The Field as a System

The traditional focus of Gestalt theory and Gestalt therapy was the individual. The Gestalt groups that Fritz Perls conducted consisted of a series of individual encounters with the leader while the other group members observed, perhaps being emotionally involved, but not participating. Little if any attention was paid to group process (Feder and Ronall, 1980, p. ix).

Despite this initial focus, the inherent systems orientation and holistic framework of Gestalt theory is powerful and attracts applications to wider groupings. Practitioners at the Cleveland Gestalt Institute have linked Gestalt to general systems theory. In this view, organisms, whether they are individuals, bosses and subordinates, a team, a department, or a whole organization, are viewed as systems with a boundary (Miller, 1978, p. 4). Systems in this view are a set of relationships in action. Their boundary both defines the system and marks the area in which it transacts business. Boundaries in this sense are not fixed—they belong to the encounter. These crucial demarcations are also a matter of perception, and it is this perception that opens the possibility for influence and change. Members of the system draw their own boundaries, sometimes with awareness and sometimes without. One significant contribution of practitioners with a Gestalt orientation is to help bring these boundaries into awareness.

Working at Multiple Levels of a System

Just as anything experienced as a whole may be a Gestalt, functioning systems can also be subsystems of a larger system (Miller, 1978, p. 52). The basic proposition of looking at how each part works with the whole applies at every level, *and it applies simultaneously*. The practitioner using the Gestalt approach has the opportunity and the considerable challenge of moving from one level of analysis to another.

A consultant was called in to work with two supervisors who seemed to be in continual conflict. The consultant started with the problem as defined and held several meetings with the supervisor using active listening and data feedback. It soon became clear that the two supervisors, both white males, represented different views in the work group and the larger organization regarding unresolved issues of race and gender in the overall work force. The consultant used this experience to trigger the management to deal with the overriding issues of race and gender.

This issue was presented at the interpersonal level. The skill of the consultant was to see its relationship to issues at the group and organizational level. The same process can work between any levels of the system. In the next example, a consultant called in to work at the divisional level helped those involved to work more effectively by illustrating how the divisional problem they experienced was actually system-wide.

A consultant was called in to work with a division's managers; they were in conflict with members of other divisions and corporate headquarters because their division was facing a reorganization that, at best, would result in a change of their assignments or, more likely, would result in a pay cut or layoffs. For these reasons, they were working less effectively. The consultant used a series of structured experiences that helped the managers to become aware that all of their concerns were system concerns. The trauma they were facing was system-wide, and the individuals they were working with at other levels of the organization were facing the same perils. This, in itself, did not solve the problem, but it did help the managers to change the nature of their communications with others.

Clusters Three and Four: The Cycle of Experience and Contact

In Gestalt theory, figure formation is part of a *cycle of experience*. Perls hinted at the notion of such a cycle when he described a sequence of "pre-contact," "contact", and post-contact" (Perls, 1969a, p. 44). The idea was refined by Paul Goodman (Perls, Hefferline, and Goodman, 1951, pp. 400–404) and further developed and refined by eight faculty members of the Cleveland Institute who had been trained by the Gestalt pioneers (Edwin Nevis, personal communication, October 19, 1995).

The cycle of experience is pivotal in converting Gestalt theory for use in organizations, and it is a focal point of this chapter (see Exhibit 8.1). I have included two diagrams of the cycle of experience from Edwin Nevis's *Organizational Consulting: A Gestalt Approach* (1987). The first circular chart (Figure 8.1) is most commonly used. The second wave chart (Figure 8.2) has the same points of reference but is included because it illustrates the likely heightening and lessening of psychic energy as the cycle takes place.

In Exhibit 8.1 I will first illustrate the cycle; then I will provide three examples corresponding to the stages in the cycle that show how a consultant would use the cycle to diagnose and intervene.

Figure 8.1. Gestalt Cycle of Experience:
Flow of a Unit of Uninterrupted Experience.

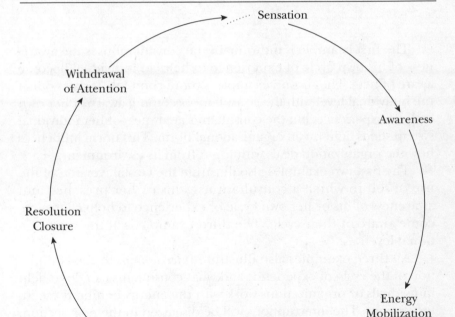

Figure 8.2. Flow of Continuous Experience.

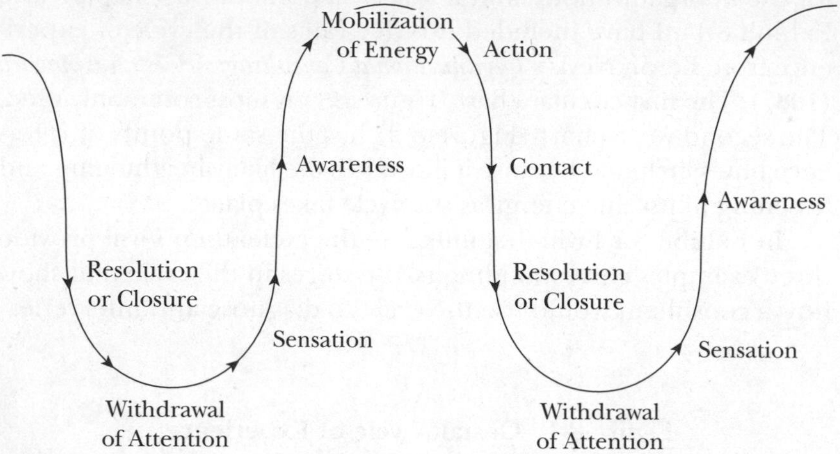

Mobilization
of Energy   Action

Awareness   Contact

Awareness

Resolution
or Closure   Resolution
or Closure

Sensation   Sensation

Withdrawal
of Attention   Withdrawal
of Attention

The first example is individual. The consultant uses the awareness of his own cycle of experience to help an individual become aware of hers. The second example is more complex. It starts out at the individual level with the consultant becoming aware of her own cycle of experience, but the consultant's awareness of her individual system sheds light on an organizational norm. This norm influences how the organization deals with input from its environment.

The first two examples also illustrate the Gestalt version of the use of self in which a consultant uses his or her presence and awareness of his or her own cycle of experience to help clients become aware of their cycle. The third example is at the organizational level.

All three examples also illustrate *interruptions* to the completion of the cycle of experience and what consultants can do to help individuals or organizations work with the energy behind these interruptions. The interruptions will be discussed in the next section.

Cluster Five: Interruptions to Contact

Interruptions to contact might be called resistance in other theoretical systems, but in Gestalt resistance is not the negative opposition to experience or help that it is in many other systems. The Gestalt view of what is usually called resistance is especially important for the organizational consultant who cannot hold the client to an enforced therapeutic hour while resistance is "worked through." Resistance in Gestalt theory is considered to be another expression of the organism, and although such expressions might delay, weaken, or distort the cycle of experience, they are still honored as authentic expressions.

This is illustrated in all three examples as the consultant counters attempts to immediately and prematurely eliminate the interruption or resistance and quickly solve the problem. In the individual example, the consultant encourages the artist to fully explore the urge to act like a helpless little girl. In the individual-organizational example, the consultant encourages the organization members to stay with and examine what it was that promoted the organizational norm of accepting suggestions from the community without critically examining them. In the organizational example, the consultant slows the process down so that the national professional organization does not paper over the issue of race and gender with a flowery resolution.

In each instance the consultant draws on what Arnold Beisser has referred to as "the paradoxical theory of change," which states that "*change occurs when one becomes what he is, not when he tries to become what he is not*" (Beisser, 1970, pp. 77–80) Beisser is referring to the same process that governs polarities, where feelings or reactions are usually paired with a less visible opposite and where, to experience a feeling or reaction that is being blocked, one must first *fully* experience the opposite polarity. Before the artist can experience herself as a mature woman, she has to fully experience herself as acting like a little girl. Before the community agency can critically examine proposals from the community, it has to fully become aware of and experience the process of uncritical acceptance. Before the national professional group can become an organization with a policy or program regarding race and gender discrimination, it has to experience itself as an organization *without* such a policy.

Six Interruptions to the Cycle of Experience

Each of the following six interruptions or resistances to the cycle of experience is examined in terms of the function it fulfills and

Exhibit 8.1. The Cycle of Experience.

Sensation

The first step for the organism in the cycle involves the senses: sight, hearing, touch, smell, and taste—all the experiences taken in by the senses. These faculties are usually characterized as passive recipients or neutral reporters of what occurs in the environment. Gestalt psychology, however, demonstrated that the senses also select. Gestalt theory is unique when compared to other theories in this volume in its emphasis upon what is evident on the surface—be it a facial gesture, a change in breathing, or a host of other surface expressions. To support this view, Perls described how what is happening on the inside of an individual is also evident on the outside:

When a man is actually attacking an enemy, he shows enormous overt body activity. He contracts his muscles, his heart beats faster; adrenalin is poured into his blood stream in large quantities, his breathing becomes rapid and shallow, his jaws are clenched and rigid, his whole body becomes tense. When he talks about how much he dislikes this enemy he will still show a large number of overt physical signs, although there will be fewer of these than when he is actually fighting. When he feels anger, and thinks about attacking an enemy, he still shows some overt physical signs. But these signs are less visible and less intense than they were when he was actually fighting, or when he was talking about it. His behavior is now of still lower intensity (Perls, 1973, pp. 13–14).

The senses are thus triggered by internal or external experience and, if not blocked, will give us a rich background from which we can develop the appropriate figure. The fact that mental and physical actions mesh means that the consultant has a window to the inner psyche. For Perls the act of simply observing the obvious is a great unused potential (Perls, 1973, p. 15).

At the organizational level, the consultant or organization members use their senses in the overall process to *scan* the organization and its environment.

Individual Example

A commercial artist at an advertising agency where a consultant was doing team building asked for a private conversation. In that conversation, she complained that the department head was a male chauvinist, would not take her seriously, and treated her in a condescending manner. In the course of that conversation, the consultant began to experience physical heat or warmth. He was starting to get "hot under the collar," but he did not comment on this feeling.

Individual/Organizational Example

A consultant was asked to help a community action agency with its outreach program. The agency had numerous programs and was very responsive to all of the suggestions from the community, but the neighborhood residents were still dissatisfied. Community speakers stated that no matter what the agency did, it was never quite right. As a consultant in a meeting in which the agency's numerous and diverse programs were reviewed, she felt a tightening in her throat.

Organizational Example

A consultant was called in to help a nationwide professional organization in its strategic planning. The organization had previously been a leader in its field, but it was now falling behind both professionally and financially.

The consultant and some members noticed that while the organization was formally supportive of racial and gender equality, the majority of its members as well as its own power structure were mostly white males.

Awareness The end result of awareness is that, out of the multitude of possibilities in the ground, something emerges as a figure. The process involves selection, heightening, and focusing. It is also a combining process. The messages from the senses are combined with values, language and desires, and the results of interactions (Melnick and Nevis, 1992, p. 65).

At the organization level, the consultant and/or organization members assess and conceptualize this information. The art of the practitioner at this stage is:

1. To be able to discern when an individual is out of touch with his or her own experience
2. To stay in the present, tolerating whatever confusion, frustration, or turmoil exists so that the system can mobilize its own energy
3. To make contact with one's own senses and emotions, including an understanding of one's own blind spots, to be aware of how one is reacting to the person and the situation
4. To have the ability to sense and track how others are using or avoiding their own sensory data and emotional reactions
5. To be able to share one's experience, keeping close to the original data in an interesting, nonthreatening manner that allows for more than one interpretation (Nevis, 1987, pp. 88–104)

Exhibit 8.1. The Cycle of Experience, cont'd.

Individual Example

The client continued to talk to the consultant, and the pitch of her voice became higher. The tone of her voice took on the sound of a little girl.

As the conversation progressed, the consultant became aware of a feeling of anger. He was angry because the artist was acting like a helpless child, asking him to fix the problem and behaving as if she had no competence to do anything about it herself. The consultant did not, however, immediately share these observations.

Individual/Organizational Example

Each speaker continued to present the demands of the community in a calm, matter-of-fact voice, stating that the agency was obliged to respond to each complaint.

As each new program was described the consultant became aware that she was feeling the same way she did when she had had indigestion. She was literally gagging on a whole series of undigested, unrelated, and uncoordinated comments.

Organizational Example

Strategic planning continued, and most members did not notice the discrepancy between the goals and action in regard to race and gender. If it was brought to their attention, these members offered explanations or indicated that the situation was bound to improve in time.

Some members of the organization, noticing this discrepancy between ideals and action, held informal caucuses at the strategic-planning meetings. A few members were added to the small group, but the majority of members did not join in this discussion. Some did not view this discrepancy as a problem, others did not believe that it could be solved, and for most, the issue was not figural.

Excitement/Mobilizing Energy At this point the organism has developed an awareness that something is happening and needs to be attended to. Energy now needs to be mobilized to take care of it. For the consultant, the art of mobilizing energy is finding the balance between holding back or even diffusing emotional situations and heightening and expanding emotional energy when it is called for. In utilizing Gestalt in an organization, the consultant needs the ability to deal with emotional energy in both ways and to choose the appropriate time for each. This brings into play the full emotional resources of the consultant, because the process of mobilizing energy can bring into play silence, tension, anger, affection, joy, and everything in between (Nevis, 1987, pp. 88–104).

At the organizational level, this means that the energy that is being displayed has started to coalesce around a subgroup, and this subgroup is starting to discuss and think of action.

Individual Example

The consultant then checked his own feelings and observations. Did the behavior of the artist trigger some old reactions in himself about what he viewed as a "dependent woman," in which case his comments would simply be working his own old issues? Could he identify specific behavior that would help the client to understand how he, the consultant, had gotten the impression of a helpless little girl? Within the limitations of his own awareness, he satisfied himself that he was not working his own issues and that he could identify behavior specific to the client.

Individual/Organizational Example

The consultant realized that if she felt choked hearing about these programs, then possibly the agency members who administered them might have similar reactions. She decided that she needed to check out this possibility and designed an organizational values-clarification exercise that would help agency members to identify their view of the agency's commitment to its many programs.

Organizational Example

At their caucuses, organization members interested in changing the organization's behavior in regard to race and gender began brainstorming visions, strategies, and plans.

At a meeting to discuss the preliminary strategic planning report, some members brought up the issue of the discrepancy between the organization's goals and its behavior in regard to race and gender. Opinion seemed to be split on how to respond to this issue. One member introduced a flowery resolution which would make the organization's goals even more idealistic but would then take the issue off the agenda.

The consultant asked the group if they were willing to hold off on their final report until they had explored this issue further. The consultant continued to hold the issue in front of the group without taking sides. The consultant's goal was to remain neutral in regard to this issue but to help the group to be aware of their efforts to dispose of the issue without full consideration.

Exhibit 8.1. The Cycle of Experience, cont'd.

Action is the final step at the individual or organizational level that leads to contact. It is the comment or movement that takes the mobilized energy and makes contact possible.

Individual Example

During a lull in the conversation, the consultant said, "I'd like to let you know what has been going on inside of me as we talk. I felt as if this whole problem was being given to me as if I could solve everything. I know that this might sound farfetched to you, but it was almost as if I were a daddy who could fix things." The client's first reaction after hearing this was to ask the consultant to help her wrap up the problem with some quick behavioral changes that would forever end her being treated like a little girl. The consultant was positive but cautious, urging the client to experience the feeling of being a helpless little girl. He did this by asking her to become more aware of how she felt when she behaved this way and to

Individual/Organizational Example

The values-clarification exercise indicated a clear preference for "responding to the community." After this exercise, the consultant described her feeling of being choked. She then pointed out that this choked feeling might be the same as the organization's reaction when it uncritically accepted new proposals. As a result of the consultant's comments and the values exercise, some members became aware that the *organizational norm* was to accept suggestions without real consideration. Agency members were now eager to establish rules to prevent such behavior in the future. The consultant pointed out that members were continuing to follow the organizational norm of accepting suggestions in the same undigested

Organizational Example

Late one evening in one of the final planning sessions, a small group made the suggestion that the organization adopt policies that:

1. Ensured that all new members coming into the organization would be more diverse in race and gender

2. Ensured that the rules that governed how members worked together in the organization's programs would change to guarantee that teams of members would be of diverse race and gender even if the organization's present membership was not that diverse

Because the hour was late and because the goal of racial and gender equality was on its surface so attractive, one member who had previously explore what the payoff was for acting like a little girl. The consultant had identified one end of a polarity, focusing on the dimensions of helplessness and self-direction.

way that they accepted new proposals. She asked them to delay that action step until they had a better understanding of the problem and had explored why they behaved this way. This suspension was awkward, but it also led toward contact.

opposed the steps suggested that the new policy be quickly adopted. (In effect, the organization would be swallowing the new policy whole without chewing it.)

The consultant suggested a role play illustrating how the organization would look in two years, five years, and ten years if this policy were adopted. After some heated discussion, the members agreed to try the role play the next morning and put the issue over.

Contact

In contact, something has become figural and is meeting something else across a boundary, and energy is mobilized to deal with it. This is the stage when new and sometimes risky behavior emerges. It is also the pivotal point in the cycle.

For Perls, if we make a Gestalt-like contact with something, then neither we nor what we have made contact with remains the same. In his earliest works, Perls likened psychological functions to the physiological process of eating. If we come in true contact with a person, an idea, or anything else, then we must digest or assimilate our reaction to that entity. In order to be digested or assimilated, the object must be chewed (broken) up. The analogy that Perls used was choosing between swallowing one's food whole or thoroughly chewing it so that it can be truly assimilated. This occurs mentally when we change mental structures before incorporating them into our self. This is contact, a mutual interaction in which no participant escapes change.

Such contact does not necessarily mean that the need is satisfied or a problem has been solved, although this may happen. Contact means that what could be is no longer a matter of speculation. The organism and the object in the environment have come together at the boundary.

Exhibit 8.1. The Cycle of Experience, cont'd.

It may be that the situation itself will be enough to promote such a process, but it is also the time when the consultant's presence can be the decisive factor. If the goal is for individuals or groups to become aware of and utilize aspects of themselves that they have not been aware of or used before, the presence of the consultant can be the pivotal ingredient. This means that the consultant must be able to present himself or herself, in Edwin Nevis's words, in a "compelling and intriguing" manner (1987, p. 70). Another way of saying this is that the consultant must be able to present his or her feelings, fantasies, and experiences in a way that *enables* others rather than merely *impressing* them. The consultant must be able to be tough, confrontational, and supportive at the same work session.

Individual Example

After the consultant's statement, it was unclear what kind of contact would take place. The first reaction of the client was a hushed silence; then her eyes began to glisten. The consultant was concerned that this conversation would simply replicate what had gone on between the client and her boss. If it did, he would have to decide whether he could successfully point this out to the client. After a long pause, the client said, "Give me some more examples. I don't mean to do that, but if I do, I guess I ought to know about it." The client had

Individual/Organizational Example

In the next discussion the participants began actively to discuss whether their norms encouraged them to accept community suggestions without adequately discussing them. For the first time since the consultant had been with the group, the members began to talk about ranking the new suggestions in terms of their relative desirability and practicality. Organization members also began to discuss their own motivation (a desire to respond to the community) for accepting community proposals without analyzing them or relating

Organizational Example

The role play surfaced a number of consequences of these new policies. Specifically, the new membership policies would make it difficult for old members to bring in friends who were in the same demographic group, and although Caucasian members appreciated the *principle* of having diverse staffs in the workshops, they did not want to give up working with people they knew who also happened to be Caucasian.

The role play also triggered a number of organizational issues regarding how the organization had identified the helpless end of her helpless-self directing polarity. Contact had taken place at two levels: the client had heard the consultant and was also beginning to get more in touch with herself.

them to ongoing programs. Some stated that they simply accepted proposals because they thought others accepted them, even though they had doubts about their practicality. The consultant was operating alternately at the individual and organizational levels. The group had made contact with their unspoken norms.

been run, the power position of the older white males, and the older white males' concern about whether there would be a place for them in the organization if the new policies went into effect.

This role play thus brought up differences, and since true contact involves meeting over a boundary between unlikes, true contact had taken place. The issue was not settled, but members of unlike subsystems within the organization had met at the contact boundary (Latner, 1992, p. 24), and neither the subsystem nor the organization would be the same.

Withdrawal and Closure Withdrawal and closure are two aspects of ending. It is not always easy to separate them. Withdrawal involves the emotional aspect of ending. The focus of attention and the energy of the organism are withdrawn from the figure. Withdrawal involves acknowledging and heightening awareness of the emotional impact of this process. Like so many aspects of Gestalt, it involves acknowledging something that is obvious, yet unnoticed. Again, the consultant has the opportunity to draw upon his or her own feelings and reactions as a means of helping clients to become aware of their reactions.

Meaning must be extracted from what has occurred. Closure is the act of extracting that meaning. It involves anchoring the change in an individual behavioral repertoire through discussion and cognitive understanding. The consultant must be able to ground the emotional learning practically and conceptually. This means relating what has been done to the overall client system in the present and in ways that take into account how the system will change in the future. It also means giving the client an appropriate conceptual structure with which to link this experience to others.

Exhibit 8.1. The Cycle of Experience, cont'd.

Individual Example	Individual/Organizational Example	Organizational Example
Closure with this client involved some discussion of how people sometimes continue to behave in ways that were appropriate at an earlier time in their life but now carry some disadvantages. The consultant also discussed how playing the role of the little girl might have fit in with some of the other dynamics and expectations in the office and how the behavior of the client in this encounter identified the other end of the polarity. Withdrawal also involved the consultant's encouraging the client to reflect on how she had felt during this encounter.	Closure with this group involved a more thorough understanding of both individual and organizational dynamics. The group looked at the general operation of the organization and identified rules, norms, and processes that encouraged them to swallow ideas without enough consideration. Withdrawal involved a brief discussion of what the organization learned about itself and how the individual members felt as they gained this new information.	The organization had identified and examined an important problem relative to several of its subsystems. There was contact between the subsystems, but the issue was not settled, nor was a decision reached during this cycle. The organization, however, did change and was now ready to enter its next cycle on this issue with more clarity.

In these examples, organisms, one individual and two organizational, did not complete their cycle of experience. Their cycle was blocked. The artist could not complete an interaction with a colleague without feigning helplessness, and the community organization could not critically evaluate suggestions from citizens' groups. The professional service organization could not properly consider its own policy suggestions. Such resistance and blockage of the cycle of experience is not rare. It is common. What is distinct is how Gestalt theory taps into the energy behind that resistance.

the way it blocks the cycle of experience. Following this examination, we will further explore the Gestalt concept of "honoring resistance" and the paradoxical theory of change. The six interruptions or resistances are:

1. When individuals and organizations uncritically accept values, ideas, suggestions, and so on from the environment (introjection)
2. When individuals and organizations assign an unwelcome impulse to another person or group (projection)
3. When individuals or organizations erase the boundary between themselves and their environment (confluence)
4. When individuals and organizations turn inward what they would like to turn toward someone or something else (retroflection)
5. When individuals or organizations turn away or push experience aside (deflection)
6. When individuals or organizations obstruct sensory awareness (desensitization)

Introjection

Introjection is the original mode of learning. We unconsciously adopt our parents' language, manner of speaking, and way of behaving. The young introjector spends little time or energy specifying preferences. This posture assumes the unlikely condition that the environment will automatically give us what we need and want. Later in life we are able to be more discerning in what we accept; however, the process remains as we learn from mentors, role models, and other figures (Polster and Polster, 1973, p. 73).

Perls uses the analogy of eating food to explain how individuals function psychologically. If we swallow food whole without chewing it, we might temporarily satisfy our hunger but we usually suffer some consequences. We have not taken the time and energy to do what is necessary to make the food part of our system, and it is quite possible that it will make us feel uncomfortable, eventually be regurgitated, or both. In either case, we will not receive the nourishment for which the food was intended. Similarly, concepts, facts, and standards of behavior all come from the outside world, but if they are to become available in a truly assimilated way, they cannot be swallowed whole. They must be questioned, experienced, analyzed, and put together in a form in which we can use them as though they are ours. The environment is a ready supplier of all kinds of psychological food, such as facts and values. However, this food will seldom, if ever, be in a form that fits our needs and our personalities in all the situations we face. We must do something to make this psychological food our own. If we do not, it cannot be used as energy to fuel the cycle of experience.

Introjection takes place at the organizational level when organizations accept, without chewing, procedures and standards, management theories, belief systems about how the organization works, ideologies, and total belief systems. The community organization in the description of the cycle of experience was introjecting program suggestions from the citizens' group.

Introjected ideas may temporarily solve the organization's hunger about what to do, but soon the fulfillment wears off and the hunger returns. Further evidence for one such type of introjection—management theories—can be found on the bookshelves of many managers and CEOs. This introjection takes the form of rows of loose-leaf training manuals for a series of off-the-shelf improvement systems that the organization purchased and swallowed but never digested. These ranged from Management by Objectives in the 1970s to Total Quality Management and reengineering in the 1990s. The reason that none of these systems really satisfied the organization's hunger for change is that they were swallowed without criticism or analysis and without changing their form to meet the organization's needs (Merry and Brown, 1987, p. 122). Gestalt theory identifies the process of introjection and offers an antidote: it triggers the cycle of experience so that the individual or organization adequately digests the needed material from its environment.

Projection

Projectors disown aspects of themselves, ascribing them to the environment. If the environment is diverse enough, projectors may sometimes be correct, but much of the time they will make serious mistakes, abdicating their own part in the direction of energy and experiencing themselves as powerless to change something that is disagreeable (Polster and Polster, 1973, p. 71). Projectors disown their own feelings because of some belief or urge that one "shouldn't" feel a certain way. To resolve this dilemma, projectors attach these feelings to another person and become exquisitely aware of this quality in others (Polster and Polster, 1973, p. 78).

Projection disrupts the cycle of experience because the energy that would make it work is propelled outside the organism. On the surface, examples of projection in Gestalt theory are similar to those in Freudian theory. The intrapsychic explanations, however, reflect the different focus of each theorist. For Freud, the explanation was primarily internal: a weak ego unable to handle the impulses of the id and the superego. For Perls, the focus shifts to the boundary between the organism and its environment, an organism that is unable to manage the energy generated by its contact with the rest of the world. Perls also notes that conscious anticipation of another's moves, as in a chess game, is not projection. When someone consciously thinks, "If I were he, this is what I would do," it can be a healthy process (Perls, 1973, p. 36). Similarly, in the Gestalt view, creative problem solving and visioning are examples of healthy projection.

Projection also takes place in several ways at the organizational level. An organization can project on part of its environment:

A steel manufacturer that had not modernized blamed the Japanese for exploiting its weakness and the U.S. government for not protecting it from what it termed "unfair competition."

An organization can also project on part of itself:

A university department with long-standing practices of ignoring the needs of its students blamed what it called the "bean-counting mentality" of the registrar for student dissatisfaction and declining enrollments.

Whatever the form of projection, it can halt the cycle of experience. The feeling, concept, or reaction that is disturbing to the organism is placed elsewhere, and the individual or organization thus never has the opportunity to encounter an impulse that could lead to its growth and change.

Confluence

Confluence involves a breakdown of the boundary between the individual and some aspect of the environment. It is conformity carried to its extreme. The individual goes along with the prevailing opinion in order to avoid conflict or some other reaction.

Confluence produces peace and harmony at the price of losing awareness of some aspect of oneself. At times—such as those when one is in a powerless position—this trade-off can be attractive.

Like the other interruptions to the cycle, confluence can be a useful part of the human condition. In order to accomplish a common purpose of a group, team, or organization, one usually must submit in some way. But confluence becomes a problem when submission is an unaware process. When a spouse says, "I don't know why my partner left. We never had a fight in all the years we were married!" or a parent comments, "But he was such a good child, he never talked back!" this suggests a parent or spouse who acted as if the other person thought, felt, and valued just as she or he did. The analogy is that of an unarticulated contract with hidden clues and fine print, which perhaps only one partner knew about (Polster and Polster, 1973, p. 93). In the cycle of experience, the triggering energy of an emotion is lost when an individual cannot be sure where it is coming from.

Confluence can also be at the base of conflict between groups, organizations, and even nations. If, for example, a nation demands that others share its outlook point for point, then it is difficult to work out the real differences that do exist because they are never heard or perhaps never even stated. Jerry Harvey's Abilene paradox describes a scenario involving his wife's family that has acquired legendary status in the world of organizational consulting (Harvey, 1988, p. 15):

> While Harvey was visiting his wife's parents in Coleman, Texas, both couples took a 106-mile round trip to Abilene, Texas, in an unair-conditioned car in 104-degree heat to have dinner in a cafeteria with terrible food. Later it was discovered that no one really wanted to go; each of them had said that they wanted to go only because they thought that everyone else did.

Harvey stated that the above process reflects the inability to manage agreement. In Gestalt terms it is confluence for each of the family members to be unaware that they have fused their boundaries with others. They each submerged their wishes to follow what they thought was the group consensus. The community organization that uncritically accepted suggestions from citizens' groups in Exhibit 8.1 is another demonstration of confluence.

Retroflection

In retroflection, individuals do to themselves what they would like to do to someone else or what they would like someone else to do to them. Retroflection originates from a past perception of an extremely high penalty for honest expression. It can continue later in life when the perceived choice may be to turn anger inward rather than to lose a job or destroy a relationship.

Like the previously discussed processes, retroflection can be a useful part of human functioning. The parent who presses a clenched fist to his or her forehead and, in doing so, avoids brutally beating a child is turning something toward the self instead of toward someone else. In a less dramatic example, the process of thinking and decision making involves retroflection as individuals step outside of themselves to ask, "Do I want alternative A or alternative B?" (Polster and Polster, 1973, p. 85).

Retroflection as a concept dramatically illustrates the difference between the Gestalt and the Freudian (and many other) views of the psyche. Freud started from the premise that the internal psyche is composed of parts that are at war with each other (the superego is continually restraining the id). Such a position would support as unavoidable the view that the self must control a separate and alien part of the psyche. Perls, in contrast, views the psyche as a single mechanism that either is effectively fulfilling its needs or is not. Retroflection gets in the way of effective functioning because internal needs are treated as something foreign, to be controlled or exorcised rather than fulfilled, and external demands are incorporated into the organism as if they were its own.

Merry and Brown (1987, p. 149) quote Perls, who described a community of religious Jews who blamed themselves for every mishap. Perls said, "What struck me most about the community was its inability to receive help. It has always been a loner. It had never been able to make demands or work on receiving the public funds that were coming to it. It suffered its problems and misfortunes in silence, never looking for outside assistance. When the electricity supply was causing problems, the bus service was bad, and roads were not being taken care of, the community never lifted a finger to deal with these. It seemed unable to make demands on outside bodies."

By understanding the process of retroflection, the practitioner is in a position to help an individual accept his or her own internal functioning and direct toward the outside what is appropriate.

Deflection

Erving and Miriam Polster added a fifth way to break the cycle of experience. Deflection involves taking the heat off contact by such means as excessive language, laughing after an angry comment, or not looking at the other person in the eye. Deflection is heightened in modern life when abstract, rather than specific, issues are addressed and when individuals come up with bad examples or none at all. Both parties to a deflected communication experience a loss. The speaker does not have the satisfaction of saying what he or she is experiencing, and the listener misses the power and meaning of what is stated. Deflection can be especially insidious because it is hard to detect when individuals are talking *about* but not *to* (Polster and Polster, 1973, p. 89).

In organizations, talking about "conditions" when one means a drastic downsizing is an example of deflection. Deflection can also be incorporated into the norms and processes of the organization.

> Gary Patterson was a divisional manager in a large telecommunications organization. In the mid 1990s, the organization moved from a directive to a team style of managing, and Gary was one of the few midlevel managers who was not laid off. He had gone through the requisite training for work with self-directed teams, and he adopted much of the language of the new approach. Still, he had not really been able to let go of his old directive style of managing. When he issued one of his old-style directions, he joked, "Well, you know, this may sound directive," and then he laughed and so did his younger team members. Behind Gary's back, the younger team members did the work to build the necessary consensus to implement Gary's orders. They often joked to each other about Gary being too old to learn anything new; however, they never mentioned to Gary or each other how they were continuing to support Gary's old style of directive management. Gary's jokes were a deflection that helped to divert attention from his continued use of the old style of directive management. His younger colleagues supported that deflection by going behind his back to build consensus.

Desensitization

John Enright describes desensitization as a type of interruption that is best known by its deliberate use by Skinner-oriented behavioral therapists. These therapists use desensitization to prevent individuals from reacting to a particular stimulus. As an example, individuals who are afraid of air travel are deliberately exposed to simulations of the process of air travel until they fail to react to the stimuli or become desensitized to them.

In the Gestalt context, desensitization refers to involuntary and unaware sensory blocking. Examples include "visual blurring, chronic 'not hearing,' sensory dullness, and frigidity" (Enright, 1970, p. 112). At the organizational level, desensitization might occur in an urban school that has been so overwhelmed with the external conditions that make it difficult for its students to learn that it is has become numb and continues with the same programs and policies designed for a different student body in a different era.

How to Help Individuals and Organizations Complete Their Cycle of Experience

Gestalt-oriented consultants can and do utilize many of the organizational and group process interventions, such as action research, that were described elsewhere in this volume. The special contribution of Gestalt theory is to focus on the cycle of experience and help systems to mobilize their energy to complete their own cycle. Whether the organism is an individual, a group, or an organization, it always has energy at the level of the total system.

The organism, however, does not always have access to that energy. It's possible that the sensation process is dulled and the organism is not even aware of the energy, or the cycle is interrupted by any of the six devices we have described. This was illustrated in our three examples by:

1. The individual level of awareness of the commercial artist whose awareness of herself as a mature woman has not been mobilized
2. The community organization that has introjected norms that urge it to uncritically accept all suggestions from the community
3. The national professional organization that has not mobilized its energy to develop a policy regarding racial and gender inequality

Edwin Nevis points out four powerful behaviors or stances that enable the practitioner to mobilize her or his own energy to help the organism, individually or collectively, to become more aware of its energy and to mobilize it (Nevis, 1987, pp. 69–187). These tools are:

1. *Presence,* or the overall impact of the consultant
2. *Undirected awareness,* or the ability of consultants to use their own subjectivity and being as a means of gathering data
3. *Honoring resistance,* or the attitude and ability to accept the ambivalence of others toward one's goals
4. *Evocative behavior,* or the ability of consultants to use their being to trigger the natural energy in a system

Presence

Nevis defines *presence* as "The living out of values in such a way that in 'taking a stance,' the intervenor *teaches* these important concepts. That which is important to the client's learning process is exuded through the consultant's way of being" (Nevis, 1987, p. 70). Presence thus includes "rightness": "whether shy and introverted or outgoing and extroverted, their [the consultants] presence coveys a *right* to be where they are" (Nevis, 1987, p. 82).

The consultants' right to be there is based on—and includes—a clear foundation for thought and action. This foundation can be scientific and rational, intuitive and mystical, or anything in between, but a link to some body of knowledge and methodology is an essential element of presence. Finally, presence includes the ability to link the source of knowledge to the problems and needs of the client.

In this description, Gestalt presence bears some similarity to Carl Rogers's notion of congruence. Both qualities involve internal consistency, and both have a powerful external impact. It is clear that with both congruity and presence, one "walks the talk." An individual's behavior embodies his or her ideas. However, an important difference exists. For Rogers, congruity is used to trigger a client's inner journey of awareness and self-acceptance. The emotional trigger for this journey is the *accepting presence* of the consultant in the role of listener. In a Gestalt approach, presence is used to attract the client's attention to a particular aspect of his or her own internal process, or to compel the client to attend to the consultant. It also provides an attractive model with respect to desirable skills or an interesting way of being in the world. The resulting mobilization of energy may be either inward toward self-exploration or outward toward coping with a problem in clients' relation to their effective function in doing their work (Edwin Nevis, personal communication, October 19, 1995).

Rather than acceptance, the crucial triggering quality in Gestalt is excitement and interest. Effectiveness for a consultant in this setting "rests on having a compelling or intriguing presence, on creating client curiosity about both the consultant and the client system itself. . . . Without some minimum level of contact, some degree of being 'touched' by the consultant, the system probably will not mobilize to learn" (Nevis, 1987, p. 79). "Compelling" or "intriguing" does not mean shallow or superficial entertainment. What captures the client's interest must also be associated with a solid approach to learning and change. The excitement does not come simply from showmanship but from a presence that has internalized the cycle of experience and that captures the client's interest in a vision of how things can be.

Undirected Awareness

Presence involves the consultant's being. Undirected awareness relates to the consultant's stance toward the world, a stance that says that the consultant will remain open to the possibility of *personal involvement* in whatever data the system makes available. Whereas Rogers approached the client and the rest of the world with a normative assumption about the essential goodness of humans, the Gestalt approach is to approach the world with no assumptions, but with a strong effort toward a stance that is open to whatever the senses report.

Nevis contrasts the nineteenth-century fictional British sleuth Sherlock Holmes with the contemporary television detective Colombo (Nevis, 1987, pp. 109–111). Holmes is precise, superior in perception and logical reasoning, and neat in appearance, and he always knows just what he is looking for. Colombo is naive, rambling, slow-moving, and disheveled in appearance, and he does not appear to be working from any sort of predetermined or logical framework. Holmes is like a well-trained bloodhound, seeking the logical sequence of data that will solve the mystery. Colombo is like a sponge, immersing himself in the milieu until something turns up. Holmes educates himself by being in control of his environment, whereas Colombo allows himself to be educated by his environment. Holmes's awareness is clearly directed; Colombo's is undirected. Both types of investigation yield important data about organizations.

The approaches are not mutually exclusive. A practitioner might well be carrying out interviewing using *directed research,* with questions based on a carefully defined premise. At the same time, this practitioner might also be carrying out undirected research by:

- Being aware of his or her own reactions while interviewing
- Being aware of the degree of real contact made with those she or he is interviewing or even having casual conversation with
- Simply wandering around and letting things into his or her experience
- Developing hypotheses and checking them out as she or he goes along
- Involving himself or herself with the client in an active way, as when Colombo admires a painting or a piece of furniture

If Colombo and Holmes were investigating a troubled team, Holmes might discover that the leader failed to set an agenda for meetings. Colombo's undirected awareness might discover the way each team member played a part in encouraging the leader not to set an agenda (Nevis, 1987, pp. 109–110). The point is not to let whatever governs directed awareness—a theory, a value, a hunch, and so on—screen out data that do not fit the framework. The consultant's own sensations, feelings, and internal states can yield a great deal of data about the organization, and making these reactions available to the client is an important way to gather data, communicate presence, and make contact.

Honoring Resistance

What some other methodologies call resistance, Gestalt views as "creative adjustment," or the organism doing what it must to survive (Latner, 1992, p. 29). Gestalt therapy also embodies the paradoxical theory of change cited earlier. The notion is that an individual, group, or organization that purports to have a desire to change, but thus far has been unable to, is likely to have its desire to change offset by a desire to stay the same. A consultant who lines up on the "change agent" side is simply being drawn into one side of an internal struggle (Beisser, 1970, p. 78). The Gestalt frame of reference thus helps a practitioner to be effective in situations that might otherwise seem to be at a standstill.

A consultant with a Gestalt orientation worked with an executive group that had great difficulty getting together for a meeting. The ostensible purpose of the consultation was to plan a program to deal with a troublesome problem in the work force. After several fruitless efforts to get the group together, the consultant wrote a memo to each executive, noting the difficulty in finding a common time for a meeting. In the memo he designated a conveyor for the meeting and stated that the issues involved in getting together to meet might shed some light on how the organization was dealing with the ostensible issue of the problem in the work force. He requested that when the group did get together, the first order of business should be to examine the difficulty involved in their finding a time to meet.

At the meeting, the executives offered a number of plausible reasons for the difficulty, none of which had anything to do with their feeling ambivalent about meeting. They also expressed some resistance to discussing the matter any further, saying, "We're together now, so let's get down to work." The consultant persisted, asking them if they would be willing to do a brief role play. They agreed.

He asked them to think of the time when they felt most energized about having the meeting and to role-play what they would have said or done at that time in order to find a common meeting time. A number of creative and practical suggestions occurred, including meeting from 6:00 to 9:30 P.M. on Friday evening or having a breakfast meeting at a nearby hotel from 7:00 to 9:30 A.M. and finally meeting early Sunday evening.

These suggestions helped the group members to be aware of their ambivalence and, hence, their resistance to working with diversity. The consultant then asked them to compare their process in getting together for the meeting with what happened in the organization when they tried to deal with the problem in the work force. They found surprising parallels.

Evocative Behavior

Presence gets the client's or the organization's attention. Undirected awareness brings important data to the consultant's attention. The evocative-provocative continuum is the skill ingredient that helps the client use these data as a basis for action.

When operating in a provocative mode, the consultant, through compelling behavior, causes something to happen (for example, confrontative feedback to a manager to which the manager feels he or she must respond). When operating in an evocative mode, the consultant attempts to heighten the system's interest in its own process, with the assumption that, with new awareness, new behavior will emerge (for example, paraphrasing a manager's remark back to him or her). Provocative behavior can be assaultive, as in Synanon therapy, in which members are attacked verbally. It can also be confrontative, as when the consultant takes a clear stand, confronting someone with data or reactions but doing so without physical or verbal attacks or coercion (Nevis, 1987, pp. 126–133). Evocative behavior can be relatively passive, as in Albert Bandura's behavior modeling (described in Chapter Six). It can also be more active, as when the consultant states her or his own feelings or asks members of the group to go around the circle and state their interest in a particular idea.

The contribution of the Gestalt approach is to make both approaches legitimate in organizational work and to provide a more precise method for the consultant to use his or her own self to evoke awareness from a client. In the previous example, the executives' own unacknowledged ambivalence about working on the work force problems was making it difficult for them to find a common time to meet. If the consultant had stated his own difficulties and ambivalence about working on that issue, he might have evoked a similar awareness from the executives.

Gestalt and Conflict

The framework of the cycle of experience can be used to work with conflict at several levels. At the individual level, the focus is often on submerged emotion that gets in the way of direct communication. This approach is rooted in the holistic view of the early Gestalt theorists as illustrated in the following exercise (Perls, Hefferline, and Goodman, 1951, p. 98):

> Attempt to mobilize some particular pattern of body-action. For instance, tighten and loosen the jaw, clench the fists, begin to gasp.

You may find this tends to arouse a dim emotion—in this case, frustrated anger. Now, if to this experience you are able to add the further experience—a fantasy, perhaps—of some person or thing in the environment that frustrates you, the emotion will flare up in full force and clarity.

Conversely, when in the presence of some frustrating person or thing, you may notice that you do not *feel* the emotion unless or until *you accept as yours* the corresponding body-actions; that is, it is *in* the clenching of the fists, the excited breathing, and so on, that you begin to feel the anger.

Prolonged interpersonal conflict is often the product of individuals expressing what they believe they *should* be feeling rather than what they are actually feeling. Stanley Herman and Michael Korenich (1977, pp. 31–33) illustrate how individually based Gestalt can be used in this situation:

> A member of a management team continually spoke in halting and abstract generalizations. In response to questions from the group, the manager indicated that he was not aware that he was communicating in this style. The consultants then asked him if he would be willing to make statements to the others in the most abstract style that he could, an example of the paradoxical theory of change. He agreed, and as he did so his voice style and manner gained increasing strength and humor. He was now taking charge of what he was doing, and he became quite animated and energetic. Later, with more discussion, the manager became aware that he used an abstract manner of communicating to avoid being challenged.

In Gestalt terms, the manager completed a cycle of experience in which he increased his contact with those in his environment. Instead of speaking in abstract terms to keep them at a distance, he communicated in a different way, one that allowed contact. The first and essential step in this cycle had to be his own awareness of his internal experience. This awareness came from the consultants who encouraged the very behavior that was presumably causing the problem.

Herman and Korenich (1977, pp. 117–121) suggest the following guidelines to this approach to individual conflict:

- Establish the readiness of the parties to deal with the issue. If they are not ready, help them to explore their reluctance, but *do not pressure them to change their mind.* This is based on the Gestalt view that individuals move to a new stage of the cycle of experience, not through external pressure, but by deepening the awareness of the stage they are in. This occurs even if that position is one of resistance to acknowledging the issue.
- Encourage participants to be as specific and concrete about their concerns as possible. Individuals are more likely to fully experience their concerns, fears, and so on if they tie them to the tangible events they are worried about. This could include specific discussion of each party's fear of a worst or most catastrophic outcome.
- Encourage participants to make personal statements they are really able to stand behind rather than impersonal attributions or "we" statements. Conflicts that have a history of not being resolved are more likely to be based on camouflaged fear. Speaking personally and specifically puts these hidden concerns on the table where they can be dealt with.
- Be willing to accept a temporary lack of resolution rather than force a false smoothing over.
- Be aware of your own anxiety level when it comes to reaching for a happy ending that does not really resolve the conflict.

The Gestalt view of examining behavior at multiple levels is particularly helpful when working with conflict. Simmering conflict at one level is often indicative of conflict at another level, as indicated previously in the example of the two supervisors whose seemingly individual conflict was instead an example of a larger organizational conflict.

Gestalt and Joining a Group or Organization

On the continuum between the individual and the group or organizational level, the Perls's early theory and Fritz Perls's later activities at Esalen emphasized the importance of the individual. The theory then grew; the later developments of the Cleveland group can be applied at the individual, group, and organizational levels.

The special strength of this development of Gestalt theory is that it can be used at multiple levels. In this way, an issue of joining can be "worked" within the individual, between individuals, or as part of a group or the organization as a whole. At any of these levels, the theory can be used to identify whether individuals have joined in *fact* when they have not joined in *spirit*. Such inclusion leads to problems with commitment, confused roles, and eventual dysfunction. Gestalt theory approaches this problem through its emphasis on clarifying boundaries.

Boundaries separate the individual from the group or organization. They are both physical and psychic. The permeability of the psychic boundary varies with the individual and the situation. If the boundary is rigid and impermeable, the individual's involvement with the organization will be limited. If, on the other hand, the boundary is overly permeable, the individual can lose the sense of self and identity that is the basis for commitment to the group or organization. The contribution of Gestalt boundary interventions is to help individuals become more aware of the location and permeability of boundaries. With this awareness, they will be better able to adjust their behavior and reactions.

Shirley Madden was a congressional candidate in a suburban district in Wisconsin. She was articulate and charismatic and had the type of personality that attracted volunteers. The problem was that these volunteers were not following through with their commitments, and the campaign was suffering. Mailings were not getting out, numbers on phone lists were not called, and there was a lack of research on several important issues. The volunteers agreed to spend a morning in a workshop session in which a consultant led them through exercises to make them become more aware of their experiences as they worked on the campaign (the sensation and awareness steps in the cycle of experience). The strongest force for the volunteers turned out to be the opportunity to work directly with Shirley. When they were with her, they lost some of their sense of themselves and made promises that they did not keep. The boundary between them and the candidate was almost completely permeable. On the other hand, the boundary between them and the campaign (without the candidate's personal presence) was quite rigid. With awareness of these boundaries, some of the volunteers resigned from active volunteering but continued to support the candidate, and others were able to make commitments that they kept.

Gestalt and Psychological Growth

The special contribution of Gestalt theory to psychological growth rests on the assumption that an organism will act to meet its own needs. This assumption draws attention to what individuals, groups, and organizations are doing, and then asks the question, "What need is this serving?" The answer to this question leads to another important Gestalt concept, *ownership* or *responsibility*. Individuals and organizations cannot change what someone or something else is forcing them to do. They can only change what they *choose* to do. Gestalt's special contribution, through such devices as evocative behavior, honoring resistance, and undirected awareness, is that it helps individuals and organizations to understand and accept the degree to which they choose to behave as they do and to accept responsibility for their decisions. With this notion of responsibility, they are then free to change and to grow psychologically.

The community organization in the individual-organizational example in Exhibit 8.1 indiscriminately accepted suggestions from the various citizens' groups. If someone were to ask organization members if they were doing this, they would probably say that they were not, because they were not aware of what they were doing. The consultant used her own physical reactions of choking and a values-clarification exercise to vividly illustrate what they were doing. Then, when the organization wanted to indiscriminately accept the consultant's analysis, she pointed out that they were again doing exactly what she was talking about. This was a graphic and dramatic illustration that helped both the individuals and the organization to complete the cycle of experience and grow psychologically.

Conclusion

Gestalt theory as it has developed today is one of the most applicable theories for organizations in this volume. Gestalt highlights wholes and total relationships: everything in people—in their thoughts, feelings, and physical reactions—and everything around them, including other people and their entire environment. The interrelationship of everything might be an accurate description of a Gestalt reality, but it's not a very manageable concept. It's hard to go into an organization and accomplish a task by focusing on the interrelationship of everything. Fortunately, Gestalt theory also provides ways to reduce this notion to manageable proportions. These are the emphasis on here-and-now behavior, which greatly narrows down the field, and the cycle of experience, which identifies significant points at which the experience of individuals or organizations can be influenced.

Annotated Bibliography
Original Sources: Readable Perls

Perls, F. S. *Ego, Hunger and Aggression: The Beginnings of Gestalt Therapy.* New York: Random House, 1969.
This first book, with two chapters by Laura Perls, states the philosophical case for a holistic view of human behavior. The writing is at times choppy, and all ideas are not followed through, but it gives the reader a good sense of many of the assumptions behind Gestalt therapy.

Perls, F. S. *Gestalt Therapy Verbatim* (J. O. Stevens, compiler and ed.). Lafayette, Calif.: Real People Press, 1969.
This book captures the spirit of Gestalt therapy as it was practiced by Fritz Perls in the 1960s. It includes both verbatim therapy sessions and brief explanations of the theory.

Perls, F. S. *In and Out of the Garbage Pail.* Lafayette, Calif.: Real People Press, 1969.
This is Perls's autobiography. The book is every bit as frank, open, attention-grabbing, and exaggerated as the public Perls. It is enjoyable reading and again presents an important part of the history of the Gestalt approach.

Perls, F. S. *The Gestalt Approach and Eye Witness to Therapy.* Palo Alto, Calif.: Science and Behavior Books, 1973.
The last book published by Perls states the theory in his own words.

Rosenblatt, D. "An Interview with Laura Perls." *Gestalt Journal,* 1991, *14*(1), 7–26.
Although she was a significant figure in the development of Gestalt, Laura Perls did not publish a great deal. This is one of the few places in which one can read of her experiences.

Secondary Sources: Books About Fritz and Laura Perls and Their Theories

Clarkson, P., and Mackewn, J. *Fritz Perls.* Newbury Park, Calif.: Sage, 1993. As part of the Sage series on psychological theorists, this book is well written and balanced, with equal attention to Perls himself and to his theories.

Latner, J. "Origin and Development of Gestalt Therapy." In E. C. Nevins (ed.), *Gestalt Therapy: Perspectives and Applications.* Cleveland, Ohio: New York: Gestalt Institute of Cleveland Press, 1992.
This book is an excellent current summary of Gestalt theory.

Polster, E., and Polster, M. *Gestalt Therapy Integrated: Contours of Theory and Practice.* New York: Vintage Books, 1973.
This popular book brings together much of the post–Fritz Perls thinking about Gestalt theory and its application. It is relatively short, has many examples, and is clearly written.

Wheeler, G. *Gestalt Reconsidered: A New Approach to Contact and Resistance.* Cleveland, Ohio: Gestalt Institute of Cleveland Press, 1991.
This is a scholarly and critical analysis of the various approaches and versions of Gestalt theory.

Organizational Applications

Merry, U., and Brown, G. I. *The Neurotic Behavior of Organizations.* Cleveland, Ohio: Gestalt Institute of Cleveland Press, 1987.
This book emphasized interruptions to the cycle of experience, such as projection, and how this process plays out at the organizational level.

Nevis, E. C. *Organizational Consulting: A Gestalt Approach.* New York: Gardner Press, 1987.
If you can read only one book on Gestalt applications in organizations, this is your best choice. It deals with theory, history, and original material on how to convert therapeutic approaches to appropriate interventions at the organizational level.

Bibliography

Beisser, A. "The Paradoxical Theory of Change." In J. Fagan and I. R. Shepherd (eds.), *Gestalt Therapy Now: Theory, Techniques, Applications.* Palo Alto, Calif.: Science and Behavior Books, 1970.
Clarkson, P., and Mackewn, J. *Fritz Perls.* Newbury Park, Calif.: Sage, 1993.

Enright, J. B. "An Introduction to Gestalt Techniques." In J. Fagan and I. R. Shepherd (eds.), *Gestalt Therapy Now: Theory, Techniques, Applications*. Palo Alto, Calif.: Science and Behavior Books, 1970.

Feder, B., and Ronall, R. *Beyond the Hot Seat: Gestalt Approaches to Group*. New York: Brunner/Mazel, 1980.

Goodman, P. *Growing Up Absurd: Problems of Youth in the Organized Society*. New York: Vintage Books, 1956.

Harvey, J. B. *The Abilene Paradox and Other Meditations on Management*. Lexington, Mass.: Lexington Books, 1988.

Herman, S. M., and Korenich, M. *Authentic Management: A Gestalt Orientation to Organizations and Their Development*. Reading, Mass.: Addison-Wesley, 1977.

Latner, J. "Origin and Development of Gestalt Therapy." In E. C. Nevis (ed.), *Gestalt Therapy: Perspectives and Applications*. Cleveland, Ohio: Gestalt Institute of Cleveland Press, 1992.

Melnick, J., and Nevis, S. M. "Diagnosis: The Struggle for a Meaningful Paradigm." In E. C. Nevis (ed.), *Gestalt Therapy: Perspectives and Applications*. Cleveland, Ohio: Gestalt Institute of Cleveland Press, 1992.

Merry, U., and Brown, G. I. *The Neurotic Behavior of Organizations*. Cleveland, Ohio: Gestalt Institute of Cleveland Press, 1987. (Distributed by Gardner Press.)

Miller, J. G. *Living Systems*. New York: McGraw-Hill, 1978.

Nevis, E. C. *Organizational Consulting: A Gestalt Approach*. New York: Gardner Press, 1987.

Perls, F. S. *Ego, Hunger and Aggression: The Beginnings of Gestalt Therapy*. New York: Random House, 1969a.

Perls, F. S. *Gestalt Therapy Verbatim* (J. O. Stevens, compiler and ed.). Lafayette, Calif.: Real People Press, 1969b.

Perls, F. S. *In and Out of the Garbage Pail*. Lafayette, Calif.: Real People Press, 1969c.

Perls, F. S. "Four Lectures." In J. Fagan and I. R. Shepherd (eds.), *Gestalt Therapy Now: Theory, Techniques, Applications*. Palo Alto, Calif.: Science and Behavior Books, 1970.

Perls, F. S. *The Gestalt Approach and Eye Witness to Therapy*. Palo Alto, Calif.: Science and Behavior Books, 1973.

Perls, F. S., Hefferline, R. F., and Goodman, P. *Gestalt Therapy: Excitement and Growth in Human Personality*. New York: Julian Press, 1951.

Perls, L. "A Talk for the 25th Anniversary." *Gestalt Journal*, 1990, *13*(2), 14–22.

Polster, E., and Polster, M. *Gestalt Therapy Integrated: Contours of Theory and Practice*. New York: Vintage Books, 1973.

Rosenblatt, D. "Introduction." *Gestalt Journal,* 1980, *3*(1), 5–18.

Rosenblatt, D. "An Interview with Laura Perls." *Gestalt Journal,* 1991, *14*(1), 7–26.

Shepard, M. *Fritz.* New York: Saturday Review Press, 1975.

Stoehr, T. *Here Now Next: Paul Goodman and the Origins of Gestalt Therapy.* San Francisco: Jossey-Bass, 1994.

Wheeler, G. *Gestalt Reconsidered: A New Approach to Contact and Resistance.* Cleveland, Ohio: Gestalt Institute of Cleveland Press, 1991.

Zinker, J. *Creative Process in Gestalt Therapy.* New York: Brunner/Mazel, 1977.

Chapter Nine

Murray Bowen
Emotional Systems

Why Murray Bowen? An Overview of Organizational Applications

Bowen Family System Theory (BFST) originated with a focus on families and evolved to concentrate on the "emotional and relationship system" that describes the interaction of individuals in a wide range of social and work-related situations (Bowen [1966] 1985i, p. 158). Instinct-based emotion provides an additional and powerful dimension that organizational practitioners can use to understand how the behavior of organization members is invisibly linked in a wide range of situations.

Bowen Family System Theory as an Organizational Image or Metaphor

BFST suggests two types of organizational images or metaphors. The more obvious is the organization itself as a family. One's family of origin is the most prolonged exposure most individuals have to the dynamics of succession, peer (sibling) rivalry, cooperation,

---

Note: This chapter relies on the following three papers to illustrate the applications of Bowen Family System Theory in the workplace: Gilmore, T., "A Triangular Framework: Leadership and Followership"; Kerr, M., "Applications of Family System Theory to a Work System"; and Wiseman, K., "Emotional Process in Organizations," all from K. Wiseman and R. Sagar (eds.), *Understanding Organizations: Applications of Bowen Family Systems Theory.* Washington, D.C.: Georgetown University Family Center, 1982.

conflict, cooperation, and collusion. The family image or metaphor can serve as a way to understand the personal dynamic in these processes. Less obvious, but unique to BFST, is the framework of viewing the group or organization as an emotional (instinctive) system. The image of an emotional system highlights such significant instinct-based areas as ritual, fighting, fleeing, and deceptive behavior.

With the emotional system as a framework, practitioners can pare away the intellectual rationalizations that sometimes obscure the instinctive base of such behavior.

Bowen Family System Theory as a Point of Influence for Dealing with Conflict

BFST defines the powerful stance of emotional detachment, which means staying in emotional contact with all parties to a conflict but avoiding involvement in the emotional forces of the conflict. This stance gives the consultant a unique and powerful vantage point from which to influence the outcome as well as behavior in general.

Bowen Family System Theory as a Point of Influence for Dealing with Psychological Growth

BFST adds the dimensions of a wider definition of instincts, a link to all species, a multigenerational time perspective, and a role definition for the consultant of serving as a coach to the process of psychological growth. With its link to the life sciences, BFST provides individuals with an opportunity to link their differentiation of self with other fundamental life processes.

Bowen Family System Theory as a Point of Influence for Dealing with the Dilemmas of Joining

One dilemma of joining or belonging to a group or organization takes place when a conflict exists between organizational goals and the emotional support individuals experience from joining with one another. BFST enables practitioners to view such disparities in terms of a conflict between two basic life forces: individuality and togetherness. In BFST terms, when responding to the life force of individuality, an organization member would be developing and living by well-thought-out life principles and values. When responding to the togetherness force, the member would be seeking comfort thorough closer contact with others. Practitioners can use this framework to help managers more effectively balance their need for support with their lifelong quest to define their principles and values.

Bowen Family System Theory as a Basis for Other Organizationally Relevant Theories

Murray Bowen often stated that he believed that there were more similarities than differences between humans and other forms of life. This viewpoint led Bowen and others to incorporate findings from biology, zoology, and other life sciences into their theory. BFST also focuses upon Toman's theory of sibling position (1969). The life stance and coping skills that one develops as a result of sibling position (for example, one's style of assuming responsibility) is clearly work-related. Practitioners can use Toman's and others' theories of sibling position to good advantage in organizational training and consultation.

Limitations of Bowen Family System Theory for Use in Organizations

The chief limitation of BFST for use in organizations lies in its choice of a different psychological process from that of most other change strategies. Most of the other organizational strategies are humanistically based and emphasize feeling awareness as a means of enhancing individual effectiveness. The bulk of the remaining approaches emphasize insight into the unconscious (Freud and others) or reinforcement of behavior (Skinner). BFST emphasizes a thinking process in which individuals reflect upon the emotional instinctive basis of their own behaviors, particularly in situations of anxiety. It also makes a deliberate effort to avoid the sense of positive sentiment, support, or togetherness that is common to most other approaches.

The origins of behavior are seen to be in an individual's multigenerational family history. Examining family history in this way is not an accustomed focus within organizations. The result is that it is hard to combine BFST with the most widely used group- and feeling-based strategies of organization development. Although most existing approaches do not preclude discussing one's family history, none involve other family members. To gain the internal awareness and perspective needed to help others understand their place in an emotional system, practitioners must do the same thing themselves. They must initiate a process of differentiation of self from members of their family of origin and/or extended family. At the present time, not many consultants have gone through such a process. However the chapter also illustrates how consultants who have initiated such a process themselves can help managers to function more effectively in their organization's emotional system without having the managers go through a similar process with their families of origin.

How Murray Bowen Developed His Theory

Murray Bowen was born in Waverly, Tennessee, in 1913. He completed his undergraduate and medical education at the University of Tennessee and internships at Bellevue and Grasslands hospitals in New York. After five years of active duty in the U.S. Army during World War II, he trained in psychiatry and served on the staff of the Freud-oriented Menninger Foundation in Topeka, Kansas. As a member of the Menninger Clinic, he became involved in psychoanalytic training, which included a personal or training analysis. However, for Bowen, as for other theorists in this volume, the Freudian approach provoked first questioning, then an attempt to fill in what were perceived as theoretical gaps or deficiencies, and finally the development of the author's own theory.

Bowen brought several attributes to theory building. From childhood he had a talent and interest in solving difficult puzzles. One talent in solving seemingly "unsolvable" puzzles is the ability to redefine the situation—to see the whole puzzle as well as the individual pieces in a new context. This quality would prove valuable in rethinking relationships as part of an emotional system. He also had a lifelong interest and wide reading in the sciences, history, and medicine. At an early point in his career, he began to seek an-

swers that existing psychiatry and psychoanalysis could not provide
(Bowen, [1976] 1985g, p. 353):

> The evolution of my own theoretical thinking began in the decade
> before I started family research. There were many questions con-
> cerning generally accepted explanations about emotional illness.
> Efforts to find logical answers resulted in more unanswerable ques-
> tions. One simple example is the notion that mental illness is the
> result of maternal deprivation. The idea seemed to fit the clinical
> case of the moment, but not the large number of normal people
> who, as far as could be determined, had been exposed to more
> maternal deprivation than those who were sick. . . . Psychiatry acted
> as if it knew the answers, but it had not been able to develop diagno-
> sis consistent with etiology. Psychoanalytic theory tended to define
> emotional illness as the product of a process between parents and
> child in a single generation, and there was little to explain how se-
> vere problems could be created so rapidly. The basic sciences were
> critical of scientific explanation that eluded scientific study. If the
> body of knowledge was reasonably factual, why could we not be
> more scientific about it? . . . These and many other questions led me
> to extensive reading in evolution, biology, and the natural sciences
> as part of a search for clues that could lead to a broader theoretical
> frame of reference. My hunch was that emotional illness comes
> from that part of man that he shares with the lower forms of life.

These doubts laid the foundation for what have come to be some
of the unique aspects of Bowen's theory: a strong link to evolutionary biology and a widening theoretical focus to define the emotional process through multiple generations of the nuclear family.

Bowen started formulating his theory while at the Menninger
Foundation in Kansas, but in 1954 he left the Foundation and
moved to the National Institute of Mental Health (NIMH) in
Bethesda, Maryland. Here he supervised a five-year project in
which schizophrenic offspring and their entire families lived in a
research ward for periods of one to three years. NIMH funded the
program on the basis that it would develop a more effective treatment for schizophrenia. The actual outcome was both more and
less than official expectations. Although much was learned about
schizophrenia, the project did not produce a definitive treatment
or cure. At the same time, a great deal was learned about the emotional process in the family as well as in the administrative systems

that constituted the family's environment. This program allowed Bowen to observe the mutual influence of symptoms and behaviors throughout the entire family. In doing so he noticed that the processes in the schizophrenic families appeared similar to those in families with less intense problems. It was just easier to see them in the extreme (K. Kerr, 1982, p. 2). The experience of this project helped Bowen to confirm and extend the general theoretical formulations he began earlier at Menninger.

In 1959 Bowen left NIMH and established the Family Center at Georgetown University Medical School. Here the work of Walter Toman (1969) on sibling positions was incorporated into the theory of family systems; the theory became available to a wider group of clinicians through a training program, an annual symposium, and a series of publications. Bowen was not alone in shifting his focus from the psychodynamics of the individual to the family as a system. While he was conducting his research and formulating his theory, others were moving along the same lines. By the late 1950s, it was possible to identify a "family movement," with many researchers and theorists moving along different lines to study emotional processes in the family as a unit (Hoffman, 1981, p. 17).

By the early 1970s, the term *family systems* was being used to describe a wide range of theoretical approaches, some emphasizing affective or feeling approaches and some based on general systems theory. Bowen's work had neither of these characteristics, and, although he was initially opposed to naming theories after individuals, he decided that it was important to differentiate his theory from these others. In 1975, "Family System Theory" was formally changed to "Bowen Family System Theory." Bowen continued his private practice and his active work in the Georgetown Family Center until his death in 1990.

Bowen Family System Theory's Point of Influence

The other theories in this volume focus on the structure and dynamics of the individual personality and view interaction with others as governed by that personality. The distinctive feature of BFST is that the focus is widened to the emotional system and how the individual is embedded in it. BFST's point of influence is the emotional system that humans share with other forms of life. This system links them together in a way that transcends groups and organizations and influences individual and collective behavior.

Using Bowen Family System Theory to Understand Human Interaction

It has been acceptable for some time to discuss thoughts in the workplace, but discussion of feelings was relegated to off-duty hours. The Hawthorne experiments in the 1920s were the first of a series of management theories and change frameworks to study the experience and expression of feelings in the workplace. The Hawthorne experiment and later studies resulted in a widening of the areas of human functioning that were considered acceptable to express and discuss in organizations. BFST widens that area even further, stating that "When one considers emotion on this level it becomes synonymous with instinct, which governs the life process of all living things (Bowen [1971] 1985c, p. 198). The theory views instinctive emotion as distinct from feeling and offers a framework for making this vital aspect of human functioning available for understanding and a limited degree of control.

Preview: When to Use Bowen's Point of Influence in the Workplace.

All three systems in BFST—intellect, feeling, and emotion—
are illustrated in the following scenario at the Chicago O'Hare International Airport:

> The day was long, and, because of a series of mechanical problems, many
> flights had been delayed or canceled. The problem was compounded by the
> airline's practice of giving only fragmentary information to its passengers.
> This meant that many passengers had the experience of being told that their
> flight would be delayed for "just a few minutes," only to find out an hour or so
> later that the flight was now canceled, too late for them to change their ticket
> for a flight on another airline. One focal point for much of this frustration was
> Ric Stearns, an agent in the Chicago terminal. It was bad enough to face peo-
> ple all day whose plans had been disrupted by canceled flights, but, when some
> of these people accused him of deliberately lying to them in order to prevent
> their switching to another airline, it was just too much. The final blow for Ric
> came when a farm implement salesman said, "Look, you two-faced ;!#» #»&
> %, don't smile and tell me that you're sorry that I've been inconvenienced.
> Your lying just cost me ten thousand dollars." Ric glanced at the salesman
> with a blank look, started rearranging some papers on the counter, put up the
> "closed" sign, and mumbled, "It's time for my break." The salesman stormed
> off, but he remembered Ric's name, wrote a letter accusing Ric of "drug use on
> the job," and threatened to sue the airline.

The Emotional System

Emotions as we are describing them are quite different from
feelings—as described in other chapters in this book—and BFST
emphasizes this distinction. Emotions come from our instincts;
feelings are our internal awareness of these emotions. The emotional system was the first to develop in the evolutionary process
and in most instances it can override the thinking and feeling systems (Bowen, [1975] 1985b, p. 305). In evolutionary terms, before
there were thoughts, and even before there were feelings such as
guilt, frustration, or joy, there was behavior. The organism had to
do a number of things to survive, and from both paleontological
evidence and the behavior of surviving species of reptiles and in-
sects, it is possible today to develop a reasonable description of that
behavior: "Soldier caste ants vigorously respond to intruders into
their colony. They neither contemplate the meaning of their ac-

tion nor harbor strong nationalistic feelings. They simply act" (Kerr and Bowen, 1988, p. 30).

In this scenario, Ric acted. Without thinking or even being aware of feeling, he distanced himself physically and emotionally from the salesman. If Ric had unthinkingly responded to the salesman's attack verbally or even physically, the BFST explanation would have been the same. The emotional system had overridden the thinking and feeling systems. At the height of the interchange, the emotional systems of Ric and the passenger were clearly influencing their respective feeling and thinking systems. At a nonverbal level, the emotional systems can even seem to be responding to one another (Bowen, [1960] 1985a, p. 66).

The prime position of the emotional system is understandable if we view it in evolutionary terms. The internal circuitry of the emotional system existed long before words, and under stress, messages from this part of our mind can override the more recently developed feeling and thinking systems (Bowen, [1975] 1985b, p. 305). The emotional system can influence spoken words, but its most direct means of communicating is nonverbal. It *expresses* and *responds* to body posture, tone of voice, volume, hand gestures, and so on. As Ric and the passenger interacted, their emotional systems expressed and responded to each other, with the response centered around messages of fear and anger. In Ric's case, the message expressed a need for him to put some emotional distance between himself and the other person.

BFST is unique among the theories in this book in its attention and focus on other species. Lizards and other reptiles, for example, perform many of the behaviors performed by humans but are completely dependent on what Paul MacLean (1978) terms the instinctual part of their brain. These creatures imitate, perform routines and rituals, displace (meaning they behave inappropriately when under stress), and perform deceptive behaviors and tropistic behavior (positive or negative responses to partial representations of animate or inanimate objects (Kerr and Bowen, 1988, p. 34).

Humans, of course, also withdraw, imitate, and respond to partial representations of objects, but because humans have a much better developed thinking system (cerebral cortex), they are quick to provide *reasons* for this behavior. The passenger yelled at Ric in the name of "honesty and telling the truth." At the time, Ric was so emotionally involved that he might not have been able to offer an explanation for his behavior. Later he might say, "It is my policy never to argue with people who are irrational." This explaining process occurs quite frequently. Humans mate in the name of "love," fight in the name of some "ideal," help one another in the name of "virtue," and rear their young in the name of "responsibility." Within the framework of BFST, we could well be performing these behaviors without the explanations provided by our cognitive brain. This does not mean that our highly developed intellectual capacity or our feeling system have no influence. They clearly do, but both of these capacities perform on a foundation of deeply ingrained instincts (Kerr and Bowen, 1988, p. 28).

Recent discoveries on the development and workings of the brain offer striking parallels to Bowen's theory. Bowen is describing internal physiological systems that are broader than functions of the brain; MacLean's theory (1978) of the *triune brain* offers physiological support for Bowen's view of three interrelated systems. According to MacLean, in human evolution the first section of this brain to develop is the *reptilian* or *R complex,* which is located in a large fist of ganglia at the base of the human forebrain. This is the major part of the reptile's brain, and with it reptiles engage in the complex behaviors (imitation, ritual, displacement, and so on) described previously.

The relevant point for the student of human behavior is that the R complex continues to exist within humans. It existed and was functioning in the brain of Ric Stearns and his disgruntled passenger. The unique contribution of BFST is to illustrate how this aspect of our brain continues to influence many aspects of human behavior (mating, rearing children, fighting, fleeing, and so on). For humans, and for some mammals, however, the impact of this part of our mind is not always clear. Because we can manufacture reasons for our responses, it is tempting to confuse responses in the emotional system with responses in the feeling and thinking systems.

The Feeling System

If the emotional system consists of the instincts that the organism responds to automatically without instruction, then feelings (which are the focus for other theorists such as Rogers) are the awareness of some of these responses. The emotional system, for example, might cause us to experience stress and to react through attack, withdrawal, hyperactivity, and so on. Ric and his customer experienced anger, fear, and a number of other reactions. These responses came from their feeling systems (Bowen, [1976] 1985g, p. 356).

The feeling system also communicates with the other two internal systems. At one point, both Ric's and the passenger's feeling systems were receiving messages from their respective thinking and emotional systems. The message from the emotional system was physiological, taking the form of age-old signals of fight and flight. As a result the body stiffened, facial muscles tightened, the heart began to race, and both individuals became aware of an internal reaction they defined as anger. The feelings of anger and fear were also fueled by more complex and symbolic messages that the feeling system received from the thinking system. The feeling system was thus getting it from both sides: instinctive messages of fear and anger from the emotional system and more complex messages of pride and resentment from the thinking system.

The feeling activity is most closely associated with the section of the brain that MacLean identifies as having been developed second in the evolutionary cycle. This is the *paleomammalian* or *limbic system*. It is the limbic cortex and the structures of the brain stem with which the feeling system has its primary connections. Only humans, birds, and mammals have developed this aspect of the brain. Its main function is to connect to the glands and other parts of the body that are involved with feeding, fighting, self-preservation, sexual arousal, affectionate behavior, nursing, and maternal behavior.

The limbic system is not responsible for performing these rudimentary functions. Reptiles eat, fight, procreate, and do a number of other things with a very rudimentary limbic system. In MacLean's theory, reptiles cannot experience the *feelings* connected with these activities. In the airport example, Ric's basic reaction and behavior came from his emotional system. His response was simple instinct and reaction. The meaning that he later attached to his reaction came from his feeling and thinking systems.

We now have accounted for two important aspects of human functioning: instincts (emotions), which govern how we perform a number of important life functions, and feelings, which influence how we experience the performance of these functions. The final and remaining function is that of conceptual understanding.

The Intellectual System

The *intellectual system* is the familiar function of human thinking, abstracting, and reasoning that allows humans to develop language, to communicate, and to begin to understand and manipulate their world. An important distinction should be made between thinking that is influenced by the emotional and feeling systems and thinking that is not. For example, a manager of auditors may assess the situation in one unit and decide that, given the nature of the task and the skills, maturity, and ability of the auditors, the group should receive more autonomy (the thinking system). The same manager may go to a workshop, come home with a rosy glow about the idea of participative management, and decide that the auditors should be autonomous (feeling influencing the thinking system). Last, the manager might feel pressure and anxiety because some auditors are not working well together, withdraw from the pressure, and grant the group de facto autonomy (the emotional system influencing behavior that the thinking system may later rationalize).

In our example of Ric and the passenger, the thinking system turned some of their instinctive emotional reactions into the thoughts and ideas that heightened and reinforced the escalating conflict. The passenger's message was "Does he think I'm so stupid he can lie to me?" Ric didn't think; he just withdrew and mumbled an inappropriate explanation. From the standpoint of Bowen's theory, the emotional systems of both of these individuals were in control. The role of the thinking system was to find the words that expressed the message from the emotional system, and this it did. The passenger cursed, and Ric withdrew and *later* explained his withdrawal in rational terms.

Togetherness and Individuality: The Forces Behind Behavior

BFST also posits two opposing life forces. The emotional system expresses these two forces. One is a built-in life force toward individuality and the differentiation of a separate "self," and the other is an equally intense desire for emotional closeness (Bowen, [1975] 1985b, p. 311). These drives are both physical and emotional. Their biological parameters are evident in reptiles and mammals, and both forces shape the contours of life for humans and other species. The togetherness force pushes us toward others for attachment, affiliation, and approval. The individuality force propels humans to build the set of values, beliefs, and responses that make up their individual self. In BFST, the significance of the individuality force is that it defines the part of the self that is nonnegotiable in relationships (Gilbert, 1992, p. 13).

One contribution of BFST is that it cuts through the intellectual explanations (rationalizations) that humans use to explain their experiences and creates a framework for understanding the instinctive base of human behavior.

Sibling Position: An Important Social Modifier

Bowen's theory acknowledges the influence of early socialization by incorporating the work of Walter Toman in *Family Constellation* (1969). For Bowen, *all other things being equal,* one's family position provides important presumptive information about one's later role and behavior (Bowen, [1976] 1985g, p. 385). The position that one holds in a family, such as oldest brother, youngest sister, only child, and so on, is the first sustained experience that one has with a number of important family and work roles. Bowen focused on these roles within the family, but Toman's work is also relevant to workplace behavior. Oldest children are more likely to have early formative experiences with responsibility. Youngest children are more likely to have had experiences in the company of others. Viewed in isolation, sibling position theories do not include a number of crucial intervening variables such as the parents' relationship or the influence of previous generations. Taken together, however, BFST and Toman's sibling theory complement one another. Toman's theory helps to account for the crucial importance of one's early experience with a sibling. BFST provides a broader context, in terms of family generations and overall functioning, in which to understand sibling relationships.

Applying Bowen Family System Theory

When You Wish to Increase Your Effectiveness as a Consultant Under Conditions of Anxiety

The emotional system is a powerful force in human affairs on both an individual and a collective basis. Individually it refers to the instinctive part of each individual, which was discussed previously. Collectively it refers to the interactions between the emotional systems of individuals in a family or other grouping. The emotional system is not likely to embody organizational goals in either case. It is powerful in both settings because it can override and hamper the effective functioning of other systems. The more that individuals automatically respond to their emotional system, the less they are able to use their feeling system to relate to other people and their thinking system to solve problems and understand a total situation.

The following example shows that when emotions override thoughts and feelings *within* an individual they also can override thoughts and feelings *between* individuals. Kathleen Wiseman was an administrator in a consulting firm specializing in the quality of work life and job enrichment. The main goal of the organization was to establish collaborative work projects in settings where adversarial relationships had been the norm. This was a high-anxiety situation, and the consultants often got caught in this anxiety and then allied themselves with one of the parties in a dispute. Wiseman believes that if the consultants had been able to remain neutral and to provide a calming presence, the parties could have resolved their issues. Instead, the consultants were often "caught" by the anxiety, bringing it back to the consulting firm itself. This anxiety, plus the uncertainty of funding and a variety of personal problems, was felt in the emotional system of the consulting firm. Wiseman describes her own experiences in this organization.

> My own patterns of reacting to stress in the organization were similar to patterns of reacting to stress in my family of origin. As the oldest daughter in the family, I tend to take on the responsibilities of others, get caught in conflict, and function less and less for myself under stress. Some individuals in anxious systems tend to become "workaholic." I worked more hours, but was less effective. If a similar situation developed today, hopefully, I would be able

to identify the process and manage my own anxiety. Identifying the processes and patterns provides individuals and organizations alternatives for action.

As I look back at my functioning during the periods of highest anxiety, I remember my energy and attention being focused on the problematic personality of the executive director. To relieve my own anxiety, much time at work was involved relating stories about him to others—not to resolve a problem, but to relieve the stress. His confusing and contradictory behavior was met by my own confusing behavior. The process I describe is a subtle one. My effectiveness suffered as I got caught in the anxiety. My relationship with the executive director became distant, and issues that needed his collaboration and approval were not discussed [1982, pp. 121–131].

In this instance, the anxiety was expressed in rapid turnover of the nonprofessional staff and, eventually, in the departure of most of the professional staff. The consulting firm could be seen as analogous to an organism in which the emotional system had impaired the operations of the thinking system and the organization itself: "If the organization had been able to step back and disengage from intense relationship issues, it could have defined organizational goals for itself and tasks for achieving them, and the relationship issues would have faded" (Wiseman, 1982, p. 40).

Wiseman also describes a more successful intervention in which she used knowledge of BFST to improve the functioning of an organization. In consulting with a 500-person firm, she remained in touch but stayed emotionally neutral; this led to real organizational change. The example involves a firm that was suffering from a wide variety of problems: a 50 percent increase in equal employment opportunity complaints, lack of communication between departments, and increases in reported thefts of employees' and the company's property. As she gathered information about the company, it became clear to Wiseman that the company had the capacity to establish procedures that would alleviate these problems. This capacity was not being used because the company's president was reluctant to use the power he had. The president had recently taken over from the company's founder, a brilliant, charismatic, harddriving, and abusive despot. The former president was now the chairman of the board, and the new president was reluctant to act.

In terms of BFST, the role of the consultant was to remain neutral, but at the same time to facilitate the thinking system of the person who had the power to solve the problems: the new president. To do so, Wiseman remained respectful of the former president's abilities and kept in contact with him but at the same time raised questions to the new president that triggered his thinking, such as "What is important for you to accomplish in your job?" and "How can you become the most responsible president in this business environment?" (Wiseman, 1982, p. 44). It's important to note that she did not raise feeling, process, or relationship questions regarding the old president that would have triggered the feeling system. The goal was to get the new president *thinking* about himself as president. The strategy worked; the president responded to these questions and began to initiate policy changes that dealt with the problems.

When You Need Help in Shifting Your Thinking: Five Concepts That will Help You to Remain Detached from the Pull of an Emotional System

BFST requires a clear departure in thinking from what is now customary in today's clinical and organizational world. With BFST thinking, consultants can decrease the likelihood that they will be pulled into the emotional system of their clients. The following five concepts will help you to understand enough to begin altering your style of thinking.

Emotional Fusion, Internal and External

BFST uses the term *emotional fusion* to refer to both the internal emotional system and the collective emotional system of a family or organization. The internal emotional system fuses with the individual's thinking and/or feeling system, thereby rendering one or both of those systems less effective. The emotional systems of a number of individuals in a family, group, or organization can also fuse, thereby temporarily overwhelming the feeling and thinking systems of the individuals in these groups. In BFST terms, the emotional systems, through nonverbal reactions like the tone of someone's voice, become so reactive to each other that they *function* as if they were fused (Bowen, [1965] 1985d, p. 105).

In the airport scenario, under the stress of the moment, the emotional systems of Ric and his passenger fused internally. Their thinking systems were temporarily overwhelmed by their emotional and feeling systems. In addition, their emotional or instinctive systems also temporarily acted in concert. In the consulting example, the new president's internal emotional system was fused with the external emotional system of the company. Wiseman was able to help the president become less fused with his external emotional system as she became less fused internally.

Differentiation of Self

Self refers to each individual's ability to maintain a separation between the emotional, thinking, and feeling systems under various degrees of stress; in particular, it refers to whether an individual can utilize his or her thinking system independent of emotions and feeling (Bowen, [1966] 1985i, pp. 161–165). Such an internal differentiation of self also makes it more possible for an individual to maintain an external differentiation of self within the emotional systems of a family, group, or organization. In the example, Wiseman's individual efforts toward a differentiation of self made her more effective externally.

Basic Self and Functional Self

Basic self refers to the aspect of the self that is differentiated sufficiently so that it is nonnegotiable in relationships. The higher the degree of basic self, the more likely it is that an individual will be able to remain functionally differentiated in varying degrees of stress. *Functional self* refers to the aspect of the self that one trades in a relationship. When operating under the influence of the functional self, an individual may display more or less competence and responsibility in a situation in order to maintain a relationship. *Functional self* also refers to the degree to which an individual becomes reactive to or fused to a relationship (emotional) system (Kerr and Bowen, 1988, p. 98).

In the example, Wiseman was working with the functional differentiation of the company's president, but this work rested on the foundation of her own basic differentiation of self. Because she was able to maintain contact with the emotional system of the organization but not automatically become reactive to the tensions in the system, she was able to coach the new president to do the same.

The Family Emotional System and the Organizational Emotional System

In BFST, underlying all work-oriented emotional systems is the emotional system in our family of origin. This system is fundamental, because it is where we developed our repertoire of actions, reactions, and behaviors. The principles governing the family emotional system apply to other groupings, provided the people in these groupings have spent enough time together to develop emotional patterns. The family of origin is also the source of the individual's basic level of differentiation. This level, however, is not fixed in stone. Within limits, individuals can grow personally by increasing their internal differentiation and their ability to differentiate from external work systems. They do this by going through a process in which they systematically differentiate more and more self from their family of origin.

An important part of BFST is the Differentiation of Self Scale. The scale is a concept rather than a concrete scale or instrument. The scale describes various levels of differentiation of self and the degree of self-directed behavior that might occur at each level (Bowen, [1972] 1985e, pp. 472–475). In working toward such differentiation a therapist-coach guides the individual, who returns for visits to the family of origin to initiate change in the system by first understanding her or his own role in the system and then changing behavior related to that role. This type of individual change often leads to changes in the system.

This process is based upon the idea that change in any part of a system will necessitate change and adjustment in the rest of the system (Bowen, [1966] 1985i, p. 155). A description of this process and the theory behind it is available in Bowen's account of his efforts to differentiate a self in his own family of origin (Bowen, [1972] 1985e). Other sources are Harriet Lerner in *The Dance of Anger* (1985) and *The Dance of Intimacy* (1989) and Roberta Gilbert in *Extraordinary Relationships* (1992). Lerner and Gilbert suggest that, while attempting differentiation of self with the family of origin, an individual should receive help from a competent psychotherapist.

Both authors, however, also offer various degrees of guidance for the process.

The likelihood of success using BFST is enhanced if the change agent or consultant has internalized the principles in his or her own life. Bowen found that psychiatric residents who began to explore their own families of origin seemed to almost automatically start doing better clinical work as family therapists (Bowen, [1974] 1985h, p. 531). This is similar to the therapeutic situation in which therapists of other orientations are encouraged or required to deal with their own issues of development before they aspire to help others. This position, however, is not absolute. In applying BFST, as in applying psychoanalysis or any other theory, cognitive understanding is a valuable first step in learning about one's role in an emotional system. Bowen stated, "Most consultants to businesses and work situation can encounter leaders who are not sure of themselves and whose functioning lapses under pressure. If the leader is fairly solid, he can learn enough to help him become more effective. Even a little learning in a profitable direction may be enough to help him on a more productive course" (Bowen, 1982, p. xi).

Emotional Distancing and Emotional Detachment

It is perilous for a consultant to become emotionally reactive to the emotional system of a client organization. Withdrawal or emotional distancing is a form of such reactivity; in either case the consultant is subject to the same automatic instinctive reactions as those in the client system. The consultant therefore compromises the ability to watch and learn from the system. If this happens, it is hard to imagine effective consultation.

The solution to this dilemma is to remain in emotional contact with as many individuals or groups in the system as possible, while remaining neutral or detached regarding the various emotional issues and alliances in the system. At an early stage in the development of his theory, Bowen termed this *interested detachment* (Bowen, [1960] 1985a, p. 50). Today BFST defines detachment as a useful stance for an individual who is attempting to increase the differentiation from his or her family of origin. It is also the stance that Bowen-oriented consultants take themselves and coach their clients to take when working with an organization.

It is hard to be aware of emotional distancing when it is taking place. Detachment, however, involves the thinking system and is more likely deliberate than automatic. In her first example, concerning the consulting firm in which she was an administrator, Wiseman distanced herself from the executive director and was thus unable to discuss difficult issues with him. In her second account, that of the firm in which she coached the new president to take a stronger stand on issues, she illustrated emotional detachment. She did not just pull away from the emotional involvement but instead used BFST to maintain objectivity, understand the system, and keep herself in a position to give the same message to all members of the system. Because she was emotionally detached, the automatic aspects of her instinctive reactions were minimized. This meant that she was able to tie in more closely with her feeling and thinking systems.

When You Need to Maintain Detachment in the Midst of Emotional Triangles

Individual emotional systems are naturally reactive to stress and changes in the environment. Just as several deer in the forest stir nervously as their emotional system tells them of a potential threat, so too the emotional system of humans responds to the environment and sends messages that raise the level of anxiety.

Triangles at the Individual Level

This is the important connection between internal and external emotional systems. The external emotional system triggers a reaction in the internal emotional system. Two individuals, for example, may work quite well together in a calm environment, but when changes in external conditions force them to interact at a more intense level, their emotional systems begin to react. If that level of interaction is uncomfortable for one or both of them, three things can happen:

1. One person can distance himself or herself emotionally, in effect leaving the field.
2. One person can lower her or his level of functioning (underfunctioning), while the other raises her or his level of functioning (overfunctioning) (Bowen, [1966] 1985i, p. 155).

3. Both people can turn the emotional relationship into one of conflict.

Each of these outcomes temporarily relieves the relationship anxiety resulting from emotional closeness, but each also has a cost. Distancing obviously cuts down on interaction and contact, whereas underfunctioning and overfunctioning leave one person limiting his or her capacity to perform and the other in a permanent posture of overextension. Continual conflict is basically a focus on the other with an inability to see one's own contribution to the problem (Bowen, [1966] 1985i, p. 166).

The emotional system has another reaction in response to relationship problems. This reaction is the emotional triangle. Stressed or uncomfortable relationships are temporarily relieved by emotionally involving a third party (Bowen, [1966] 1985i, p. 160). The tendency to transform relationships between two people into relationships of three people is pervasive among human and nonhuman species (Kerr and Bowen, 1988, p. 144). We will use the work system of Ric, the airline clerk, to explore how and why triangles are such a common form of human relationships.

Ric's closest friend at work was another reservation clerk, Larry Alton. Ric and Larry ate lunch together, conversed informally during breaks, and generally seemed to be on the same emotional wavelength. When they were together it was not always easy for another person to break into the conversation. The friendship had its ups and downs. As long as things were going smoothly on the job, their friendship also went smoothly. If the job became more stressful, as when there were weather shutdowns or clusters of mechanical problems, the relationship changed, but even then it did not seem to be openly conflictual. In these times of stress, Ric and Larry reacted quite differently. Larry reacted to stress by stepping up his pace of activity and his sense of responsibility. He was ready to take care of his own responsibilities and, if given the opportunity, those of his co-workers. At such times he would often question Ric to make sure that Ric had taken care of all the details for ticket transfer and reports. Larry's response to stress was to *overfunction*.

Ric moved in just the opposite direction. As the stress level of the job increased, he became less and less emotionally connected, both to his work and to his fellow workers. He did the minimal job but began to call in sick more frequently, took longer breaks, made more errors, and didn't object when Larry began to pick up some of the slack from his area of responsibility. Ric's response was to *underfunction*.

At first glance this seemed to be a complementary relationship. Ric did less and Larry picked up the slack, but this arrangement bred problems. Larry felt stressed and wondered why Ric couldn't do his share of the work; Ric felt depressed and inadequate in performing his job and resented Larry's checking up on him. For Larry, Ric's emotional withdrawal was frustrating. He was putting himself out there, responding to the crisis in the best way he could, and offering what he considered to be help to Ric, who certainly seemed to need it. He was also hurt because Ric did not seem to appreciate his help. Instead, Ric reacted to this reaching out by doing less and less. Larry's emotional system was overfunctioning and Ric's was underfunctioning.

If Ric and Larry had been able to discuss this issue openly, they might have reached some agreement, but this did not happen. Both of them received clues from their feeling system about their emotional reactions. Larry felt anger because he was doing more than his share, and Ric felt guilt and resentment because he was being pressured to behave in a certain way. Neither person felt safe in using these feelings as a basis for discussion. If Ric and Larry were asked why they changed their level of functioning under stress, both could have come up with an explanation. However, it's unlikely that either explanation would have included their instinctive emotional response to stress. They both avoided a discussion, and the relationship deteriorated.

The resource to absorb the anxiety in the relationship was available in Helen Walton, their supervisor, who at that time was the third, "outside" member of their triangle. Though she was a supervisor, Helen had until recently been a clerk herself, and she did not like to see herself as socially above or separated from the people she supervised. In fact, she liked to join them in small talk, gossip, and general conversation. She liked both Ric and Larry but sometimes felt on the outside when they were engaged in intense conversation.

When things were going well, Ric and Larry were the inside members of a triangle, leaving Helen on the outside. But as tension between Larry and Ric increased, it was no longer desirable to be the inside member of the triangle. Now the outside position became more desirable, and Larry invited Helen into the triangle by complaining to her about Ric.

It is now evident that if we focus only on Ric and Larry, we are not seeing the whole picture. In this instance, Larry brought Helen in directly, but the recruitment of the third member of a triangle can also be more subtle. An unstable relationship can involve a third person in a problem just by allowing that person to be in earshot (Kerr and Bowen, 1988, p. 137).

Triangles can take a variety of forms. In this example an unstable twosome (Ric and Larry) was stabilized by Larry's recruiting of a third person (Helen). The third member need not be an individual. It can be an issue or an addiction—anything that can absorb the unrecognized energy in a dysfunctional relationship. When drinking or overworking make up the third member of a triangle, the addiction acts as a regulator or governor, tapering off when the emotional system is less intense and becoming more active when the emotional system heats up.

Triangles are a part of life because they allow temporary relief from anxiety and temporary stabilization of relationships. They can also be a way of temporarily dealing with, but not resolving, conflict; anxiety can travel around a triangle with the three individuals repeatedly switching positions and never allowing the real differences or issues to surface (Bowen, [1966] 1985i, p. 161).

> Helen responded to Larry's complaints by having a heart-to-heart talk with Ric about his performance and by supervising him more closely. Ric then complained to Larry about Helen's harsh methods, and Larry sympathized with Ric about Helen's manner. Ric and Larry reestablished the inside position, and for the time being Helen was again on the outside of the triangle. Thus the differences between Ric and Larry were never openly discussed.

Thomas Gilmore (1988, p. 112) describes a similar situation involving a governor's first year in office (see Figure 9.1):

> The governor was irritated with the action of a cabinet member. Instead of speaking to the cabinet member directly, he spoke to his own chief of staff. In this triangle the alliance was between the governor and the chief of staff, with the cabinet member in the outside position (Position One). When the chief of staff brought the matter to the attention of a cabinet member, positions shifted in the triangle, with the cabinet member still on the outside but not sure if the

Figure 9.1. Shifting Positions in a Triangle.

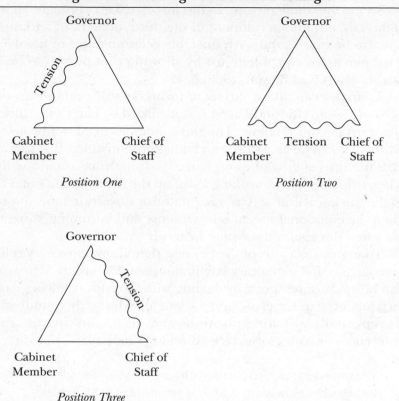

Position One

Position Two

Position Three

chief of staff was expressing his own concerns or the governor's (Position Two). When the cabinet member mentioned the issue casually to the governor, the governor replied that he was concerned but then made a mollifying comment to the effect that the chief of staff sometimes overreacted. At this point, positions in the triangle shifted again, with the chief of staff on the outside (Position Three).

In BFST, triangles are an automatic part of all nature. Ric was truly functioning at less than an optimum level during times of stress, so Larry's complaints were based on some degree of reality. At the same time, Ric's underfunctioning was *reciprocally* related to Larry's overfunctioning. In addition, Larry's timing in complaining about Ric to Helen and Helen's receptivity to hearing the complaint all fit into the "triangling" process (Kerr and Bowen, 1988, p. 149). The intensity of the two-person relationship was uncomfortable for Larry, so he brought in Helen to take up part of that tension. At the same time, Helen had felt on the outside of this relationship, and she was now very receptive to being included. In Gilmore's example of the governor, anxiety simply moved around the triangle, reflecting the ambiguities in each relationship. We will examine the role of the consultant in the midst of triangles later in this chapter.

Triangles at the Organizational Level

This process of triangling can also occur between organizational units. For example, in the incident between Ric and the unhappy passenger, the delay was caused by the excessive time it took to get parts to fix a broken hydraulic valve. Organizational triangles were a big part of this delay.

> The airline's Maintenance department was responsible for all aircraft repairs, but the decision to delay the flight, as well as the responsibility for communicating such delays, was that of the Scheduling department. Relations between the Maintenance and Scheduling departments were distant. The mechanics and their supervisors wanted to be left alone so they could do their job of repairing the aircraft. Scheduling wanted to know as soon as possible when the flight would be ready to take off, and Maintenance would not give them this information. Over time a number of incidents had taken place in which Maintenance and Scheduling had failed to communicate. Each then gradually built up perceptions of the other that made clear communication more difficult. This could be seen as two points in a triangle with some degree of tension between them (see Figure 9.2).
>
> It would have been possible for Maintenance and Scheduling to deal with this problem, but in this case it was much easier, and hence more likely, for the two departments to form a triangle with a third unit to help absorb the tension and keep the relationship stable, leaving the problem unresolved. In fact, several units did function to absorb the tension and keep the relationship between the other two units stable. If asked, Maintenance would be sure to mention the Parts department. Airlines cannot afford to have every part that might be

Figure 9.2. Interlocking Triangles in an Airline.

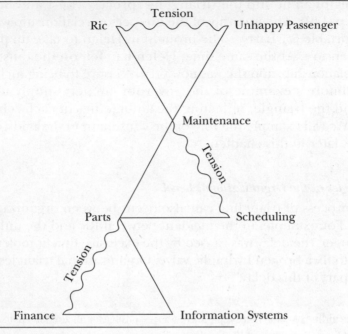

Note: Individuals and units are mixed in this figure.

needed available at every airport, so some decision has to be made regarding which parts will be stockpiled and where. Rather than working things out with Scheduling, it was much easier for Maintenance to blame the situation on the Parts department. In the meantime, individuals at the counter, such as Ric, absorbed the tension from the customers. This illustrates two interlocking triangles. The Parts department was also involved with the Finance department, which allocated the amount of money available for stocking spare parts. It might seem that given the delays that occur when parts are not available, Finance would allocate more money. At a recent series of meetings, representatives from Finance, not wanting to state why they were withholding money from Parts, stated that they would be happy to allocate more money if they could only get timely and sufficient information from Information Systems. Rather than dealing with Parts, Finance added a third member to this set of interlocking triangles.

Analysis of this situation reveals three interlocking triangles, shown in Figure 9.2. At one level, the relationship between these units is simply a matter of coordinating organizational units toward a common goal. However, if the individuals included in these units automatically back off from tension and involve a third party, we have the same sort of triangles Bowen found so pervasive in families.

Detriangling

Triangles are a pervasive and sometimes troublesome aspect of human relations, but they also provide an opportunity for consultants to work with the relationship system. The most common form of this work is referred to by Bowen as coaching individuals to "detriangle." Detriangling simply means finding a way to deflect the efforts of others to involve you in a triangle. The difficult part is carrying out the process in a way that does not create additional triangles or other relationship patterns. For example, when Larry complained to Helen about Ric not taking his work seriously enough, if Helen reacted with anger to Ric, she would simply be moving back into her outside role in the triangle. If she directly confronted Larry about his complaints by saying, "Don't complain to me about your co-workers; deal with it yourself!" she would be responding to emotionality with emotionality. This would keep her in an active role in the triangle.

To alter the triangling process, Helen would have to make a neutral comment that deflected the emotionality back to Larry. For example, she could have stated playfully, "Well, its always good to know how not to be too involved in your work." The important point about this comment is its emotional neutrality. Many Bowen-oriented consultants and therapists use humor and playfulness to loosen up tight emotional situations.

Secrets or comments from one member of a triangle to another that exclude a third are another basic aspect of the triangling process. Given this phenomenon, a powerful act of detriangling is to find a way to avoid being a depository of secrets. The process of detriangling by avoiding secrets is illustrated by Michael Kerr, who describes his role as a psychiatrist and then an administrator on a ward of an Army hospital.

Kerr was assigned to a psychiatric unit in which one physician, "Dr. Leary," was the extreme outside member of a whole series of organizational triangles. The triangles even extended outside of the formal work system to spouses. From his first day in the unit, Kerr was greeted by the entire staff with the exception of Dr. Leary. Kerr heard an endless series of negative stories about Dr. Leary. Early in the orientation, doors were shut, voices hushed, and it was explained to him that "the problem" was Dr. Leary, who was "unfriendly, hostile, and not to be trusted" (M. Kerr, 1982, p. 125). Kerr was particularly impressed that the chief informant was a Dr. Storm, who had only been at the hospital for three days. Rather than accept the group's diagnosis, Kerr worked to form his own opinion. He soon had an opportunity when he met Dr. Leary himself:

> When I first saw him, he was walking along the edge of the hallway with his head down and unsmiling. He gave all appearances of being unfriendly, uncooperative, hostile, and not warranting trust. I introduced myself. As we talked, the group's diagnosis of him was swirling in my head and his demeanor seemed to validate what I had heard. My reaction to him was tempered by a hypothesis then developing in my fragile "thinking brain" that what I was hearing about Dr. Leary was determined more by problems in the staff relationship system than by problems intrinsic to Dr. Leary. We exchanged a few pleasantries and went our separate ways [p. 125].

Kerr then began to investigate the history of the relationship system in the unit, and what he found illustrated several important principles about triangles.

First Principle: In an Emotional System Individuals Can Change, but Triangles Persist

In families, once the emotional circuitry of a triangle is in place, it usually outlives the people who participate in it. Children may act out a conflict that was never resolved between their grandparents. In organizations, the time line may not be so extended, but triangles regularly live on beyond the original participants. This was clearly demonstrated in this medical unit.

In this instance, the original "hot spot" in the triangle had been between Dr. Leary and a Dr. Wild. There had been loud verbal exchanges and even threats of bodily harm. Dr. Wild had left the military to be replaced by Dr. Storm. The two physicians knew each other, and Dr. Storm was even planning to go into practice with Dr. Wild after his tour of military duty. Dr. Storm's head had been filled with stories about Dr. Leary from Dr. Wild long before Dr. Storm had arrived. Dr. Storm stepped into Dr. Wild's spot in the relationship system without protest. The third position in the triangle was filled by unit physicians, the administrative secretary, and the receptionist.

The playing out of preexisting roles can also involve groups, organizational units, or even the memory of a previous leader. What makes these situations triangles is not simply the existence of three identifiable individuals or units but, rather, the fact that emotional contact and, hence, communication between two points of the triangle are affected because of the third point. Gilmore described the triangling process that occurred between a new governor, the governor's staff, and a memory of the old governor. Similar triangles could involve the new governor, remnants of the old staff, and the governor's new staff, outside consultants, or line managers who had contact with the governor (Gilmore, 1988, p. 117).

Second Principle: In the Presence of Enough Anxiety, Triangles Create More Triangles

If the emotional energy cannot be tempered or defused in one triangle, other triangles are created. In this instance the doctors' spouses formed an additional interlocking triangle. Within days after Dr. Storm's arrival, his wife, who had never met Dr. Leary, was informing Kerr's spouse about "the problem."

Third Principle: Humor and a Light Touch Are Very Helpful in Avoiding the Emotional Pull of a Triangle

Once someone has defined a triangle, it is possible to use a light touch to keep in contact with all points of the triangle. Kerr reports:

> For my part, I had an office next to Dr. Leary and simply made an effort to have a relationship with him. I was not feeling mad at him as others were, and although I did not always agree with the way he did things, I found him competent and responsible in relationship to me. Other staff members expressed puzzlement that I seemed to have a relationship with Dr. Leary, and they would want to know what we talked about. With a straight face I would tell them that we

discussed certain staff members whose names I could not reveal because Dr. Leary had sworn me to secrecy. I could get away saying things like this without being seen as against the staff because I was calm in doing it and had kept open relationships with everyone on the staff. When the secretary or receptionist would complain to me about Dr. Leary I would say something like, "Gee, and he says such nice things about you!" [pp. 127–128].

Fourth Principle: Triangles Allow Individuals to Mask or Replace Conflict

The head of the service, Dr. David, was replaced by a Dr. Price. Dr. David had had a relatively calming effect on the conflict and the triangles with Dr. Leary. At least he did not accelerate them. Dr. Price lacked the sense of responsibility and the organization of Dr. David. This presented a particular problem for Dr. Storm. Dr. Storm was overfunctioning. When someone else did not function as he believed that person should, Dr. Storm took it upon himself to take up the slack and perform for the other person. This type of activity usually breeds tension. In this case the tension was mostly felt by Dr. Storm, because he did not communicate his dissatisfaction to Dr. Price. He often sought out Dr. Kerr to complain about Dr. Leary but never voiced his dissatisfaction about Dr. Price. What happened was that, as the overfunctioning and underfunctioning between Dr. Price and Dr. Storm increased, it was not discussed directly, but Dr. Storm increased his conflict and complaints about Dr. Leary.

Fifth Principle: A Deliberate Detriangling Effort Can Have an Impact on the Rest of the System

As the tension increased in the system, Dr. Price went on extended leave and Dr. Kerr became the acting head of the service. He had been thinking about how to handle the issue of these dysfunctional triangles for some time, and he now had the opportunity to act.

On my first day as chief, I was totally bombarded with stories about Dr. Leary. I was not hearing those stories when I was second in command. I immediately had a better appreciation of the amount of input about Dr. Leary that Dr. Price had been trying to "field." The essence of the stories was that Dr. Leary was a terrible and intolerable problem and that I was to do something about him now, immediately, today! That morning a communication had come from

outside the department that a doctor on another service was not
satisfied with some recent consultation Dr. Leary had performed.
This outside person wanted the department to "right the wrong."
This type of communication had become routine since Dr. Price
had been chief-of- service. . . . I was alone in my office after receiving this information and was aware that Dr. Storm, Mrs. Jumpy,
Miss Languid and several technicians had gathered in the adjoining office to discuss this latest complaint about Dr. Leary. Miss
Languid had given me the communication and had then informed
others about it. I considered this a fertile situation. I was effectively
triangled and now had the opportunity to do something about it. I
went out of my office and into the adjoining office where the staff
had gathered. Speaking to Miss Languid, but loudly enough so
others could hear, I said that I considered Dr. Leary a responsible
and competent physician, which I did, and that this complaint was
to be passed on to him to do with as he saw fit. I left the room. The
message was passed to Dr. Leary. Later that day, Dr. Leary came to
my office. He said that he had talked to the physician who had
complained and had straightened out the problem. "I appreciate
your letting me know that he was not satisfied," added Dr. Leary.
I had only a few inputs about Dr. Leary the next day but handled
each of them in a similar way. Three days later I observed Dr. Leary
and Dr. Storm spend over an hour alone and talking together. Each
had apparently inquired about the other's background and interests. Two people who had been in intense conflict for one year
were now taking some interest in each other's lives [p. 130].

Here, Kerr was carrying out Bowen's theory, which indicates
that if two people who are involved in a triangle can come into
contact with a third person who understands triangles, does not
play into the emotional moves, and *remains in contact with both parties,* the triangle will modify its operation (Bowen, [1971] 1985f, p.
245). Kerr further states:

I, quite honestly, had come to see Dr. Storm and Dr. Leary as just
plain allergic to each other and had underestimated how much the
triangling had hampered any potential resolving of their relationship problems. Over the next weeks the talk amongst the staff about
Dr. Leary dwindled away to nothing. People around the hospital
remarked about the change in Dr. Leary. Dr. Leary became an increasingly social being. Periodic crises would, of course, reignite the

triangles, and I would have to devote energy to their management. Overall, however, there was a striking change in the system, and I was free to devote major energies to the work at hand [pp. 130–131].

Kerr later notes the power of triangles, once established, to reassert themselves (First Principle). When Dr. Price returned as chief of service, the triangles were reactivated and Dr. Leary was again isolated.

Managing in a World of Triangles

Triangles are an ever-present aspect of human interaction, and the tendency to seek a third party to absorb tension between two others is built into our functioning at a very basic level. Given this strong tendency, it is impossible to completely eliminate triangles. However, it is possible to minimize being unknowingly drawn into them. It is useful to develop an awareness of the triangling process and immediate, but nonconfrontational, strategies for keeping yourself out. Gilmore (1988, p. 118) suggests several ways of doing this:

[A] managing partner handled a detoured complaint from one partner about another by cutting short the one complaining, immediately telephoning the third party, and saying, "Mr. Brown is in my office with some concerns about your behavior and I thought you should come up here right away so you can work them out." In addition to working on the immediate presenting issue, the managing partner sent a clear signal about how he would respond to future attempts to complain to him unconstructively. . . . When triangled by someone complaining about an absent third party, an effective response is to ask, "What did he say when you discussed this with him?" . . . When it is acknowledged that no such discussion has occurred, as is usually the case, one can then shift to work with the complainer on finding a way to take up the matter constructively with the appropriate person.

Given the significance of triangles, it is important to be able to recognize the triangling process as soon as possible. The overall approach offered by BFST is to stay in calm contact with both of the other two individuals. Gilmore offers more specific advice regarding how to recognize and not become involved in triangles (1988, pp. 117–118):

1. Identify the main players in the triangle and in particular the hot leg of the triangle, the one that is carrying a disproportionate amount of the conflict.
2. If you experience an intense dyadic encounter, looking for a potentially underinvolved third party may shed some light on the situation.
3. Identify the third person who is often in the cool or distant position and benefiting from the deflection of affect. Are there ways to involve that person so that he or she takes a fair share of the issue?
4. Watch for over- and underfunctioning. Who is doing whose work for whom? How is the work of worry distributed? Who carries more than a fair share of worry? It is often easier to throttle down an overfunctioner than to get an underfunctioner moving. Often an underfunctioner will not be motivated until the overfunctioner stops protecting the other (often unwillingly).
5. Look for ways to stay in contact with the person with whom you are having the most trouble in the triangle. For example, might an out-of-town business trip provide opportunities to relate in a significantly different way?
6. Look for conflicts that are being detoured. Are people getting angry at someone who is less powerful (and therefore less risky to hate) than the real target of their anger?

Using Bowen Family System Theory to Promote Change

We can now illustrate how BFST can be used as an instrument of organizational change. To the extent that a family organization, or any collectivity, is *emotionally fused,* a person or people who are *less fused* and are operating with clear principles and goals can function as effective leaders or change agents. This is called *leadership by differentiation of self* and is a unique contribution of BFST. In leadership by differentiation of self, the leader stays in touch with the followers but does not become emotionally fused with them. This means that the leader is not only physically available, but is also able to maintain an intellectual and feeling connection. This connection is maintained even though the leader remains less emotionally reactive to the instinctual responses of the group.

The second aspect of leadership through differentiation of self is the leader's continued efforts to differentiate a self. This does not mean withdrawal or isolation but, rather, a continued effort to take nonreactive, clearly conceived, and clearly defined positions that may or may not agree with those of the others. It is not difficult to take such positions if the leader withdraws, but the essence of the BFST approach is to take well-thought-out and clearly defined positions while remaining in touch with and available to the group.

The final aspect of leadership through differentiation of self involves working with the inevitable resistance to change. If the group was used to leadership through emotional fusion (in BFST terms, another name for charisma), a different way of leading will represent a change in the emotional status quo. Followers who were used to having the leader emotionally fused will resist any attempt to have the leader return to a familiar pattern of behavior. This means that the leader must be able to untangle himself or herself from these attempts *without* directly resisting, which would be another way of becoming emotionally involved. This process is illustrated as we examine an example of leadership through differentiation of self undertaken by Edwin Friedman (1985, pp. 234–242), who was rabbi of a small congregation in Bethesda, Maryland.

In 1974 Friedman had been the rabbi of this congregation for approximately ten years. In that time he had gone through several phases of involvement. Even though his position was part-time, he had started by being intensely involved with the congregation, and when he found himself overextended, he cut back. There was a predictable reaction in the congregation: criticism of the rabbi and growing dissension and splits among the congregation itself. Where meetings had at one time had an air of camaraderie and playfulness, they now became deadly serious, with extended discussion over the smallest points. The crisis came to a head when members began to discuss dissolving the congregation. The members also talked about the rabbi leaving the congregation. The members who wanted him to stay requested that he go back to the heavy involvement that had marked his initial years with the congregation. He was reluctant to return to this type of involvement, but he also did not want to let go of a decade of hard work. After several days of inner turmoil, he made the decision to remain with the congregation but not to return to his old pattern of intense involvement. Instead, he decided to initiate a change effort and a new type of leadership based on the principles of BFST.

His first effort had to be to regain a connection with the relationship system of the congregation. This was not an easy task. Although he did not mention the term, Friedman in effect used a form of action research. He personally called 80 percent of the families in the congregation and invited them to a series of informal meetings at his home. He opened these meetings with a short statement describing how he perceived the crisis in the congregation and his own role in it. He then asked people for their reactions and suggestions and took careful notes. As the meetings progressed, he fed back the suggestions from the previous groups, and after the last meeting he prepared a twenty-four-page report summarizing all of the views and suggestions and sent it to the entire congregation. The purpose of this process was to act as a catalyst and encourage self-definition among the congregation. The aim was to have members clarify their views in as calm an atmosphere as possible and thereby increase their own functional level of differentiation.

The second step was to increase his own differentiation of self within the congregation. Here the effort focused on the board of trustees, from which the major impetus to dissolve the congregation had come. After his series of meetings with individual members, Friedman believed that he had enough support in the general membership to defeat a motion by the board of trustees to dissolve the congregation, but he did not wish to have a divisive vote in which a significant part of the congregation would have to perceive themselves as losing.

In the Bowen framework, one would not attempt to directly change the position of another, whether the other is an individual or a group such as the board. Rather, change is possible in a system when a differentiated self maintains contact and simultaneously redefines and differentiates a position in regard to the emotional system. The theory states that the system, after first reacting to the change, will readjust itself to the differentiated position of one person (Bowen, [1971] 1985c, p. 217). Two incidents illustrate how this process can work, one in which Friedman differentiated himself and one in which he "coached" a reluctant board chair to take a differentiated position (Friedman, 1985, p. 237).

At the next board meeting, I announced my renewed commitment to keep the congregation functioning and told the board members about the small parlor meetings I had begun. (Some of the board members, of course, had already been called.) At this meeting, which was to approve the budget for next year, the mood was one of deep pessimism. Everyone kept looking for an item to be cut; everyone kept worrying about how the membership was going down and how the deficit would get bigger. As each person spoke, the dreary atmosphere thickened and the anxiety increased. Any effort on my part to suggest that cutting this or that item would hurt the quality of programs was futile.

When everyone was through cutting and pruning, I said I wanted to make a different suggestion. Instead of defending the budget against the cuts, I paradoxically suggested that the original budget be *increased* by 25 percent. I told them that I thought their solution was defensive and could only lead to self-defeating consequences. Since I was now doing what they complained I hadn't done—exert leadership—it would never work without (I pulled the word from nowhere) an "aggressive" budget. To my utter shock, the dominoes stopped falling, and one by one everyone agreed, though everyone was also unwilling to take the responsibility for such a recommendation. The final result was the preparation of two different budgets that were then mailed out to the congregation for the membership to decide.

For Friedman, the essence of leadership was taking a position *and* clearly taking full responsibility for that position. If that is done, *provided that one stays in touch with the system,* there is a very good chance that the system will go along, and in this instance it did (Bowen, [1971] 1985c, p. 218).

Friedman also illustrated how a consultant can help another individual become a more effective leader by increasing differentiation of self (Friedman, 1985, p. 238):

[T]he president, the man at the top, while a very liberal thinker and one who tried to be fair, was simply too weak to carry the day. His liberalism, which strove for consensus, always gave strength to the extremists on the board. He obviously did not realize that reasonableness is a highly inadequate tool for change in anxious systems. Since in my family counseling practice I was increasingly successful in effecting change by not seeing the whole family together and never bothering to see the most resistant to change, I made no attempt to deal with the board as a group, or to assuage the hostility, and in some cases downright pathology, of some of the members. Instead I singled out those who I thought had strength and went to them individually. I told them how important I thought it was, despite the fact that it was not usually their style, to speak up and circuit-break the kind of anxious feedback that tends to get going in "this family."

Friedman told the chair that if he simply allowed everyone to express his or her opinion without taking a stand himself, the congregation would be split. After the conversation, Friedman didn't believe that he had made much of an impression on the board president, but events proved otherwise (Friedman, 1985, p. 239):

> It was later reported to me that at the crucial board meeting, after giving everyone a chance to speak, he [the board president] got up and said: "I don't know how the rest of you are going to vote, and I'm not going to try to change your mind, but as for me, given what the rabbi has already begun, I don't see how we can fail to give him the opportunity." Whereupon the man at the top having defined himself, one of the typically silent members of the board stood up and said, "I think this focus on Ed Friedman is bullshit. He's not the problem; it's the board that has the problem." . . . At the annual general membership meeting, the whole package, program and budget, passed with one dissenting vote (cast by the vice president in line for the presidency who had been passed over by the new nominating committee).

Friedman had coached the president in taking the small step of differentiating himself from the emotional system of the board. When he did this the board followed his lead and changed its own behavior.

Using Bowen Family System Theory to Encourage Psychological Growth

All of the theories in this volume deal with psychological growth. BFST shifts and expands the dimension regarding time and space. Timewise growth is viewed in terms of multiple generations. In regard to space, growth is widened to include the emotional system in which one is embedded, whether it is the system of one's family of origin or the emotional system of a group or organization. Within this context, BFST makes two contributions toward growth: one fundamental and long term, one situational and short term. Fundamental and long-term BFST growth involves a lifelong effort to differentiate a self from one's emotional system (family) of origin. This is a process that a consultant would do for himself or herself with the help of a therapist or coach trained in BFST. Such fundamental growth or differentiation in the practitioner is a precursor to helping others.

Given appropriate preparation, a practitioner can help organization members to operate from a more differentiated position within the emotional system of their organization. The examples of Katherine Wiseman as a consultant and Edwin Friedman in his synagogue illustrate this process. Both are powerful examples of the change potential of an emotionally detached position.

Bowen Family System Theory and Conflict

BFST deals with conflict by viewing it in the context of triangles within an emotional system. Triangles are a way of dealing with the anxiety triggered by conflict or potential conflict without resolving the difference. The general solution proposed is emotional detachment, so that the practitioner avoids playing a role as one of the corners of the triangle. The specific techniques for maintaining such detachment are suggested by the experience of Michael Kerr in an Army medical clinic and the guidelines offered by Thomas Gilmore.

Bowen Family System Theory and Joining

BFST provides a general perspective rather than specific techniques for working with the problems of joining or membership in groups and organizations. The BFST perspective is to focus on the price that individuals and organizations pay to satisfy the need for togetherness. In general BFST terms, the price one pays for the comfort of togetherness is that of losing the higher functioning of thinking and feeling that could come from a greater emphasis on developing one's potential for individuality.

In specific terms, for an organizational practitioner, this perspective would have the practitioner coaching managers and leaders to develop clear and firm positions based on well-thought-out principles and their own process of differentiating a self. The Wiseman and Friedman examples illustrated this process.

Conclusion

BFST opens the door to a realm of human functioning that has received little attention from organizational practitioners—the social influence of instincts (in BFST, this is termed *emotions*). The influence of such instincts or emotions is impressive because they limit thinking and feeling, the two human functions that make the greatest contribution to the successful operation of organizations. BFST's contribution is to highlight how the emotional system does this, and then to point out through *emotional detachment* and the various techniques of *detriangling* how the influence of the emotional system can be managed.

This is an important contribution toward helping individuals to function in organizations, and like most important contributions it has a price. The price is the need to devote enough sustained attention to truly understand and personally integrate a radically different system. This attention and immersion includes the therapeutic work of understanding one's own family of origin and the influence of that history upon her or his current degree of differentiation of self. It also includes at least temporarily suspending a dominant paradigm in organizational work, the support of *togetherness* and *awareness of feelings* as a method of operation.

The current field of organization development, particularly with regard to team building, is heavily oriented toward helping individuals to work more effectively by becoming more aware and accepting of both their feelings and their need for others (togetherness). In using BFST, the practitioner refocuses upon using thinking and emotional detachment to help individuals define clear values and principles that, although they are not hostile or aggressive to others, are not negotiable in the relationship system. This is done by helping clients to use thought to understand and limit the impact of the instinctive emotional system. This can be a stiff price for a practitioner who is used to operating on the basis of feeling awareness, but BFST promises considerable rewards for doing so.

Annotated Bibliography
Original Sources: Readable Bowen

Bowen, M. "Family Therapy After Twenty Years." In M. Bowen, *Family Therapy in Clinical Practice* (pp. 285–320). New York: Aronson, 1985. (Originally published 1975.)

Bowen, M. "Theory in the Practice of Psychotherapy." In M. Bowen, *Family Therapy in Clinical Practice* (pp. 337–388). New York: Aronson, 1985. (Originally published 1976.)

These two articles present Bowen's theory in the theorist's own words. Bowen's theory uses common terms such as *emotion* in a unique way, and if one is going to use the theory, it is important to have some familiarity with the original source.

Secondary Sources: Books About Bowen and His Theory

Gilbert, R. M. *Extraordinary Relationships: A New Way of Thinking About Human Interactions.* Minneapolis, Minn.: Chronimed, 1992.

This book applies Bowen's theory to individual relationships. The author is a member of the Georgetown Family Center. The book is soundly based in Bowen's theory and is very readable.

Kerr, M., and Bowen, M. E. *Family Evaluation: An Approach Based on Bowen Theory.* New York: W. W. Norton, 1988.

This is a significant exposition and clarification of Bowen's theory. It is particularly helpful in relating human behavior to that of other life forms.

Papero, D. V. *Bowen Family Systems Theory.* Boston: Allyn & Bacon, 1990. This is a short, readable exposition of Bowen's theory.

Organizational Applications

Friedman, E. H. *Generation to Generation: Family Process in Church and Synagogue.* New York: Guilford Press, 1985.

This is an imaginative and sometimes humorous application of Bowen's theory in religious organizations. The principles can be applied to other types of organizations.

Wiseman, K., and Sagar, R. (eds.). *Understanding Organizations: Applications of Bowen Family Systems Theory.* Washington, D.C.: Georgetown University Family Center, 1982.

This book consists of pioneering essays and case studies dealing with the application of Bowen's theory to organizations.

Bibliography

Bowen, M. "Introduction." In K. Wiseman and R. Sagar (eds.), *Understanding Organizations: Applications of Bowen Family Systems Theory* (pp. vii–xii). Washington, D.C.: Georgetown University Family Center, 1982.

Bowen, M. "A Family Concept of Schizophrenia." In M. Bowen, *Family Therapy in Clinical Practice* (pp. 45–70). New York: Aronson, 1985a. (Originally published 1960.)

Bowen, M. "Family Therapy After Twenty Years." In M. Bowen, *Family Therapy in Clinical Practice* (pp. 285–320). New York: Aronson, 1985b. (Originally published 1975.)

Bowen, M. "Family Therapy and Family Group Therapy." In M. Bowen, *Family Therapy in Clinical Practice* (pp. 183–240). New York: Aronson, 1985c. (Originally published 1971.)

Bowen, M. "Intrafamily Dynamics in Emotional Illness." In M. Bowen, *Family Therapy in Clinical Practice* (pp. 103–116). New York: Aronson, 1985d. (Originally published 1965.)

Bowen, M. "On the Differentiation of Self." In M. Bowen, *Family Therapy in Clinical Practice* (pp. 467–528). New York: Aronson, 1985e. (Originally published 1972.)

Bowen, M. "Principles and Techniques of Multiple Family Therapy." In M. Bowen, *Family Therapy in Clinical Practice* (pp. 241–258). New York: Aronson, 1985f. (Originally published 1971.)

Bowen, M. "Theory in the Practice of Psychotherapy." In M. Bowen, *Family Therapy in Clinical Practice* (pp. 337–388). New York: Aronson, 1985g. (Originally published 1976.)

Bowen, M. "Toward the Differentiation of Self in One's Family of Origin." In M. Bowen, *Family Therapy in Clinical Practice* (pp. 529–548). New York: Aronson, 1985h. (Originally published 1974.)

Bowen, M. "The Use of Family Theory in Clinical Practice." In M. Bowen, *Family Therapy in Clinical Practice* (pp. 147–182). New York: Aronson, 1985i. (Originally published 1966.)

Friedman, E. H. *Generation to Generation: Family Process in Church and Synagogue.* New York: Guilford Press, 1985.

Gilbert, R. M. *Extraordinary Relationships: A New Way of Thinking About Human Interactions.* Minneapolis, Minn.: Chronimed, 1992.

Gilmore, T. "A Triangular Framework: Leadership and Followership." In K. Wiseman and R. Sagar (eds.), *Understanding Organizations: Applications of Bowen Family Systems Theory* (pp. 73–94). Washington, D.C.: Georgetown University Family Center, 1982.

Gilmore, T. N. *Making a Leadership Change: How Organizations and Leaders Can Handle Leadership Transitions Successfully.* San Francisco: Jossey-Bass, 1988.

Hoffman, L. *Foundations of Family Therapy: A Conceptual Framework for Systems Change.* New York: Basic Books, 1981.

Kerr, K. "An Overview of Bowen Theory and Organizations." In R. K. Wiseman and R. Sagar (eds.), *Understanding Organizations: Applications of Bowen Family Systems Theory* (pp. 1–8). Washington, D.C.: Georgetown University Family Center, 1982.

Kerr, M. "Applications of Family Systems Theory to a Work System." In K. Wiseman and R. Sagar (eds.), *Understanding Organizations: Applications of Bowen Family Systems Theory* (pp. 121–131). Washington, D.C.: Georgetown University Family Center, 1982.

Kerr, M., and Bowen M. E. *Family Evaluation: An Approach Based on Bowen Theory.* New York: W.W. Norton, 1988.

Lerner, H. G. *The Dance of Anger: A Woman's Guide to Changing the Patterns of Intimate Relationships.* New York: Perennial Library, 1985.

Lerner, H. G. *The Dance of Intimacy: A Woman's Guide to Courageous Acts of Change in Key Relationships.* New York: HarperCollins, 1989.

MacLean, P. D. "A Mind of Three Minds: Educating the Triune Brain." In J. S. Chall and A. F. Mirsky (eds.), *Education and the Brain* (pp. 308–342). Chicago: National Society for the Study of Education, 1978. (Distributed by University of Chicago Press.)

Toman, W. *Family Constellation: Its Effects on Personality and Social Behavior.* (2nd ed.) New York: Springer, 1969.

Wiseman, K. "Emotional Process in Organizations." In K. Wiseman and R. Sagar (eds.), *Understanding Organizations: Applications of Bowen Family Systems Theory.* Washington, D.C.: Georgetown University Family Center, 1982.

Using Personality Theory
Understanding Behavior, Taking Effective Action, and Increasing Personal Awareness

We have surveyed the organizational implications of nine theories of personality. No one of these theories fits every practitioner in every organizational situation. This chapter will help you to draw upon the full range of these nine theories. It will highlight the appropriateness of each for different situations and different practitioner strengths and limitations and will review how each theory points toward a different aspect of the psyche. It will do this by identifying three ways in which an organizational practitioner can use a theory: for *understanding,* for *taking action,* and for *self-awareness* (Friedlander, 1976). I will then review the nine theories in terms of how each will help you to fulfill these three purposes.

The preceding chapters examined the nine theories in terms of each theory's point of influence and then grouped the theories in terms of the location (internal or external, conscious or unconscious) of each theory's point of influence. Three of the theories— those of Freud, Jung, and Horney—are internal and largely out of our conscious awareness. Three of the theories—Rogers's and Ellis's and Beck's—are internal but potentially within our conscious awareness. Five theorists—Skinner, Lewin, the Perls, and Bowen—define an external boundary between individuals and part of their environment. Their theories vary widely in terms of their conscious awareness. We will reexamine the theories in terms of how practitioners can use them to (1) understand human behavior, (2) take effective action, and (3) increase their own personal awareness (Friedlander, 1976).

Points of Influence Beyond Our Awareness
(Sigmund Freud, Carl Jung, and Karen Horney)

We have previously stated that if all human behavior was purposeful, rational, and had surface validity, we would have little need for the applied field of organization development or of organizational practitioners as we have defined them in this book. Human behavior, however, is neither so obvious nor so understandable. A vast and powerful underlying network of forces exists called the unconscious, and no organizational practitioner can ignore it. Three theorists in this volume offer a framework for understanding these forces.

The Unconscious and Understanding

Freud, Jung, and Horney each offer the practitioner a different picture of the part of our mind that exists beneath our awareness, our unconscious. Freud's picture is like an artist's conception of prehistoric times, with great beasts and smaller defenseless creatures locked into a permanent struggle for survival. The giant unreasoning id represents raw instinct; the smaller, but still powerful, superego represents morality; and the tiny and weak ego represents reason. Pasted in the corner of this primitive scene is a contemporary snapshot of a two-year-old enraged at his parents and, unable to understand why, not being able to have his way.

Carl Jung accepted and built on Freud's picture of the unconscious. Jung's picture moves ahead to the time of ancient civilizations and is rich in the imagery, colors, and elaborate symbols of that time. Looking at Jung's picture, we can examine the range of psychological forms and artifacts that Jung terms the collective unconscious. The collective unconscious is the home of Jung's archetypes, which are the enduring inner patterns that influence—but do not completely control—every repeated experience that we have as humans.

Finally, we observe Karen Horney's picture of the unconscious, a 1930s-style black-and-white photograph of a seven-year-old in a situation in which she is becoming aware of a world over which she has little control. The child is frightened, and she is trying to get her mother's attention, but her mother is occupied with something else. As we look at the child's face, we have the impression that she is imagining the kind of ideal child she would have to be to get the attention she wants so much. With this photo we have a depiction of Horney's theory of real and ideal selves.

The Unconscious and Action

How do these pictures help the organizational practitioner, whose prime concern is neither with psychotherapy nor with understanding the human condition? Practitioners, instead, must focus on how to accomplish things in an organization. Despite its seemingly esoteric nature, the unconscious is important to the action-oriented practitioner. Understanding the potential of the unconscious to both confuse and inspire is an essential basis for effective action. These three theories invite the practitioner to slow down and to move from a reactive to a reflective stance, and they offer a framework that illustrates how to deal with powerful but hidden forces. From this vantage point, practitioners are better able to develop strategies for working with individuals, groups, and organizations when patterns of behavior cannot be explained in rational terms. Each of the three theorists offers a different strategy for action that can influence behavior that is driven by unconscious impulses.

Freud describes transference and defense mechanisms as two processes that can hinder effective action. With this understanding, the practitioner can use tools from other theorists to minimize the impact of these processes. Jung leads the practitioner to a wider range of tools such as myths and symbols to tap into the creative power of the unconscious. Karen Horney points the practitioner toward the self—real or ideal. She also describes one's stance toward the world in terms of internal images and processes that influence human effectiveness. Again, the methods for dealing with these processes come from other theorists. Methods that can be used with all three theorists include simple questioning, confrontation and use of self, sharing of perceptions, brainstorming other possibilities, various types of structured experiences, self-disclosure, active listening, and providing support. This can be done either through active listening or by creating supportive groupings.

Developing Practitioner Awareness

Understanding and taking action with others are only part of the importance of the unconscious. The practitioner is subject to the same unconscious processes of every organization member. The theories of Freud, Horney, and Jung offer an opportunity and a challenge for practitioners to become aware of the influence of their own unconscious and to use that awareness as a method of helping others. In this instance, practitioners can become sensitized to their own use of defense mechanisms and transference; their Shadow as a source of trouble, an embarrassment, and a potential for creativity; and the problems that occur for them when they are influenced by their own image of an ideal self.

Influence Points Potentially Within Our Awareness: Thinking (Albert Ellis and Aaron Beck) and Feeling (Carl Rogers)

Thought is relatively acceptable in most organizational cultures and is a powerful but often neglected avenue for the practitioner to understand human behavior. Thinking has legitimacy, and many individuals are hired and valued because of their capacity to analyze. Ellis and Beck advocate applying the same sort of logical analysis to the internal process of creating thought that many organization members already use in analyzing tasks and policies. Compared to the other approaches in this volume, understanding our cognitive processes is a relatively short step from the day-to-day activities of many organization members.

As thought is primary to Ellis and Beck, feelings are primary to Rogers. For Rogers, feelings are much more than internal reactions to external events; they are an overall gauge to the whole inner psychic process as well as an integrating mechanism and an entry point for influencing that process. Rogers's theory is an overall view of the whole organism, or person, and feelings are the key input and output of that system.

Thinking and Understanding

Ellis and Beck have a similar view of the causal chain between thought, feelings, and behavior. In both of their theories, thought influences—perhaps even controls—feeling and behavior. Both theories also take advantage of the position of thought as one of the most accessible of human functions, and both provide a relatively simple and very revealing map of the human psyche in which the practitioner can trace feelings, attitudes, and behavior back to the thoughts that shaped them.

Thinking and Action

Ellis and Beck differ in how they define and work with unproductive or dysfunctional thoughts. Ellis's rational emotive behavior therapy takes a philosophical approach, defining certain types of thoughts as irrational and vigorously disputing them. Beck's cognitive therapy is more empirical, with therapist and client jointly exploring the basis and impact of the individual's thoughts. In organization development terms, Ellis emphasizes confrontation, Beck reframing.

Ellis and Beck focus on early childhood lessons and experiences and how these constructs influence later feelings and behavior. We have also noted how Robert Marshak and Judith Katz apply Ellis's and Beck's ideas in an organizational context by focusing on less personal and more task-related levels of thought. These include beliefs, assumptions and values, formal theories, paradigms, organizational and societal culture, and values. Marshak and Katz, in their Covert Processes Model™, also introduce a variety of more organizationally accepted methods of understanding thought, such as personal constructs. These include using metaphors, symbols, imagery, music, and movement. Their model offers a comprehensive and useful way to use the point of influence of thought in the more commonly accepted modalities of organizational training and consultation.

Thinking and Developing Awareness

Practitioners can use the thought process to increase their own personal awareness, and each of the theorists in this book offers guidelines for such an inquiry. Albert Ellis offers the simple but compelling ABC explanation, in which "A" signifies an action, "C" signifies a consequence, and "B" signifies the intervening belief that influences the consequences—whether they are feelings, attitudes, or behavior. Ellis enumerates irrational beliefs such as "I must perform well and/or be approved by significant others or else I am an incompetent and unlovable person." Beck invites consultants to consider the assumptions behind their thoughts by asking:

1. What's the evidence?
2. What's another way of looking at it?
3. So what if it happens?

For Beck, the answers to these questions take the form of a *schema,* which is a verbal or pictorial construct or lens that then interprets all experience in terms of the bias of the schema, such as "Unless I do everything perfectly, I'm a failure." Marshak and Katz extend the analysis by helping the practitioner to examine the influence of thought by looking at such everyday communication vehicles as metaphor, symbols, movement, and music.

Feelings and Understanding

Feelings are one link between the hidden world of the unconscious and the visible world of external behavior. Every practitioner working with human behavior needs some way of understanding and working with feelings. Carl Rogers is a good source for this link. Rogers identifies awareness or lack of awareness of feelings as well as feelings themselves as a key to understanding and influencing behavior. Rogers's model also identifies degrees and nuances of feelings that go beyond the usual day-to-day use of the term. This model, with its subtleties and shades of meaning, thus provides a way of understanding behavior at the individual, group, and organizational levels.

Feelings as a Basis for Both Action and Awareness

Action with others and awareness of self are closely bound together in Rogers's theory. Rogers describes how the practitioner can use feelings as a way of helping individuals and groups to discover their concerns, desires, values, and—ultimately—their goals. The caveat is that practitioners must at the same time be equally open to increasing awareness of their own feelings. In this context, Rogers provides two methods for increasing awareness of feelings in the self and others. The first is empathic understanding or its nonclinical application, active listening. The second is the nondirected process, an essential part of Rogers's therapy that leaves a vacuum to be filled by the emerging feelings of the therapy client or organization member. In training, workshop, or consultation settings, this vacuum encourages feelings to emerge (sometimes accompanied by anxiety). Provided that the practitioner is congruent and the culture is supportive, Rogers's methods can provide strong support for better communication, conflict resolution, and personal growth.

Four External Points of Influence (B. F. Skinner, Kurt Lewin, Fritz and Laura Perls, and Murray Bowen)

Thus far the theories we have reviewed have examined humans apart from their environment and from other individuals. The following four theories adopt a wider perspective. They each view the individual as part of some segment of their environment, which includes other people. Each theory, however draws the boundary differently, defines a different environment, and therefore suggests a different set of actions.

The widest view of the environment is that of B. F. Skinner, who focuses entirely on the environment (with the exception of genetic background). Less inclusive are the theories of Kurt Lewin and Fritz and Laura Perls. Both the Perls and Lewin focus on the self-perceived environment of each individual. Still another boundary is drawn by the theory of Murray Bowen, who defines an emotional system that links individuals through emotional or instinctive processes that humans share with other forms of life.

The Individual and the Environment and Understanding

Organizational practitioners are interested in an individual's behavior not in and of itself but as a basis for understanding what takes place in collections of individuals, particularly groups and organizations. The focus of the individual and the environment, especially as that environment includes other people, is thus especially relevant.

An added dimension to the theories of the individual and the environment is that whereas all of the theories avoid the use of the term *unconscious*, they all still present a view of humans as responding to stimuli or impulses that are in some way unavailable to their conscious awareness. Skinner's theory of operant conditioning describes the phenomenon of reinforcement as a single viable explanation for human behavior. Although at times individuals are aware of such reinforcement, often they are not. Similarly, Lewin's and the Perls's focus on the psychological field includes some phenomena that are available to conscious awareness; this focus also includes many phenomena that are not. The Gestalt theory of the Perls also focuses on bodily sensations that are both in and out of personal awareness. Bowen's theory similarly draws on "automatic" responses that are also outside of conscious awareness.

The unique contours of each theory delineate what the theory defines as relevant and what actions are suggested. Skinner focuses on the entire environment but then narrows his focus to whatever reinforces very specific individual behavior. His theory is most applicable to specific behaviors such as attendance or thanking customers. Lewin and the Perls start from the same base of an individually perceived environment but then go in opposite directions. The Perls focus more on the individual; Lewin concentrates more on the group and the organization. At the start of his career, Lewin centered his attention on individually perceived behavior in his exposition of topological psychology but later focused his writings on groups, organizations, and whole societies. The organizational field has concentrated more on his later writings. Thus, for Lewin, a whole range of collective behavior, especially group dynamics, became relevant.

The Perls's Gestalt theory keeps the focus on the individual but intensifies it to include bodily sensations, resulting in a greater emphasis on human emotion. Later practitioners have applied the Gestalt perspective to couples, groups, and organizations. Bowen's theory emphasizes the aspects of humans that are shared with other forms of life, such as the instinctive drive for togetherness and withdrawal and reactions to anxiety, ritual behavior, and so on. Bowen's theory highlights other aspects of human behavior, particularly the efforts that individuals make to separate themselves from herd behavior. Focusing on the emotional system and triangles, Bowen's theory transcends the usual arrangements of group and organization and gives the practitioner a way to study what up to now have been invisible links between individuals.

The Individual and the Environment and Action

Each theorist's definition of what constitutes the relevant environment also defines her or his approach to action. Skinner's broad definition of the relevant environment shaped his approach so that it is relatively simple. His theory focuses on reinforcement, or discovering what occurs after a behavior that will make that behavior more or less likely to be repeated. His theory of operant conditioning is most effective when the practitioner can define a specific behavior.

Kurt Lewin's field theory spawned the modern study of group dynamics, and one of the first studies was in the area of participative management. His work gave today's organizational practitioner two important tools: action research and interpersonal feedback.

Fritz and Laura Perls's work also focused on the individual but in a way that later yielded several unique tools for the organizational practitioner. The individual cycle of experience, as developed at the Cleveland Gestalt Institute, shows practitioners what can block the organism and how one can unblock it at any level: individual, group, or organizational. Once it is unblocked, the organism can utilize its natural energy for change. The stance of the Gestalt therapist toward what is usually termed resistance illustrates how the organizational practitioner can use what others view as a negative force in a positive way.

Murray Bowen's focus on the instinct-based emotional system also yields unique tools. The position of detachment, as opposed to distancing oneself from the emotional system at home or at work, and the process of detriangling are also unique organizational tools.

Developing Awareness

Each theorist studying the individual and the environment concentrates on a different approach to individual awareness. B. F.

Skinner, though avoiding acknowledgment of such an abstraction as "the internal self," provides the motivation and the methodology for keeping track of individual behavior. Paying careful attention to specific behaviors—whether they are personal, such as noting what one eats, or organizational, such as noting how often one performs a task—has the indirect consequence of increasing awareness.

Kurt Lewin's widened focus on the individual field and emphasis on group dynamics also opens the possibility of learning about oneself through feedback at the individual and group levels and learning about action research at the organizational level. The Perls's focus on the interrelationship of the total organism, thought and feeling, mind and body, and individual and environment, opens the possibility of increasing awareness of what might be influencing an individual at a particular moment. Finally, Murray Bowen's emphasis on the influence of multigenerational transmission on differentiation of self opens the door to looking at one's extended family of origin as a source of self-understanding. In addition, taking a position of detachment and neutrality helps individuals to study themselves and their reactions in various relationship situations and thereby increases their self-awareness.

Bibliography

Friedlander, F. "OD Reaches Adolescence: An Exploration of Its Underlying Values." *Journal of Applied Behavioral Science,* 1976, *12*(2), 7–43.

Name Index

Subject Index

A

applications of, to conflict management, 111; organizational applications of, to gender issues, 111, 127–129, 135–137; organizational applications of, to high performance, 121–122; organizational applications of, to individual dysfunction, 126–127, 134–135; organizational applications of, to joining, 112; organizational applications of, limitations of, 112–113; organizational applications of, to management styles, 122–126, 130–134; organizational applications of, overview of, 111–112, 115; organizational applications of, to psychological growth, 111–112, 129–130

Human nature, Rogerian theory of, 192–194. *See also* Self-actualization tendency

Human potential movement, 298

Humor, 365–366

Hysteria, 23–24

I

Id, 4, 26

Idealized self, 5, 118–119; and action research, 288; and despised self, 118–119; grandiose, 118–119; organizational applications of, to individual dysfunction, 126–127, 134–135; organizational applications of, overview of, 111–112; as organizational image, 135, 288; organizational importance of, 114. *See also* Horney's theory

Idealizing transference, 36, 40–41

Identification, in Freudian theory, 27

Identity, and group affiliation, 252, 274, 284–285

Identity boundary, 11

Images of Organization (Morgan), 183

Images: figure-ground relationship

and, 262; in Gestalt theory, 262, 292–293; use of, in Beck's therapy, 170; use of, in Covert Processes Model, 171–175; use of, in Ellis's therapy, 161–162; use of, in Lewin's theory, 251. *See also* Organizational metaphor

"Impact of Kurt Lewin's Life on the Place of Social Issues in His Work, The" (Lewin, M.), 289

In and Out of the Garbage Pail (Perls, F.), 295–296, 333

Individuality versus togetherness, 338–339, 348–349. *See also* Bowen Family System Theory; Differentiation of self

Inferior function, 98, 103–106

Innocent archetype, 87, 88

Insight, Gestalt, 260–261

Instinct: in Bowen Family System Theory, 344–346, 349, 375–376; in Freudian theory, 3, 4, 24–25. *See also* Emotional system

Institute for Rational Emotive Therapy, 148

Institutionalized group, 39–40

Integration, 69–71

Intellectual system, in Bowen Family System Theory, 348. *See also* Bowen Family System Theory

Intentional groups, 41; learning process of, 41–42

Interested detachment, 355–356

Intermittent reinforcement, 237–239

Interpersonal Behavior: Communication and Understanding in Relationships (Athos, Gabarro), 215

Interpersonal relationships, in Rogerian theory, 186, 194–195

Interpretation technique, 41–42

Interval, in reinforcement schedules, 237–239

Interventions: behavioral, using operant conditioning, 228–231; for conflict management process, 12–14; for dealing with defense